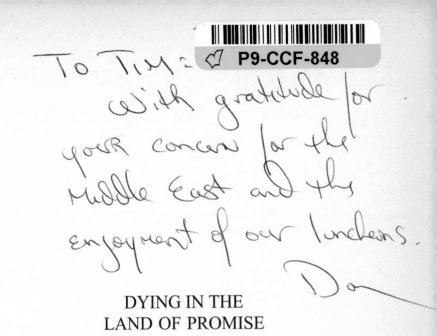

P9-CCF-848

# DYING IN THE
# LAND OF PROMISE

Donald E Wagner

*All that I have is a voice to undo the folded lie*
W H Auden

# DYING IN THE
# LAND OF PROMISE

*PALESTINE*
*and*
*PALESTINIAN CHRISTIANITY*
*from*
*PENTECOST TO 2000*

## Donald E Wagner

**MELISENDE**

*Dying in the Land of Promise*
by Donald E Wagner

First published 2001 by
Melisende
39 Chelmsford Road
London E18 2PW
Tel. +44 (0)20 8498 9768
Fax +44 (0)20 8504 2558
E mail: melisende@cwcom.net
www.melisende.cwc.net

ISBN 1 901764 50 8

*Cover photo: we gratefully acknowledge the Christmas Lutheran Church and International Centre in Bethlehem, Dr Mitri Raheb Pastor and Director, for the use of the mural on the cover, painted by the Palestinian artist, Sulaiman Mansour.*

Editor: Leonard Harrow

Printed at the St Edmundsbury Press, England

*To my children—Anna, Matthew and Jay,*
*and to all Israeli and Palestinian children,*
*that your generation will hunger and thirst for*
*the justice and peace that has escaped us thus far*
*in the Holy Land and in our world.*

# CONTENTS

# LIST OF MAPS

# ACKNOWLEDGEMENTS

A work such as this is inevitably dependent upon a larger community, which indeed was the case from inception to completion. In this regard I must express my most sincere gratitude to the Palestinian Christian friends in Jerusalem, and in particular my colleagues at *Sabeel*, who sacrificed valuable time to give me feedback on the initial drafts of chapters one through five. Norma Karmi and Hilary Rantisi, the always efficient administrators, arranged a January seminar in which such luminaries as Naim Ateek, Cedar Duaybis, Jonathan Kuttab, and Sabeel friends Douglas Dicks and colleagues from the Christian Peacemakers Teams helped correct and redirect my initial efforts. Roxanne Assaf arranged several appointments to make my week in Jerusalem, Israel, and Palestine very efficient, and in particular I want to thank Mr Fuad Farah of the Palestine Orthodox Congress in Nazareth and Fr Elias Chacour for their invaluable feedback and documents on their important work.

In London I appreciate the January feedback and ongoing emails from Fr Michael Prior, who hosted a luncheon and seminar on the initial chapters at St Mary's College, University of Surrey. Attending were Revd Dr Stephen Sizer, Mary Davies, Dr Nur Musalhah, Dr Duncan Macpherson, and my editors and publishers Alan Ball and Leonard Harrow of Melisende. I extend my deepest gratitude to them for their patience and skills in guiding me through to the final product.

Three academic friends gave valuable feedback on historical and political aspects of the study at various states: Drs Rosemary and Herman Ruether and Dr Ghada Talhami. I received valuable editorial comments from Bill Taylor, George Kovats and Betty Jane Bailey, the latter making an extraordinary effort from Bethlehem.

My staff at North Park University in Chicago was extremely helpful at various stages. My assistant, Silvija Klavins-Barshney was able to track down maps and assist me at various stages of a crowded academic schedule with little time to write. My Palestinian student assistant, Rana Khassis, was always volunteering to do whatever she could to help, as was Karna Eklund. My academic Dean, Dr Daniel de Roulet, was graciously supportive in allowing me the necessary time during the spring semester (2000) to work at home two mornings a week. A special word of gratitude goes to my theological reflection and Covenant group: Drs Dave Handley, Terry Halliday, Christopher Miller, and Ken Vaux, for their counsel and spiritual support.

Rounding out the community were my dear children, Anna, Matthew, and Jay, whose love and encouragement gave me energy and support. A special word is extended to Matt, my teenage computer genius, who patiently stuck with his semi-illiterate dad, rescuing me on a regular basis as I randomly moved among four computers, all with different software, to complete the project. Only by the grace of God and a wider community could such a volume be conceived and completed. Whatever shortcomings in the original design and in the analysis belong entirely to me, and I look forward to your feedback as I expect to probe this subject matter much more in the future. To all of those mentioned and to so many others, I extend my sincerest thanks.

*Donald E Wagner*
*Chicago, December 2000*

# PREFACE
## *Naim Ateek*

In Jerusalem on the day of Pentecost, the Church was founded by the reality of the resurrection of Christ and by the power of the Holy Spirit. From its inception, it was a crucible of believers from the variety of the racial and ethnic backgrounds of which Palestine was composed, namely, the Jewish, Roman, Greek, Samaritan, Arab, Phoenician, as well as other Canaanite groups. In fact, some historians have estimated that the population of Palestine at the time of Jesus was approximately two million, out of which only fifty percent were Jewish. The rest belonged to these other ethnic groups.

After the conversion of Constantine in the beginning of the 4th century and the official recognition of Christianity, the number of Christians in Palestine grew rapidly. Within a hundred years, Palestine had become a predominantly Christian country with hundreds of churches and monasteries built throughout the land. In spite of the theological controversies of the 4th and 5th centuries, the church in Palestine experienced numerical majority in the land of Christ.

The demographic changes that affected Palestinian Christians beginning with the 7th century and up to the present have, indeed, been phenomenal. They have turned the majority into a minority in their own land. The reasons have been varied and sometimes complicated. They combine factors that are political as well as religious, internal as well as external, personal as well as communal. A quick outline of developments would include the Arab Islamic conquests, the coming of the Crusades, the successive occupation of the country and the brutality of many of its rulers, the inner divisions of the Christian communities, the economic hardships which periodically hit Palestine, the establishment of the State of Israel, and the emigration of many Christians. All of these factors and more contributed to demographic changes in the country and the depletion of the number of Palestinian Christians.

Today, Palestinian Christians have become dispersed throughout the world and especially in Western countries. Many of them have been forced to abandon Palestine as a result of the Palestinian-Israeli conflict. Most of them still long to return to Palestine. Many of them cannot even visit due to Israeli restrictions. And the Palestinian Christians who are now living in the State of Israel and on the Gaza Strip and the West Bank including East

11

Jerusalem make up barely two percent of the total population. They are proud of their Christian heritage in the land, and have borne a witness for Christ in good and ill times and continue today to contribute to the well being of their country.

During the last hundred and fifty years, the indigenous Christians of the land have been joined by a good number of expatriate brothers and sisters from other parts of the world. They built and pastored churches, opened schools, hospitals, and many other charitable institutions to serve the Christian community as well as the wider communities in the land. Through the help of these institutions, the Palestinian Christians have been able to preserve a good standard of education and a quality of life, which allowed many of them to play an important role in the development of their societies as well as in the political arena. Even when many Palestinian Christians were forced out of their land due to the establishment of the State of Israel, these institutions, largely Catholic and Protestant, continued in their ministry of protecting the Holy Places, educating the young, healing the sick, looking after the orphans and the elderly and so on.

It is important to point out the great difference between the occupation of Palestine in past centuries and the more devastating effect of the Israeli occupation on Palestinians in general, and Christians in particular. In the past the many occupiers of the land, by and large, allowed the indigenous population to live its life on its land. Indeed, they exploited the people, the land and its resources but it did not expel the inhabitants. The Israeli occupation however, and out of its own Zionist ideology, forced the displacement of the Palestinians and confiscated most of their land. In 1948 approximately three quarters of a million Palestinians were expelled and in 1967 a further 300,000. The consequences were devastating for both the Christian as well as the Muslim Palestinian community.

One of the great tragedies in the story of the Palestinians and more particularly Palestinian Christians is the fact that many people in the world do not know they exist. So, before one starts to introduce their political plight, there is a need to establish their existence—who are they, where did they come from, how long have they lived there, i.e., their history. Many of us Palestinian Christians who have been travelling to the West attending conferences and lecturing recall the surprise on the face of many Western Christians when they discovered the existence of Palestinian Christians; or the shock on our faces when we were presented with the question, 'When did you become a Christian?' In other words, Palestinian Christians were non-existent in the memory and concern of most of their brothers and sisters in the West. Even now we still find people who cannot comprehend the presence of Christians in Palestine.

Be that as it may, it is important to point out that there has been a growing interest in the plight of the Palestinians and Palestinian Christians in particular over the last 20 years. This has been due to a number of factors. To begin with, the high profile of Israel in the West after its impressive victory in the 1967 war gave it constant coverage in the Western media. There was a general interest in what was happening in Israel and in its occupied territories. So when the *Intifada* erupted, it exposed the Palestinians to the world and highlighted their predicament. Furthermore, Palestinian Christians themselves started to tell their story. This coincided with an increasing number of tourists and pilgrims coming to visit the Holy Land. Some of them could not anymore be satisfied with visits to the Holy Places. They were encouraged to meet and interact with the 'living stones', the indigenous Christian community, of the land. They were challenged to relay these stories to their own people back home and become advocates for a just peace in Palestine. Moreover, books and articles began to be written about the injustice done to the Palestinians from both Palestinian as well as expatriate writers. It has been a slow process of informing and educating people but, I believe, it has started to yield a good dividend.

It is in this context that Don Wagner deserves great credit. He has shown great faithfulness in pursuing and presenting the truth about the Palestinians. As he tells his own story in the book, it did not come naturally for him. He was very much committed to the Zionist cause due to his dispensationalist upbringing. Yet his encounter with Palestinians made him seek the truth of their plight and finding it set him free to a commitment to justice and peace on their behalf.

I believe that one way to measure greatness in people is in their ability to change their views when confronted by the truth. We usually assume that truth automatically changes us. Unfortunately it does not. Some people refuse to change though the truth becomes known and evidence is presented to them. They prefer to continue to live in their own preconceived ideas and prejudices. Truth can be threatening to some. It demands repentance and change, a re-evaluation of one's past attitude and behaviour and a commitment to a new set of principles. It could mean a new set of friends because the old friends will not tolerate the change and will walk away. Some people cannot handle all these disruptions. It makes them very uncomfortable so they repress the truth and live the lie. It is wonderful, however, when we meet people who, like Don Wagner, have the grace and humility to allow the truth to chart their new course in life.

We have appreciated the commitment of Don to break the Western, mediated stereotype of the Palestinian and instead reveal the true, human face and present them to his American people. Moreover, he has committed himself in a special way to introduce Western Christians to Middle East Christians in general and to Palestinian Christians in particular. His organization, 'Evangelicals for Middle East Understanding', has played a significant role in this endeavour. Through its annual conference in the United States and frequent group visits to the Middle East, many people have been exposed and their lives changed. And now through this new book, Don Wagner is again using his rich personal experience accumulated over many years of faithful visits and contacts with many Palestinians coupled with scholarly research to write this comprehensive volume of the story of the small community of Palestinian Christians.

Indeed, the Palestinian Christian community living in Palestine-Israel is small in number. In fact, there are more Palestinian Christians living outside the area of historic Palestine than inside it. This has caused many of our leaders to express their deepest concern about the future of our community, as Don rightly presents it. Some talk about it in pessimistic terms. They believe that given time, the Christian community of the land will become extinct. Every now and then incredible ideas are suggested such as a mass conversion to Islam. Others have advocated a mass emigration to the West where the majority of inhabitants are Christian. Undoubtedly, the situation is alarming and for many of us very serious. However, I believe that a remnant Christian community will survive in the land and eventually will grow in number. Obviously, we will not be able to compete numerically with Jews and certainly not with Muslims. Our great responsibility is to work diligently for their empowerment. This can be done through greater unity among them. The need to de-emphasize denominationalism and emphasize our connectedness with Christ and unity in him. The need to deepen the faith and witness of the Christians and their rootedness in their own land, and the importance of maintaining a viable witness for Christ in the footsteps of our forefathers and foremothers.

In other words, we need to recapture the vitality of the Christian community in Palestine during the first three centuries. Three things characterized it. The Christians were small in number, they were vulnerable, sometimes they suffered for their faith, and they did not enjoy political clout. This pre-Constantinian way of life proved to be very effective in living a viable Christian faith. It is a life lived in total trust and dependence on God. God is ultimately its protector and guardian. When Jesus addressed his disciples calling them salt and light, he was looking at a very small number of people. It is our duty to strengthen the faith of our community so that they might truly be what Christ expects them to be. Similarly, our greatest challenge today is for the small Christian community in Israel-Palestine to be salt, light, and yeast. It is not our numerical quantity that is our greatest concern, it is our effective quality. By the grace of God the small Christian community will keep the torch of faith burning in the land of Christ and live in the strength and comfort of his words, 'Do not be afraid, little flock, for it is your Father's good pleasure to give you the kingdom' (Luke 12:32).

*Naim Ateek*
*Jerusalem, May 2000*

# INTRODUCTION

Recently I delivered a paper at a faculty research seminar that discussed the Israeli-Palestinian problem and included an extensive section on the erosion of the Palestinian Christian community in the Holy Land. After the discussion, one of our respected faculty members came up and said: 'I was reluctant to show my ignorance in public but I never realized that there was a Palestinian Christian community in the Holy Land. I had always assumed that everyone over there were Muslims or Jews. Were these Christians the result of Christian missions? Where did they come from?'

I assured my colleague that he should not be embarrassed about this knowledge gap. My graduate studies and seminary education never mentioned the full history of Christianity in the Holy Land. We studied the history of Israel and the Hebrew scriptures, the New Testament era and the early church, but we did not study the history of Christianity from the first Pentecost to the present day. It is not surprising that this highly educated and well-read university professor was unaware that an important Christian community emerged in the Holy Land and eventually they became the dominant population in the land the Romans called *Palestina*. I had a similar impression about the people of the Holy Land until I began to immerse myself in the Palestinian experience some twenty-five years ago.

When I was confronted by the complex and controversial case of the modern Zionist-Palestinian struggle I was a young clergyman and very much in the pro-Israel camp. I had grown up in evangelical Protestant churches and had generally accepted the assumptions of what is today called Christian Zionism. As a young boy I heard our pastors and Sunday school teachers proclaim that the establishment of the modern state of Israel was a divine miracle in fulfilment of certain biblical prophecies. However, by my university years I had left these views behind but my commitment to Israel and to the Jewish people remained very high. Holocaust studies in seminary led to work against antisemitism during my first pastorate in the tense urban environment of Newark, New Jersey. This was followed by taking high school and university age students to Auschwitz after I conducted extensive orientation sessions on the rise of European antisemitism and the Nazi's 'final solution'. I remain committed to the Jewish people and will join them in the ongoing struggle against the deadly curse of antisemitism, but I soon discovered another side of this equation.

When I initially encountered the Palestine question in the mid-1970s, I dismissed Palestinians as the worst of contemporary antisemites. The 'Munich Massacre' at the Olympics and other terrorist actions simply reinforced the connection between Palestinians and terrorism. Of course, I had no knowledge of the history of the Palestinians or, more importantly, of full story concerning the events that took place in Palestine from the rise of Zionism until the present time. It was not until I heard a series of thoughtful academic presentations by Palestinian and Israeli historians and began an academic study of the situation that my opinions began to change. One visit to the Middle East where I saw the Palestinians scattered in squalid refugee camps across Lebanon, Syria, Jordan, and the West Bank enabled me to see first-hand the history I had been reading. I was appalled not only by how I had been deceived by the one-sided accounts that I had received by I was angry about my own government's role in undermining a just solution for the Israeli and Palestinian people, and perhaps equally troubled by Britain's previous role of 'divide and run' during the Mandate.

Within two years of my initial visit to the Middle East I decided to leave my position as a pastor on the staff of a large suburban congregation and spent the entirety of the 1980s as the National Director of the Palestine Human Rights Campaign. In this role I became both a target of the opposition as well as an advocate, joined thankfully by many progressive Israeli and American Jews while finding significant moral support from Arab Americans and a variety of others. Initially, one of the most difficult communities to engage broader discussion of the Palestine question was the community in which I grew up, conservative Evangelical Christians. American evangelicals are a complex and diverse community that many observers believe constitute over 20 percent of the 225 million Christians in the United States. The most conservative wing of the evangelical community is perhaps the most resistant to change on Middle East issues (and many other theological and social matters) due to their theological predispositions concerning to the modern state of Israel. Simply put, most of this community, which represents approximately 20 percent of US evangelicals, believes the modern state of Israel is prophetic fulfilment of the Israel of the Bible. Perhaps more problematic for the political and historical matters discussed later in this book is their belief that all Jews and this largely secular political state have a divine right to the land called Israel and Palestine. Many Evangelicals add the predispensational argument that Israel will be God's primary instrument at the end of history to carry out God's purposes, paving the way for the second coming of Jesus the Messiah. This is the community and the beliefs with which I grew up and today they represent the largest bloc of pro-Israel political and moral support in the United States subscribe to some form of these millennial perspectives and are called Christian Zionists. My previous books: *Anxious for Armageddon, Peace or Armageddon* (with Dan O'Neill), and *All in the Name of the Bible* (with Hassan Haddad) were addressed primarily to this community.

*Dying in the Land of Promise* seeks to address a wider audience. The present volume is an attempt to provide the average layperson, the first-time or the seasoned traveller to the Holy Land, professors, students, clergy, pilgrims, or anyone interested in the Middle East, with a dual narrative. First, I tell the story of Palestinian Christianity from its inception at the first Christian Pentecost until the present day. The second narrative, the history of the Zionist (Israeli)-Palestinian conflict, begins one third of the way through the book and overtakes the initial narrative both in the amount of space I give and its obvious importance. This is in a sense symbolic of what has occurred to Palestinians as a people and to Palestinian Christians in particular, as they have been overtaken by these events, many of which were imposed upon them by both distant and nearby occupiers. The 'dual narrative' attempts to strike a balance between a style that is simply told but one that is based upon contemporary historical and political scholarship, utilizing the best of Israeli Jewish, Palestinian Arab, and western sources.

Throughout the text I intentionally use the term Palestinian Christians to describe the Christian community that has emerged in the Holy Land, which was named Palestine by the Romans in the early second century, and somewhat loosely retained this affiliation through the Ottoman empire and the period of the British Mandate (1922-48). I recognize the potential controversy that this 'naming' of these Christians may generate for some but there are few acceptable alternatives. First, they are the largest Christian community in the Holy Land and this is the term that they use to describe their many historic churches. Outside of the Armenian and Syriac churches and the Messianic Jewish community, virtually all of the Christians in the Holy Land self-identify with the term Palestinian. Second, the term Palestine was employed by the Romans after 135 to designate the Holy Land, thus beginning at this point in the second century, the indigenous residents would rightly be Palestinian, and perhaps add an additional term for precision: Armenian, Syriac, Jewish, etc. Critics might make the case that while you can call this community 'Palestinian Christian' today, you cannot read this back into history and apply it to an earlier period. I would argue that the Romans called the district *Palestina* so the inhabitants are rightly called Palestinian when describing these people today. This is not a political usage and to be more precise one can simply call it an adjective, and add more precise nouns: Armenian, Orthodox Christian, Syrian Orthodox, Jewish, etc. Third, biblical scholarship uses the designation 'Palestinian Judaism' to describe the first and early second century developments within the Jewish community the Holy Land. This usage is not disputed and is not perceived as a political reading of the people or land. Hence, the matter of calling the Christians of this land and of the same era 'Palestinian' should not be questioned.

The book follows a historical approach beginning with the initial Christian Pentecost in the first century and concludes with the Oslo Accords with its various procedures, protocols, and quest to bring peace to the Holy Land. Throughout the work I am asking how local events have affected this Palestinian Christian community. Statistics demonstrate that in this present generation, Christianity is dying as a living religion in Israel and Palestine. The Anglican Bishop of Jerusalem, the Rt Revd Riah Abu El-Assal, himself a Palestinian, writes 'if we do not find a solution quickly, the land where our faith was born and survived for two thousand years will soon be empty of indigenous Christians. The living faith will be represented only by dead stones and their imported custodians.'[1]

In his critically acclaimed and important book *From the Holy Mountain*, British travel writer William Dalrymple trekked across Turkey, Syria, Lebanon, Israel-Palestine, Jordan and Egypt during 1996-7, seeking to find the current state of Christianity in these countries where the faith once had flourished. In a particularly graphic statement, Dalrymple reflects on what he discovered among the Christians in the Holy Land: 'the single most dramatic decline in the Christian population (next to Anatolia) is Palestine.'[2]

The numerical decline of Christians in the Holy Land has become particularly acute during the last fifty years. Accurate data about the decline has become a sensitive political and ecclesiastical matter which presents numerous obstacles to a scholarly investigation, clergy and academicians alike. Those looking for indisputable statistics on the Palestinian Christian community will be disappointed if they are looking for a final word from this text. However, I will point to the best estimates that are available at various historical periods and would simply note that this is a matter for independent researchers and sociologists. I rely heavily on the work of Professor Bernard Sabella of Bethlehem University, whose surveys and research are generally recognized by Palestinian Christians and most scholars as the most reliable statistics available. Suffice it to say, that the decline of Palestinian Christianity since 1948 is a striking matter of concern and the data indicates that the community has dropped from approximately 18 percent of the overall population to roughly 1.9 percent as we end the year 2000.

---

[1]  Riah Abu El-Assal, *Caught In Between*, SPCK, London, 1999, xv.
[2]  William Dalrymple, *From the Holy Mountain*, Owl Books/Henry Holt and Company, New York, 1999; 319.

There is no reliable data concerning the religious affiliation of the populations in Palestine prior to the British census of 1922, but estimates of the Christian population in the year 1900 in all of Palestine, including Galilee, the Mediterranean coast, Jerusalem, West Bank and Gaza Strip, range from a high of 18 percent to a modest 10 percent. These estimates are based on the Arab Palestinian Christian population in the Ottoman province known as Palestine in relation to the Jewish and Muslim populations. Recent sociological studies in the Palestinian territories (East Jerusalem, West Bank, and Gaza Strip) claim that the Palestinian Christian population has dropped to a mere 2.4 percent of the total Arab population.[3]

The major expression of the Christian community's sense of hopelessness lies in the high levels of Christian emigration to Europe, North and South America, and Australia. One of the leading Palestinian theologians, Dr Mitri Raheb, Pastor of the Christmas Lutheran Church in Bethlehem, has noted that this is both a local and a regional problem:

> The problem of Christian emigration is terrifying for the whole Christian community in the Middle East, but especially for Palestine. Last year (1994) we published the most detailed study on this subject, 120 pages. What we found is that this problem could make the Holy Land a so-called Christian Disneyland, with nice, old churches where groups can come and wander, but without any real, living community. The Holy Land will lose its sense of significance if there are no Christians there.[4]

One might examine the emigration patterns of Bethlehem, which prior to 1948 was approximately 90 percent Christian, and discover that in the year 2000, there are more Palestinian Christians from Bethlehem living in South America than in Bethlehem itself. Or consider Ramallah, once a major Palestinian Christian city and a centre of culture and commerce for its district just north of Jerusalem. Today there are more Christians from Ramallah living in the United States than in Ramallah, having become productive citizens in such cities as Detroit, San Francisco, San Jose, Chicago, Jacksonville, Florida, and Knoxville, Tennessee. In fact, the metropolitan San Francisco and Detroit areas alone contain more Ramallah Christians than does Ramallah, Palestine.

Those Christian Palestinians who remain do so with mixed feelings. Most see their families find better lives in the West, and either silently or

---

[3]  Naim Ateek, Cedar Duaybis, and Marla Schrader (eds.), *Jerusalem: What Makes for Peace?*, Melisende, London, 1997, 132-134.

[4]  *Christianity Today*, October 2 1995, 34.

overtly they long to join them. With a strong cultural commitment to the nuclear and extended family, most Westerners cannot fully appreciate the magnetic pull that comes to Palestinian families who see their flesh and blood make the difficult but generally successful decision to emigrate. Those who remain in Palestine generally do so either out of a deep commitment to their people, churches, and land, or they lack the economic means to leave.

While most Palestinian Christians have made their new homes in Europe, Canada, South and Central America, Australia, and the United States, the policies of these Western governments have generally been hostile toward Palestinian aspirations. Perhaps more difficult for Palestinian Christians to understand is the overwhelming religious and political support that Western Christians grant to Zionism and the State of Israel. The fact that this support often comes at the expense of Palestinians is a matter that remains relatively unknown to Western Christian conscience. Even issues of such magnitude as population transfers, loss of land, extended closures and economic blight are generally non-issues in the West.

As I conclude this text during Advent, 2000, the Palestinians and Israelis are experiencing a disturbing war of attrition that has claimed nearly 300 lives, 90 percent of which are Christian. An ecumenical Christian leadership delegation has been visiting both Israeli and Palestinian communities, and were particularly disturbed by the scenes of churches, homes, clinics, and social service organizations that have been destroyed as a result of Israeli tank and aerial bombardment. Palestinian Church leaders have declared that Christmas will not be celebrated this year, due to the large numbers of their community who have been killed, maimed, or are suffering from economic deprivation. United Nation's ambassador to the Middle East, Terje Rod Larsen, a key player in the Oslo peace process, declared on 4 December 2000, that roughly 50 percent of Palestinians in these areas are living on 8 shekels per day (approximately $2 US). As the US Christian delegation entered Bethlehem in early December, they were struck by a roadside sign that said: 'Merry Christmas, Thank the United States.' On the sign were pictures of dead children and US manufactured Apache helicopters, used by the Israeli army in the raids on Bethlehem and other areas. Some of the Bethlehem Christians the delegation interviewed expressed their anger at the silence of western Christians who stand idly by as Israel targets Palestinian Christians, encouraging them to emigrate so their land will become available to the state of Israel. The Armenian Patriarch of Jerusalem once stated: 'We feel an increasing sense of alienation from the Christians in the West, particularly those in the United States. While your government supplies Israel with the necessary economic and political tools for our demise, you do nothing to keep us here amidst these troubling developments. We sometimes feel that you do not care if we live or die.'[5] These strong words reflect this growing sense of abandonment felt by Palestinian Christians in the Holy Land, who often visit the Holy sites but show no interest in their fellow sisters and brothers in Christ.

Fr Elias Chacour, a Nobel Peace Prize nominee and builder of schools and communities in Galilee, recently told our tour group: 'We are dying here while Christianity thrives in your [Western] countries. We do not want your pity or even your charity. We simply want your hearts, prayers, and love— and perhaps your respect that we exist in this dreadful state. Until now, we have only a few who have sent a message of true compassion in the spirit of Christ—otherwise we believe you do not care about us.'[6]

At the same time, the Israeli media and much of the Western religious press have given significant media coverage to small groups of Western fundamentalist Christian Zionist organisations and their spokesmen, who generally give Israel their unqualified support. Such prominent Christian spokesmen as televangelist Pat Robertson, 'Focus on the Family' leader Dr James Dobson, and the Revd Jerry Falwell, have given Israel significant assistance by advancing their public opinion campaigns, facilitating political support for Israel in the US Senate and House of Representatives, as well as financial assistance through tourism and other measures.

In Jerusalem, many of these interests are advanced by a Christian fundamentalist group called the International Christian Embassy-Jerusalem, which sees its role 'To comfort and support Israel'. Such support often takes the role of bringing Russian Jews and to live in exclusively Jewish colonies on Palestinian land. ICEJ has even raised funds for illegal settlements in the Bethlehem area on land taken from Palestinian Christian and Muslim farmers, granting them no compensation. Such actions have projected a negative image of Western Evangelical Christianity and sometimes of Christianity itself to Muslim leaders, who have difficulty distinguishing one form of Christianity from the other. Such developments can project the impression that Christianity is a Western, Zionist-supporting religion in a region of 250 million Muslims. As a result, tension can increase on the local Christian minorities and they are often viewed as 'a fifth column' in the Arab-Muslim Middle East, supporting Zionism over Arab aspirations.

In the chapters before us, I will register my plea to all concerned persons, but particularly Christians, Muslims, and Arab or Jewish residents of Europe and North America, to hear and respond to the crisis in the Holy

---

[5]  Dalrymple, *op. cit.*

[6]  Fr Elias Chacour in a speech to the Evangelicals for Middle East Understanding, Open Doors Group, 17 May 1997, at Prophet Elias College, Ibillin, Israel.

Land. In some ways, newcomers to the complicated Arab-Israeli conflict might understand the issues more clearly by examining this small slice of the problem, the 'slow death' of Palestinian Christianity. I have drawn upon my experiences but more importantly, I have turned to the research by academics, to interviews I have conducted in recent visits to Israel and Palestine, and to the everyday experiences of Palestinian Christians from all walks of life, all denominations, both those living in the diaspora or remaining in Palestine.

Chapters 1-3 review the early history of the Palestinian Christian community from the first Christian Pentecost to their experience under Islam. Chapter 1, 'Identity and Continuity', explores questions of identity in relation to the modern state of Israel and Zionism, and the relationship with Islam. Six short profiles of contemporary Palestinian Christians provide personal accounts of different leaders from this community. The second chapter, 'From Pentecost to the Rise of Islam', begins with the Apostolic Era' (30-64), continues through Roman persecution, the developments under the 'Christian' Byzantine empire, the rise of the monastic and pilgrimage traditions in Palestine, and the coming of Islam. Both the strength of Palestinian Christianity at its peak and the beginnings of fragmentation are seen through this chapter. Chapter 3, 'Palestinian Christians Under Islam', begins with the peaceful entry of the new Arabian religion into Jerusalem and the submission of the (Orthodox) Patriarch to the caliph. Initially the relationship with the Muslim leaders brought theological dialogue and was characterized by tolerance and respect. By and large, Islam was very tolerant with both Christians and Jews, but we note certain exceptions that can only be characterized as oppression and persecution, such as the reign of the 'mad' Caliph al-Hakim (996-1021). Perhaps the most tragic and enduring blight on the record of Christian presence in the Middle East are the Crusades, still remembered as a European Christian intervention in the Middle East. The chapter ends with the longest of the Muslim eras, the Ottoman empire, punctuated as it was by western political intervention, missionary activity, and then Napoleon.

Chapters 4-6 focus on the rise of Zionism in Europe as a response to western antisemitism, while I continue to keep an eye on the Palestinian Christians. Chapter 4, 'Foundations of Injustice', examines the situation in Europe in the 19th century that gave rise to various forms of nationalism and the curse of antisemitism. In Palestine, the dying Ottoman empire stimulated the dominant Palestinian Arab community to explore thoughts of independence, and Christians were in the forefront of these developments. The chapter demonstrates the support given to Zionism by Great Britain and the acceleration of Jewish settlement. The political manoeuvres and various promises made to Zionists and to Palestinians during the decade of World

War I deepened the seeds of conflict that would soon explode in crisis. Chapter 5, 'The Ambivalence of Hand and Voice: Palestine Under Britain, looks at the British Mandate era (1922-48), and the critical decisions that altered the situation in favour of the Zionists, at the expense of the Palestinian majority. The Christians of Palestine were caught in the sweep of events that would see them begin to lose significant numbers, property, and influence. Chapter 6, 'Zion's Triumph, Palestine's *Nakba*/Catastrophe', offers a critical and controversial look at the events surrounding the establishment of the state of Israel and the violence that ensued in the Holy Land. It is during these tragic three years that the Palestinians and the Palestinian Christians suffered their single worse loss of land and population in Palestine.

Chapters 7-9 turn to the events in the last 50 years since Israel has become not only a reality but the strongest military force in the Middle East. Chapter 7 looks at what many analysts consider the most important aspect of the Zionist-Palestinian conflict, the issue of land and land loss. Various strategies employed by the new Zionist state against Palestinians and especially Palestinian Christians in Galilee are discussed, including ways in which Christian leaders have collaborated with the Jewish state at the expense of the local Christians. Chapter 8, ''The Negation of Time and Space' takes a more philosophical and theological look at the same period, reflecting on how Zionism, as a form of Jewish nationalism, overpowered Palestinian national identity but had as one of its primary goals the defeat of Palestinian national consciousness and its political and institutional expressions. The *Intifada* of 1987-91, for a brief moment turned the Palestinian political decline into a revived national resistance inside Israel and the Occupied Territories, the Gulf War seemed to undermine all the gains. Chapter 9, 'The Oslo Process', reviews the promise and present peril of the peace process that began secretly in Oslo and led to the now famous White House signing on 13 September 1993. The chapter studies why the Oslo process is failing and the likelihood that it will bring an Apartheid-like situation to the Palestinian areas rather than peace. In this deteriorating economic and political context, Palestinian Christianity is indeed dying, and as many say, has only a generation before it disappears.

The concluding chapter (10), 'Death or Resurrection', searches for a spiritual and practical calling for Palestinian Christians and those international friends who would be in solidarity with them through this time of agony. The chapter asks whether there is are unique and perhaps not so unique roles for Palestinian Christians to play in terms of being a sign of 'redemptive suffering', reconciliation, and seeds of renewal. It becomes clear that there must be strong support from the Palestinian Christian Diaspora and international partners if there is to be any renewal. The Epilogue issues a 'Proposal' to be discussed by Palestinian Christian leaders and the grass-roots, as well as international partner agencies and concerned friends, to consider practical and immediate steps that can be taken to become more intentional in acts of solidarity that seek the transformation of Palestinian Christianity in our time. The Proposal, like the text that precedes it, are submitted as an often imperfect but hopefully stimulating challenge that seeks discussion, further research, and action. One sign of that action will come from the Palestinian Christians themselves, such as the *Sabeel* Liberation Theology Centre, whose 'Jerusalem Document' is included as an Appendix and provides a theological, moral, legal, and political analysis, all within seven pages.

A work of this length and scope is dependent on a wider community that has become 'family' over 25 years of travel, study, and service. The Palestinians, both Christian and Muslim, as well as the progressive Jewish community in Israel, have become a significant of my life and vocation. Much of the analysis and the content that follows owe an enormous debt to them. However, I must take full responsibility for what is written, as it may have overstated or poorly articulated. All conclusions put and every assumption is mine, and while intended to be truthful, I confess that there are times ones vision is limited. Nonetheless, what follows is my humble attempt to engage the reader and a broader community around issues that seem to me urgent.

# Chapter 1
# PALESTINIAN CHRISTIANS:
# IDENTITY AND CONTINUITY

Not long ago, the popular former Mayor of Jerusalem, Teddy Kollek, an Austrian Jew, made the startling claim that Palestinian Christianity, in fact Christianity itself, is not indigenous to Palestine. After all, with Jesus' birth in Bethlehem and his death and resurrection in Jerusalem, it would seem that Mr Kollek's words would be readily dismissed. However, there is a more subtle and perhaps calculated challenge for the indigenous Palestinian Christians and their churches than one may initially grasp. Here are the former Mayor's exact words:

> Christianity ... sprang up and developed far from the scene of Jesus' last ministry, notably in Antioch and other parts of the Middle East and the eastern Mediterranean, where his disciples recounted his teachings, his parables, the stories of his miracles in his lifetime and his resurrection and ascension. Jerusalem itself ... remained comparatively untouched by the views expounded by the latest victim of Rome.[1]

This stinging critique has at least three components that challenge Christianity. First, Kollek claims Christianity is not indigenous to Palestine. It may have been born in Jerusalem and was present in many other cities and districts at one point in history, but it 'developed far from the scene of Jesus' last ministry.' He mentions Antioch, but the thrust of his case is that Palestine and Jerusalem are not home to Christianity. In other words, let Christians claim Antioch, Athens, or Rome, thereby making the case that Christianity is essentially Western. Second, Kollek goes on to imply that Christianity cannot claim a continuous presence in Jerusalem or the 'Holy Land'. This statement would open the door for him to assert that only Judaism can make that claim, one of the arguments used by Zionists to justify their claims to the land they call Israel. In essence, the land, its cities, resources, and contemporary political sovereignty belong to the Jews. Others might be welcomed to live under Jewish-Israeli sovereignty, but we must be clear as to who is in charge.

---

[1] Quoted in Kenneth Cragg, *Palestine: The Prize and Price of Zion*, Cassell, London Publications, 1997, 218.

Third, there is a subtle assumption by Kollek that Christianity is a 'derived religion,' Judaism being its historical superior and by implication the more authentic and complete religion. Christianity grew out of Judaism, without question, but Christianity also has its own unique revelation in Jesus Christ and its universal message of God's love for all humanity. Christianity may have its roots in Judaism but not in the derived sense of dependency nor in a manner that would undermine its authenticity. Some branches of Judaism and most Zionist traditions, whether secular or religious, do not grant Christianity legitimacy in Israel and Palestine, particularly when it comes to land claims and historical attachments to Israel. Thus a political argument is made from Mr Kollek's simple but profound statement which essentially provides Israel with jurisdiction over the land, including the holy places. These issues have important ramifications for the residents of Israel and Palestine today. If Palestinian Christians and Muslims in Bethlehem wish to pray at the Church of the Holy Sepulchre or al-Aqsa Mosque in Jerusalem, or Christians from Ramallah wish to attend the Christmas Eve celebration in Bethlehem, Israel can deny them entry. In fact, since March 1993, the overwhelming majority of Palestinian Christians living outside the boundaries of Jerusalem have not been allowed to visit family, obtain medical services, or pray in Jerusalem, the most important city for Palestinian Christians and Muslims. However, you and I, as Europeans or Americans, like any Israeli Jew, can travel wherever we desire in Israel and the Palestinian areas.

Another major challenge to Palestinian Christianity (and all Christians) comes from Islam, by historical definition the youngest of the Abrahamic monotheisms (according to Muslim belief, Adam was the first Muslim, making Islam the oldest). The challenge of Islam also goes to the core of Palestinian Christian identity and asks three very different questions. First, if Christianity is so divided by its multiple theological splits and competing ecclesiastical bodies, how can it be true to the one God it serves? The history of divisions in Christianity give Islam a strong case which is felt acutely in the Middle East where Christianity's diminishing numbers seem to make the case that its doctrines are foolish and perhaps false. Islam's second challenge is also theological for it makes the case that the Qu'ran was given to the Prophet Muhammad as the final revelation in order to correct various aberrations of belief and practice that had entered Judaism with its elevation of the Jews as 'The Chosen People' and Christianity with such unacceptable doctrines as God's incarnation in Jesus, his resurrection from the dead, and the Trinity. Islam rightly challenges the variety of biblical texts and the variety of translations of the Bible to ask: 'how can you trust the Bible as the Word of God when you have so many sources and versions?' Islam on the other hand points to the Qu'ran, which Muhammad received directly from Allah through the angel Gabriel, and because Muhammad was illiterate, he was a pure recipient. Muhammad recited the revelation perfectly and accurately. Others wrote it down exactly as it was recited from Muhammad, thus the Qur'an means 'the recitation'. It is believed to be the true revelation of Allah and corrects those places where Judaism and Christianity diverted from the true message. These are only a few of the theological challenges that Islam brings to Christianity, but the power of its message represents a constant critique and challenge to Palestinian Christians and Middle Eastern Christians in general.

Islam also claims dominance in social, political, and religious arrangements through the *dhimmi* system. Christians live under Islam and its legal system *(shari'a)* as a religious community that is protected by a contract called the *millet* ('religious community'). However, like Zionism, Islam must exercise political and religious sovereignty where it is dominant. Christian submission and at times humiliation under Islam remains the case in some Islamic countries where a more conservative interpretation of *shari'a* applies. Dr Habib Malik, son of the great Lebanese statesman and architect of the United Nations, Dr Charles Malik, articulates a more severe critique of Islam than most Middle East Christians would offer:

> Over the centuries, political Islam has not been too kind to the native Christian communities living under its rule. Anecdotes of tolerance aside, the systematic treatment of Christians and Jews (who fall under the Islamic category of *dhimmi*) as second-class citizens is abusive and discriminatory by any standard. Under Islam, the *dhimmi* are not allowed to build new places of worship, or renovate existing ones; *dhimmi* women are available for marriage to Muslims while the reverse is strictly prohibited; the political rights of *dhimmis* are absent; and the targeted *dhimmi* community and each individual in it are made to live in a state of perpetual humiliation in the eyes of the ruling community.[2]

Islam has its own claims to Jerusalem through the Prophet's 'Night Journey' and due to the fact that it has ruled over Jerusalem and Palestine longer than the other Abrahamic monotheisms. Today, the biggest political alternative to the Palestinian Authority is the Islamic movement Hamas, whose goal is to establish an Islamic state in all of historic Palestine with Jerusalem as its capital, with the state linked to an Islamic empire across the Middle

---

[2] Habib C Malik, 'Christians in the Land Called Holy', *First Things*, January 1999, 11.

East. While Muslims point to a record of greater tolerance toward Christians and Jews when it ruled Palestine, many Palestinian Christians and secular Muslims wonder about their future status in a revived *dhimmi* arrangement under Hamas. Many Palestinian Christians argue that such an arrangement will be an improvement over present conditions, while others doubt it. They ask: 'What assurances do I have now that I will not be caught in a situation such as Southern Sudan or Upper Egypt, where extremists are using Islam for their political agendas?'

I raised this question at a personal interview at the home of Shaikh Ahmad Yassin, founder and leader of Hamas. He responded to my question about the future of Christians, stating, 'Christians will have complete freedom in our state, even more than they have now.'[3] But one must wonder about the 'fine print' in the arrangement. Will Christians be represented in government? Will there be a bill of rights or constitution to safeguard their rights, or will Islamic law *(shari'a)* be the only basis for human and civil rights? The challenges to Palestinian Christian identity and continuity come not only from Judaism and Islam, but from 'fellow' Christians. Allow me to mention only two of the challenges. First is the issue of division and competition within the Christian community. Those who have visited the Church of the Holy Sepulchre are well aware of the unfriendly competition and territorial battles that the Christians maintain there, to the embarrassment of most Christians. The indigenous Palestinian Christians have been divided within themselves for centuries, which is true, but many of the divisions evolved from outside political or religious powers who imposed control over doctrine or church property, and rarely acted in the interests of the local community. Here lies an important second problem emerging from Christians, and it is still haunting local Christians. We will see that a form of colonial control of several churches has become a major point of contention over such issues as the sale of church property, the language of the liturgy, and whether Palestinian priests and bishops control the decision-making of the local communities.

These are among the complex issues that shape, weaken, confuse, and characterise the struggle of Palestinian Christians for their identity and continuity in their homeland. Whether under Israel's Zionism in its various manifestations of political and religious power or in the Islamic Middle East, the Christian individual and the church collectively are vulnerable in their weakness. Christians are the minority community in every Middle Eastern country and as such they must struggle with issues of discrimination and second-class status while they have little or no political power. As Westerners

---

[3] Interview by the author with Shaikh Yassin Ahmad in his home in Gaza City (Palestine), 27 May 2000.

try to understand these issues, they must put aside assumptions of civil liberties, equality, and protection under the law. In the Middle East, the playing field of citizenship and the nature of the societies are very different from that to which we are accustomed. A very different Christian challenge is the increasing presence and visibility of Western Evangelical Christian Zionists, who support the political actions and dominance of the State of Israel, as if the modern state is a fulfilment of biblical prophecy. Such groups as the International Christian Embassy-Jerusalem, Bridges for Peace, and many British or North American Christian Zionist organisations are gaining visibility in the Middle East through their television and radio broadcasts. Thus Christianity is projected into a predominantly Muslim world as a Western, Zionist religious movement rather than an indigenous Arab religious community that predates the arrival of Islam. When the identity of Christianity becomes that of a Western, Zionist fundamentalism, local Palestinian Christians (and other Middle Eastern Christians) find their identity and historic continuity under suspicion.

So who or what is a Palestinian Christian? Let us listen to the stories of six Palestinian Christians, each very different from the other, but all represent various aspects of Palestinian Christianity today.

## 1. Nora Kort

Consider Nora Kort, an articulate Greek Orthodox woman and a lay-leader in her church, who is a child of Jerusalem's Christian community. Nora was six years old when the modern State of Israel was established. During the hostilities of 1948, her family was forced out of their home which was located in the affluent Western side of the city. They lost everything, including their house and most of their possessions, and were forced to create a new life in Arab East Jerusalem. Nora explains: 'I have five identities. I am a Palestinian, a Christian, a Greek Orthodox, a Jerusalemite, and an Arab living under Israeli occupation (but not a citizen of Israel). As an Orthodox Christian, I trace my roots to the first Apostles of Jesus, so the Orthodox Christian community has an unbroken connection with the first Disciples and most important, with Jesus himself. But unfortunately, my church has been dominated by the Greeks and they have not been good stewards of our Palestinian Arab traditions or for our property.' As a Palestinian Christian and a woman, Nora must negotiate various layers of cultural and political identity as she goes about her work as a community organiser and leader of a charitable organisation in Jerusalem's Old City. By claiming that her primary identity is Palestinian, Nora notes that she was born and raised a Palestinian Arab and has identified herself completely with the geographic area called the Holy Land, Israel, or Palestine. These competing titles and claims are part of the confusion facing Nora. She sees Palestine with a long-term historical perspective as a land shared by ancient Semitic tribes and languages, including the Canaanites who welcomed Abraham in Jerusalem and Hebron. Thus her identity has a territorial dimension, and while it is filled with political and religious conflict, this territory known historically as Palestine or Israel is her home.

Why use the term 'Palestinian Christian' as opposed to Israeli or Arab Christian? At the very least, it means that Nora has been shaped culturally and to an extent religiously by a people and history called Palestinian. The people who live in the land called Palestine from the Roman era who identify with the land, its people, and its history, are called Palestinians.

## 2. Revd Dr Mitri Raheb

Nora's neighbour from Bethlehem, Pastor Mitri Raheb, received his Ph.D. from Marburg University in Germany. Pastor Raheb's family has lived in the Bethlehem region for several hundred years. The name Raheb means 'monk' in Arabic, indicating there were once monks in the family. Mitri is Greek, so they know the family was once Greek Orthodox. Mitri's great-grandfather, Constantine, and his wife died tragically at a very young age and left a small son named Mitri, who was raised in a Lutheran orphanage founded by the German missionary Johann Schneller. Grandfather Mitri wished to remain faithful to his Greek Orthodox heritage, but upon graduation from high school, discovered that the church hierarchy was more interested in their holy sites than the people. He challenged the bishops and priests and found the foreign control of the church insurmountable, so he joined the Lutheran Church in Bethlehem.

The Revd Dr Mitri Raheb, now a third generation Palestinian Lutheran from Bethlehem, is today pastoring in his native city as leader of a dynamic and creative ministry based at the Christmas Lutheran Church, just a few blocks from Manger Square. Among his central concerns is the development of an authentic, indigenous Palestinian Arab liturgy with accompanying music and art, and to recover their ancient roots as Palestinian Christians. In his thoughtful book, *I am a Palestinian Christian*, Pastor Raheb writes:

> My identity was stamped by the fact that I was born in this particular place. I feel I have something like a special relationship to David and to Christ—a relationship developed not only by way of the Bible, nor only through faith, but also

by way of the land. I share my city and my land with David and with Jesus. My self-understanding as a Christian Palestinian has a territorial dimension. I feel that I am living in a continuity of locale with these biblical figures, sharing the same landscape culture, and environment with them. One need not make a pilgrimage, since one is already at the source itself, at the point of origin.[4]

The land between the Mediterranean and Jordan River was called by the Romans *Palestina* after the year 70 AD, and perhaps earlier. Thus the people of this region are sometimes called Israelites or Canaanites, but after the Roman era they can also be called Palestinians, whether they are Jews, Christians, or after the seventh century Muslims.

The geography of Palestine defines and restricts Nora and Mitri, but it also gives further definition to their Semitic roots, for Nora and Mitri are as Semitic as are the Jews of Israel and New York. The term Semite was initially used as a linguistic designation for various languages of the eastern Mediterranean, such as Akkadian, Hebrew, Assyrian, Syriac, Aramaic, and Arabic. Subsequently, those who spoke a Semitic language could be called Semites, although in recent decades the term has been applied exclusively to persons of Jewish background, whether or not they were religious or ethnic Jews.

Palestine's location at the crossroads of Africa and Asia, as well as at the juncture of the European-Mediterranean basin and Southwest Asia, has left this land prey to a literal parade of outside nations and empires. Each empire has left a significant aspect of its culture and in certain cases its religion, language, and ethnic heritage with the local population. The land has been inhabited by, among others, Canaanites, Philistines, Hebrew (Jews), Nabateans, Byzantines, Arabs, Turks, and British. Now the Jews have returned in a new form, with many from the European and Middle Eastern diasporas. In reality there are no pure ethnic Palestinians, Jews, or Israelis, but a mixture of bloodlines and cultures. One can see blond Palestinians and Jews, red-headed Palestinians in Gaza and many red-headed Jews of Ashkenazi heritage. There are African Palestinians and Ethiopian Jews, Yemeni Jews and various shades of colouring and linguistic or ethnic heritage in both communities. Many Palestinians joke that for them the red or blond hair is a legacy of the Crusades.

As for Palestinian Christians, this 'Semitic' ethnic inclusivity is

---

[4]   Mitri Raheb, *I Am A Palestinian Christian*, Fortress Press, Minneapolis, 1995, 3.

clearly reflected in the account of the birth of the Church. According to the Acts of the Apostles, 'there were devout Jews from every nation under heaven living in Jerusalem' for the Jewish Feast of Pentecost. Included in the gathering were 'Parthians, Medes, Elamites and residents of Mesopotamia, Judea and Cappadocia, Pontus and Asia, Phrygia and Pamphylia, Egypt and the parts of Libya belonging to Cyrene, and visitors from Rome, both Jews and proselytes, Cretans and Arabs' (Acts 2:9-11). Today one would say that this Jewish and Gentile gathering came from Europe, Central Asia, Persia, Africa, and the Middle East.

This remarkable mosaic of bloodlines, ethnic groups, nations and cultures at the first Christian Pentecost characterised early Christianity and influenced its message of universal acceptance of all races and peoples. St Paul stated the universal inclusivity of Christianity in Galatians 3:28: 'There is no longer Jew nor Greek, there is no longer slave nor free, there is no longer male nor female; for you are all one in Christ Jesus.' Sadly, the Church has rarely lived up to this ideal, becoming a bastion of racism in the United States, a champion of apartheid in South Africa, a supporter of Hitler's antisemitism, and too often subjecting its message of universal acceptance to one form of nationalism or racism after the other. This universal inclusion of the early Christian message is in marked contrast to the ethnic particularism or 'chosenness' that has reappeared in most tributaries of contemporary political Zionism.

### 3. Edward W Said

Many Palestinian Christians have a complicated identity and have had to spend a considerable portion of their lives trying to make sense of it. Consider the Palestinian scholar and writer Dr Edward W Said who is Professor of English and Comparative Literature at Columbia University in New York City and known for his scholarship in such fields as English literature, classical music criticism, and Middle East politics. He was born in Jerusalem into a well-to-do Christian family. Today, he is perhaps the most influential Palestinian in North America and possibly the Western world. Recently Said has written a biography titled *Out of Place*, the very title of which captures his struggle for identity and roots.

Professor Said's story is not exceptional among Palestinians, for it is a story of exile from historic Palestine and then a journey from place to place, culture to culture. He was born in Jerusalem and named after Edward, Prince of Wales, which reflects the orientation of his Palestinian father, who was more influenced by British culture than the Arab culture of Palestine. Edward cannot recall if his first language was Arabic or English, but the latter won out in influence and practice, even in Cairo where he grew up. His loving and tender mother was from Nazareth, where her father was a Texas-educated Baptist minister. These varied and often conflicting influences caused Said to reflect:

> Not only could I not absorb, much less master, all the meanderings and interruptions of these details as they broke up a simple dynastic sequence, but I could not grasp why she (his mother) was not a straight English mummy. I have retained this unsettled sense of many identities—mostly in conflict with each other—all of my life, together with an acute memory of the despairing feeling that I wish we could have been all-Arab, or all-European and American, or all-Orthodox Christian, or all Muslim, or all-Egyptian, and so on.[5]

This agonising quest for identity, complicated by a series of dislocations with new cultural and linguistic influences, can be repeated by more than half of the seven to eight million Palestinians of the world.

Thus far we have observed the complicated web of identities that Palestinian Christians (and Muslims) must work through in order to grasp a clear sense of their roots. Professor Said, having been uprooted from historic Palestine and raised in Egypt, was detached from his origins. His father's British values and even his names—Edward (after British royalty) and the Arabic Said—further complicated his self-understanding. Language, a British and American education, plus psychological and developmental pressures to 'fit in' added to his burden. Combine these pressures with the Western and Zionist bias against Palestinian Arab identity, plus the virtual negation of the idea of 'Palestine', and one has a nearly insurmountable mountain to climb.

Through it all Said has achieved excellence in three fields (English literature, classical music, and Middle East politics). After two decades of disinterest in his political writings, Said is now taken seriously by the *New York Times* and many mainstream journals and newspapers in Europe and the United States. Born a Palestinian Christian but today a thoroughgoing secularist, Edward Said is nonetheless another product of Jerusalem's vibrant Christian community which is slowly being squeezed out of the Holy City.

### 4. Bishop Riah Abu El-Assal

One might ask, how can Palestinian Christians be Arabs? Are not all Arabs Muslims? The answer is an emphatic 'NO.' Bishop Riah Abu El-Assal of the

---

[5]   Edward W Said, *Out of Place*, Alfred A Knopf, New York, 1999, 5.

Anglican Church is fond of claiming: 'Before Muhammad was, I am.' As already noted, there were Jews or proselytes at Pentecost who came from the Arabian peninsula (Acts 2:11). They were technically called Arabs. The British scholar Spencer Trimingham has traced the roots of several Christian tribes in Arabia. We also know that St Paul was mentored in Arabia after his conversion on the road to Damascus, which Trimingham believes was in the Nabatean empire, surrounding Petra in southern Jordan today.

Trimingham also notes that there was a significant Christian community in the Najran in southwestern Arabia (western Yemen today) where the Monophysite type of Christianity had found a home. He cites the Arabic Nestorian work the *Chronicle of Seert* as tracing the conversion of the merchant Hannan, the first Christian leader of the Najran, who brought his beliefs home and converted his family, formed a house church, and soon the tribe and region became Christians.

Trimingham also cites a Himyarite king, Abed Kulal, who was converted by a Syrian Christian and lived in the 460s. It is believed there were significant Nestorian, Coptic, and Abyssinian (Ethiopian) mission efforts in Arabia between the 1st and 4th centuries AD resulting in a series of Christian tribes, monasteries and churches being established prior to the time of Muhammad. The Church in Najran was associated with the monastery Deir Najran, which is called Ka'bat Janran (Church of Najran) in extra-Quranic Muslim sources. In 530, King Abraha consolidated his power in the coastal region of what is today Yemen, and converted to Christianity. His announcement of his rule used a trinitarian Christian formula: 'By the power of the Merciful One, and his Messiah, and the Holy Spirit,' (Abraha announces) 'he is King of Saba and Dun Raidan and Hadramawt and Yamanat, and of the Arabs of the highlands and lowlands.'[6]

But Christianity did not last in Arabia, due to its serious divisions which were exacerbated by the Byzantine empire's attempts to enforce its Chalcedonian Christianity on the region in conjunction with various military invasions and attempts at conquest. The divisions were so deep that most Christians either left or were expelled during a subsequent Persian invasion and the coming of Islam. Many believe that most of the Christians of Arabia fled to north-central Arabia, or what is today Jordan. Others may have travelled to Palestine during this turbulent period. Palestinians have evidence of the migration of Arabian Christian tribes to Palestine in the 5th century, some settling in the Ramallah district and others in the Bethlehem region. There are several Christian Bedouin communities in Jordan today who trace their roots to the Arabian peninsula.

---

[6] J S Trimingham, *Christianity Among the Arabs in Pre-Islamic Times*, 301ff.

## 5. Fr Emile Salayta

Fr Emile is a Catholic priest in the Palestinian village of Bir Zeit and also Director of Education for the Latin Patriarchate, covering all Catholic schools in Palestine and Jordan. The articulate and winsome young priest has brought a spirit of renewal to the parishes and schools with which he works. Several US evangelical leaders and churches have formed a close relationship with Fr Emil, whose message is of personal salvation in Jesus Christ and a call for justice for the Palestinian people. The National Presbyterian Church in Washington, DC has been twinned in an exciting sister church relationship with Fr Emile's Catholic parish in Bir Zeit. Both communities have been enriched and inspired by the relationship and have grown in fellowship and solidarity with each other's promise and pain. The American Christians who meet Fr Emile are often unable to comprehend that he is an Arab and a Bedouin.

By the time of Muhammad's death in 632, the entire Arabian peninsula came under Islamic rule. Christian and Jewish tribes were allowed to retain their faith if they desired, according to terms agreed with Muhammad. However, by 644, the second 'Rightly Guided' Caliph 'Umar, rejected the treaty and forced Christianity out of the peninsula. With the entry of Islam into the Holy Land in 636, the Arabic language and its culture gradually gave new definition to the residents of Palestine. Most of the population gradually accepted Islam, perhaps 80 percent, leaving around 18 percent Christians and a tiny Jewish community until the 20th century. The Arabic language was adopted in Palestine alongside Greek in the Church, but gradually spread throughout the Middle East and North Africa as the successors of Muhammad extended the new religion and language from the borders of India to the frontiers of Spain. The Islamic studies scholar Kenneth Cragg writes:

> It seems fair to assume that the ethnic factor had become very attenuated through the centuries and that what Islam brought was not primarily an accession of Arab blood but rapid Arabisation via language. It was Arabness through Arabic that within a century or so became the vital factor in the making of identity.[7]

When Palestinian Christians like Fr Emile, Nora Kort or Mitri Raheb relax with their families or close friends, they converse in Arabic and share a rich body of folksongs, dances, and literature that have shaped their

---

[7] Kenneth Cragg, *The Arab Christian*, Westminster/John Knox Press, Louisville, 1991, 14.

worldview. There are clear cultural practices that have emerged through the centuries that have become the norm in Arab societies, including conservative gender roles that are not challenged in public. Arab hospitality is unmatched in its treatment of strangers. Dress is conservative, with women rarely exposing the neckline and shoulders and men dressing well, often in sport-coats, but rarely in shorts.

When Nora worships, the prayers and scripture readings are in Arabic, but with some elements still in Greek, a matter of great tension among Palestinian Orthodox Christians. When Mitri Raheb leads the liturgy at the Christmas Lutheran Church, it is in Arabic. Thus there is an authentic Arab Christian history, with roots in the Arabian peninsula after Pentecost and establishing various communities and tribal roots throughout the region. Arab Christian tribes made their way to Jordan and Palestine prior to the coming of Islam. However, clearly after the arrival of Islam in Palestine, there was a gradual cultural and linguistic Arabisation of Palestine, giving Christianity a distinctly Arab orientation by the year 800 AD.

## 6. Cedar Duaybis

Mrs Cedar Duaybis represents another dimension of Palestinian identity: the Israeli Palestinians who became refugees in their own land in 1948. Cedar was born in Haifa and recalls the harmony that existed in the city among the Christians, Muslims, and Jews prior to the 1940s. They were essentially one community, at least until the massive Zionist settlement campaign of the 1920s-30s. Cedar grew up somewhat like Edward Said, but it was her highly educated mother who was more British than Arab. Cedar also recalls a streak of Palestinian nationalism which carried over from her grandparents, who were active during the 1908-15 period when Palestinian Christians in Haifa and Nazareth were in the forefront of the newly emerging Palestinian national movement. Although the movement died out by the end of World War I with successive campaigns by the Ottomans, British and Zionists, she still recalls its impact.

When hostilities broke out in 1948, Cedar's family, like the majority of Palestinians in Haifa and Galilee, were driven from their homes, most of which had been in their families for hundreds of years. They would never return to their homes because they were promptly seized by the new State of Israel and turned over to Jewish families. As we shall see in Chapter 8, the Israeli militias had developed a strategy called 'Plan Dalet' (letter D in the Hebrew alphabet), a carefully calculated military strategy designed to depopulate major concentrations of Palestinians and displace them with Jewish residents.

Ironically, three of the Executive Board of the promising *Sabeel* movement in Jerusalem are Israeli Palestinian Christians, who lost their homes and livelihood in 1948: Cedar Duaybis, Fr Elias Chacour (whose story is told in his book *Blood Brothers*), and Revd Dr Naim Ateek, the Director of *Sabeel* (the Palestinian Liberation Theology Centre) in Jerusalem, whose story is told in *Justice and Only Justice*.[8] Each of them, when asked 'who are you?' will answer: 'I am a Palestinian Christian, a citizen of Israel, and a refugee in my own land.' These three dimensions of identity have shaped their lives with scars and wounds that have empowered their quest for faith and a just peace for their people as well as Israeli Jews.

Thus we have observed six profiles that demonstrate some, but not all of the complicated aspects of Palestinian Christian identity:

1. Nora Kort, a Palestinian Greek Orthodox Christian woman from Jerusalem
2. Rev Dr Mitri Raheb, a Palestinian Christian who is a Lutheran with an Orthodox heritage from Bethlehem
3. Bishop Riah Abu El-Assal, a native of Nazareth and an Israeli Palestinian Anglican bishop in Jerusalem
4. Dr Edward Said, a Palestinian Christian who is primarily secular and part of the Palestinian *diaspora*, spending nearly his entire life outside the country of his birth
5. Fr Emile Salayta, a Bedouin whose family line can be traced back to Arabia but is today a Catholic priest and head of the Latin (Roman) Catholic education in Palestine and Jordan
6. Cedar Duaybis, a Palestinian Arab Christian who is a citizen of Israel, but was displaced in 1948 and lost her home, other property, and her family lost their livelihood.

Nevertheless, all six have recovered their Palestinian Arab Christian identity in significant ways, engaging their faith with the issues of justice in their homeland. All have been shaped by the Palestinian tragedy but none has abandoned his/her dream of realising a time when, if not they, then perhaps their children will live in a Palestinian state that is at peace with Israel (or evolves into a single democratic state). All are working toward these goals in their own ways, not having forgotten what they lost in the process. None of the six will be satisfied with anything less than full compensation for what they have lost and a state that is fully sovereign in its own land with leadership that represents them, is chosen by them and is free of foreign domination.

---

[8]  See Elias Chacour, *Blood Brothers*, Chosen Books, Grand Rapids, Michigan, 1984; and Naim Ateek, *Justice and Only Justice*, Maryknoll, Orbis Books, New York, 1989.

# Summary

1. Zionist ideology and its implementation challenge Palestinian Christianity in at least four ways: a) in claiming that Christianity is not native to Palestine; b) by portraying Palestinian Christianity as Western, not Middle Eastern in its origins and present character in the region; c) by exercising sovereignty over the land Zionists can design and redesign Israel and Palestine, often at the expense of Palestinians; d) by implying that Christianity is essentially Western, it then follows that it is at best derived and at worst inferior.

2. Islam challenges Palestinian Christianity in at least three ways: a) it claims Christianity is filled with divisions and thus cannot be the true revealed religion of God/Allah; b) Islam questions key Christian doctrines such as the person and work of Christ, the divine nature of Christ, and the Trinity; c) the *dhimmi* system places Christianity under the control of Islam and renders it a protected but inferior status; d) an Islamic state in Palestine, if conservative in its application of *shari'a* law, could be problematic for the future of Palestinian Christianity.

3. Western fundamentalist Christian Zionism challenges Palestinian Christianity: a) by endorsing a modern Zionist state as the fulfilment of the biblical prophecies; b) as it receives an inordinate amount of radio, television, and press attention enabling its influence to be exaggerated by projecting a Western, Zionist branch of Christianity into a predominantly Muslim region, Christianity is misrepresented as a hostile phenomenon, thus bringing additional pressures on indigenous Arab Christians.

4. Palestinian Christian identities are varied and complicated. While all are Arab, Christian, and Palestinian, some are citizens of Israel, others of the Palestinian territories; still others are part of the diaspora.

5. There were Christian tribes and districts in 'Arabia' 300-400 years before Muhammad, and Christianity has been present in a continuous basis in Palestine since Pentecost (30 AD) Arab Christian tribes arrived in Palestine in the 4th century. Thus one can state that there have been Arab Christians in Palestine (and Jordan) since the late 4th or early 5th century.

# Chapter 2
# FROM PENTECOST TO
# THE RISE OF ISLAM

One of my Palestinian Christian friends was asked at the Presbyterian church I attend: 'When did you become a Christian?' Thinking the answer would be to the credit of Protestant missionaries of recent vintage, the questioner was completely thrown off by the response: 'Well, I grew up in Nazareth and we were told that our family was Christian since the time of Jesus. In fact, my great, great grandmother, many times removed, used to baby-sit for Jesus when he was a little boy.' Of course, the comment was tongue in cheek, but he made an important point. Palestinian Christians believe they are part of an unbroken historical continuity that dates back to Jesus and the first Disciples. The chapters ahead of us will attempt to provide an historical overview of the Palestinian Christian experience from the day of Pentecost to the year 2000. The survey is neither exhaustive as history nor does it represent a strictly academic account. While it is built upon a scholarly foundation, my hope is to provide a narrative on Palestinian Christianity that is readable and reliable. Additionally, the reader will be able to trace the highlights of 2000 years of history in the Holy Land as the Palestinian Christians have experienced it.

## The Apostolic Age (30-64)

Our historical survey of Palestinian Christianity begins in Jerusalem. Luke's account in the Book of Acts notes that Jesus' Ascension took place on the Mount of Olives, just east of the Old City. As Luke reports, just prior to Jesus' departure the Disciples asked if he would now 'restore the Kingdom (of God) to Israel?' (Acts 1:6) The question was prompted by a popular form of apocalyptic theology articulated by a political movement called the Zealots who expected a military-type of Messiah to come and lead a 'holy war' against the hated Roman occupation. They believed their efforts would lead to a revived Jewish state and independence from foreign occupation.

Jesus rejected the apocalyptic-nationalist solution with a single statement: 'It is not for you to know the times or the seasons which God has fixed by his own authority' (Acts 1:7) Jesus was stating quite emphatically that the ideological programme of the Zealots and virtually any predictive

41

political interpretation of the Messianic age were not God's purpose in history. By implication, those today who would turn the Bible into a predictive tool that seeks signs of the 'end' are sadly mistaken in their view of God and scripture. Alternatively, Jesus told his followers to begin their ministry in Jerusalem, the same city that crucified him and was prepared to eliminate his followers. Because Jerusalem was the religious centre of Judaism and the location of the Second Temple, the Sanhedrin, and locus of several important events throughout Israel's history, it was important for the Christian movement to begin there, as a prophetic witness to Second Temple Judaism.

If we are to take Luke's account in Acts seriously, we might assume that the first Christians were a relatively low-profile movement that met in homes. There is no archaeological evidence of church buildings in the Palestine region until the late 3rd century, as recently reconfirmed in discoveries south of the Dead Sea in the country of Jordan. It was unlikely that Christians would build their own structures due to the opposition they encountered from the Jewish establishment and the Romans. We also know there were not only Jews but many gentiles in the new movement, giving Christianity a cultural, linguistic, and ethnic pluralism. We often think that 1st-century Palestine was entirely Jewish but it is more likely that up to fifty percent of the general population consisted of pagans, non-Jews, and various Bedouins that had settled in the region of Palestine or were transient according to grazing seasons.

Saul Colbi, the government of Israel's official responsible for Christian Communities from 1948-1969, begins his volume on Christianity in the Holy Land on a similar note:

> When the Christian era dawned, the population of the Holy Land was far from constituting a homogenous entity. It might be looked upon rather as a 'mosaic' of peoples belonging to a number of national and religious groups. The Hebrew element was predominant in the provinces of Galilee and Judea, in the central part the Samaritans were populous, the Phoenicians inhabited the coastal strip, and the Nabataean Arabs dwelt in the southern region on the edge of the desert. Besides, considerable Hellenistic colonies had been established throughout, particularly along the maritime plain, and there was also the Roman factor represented by the civil servants of the empire and by the legions stationed in Palestine.[1]

---

[1]  Saul P. Colbi, *Christianity in the Holy Land: Past and Present*, Tel Aviv, 1969, 11.

The second chapter of Acts reflects a rich diversity in its account of the birth of the Jerusalem church on the day of Pentecost, as noted in Chapter 1. The early community consisted of residents from Eastern and Central Asia, the Arabian peninsula, the Fertile Crescent (Mesopotamia), Asia Minor (Turkey), Europe, and today's Middle East from Iraq and the Arabian peninsula to North Africa. Many of these early believers were pilgrims who had visited Jerusalem for the Passover Festival and stayed through the Feast of Pentecost (*Shivot*, a festival commemorating the giving of the Torah at Sinai). Here we see the Semitic custom of pilgrimage to sacred places at holy seasons, a practice that would be repeated by both Christianity and Islam. New Testament scholar Joachim Jeremias reports that Jerusalem would swell to ten times its normal size during this period.[2] Most of the pilgrims would return to their native lands after Pentecost. We can conclude that those who had converted to the new Christian movement and were present at the first Christian Pentecost became the first Christian missionaries. However, it is possible that many chose to remain in Jerusalem and the Holy Land in order to assist the newly forming churches.

Leadership in the Jerusalem-based Christian community gradually shifted from Peter, one of the original Twelve Disciples, to James, the half-brother of Jesus. The Book of Acts indicates that James encouraged the new movement to make a strong cultural and religious connection to their Jewish roots by maintaining such practices as worship in the Temple, circumcision, keeping the Jewish Sabbath, and following the liturgical seasons and rites of Judaism. The historian Eusebius (d. 340) confirms this:

> Until the time of the siege by Hadrian there was an extremely significant church of Christ at Jerusalem, which consisted of Jews.[3]

Under Paul's influence Christianity gradually moved toward the gentile world, a process that would alter the character and theology of the early Church during the next two hundred years, eventually abandoning many of the Judeo-centric practices. Undoubtedly, a tension remained within the Christian community in the Holy Land, at least until there was partial resolution at the Jerusalem Council mentioned in Acts 15 (approximately in the year 50), where the two streams of Christianity agreed to go their separate ways. Thus Christianity became a blend of the Judaic and Pauline forms, but

---

[2] Joachim Jeremias, *Jerusalem in the Time of Jesus*, Fortress Press, Philadelphia, 1969, 59.

[3] Eusebius, *Church History*, 3.5.108.

also adapted to the various cultures where it found its new homes. In other parts of rural Palestine, however, it is likely that a lively dialogue continued between Christians and Jews, as much of the hostility was concentrated in the Jerusalem Jewish hierarchy. An example would be the mixing of Christian and Jewish traditions which seemed to occur in the Essene community at Qumran, where John the Baptist and Jesus himself may have been visitors.

The early years of the Palestinian community were shaped by persecution, the search for doctrinal clarity, and identity formation. According to tradition, James the Less became the leader of the community, possibly following the execution of James the Brother of Jesus. James the Brother of Jesus was martyred in the year 62, an event still commemorated by the Armenian Orthodox Church at St James' Cathedral of Jerusalem's Old City, the seat of the Armenian Patriarch of Jerusalem. The execution of these two early Christian leaders indicates that persecution was significant and could be imposed frequently by either the Jewish authorities or by the Roman occupiers. Eusebius provides a list of thirteen bishops of Jerusalem who presided until 135, when the Bishop Symeon replaced James in 62.

Jerusalem was not the only important centre for Christianity in Palestine. Various traditions indicate that small communities settled in Bethlehem, Caesarea, and Acre. In these latter communities, the Christians may have included many gentiles due to Greek and Roman colonisation and were influenced by Hellenistic or Roman culture. Acts 21, 23 and 25 show that the Roman authorities did not persecute the Christians in Caesarea, but they did place Paul under house arrest prior to transferring him to Rome. However, there are no other reports of outright persecution in Caesarea and the possibility exists that there was a significant Christian community by 50-60. Some New Testament scholars are looking at the possibility that early Palestinian Christianity was primarily rural and became significant in the hundreds of villages scattered throughout Galilee, Judea, and Samaria. They suspect there was little persecution of Christians by Jews in these areas and there may have been a constructive dialogue between the two, such as occurred at Qumran. This rural nature of early Palestinian Christianity and Christian-Jewish relations will become important agendas for Biblical archaeology and New Testament scholarship in the coming decades.

The move to rural areas may have been prompted by the Roman procurator for Palestine, Gessius Florus (64-66), who increased Roman oppression of the Jewish community, provoking a rebellion in the years 66-70. While the Christians did not participate in the Zealot's revolt, they were caught in the crossfire. Undoubtedly, Romans did not always distinguish Jews from Christians and there were many deaths, persecution and imprisonment of Christians as well. Eusebius notes that most Christians fled from Jerusalem, with many going to Pella, which is south of the Sea of Galilee, east of the River Jordan.[4]

Other scholars such as Fr Jerome Murphy-O'Connor, the Dominican biblical scholar from the École Biblique in Jerusalem, argue for a more complex scenario. O'Connor notes that the wealthier Christians and Jews were able to buy their way out of Jerusalem. Many tried to escape but were killed. Christians were warned by an oracle of the impending siege, also mentioned by Eusebius, and many fled to the mountains surrounding Jerusalem. The oracle read: 'When you see him, the abomination of desolation, let the reader understand, then flee to the mountains.'[5] Thus the majority of Christians may not have travelled as far as Pella, but found safety in the Judean and Samaritan hills in every direction from Jerusalem. The Romans began the final siege in the fall of 69 and concentrated on Jerusalem, reducing the remaining population to starvation and finally sacking the city. The Temple was destroyed and most of the living were slaughtered. Historians tell us that most of the Christian community survived with many fleeing before the siege began, returning once it subsided in the spring of 70.

Political tension rose again in the year 131 and this time the Zealots tried to force the Christians of Jerusalem into an alignment against Rome. Justin wrote just 20 years after the Bar Kochba revolt (131-5) and indicated that Jerusalem Christians were under pressure to reject Jesus as Messiah and accept Bar Kochba as the true deliverer. Most Christians resisted the Zealot pressure and many were spared when the Emperor Hadrian ordered the city to be razed. Hadrian then issued an edict that Jews were forbidden to take up residence in the new Roman city of Jerusalem, renamed Aelia Capitolina. The decree read:

> It is forbidden for all circumcised persons to enter or stay within the territory of Aelia Capitolina; any person contravening this prohibition will be put to death.[6]

While the Christians were spared the oppressive measures imposed on the Jews, they were subjected to other forms of control and subjection. For example, the Romans built a large Temple over the tomb of Christ, which was a major affront to the community, and a sign of the severe occupation that lay ahead.

---

[4] Eusebius, *ibid.*, 2:23.18.

[5] See Jerome Murphy-O'Connor, 'Pre-Constantinian Christian Jerusalem', in *The Christian Heritage in the Holy Land*, Anthony O'Mahony with Göran Gunner and Kevork Hintlian (eds), London: Scorpion Cavendish, 1995), 16-17.

[6] *Ibid.*, 18, note 34.

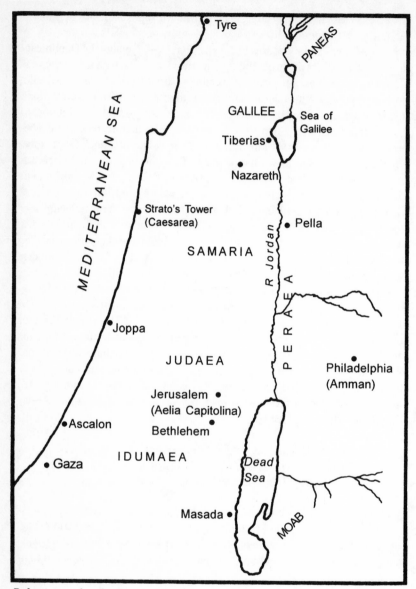

*Palestine under the Roman Empire*

From this point there appears to be no Jewish community living in Jerusalem, although one wonders how thorough the Romans were in conducting military inspections. The line of Jewish Christian bishops in Jerusalem ended at this time and given the Roman edict, we can surmise that the Christian community became predominantly gentile. Some Jews, including Jewish Christians, were able to establish colonies in Galilee, which the Romans seemed to tolerate, but not in Jerusalem. Not to be overlooked is the fact that, while there was an interruption in the historical continuity of the Jewish community in Jerusalem beginning in 135, there has been a continuous presence of the Palestinian Christian community from the day of Pentecost until today.

We can also state that the account of Christians in Palestine is appropriately called a Palestinian Christian history. Rome called this region *Palestina* which would include on today's map Israel, the West Bank, the Gaza Strip and East and West Jerusalem. The Christians cannot be strictly called Arab as yet, because there were only a few Arab tribes who had settled in Palestine at this time. A better term is simply to use Palestinian Christian, which would include the Jewish and gentile Christians of this district.

During the next 130-140 years the majority of the populace was pagan. Persecution of Christians was sporadic, depending upon the emperor in Rome and need of the Roman authorities in Palestine to enforce the persecution orders. One of the first developments during the period 135-250 AD was the tradition of Christian pilgrimage, a concept that had been borrowed from Judaism and the religions of the ancient Near East. We generally credit St Helena with starting the pilgrimage tradition, but as early as 212 the Bishop of Cappadocia, Alexander, came to Palestine with the stated intent 'to worship there and to examine the historic sites'. Alexander found Palestine so inspirational that he decided to remain in Jerusalem, initially as the auxiliary bishop under Narcissus, whom he eventually replaced. For the remainder of his career, Alexander encouraged pilgrimage. Eusebius mentions a library developed by Bishop Alexander for the pilgrims and acknowledges that he drew upon its sources when writing his famous *Ecclesiastical History*. Eusebius is the primary source during this period. He was born in coastal Caesarea around 260, became a great scholar and later bishop in the same city, and died there in 339. Thus he saw Palestine from the end of the Decian persecution to a period of relaxation, but then another period of persecution from Diocletian until his death.

Another pilgrim who benefited from Bishop Alexander's leadership and encouragement of the new Christian pilgrimage tradition was Origen of Alexandria (185-254), the great theologian of Egypt's Orthodox tradition (called the Coptic Orthodox Church after the 4th century). Origen was the son of a martyr and succeeded the highly regarded Clement as head of the catechetical school of Alexandria. Origen was an ascetic who castrated himself, later questioning the value of this irreversible act. He moved to Palestine in 230 but shortly thereafter the (Greek) Orthodox Patriarch Demetrius deposed him for being 'irregularly ordained', which simply meant that the Orthodox in Jerusalem did not accept the Egyptian Church as authentic. Origen moved to Caesarea where he founded an important theological academy and developed one of the first Christian theologies of monasticism, drawing on biblical personalities and motifs.

Always a controversial figure, Origen was known as the greatest theologian and biblical scholar of his time. Eusebius, who was a student of Origen, claims that his mentor had studied briefly under the Platonist Ammonius Sakkas. Origen seems to have utilised some Platonic concepts but subsumed them under a Christocentric theology and piety. He understood the task of the ascetic was to seek complete mystical union of the person with the divine Logos. Some of Origen's views on the divine Logos reflected the theological debates of his day. For example, he taught that the soul of Jesus united with the Divine Logos before the historical act of the Incarnation, and that the general resurrection of the saved Christians would be like the Seraphim, or that the sun, moon, and stars and celestial waters have souls and intelligence.

While his theology appears to be unorthodox when compared to Byzantine theology or contemporary evangelical Protestant beliefs, Origen was Christian to the core, but within the philosophical thought-forms of his time. He was entirely Christocentric, was devoted to the Church, to a strict monastic Christian ethic, and was committed to evangelism, believing even during persecution that the empire would one day be Christianised. After Origen died, his disciple Pamphilios of Caesarea (240-309), a later, much respected Christian martyr, wrote an *Apology* based on Origen's theological works, which popularised Origen's theology among the monasteries and priests of Palestine. It was not until 543 that the Emperor Justinian ordered his works to be condemned at the Council of Constantinople.

By the mid-3rd century the fortune of Christians in Palestine swung from relative freedom under the usual restrictions of Roman occupation to outright persecution. The Emperor Decius (249-251) launched the first systematic persecution of Christians in selected parts of the empire. The Christians in Palestine were especially targeted, among whom was Bishop Alexander, who was martyred in prison in 251. After the brief period of darkness the pendulum swung toward the cessation of persecution under Emperor Gallienus (253-261) and remained relatively peaceful until the 'Great Persecution' under Diocletian (301-3).

To place the Great Persecution in context, the Roman empire had been tightening its rule since the year 275, evolving a new constitution under a series of military dictatorships. A conservative form of pressure came from the Roman Senate and various intellectuals to restore Roman virtues, law, increase the building of roads and government buildings, governance through military might, and even restore worship of the old Roman pantheon of gods whose stock had steadily declined. These conservative voices blamed the rise of Christianity and Manicheanism for the decline in Roman virtues and recommended a return to traditional morality, religion, and a tightening of Roman law. New coins were minted during the 294-6 period and reflect the uniformity of Roman military power and the pantheon of gods. A silvered bronze coin of the period has the inscription *Genio populi Romani* ('To the genius of the Roman people'), with an image of the god Jupiter standing with a sacramental dish in one hand and a horn of bounty in the other. The sense of economic abundance, state power, and blessing of the gods, ('state religion' we would call it today) were unified. A commentary on Roman law during this period stated: 'Our laws protect nothing that is not holy and venerable, and thus Roman majesty has attained so great a plenitude by the favour of the divine powers.'[7]

After the Roman armies defeated the Persians in a series of battles during 297, Diocletian and his advisors were less concerned about the Manichean mission cells (which they associated with Persian political tactics) and other external threats, so they concentrated on what they perceived as the disturbing growth of Christianity throughout the empire. These conservative forces within the Senate and Roman society may explain why Diocletian launched the most severe persecution of Christians on 23 February 303. In addition, Diocletian was a committed pagan and a ruthless political animal, willing to use a weak minority community to his political advantage. Attacks on Christian communities and leadership began slowly, but once the anti-Christian edict of 23 February 303 was issued, persecution became severe. Throughout the empire there were reports of churches being destroyed, sacred scriptures and theological works being burned, Christians removed from public office, and worship of the Roman gods and the Emperor being enforced. Christians became the scapegoats for various problems from bad weather to economic reversals. Many charges against church leaders or Christian civic leaders were manufactured to justify their imprisonment or execution.

Eusebius simply attributes the persecution to God's need to discipline the Christians, who had grown slothful:

---

[7] *Codex Gregorianus V*, from S Riccobono, *FIRA* II, 558-60, as quoted in W H C Frend, *The Rise of Christianity*, Fortress Press, Philadelphia, 1984, 454.

> … as a result of greater freedom, a change to pride and sloth
> came over our affairs, we fell to envy and fierce railing against
> one another, warring upon ourselves, so to speak, as occasion
> offered, with weapons and spears formed out of words; and
> rulers attacked rulers and laity formed factions against laity,
> while unspeakable hypocrisy and pretence pursued their evil
> course to the furthest end.[8]

Eusebius' words certainly have a contemporary ring with reference to the struggles within most Christian communities in Palestine today, as these relatively small populations fight amongst themselves for what amounts to petty ecclesiastical power struggles in exchange for minimal Israeli political favours. It seems that most religious communities have similar problems, whether under military occupation, such as the Roman or Israeli, or in affluence and abundant freedom.

Eusebius also reports that many of these practices were enforced in Palestine. Christians began to flee from urban centres like Jerusalem, Caesarea, and Acre, to small towns and the deserts. Eusebius' *On the Palestinian Martyrs* indicates that during the first year of persecution, Christian priests and bishops bore the brunt of suffering, but by 304 all the Christians of Palestine were at risk. A new edict demanded an end of Christian worship, which needed to be replaced by emperor worship and sacrifice to the gods or face death. Thus the Roman soldier's interrogation would be: 'Who is your Lord?' Christians are said to have reverted to the simple creed made popular during Nero's persecution of the 60s, *Kurios 'o Kristos* (Phil. 2:11).

Following the death of Diocletian, and perhaps due to a furious competition for power among would be successors, the empire began to decline. Emperor Galerius pursued the policies of Diocletian, including the severe persecution of Christians, but concentrated his campaigns in the eastern provinces, such as Palestine. The martyrdom of the respected Origen and then Pamphilius of Caesarea in 309 sent shockwaves throughout the monasteries and Christian communities of Palestine. Inspired by the Christian witness in Egypt and elsewhere in North Africa, a resurgence of faith and willingness to face martyrdom emerged during these years of severity.

---

[8] Eusebius of Caesarea, *Ecclesiastical History*, Volume II, Book VII, 1.7, English translation by J E L Oulton, Harvard University Press, Cambridge Mass., 1932.

## *Constantine and Byzantine Christianity (313-636)*

A new chapter was about to open for Christians in Palestine, but the script was being written in Europe, a historical process that forms a subtext for this study. Emperor Maxentius had become unpopular, due in part to increased taxation and a variety of domestic political errors. Increasingly, there were indications the empire was coming apart, with an East-West cleavage now underway. On 29 October 312, the threat of Roman persecution lifted as Constantine defeated Maxentius at the Milvian Bridge near Rome. Constantine credited the sign of Christ, the *Chi Rho*, with the victory and as a result persecution was to be relaxed. The Edict of Milan was issued in 313, thus officially ending persecution, but its initial impact was only in the western part of the empire. In 324, Constantine defeated Licinius near what is today Istanbul, a site destined to be named as the centre of the new eastern empire, Byzantium. Constantine was able to consolidate the remainder of the empire and a new status began for Palestinian Christianity, as the proclamation for religious tolerance was finally published in Caesarea in 324.

According to Eusebius, there were only three Christian centres in the region at the time of Constantine's edict: Caesarea, the Jordan River Valley (where Jesus was baptised), and Gethsemane. Acre remained a small but important centre with a small community of Phoenician and Galilean Christians. Jerusalem had a tiny Christian community and was still known as Aelia Capitolina. Perhaps the largest Christian community was in Caesarea, but it had been dealt a severe blow by the Diocletian persecutions. The Bishop of Caesarea, Eusebius, emerged as the leading theologian and historian of his decade. His mentor Origen had imbued him with the same passion for probing theological rigor, a prolific writing career, resistance to imperial political pressure and the strong leadership style that had characterised his teacher. In addition to his invaluable *Ecclesiastical History* which was followed by the *Martyrs of Palestine,* Eusebius wrote influential apologetical works against pagan critics of Christianity, such as *Preparation for the Gospel* and *Against Hierocles* and *Prophetic Extracts.* The latter two books included thoughtful appeals to 'Christian seekers' and recent converts. Emperor Constantine was so impressed by Eusebius works that he frequently sought his counsel. The Church historian W H C Frend credits Eusebius with developing 'the Christian political philosophy of the Constantinian state' between the years 311-320. He based the theology on his perceived unity of the providence of God, the Church and the Roman empire.[9]

---

[9] Frend, *ibid.*, 478.

With the events surrounding Constantine's ascension to power and the end of the persecution of the Christians, the new empire took note of certain sites in the Holy Land: Jerusalem, Caesarea, and Bethlehem. In 325 the Council of Nicaea was held and Canon 7 recognised Jerusalem as the 'Mother Church' of all Christianity. The council ordered the Temple of Venus to be destroyed and excavation was to begin at the site. One particular tomb was identified as the Holy Sepulchre of Jesus and it was decided to build a great church on the site. This activity was followed by the replacement of the Temple of Adonis in Bethlehem with one that was built over the cave claimed to be the birthplace of Jesus.

Shortly thereafter, Constantine's mother Helena visited Palestine and spent considerable time in Jerusalem. While reports of her discovery of the 'True Cross' at the Sepulchre site may be exaggerated, the effects were to extend the Constantinian programme that favoured Christians and provide a marketing tool for Christianity. As Helena returned home, pieces of the 'True Cross' were left as relics of the new faith, with hundreds of cross fragments left across the Middle East and Europe. Leaving aside the question of authenticity of the 'True Cross,' the effect was to stimulate enthusiasm toward Christianity, to unify the new empire, and to encourage Christians with 'means' to consider the possibility of making their own pilgrimage to the Holy Land. In addition to the Basilica at the Holy Sepulchre, Helena was influential in the Basilica of the Nativity in Bethlehem and the Church of Eleona (Olive) on the Mount of Olives, which was destroyed in the early 7th century. Additionally, Constantine's mother-in-law, Eutropia, is credited with building a church in Hebron in honour of St Abraham, probably over a synagogue. Today the site is the controversial Ibrahimi Mosque, divided between Islam and Judaism.

Underscoring Helena's efforts was a new literary style that flourished in these years: hagiography. A number of biographies and autobiographies were written such as Eusebius' *Life of Constantine*, which historian Peter Brown views as political spin-doctoring: 'a work whose capacity to irritate the modern historian springs precisely from its Late Antiquity aim: how to present the career of a successful autocrat as a model of the pious life.'[10] We see evidence of this in the lifestyles of the rich and famous today, including such contemporary politicians as the Bible-toting President William Jefferson Clinton, whose public image often needs an occasional sacred adjustment.

Various accounts by pilgrims in the early years of Constantine's reign offer evidence of a growing Christian community which became known

---

[10] Peter Brown, *The Making of Late Antiquity,* Harvard University Press, Cambridge, Mass., 1979, 14.

for the abundant Palestinian Christian hospitality offered to pilgrims. Helena's example also inspired women pilgrims, particularly those of means, not only to visit the Holy Land but to remain with Christian communities for extended periods of study. The journals of the famous pilgrim Egeria note the changing landscape of Jerusalem with churches marking Jesus' healing of Lazarus at Bethany, the church at Gethsemane, and the great basilica at the tomb of Jesus. She comments on the elaborate liturgies and traditions that were emerging, especially during Holy Week. The long and prosperous leadership of Bishop Cyril of Jerusalem deserves gratitude for these developments.

One of the great minds that settled initially in Jerusalem was the irascible Jerome, theologian and biblical scholar of extraordinary abilities, best known in the West for his translation of the Bible into Latin (the Vulgate). Jerome did not find Jerusalem to his liking, describing the city as 'crowded, with its council, its garrison, its prostitutes, actors, jesters, and everything which is usually found in other cities.'[11] Jerome moved to Bethlehem in 386, encouraged possibly by the Roman noblewoman Paula and her daughter Eustochium, who shared their wealth to build the first monasteries in Bethlehem and a hospice for pilgrims. Jerome remained in Bethlehem until his death in 420, establishing a strong monastic tradition and his scholarship drew many others, including a number of leading women of Roman society. There was also a significant tradition of monks making the pilgrimage to Bethlehem.

The dramatic growth of monasticism in Palestine was one of the distinguishing features of this period. Origen may have been the initial influence but there were others, primarily from Egypt, who brought the rigor and ascetic spirituality from Egypt's rich coenobitic tradition of the western desert. We know of Epiphanius, a Palestinian Christian, who was influenced by the Egyptian monks but returned to Palestine around 330 to establish a monastery near his village of Eleutheropolis, a Hellenistic town that is present-day Bet-Guvrin in Galilee. He later became bishop of Salamis in Cyprus.

The monasteries were important centres for pilgrimage, learning, and spiritual formation. After Helena's pilgrimage, bishops and monks from the Middle East, Africa, Europe, and Asia began to come and spend extended periods in Palestine. The publication of Athanasius' *Life of Antony* (circa 370) gave international recognition to Egyptian monasticism, and certainly boosted the new Palestinian monastic tradition. It soon became a tradition that many monks, bishops, and priests from Europe, Africa, and the

---

[11] Jerome, E. 58.4.4, quoted in Peter Walker, 'Jerusalem and the Holy Land in the Fourth Century', G Gunner, *et al.* (eds.), *The Christian Heritage in the Holy Land*, Scorpion Cavendish, London, 1995, 29.

Mediterranean world yearned to settle in Palestinian monasteries for their remaining days and were buried in the Holy Land. O'Mahony indicates that during this period pilgrims and monks arrived in Palestine in record numbers from as far away as Asia, Africa, Armenia, Georgia, Persia, India, Ireland, Scandinavia, Iceland, and Russia. He adds that the Judean desert was populated with monks from all over the Christian world, with approximately 3,000 monks in some sixty monastic settlements in Judea alone.[12]

Another important Palestinian Christian centre, now forgotten, was Gaza. Jerome gives evidence of this in his biography of the monk and St Hilarion who was born in Gaza and travelled to Egypt to live with the desert fathers. Some claim his was the first monastery in Palestine, established in 290, at a site that is today the impoverished Shati (Beach) camp for Palestinian refugees.[13] The monastery of St Hilarion, a disciple of St Antony, led to the establishment of several others in the Gaza district. Also, the third oldest church in the Holy Land (after the Churches of the Holy Sepulchre and Nativity) is located in Gaza, St Porphyry Orthodox Church of Gaza City, whose cornerstone reads that in the year 407 Bishop Porphyry was able to convince the Emperor Arcadius after the Council of Nicaea to build the church on the site of a destroyed pagan temple, following the pattern of the Church of the Holy Sepulchre. There was a steady flow of pilgrims and monks from Egypt to Palestine and *vice versa*, with Gaza becoming an important way station on the route.[14]

The Gazan monasticism was inclined slightly toward the harshness of the Egyptian Desert Fathers and by the 8th century was known for its high spirituality and rigorous discipline. Euthymius and John the Armenian, both saints, were known for their rigor and the Egyptian style of coenobitic spirituality. The monasticism of the Judean desert evolved in a slightly different direction as the monks were less withdrawn from society and actually became engaged in the life of the churches. Jerome may have set that standard early but most Palestinian monasteries of the Judean region encouraged their monks to be available to pilgrims, to assist the local churches in their ministries and to occasionally be part of life in urban settings. Hundreds of monks came to visit Jerome, many from far away Armenia, Georgia, and Syria, with many deciding to settle in the monastery.

---

[12] Anthony O'Mahony, 'Palestinian Christians: Religion, Politics and Society, c. 1800-1948', Anthony O'Mahony, (ed.), *Palestinian Christians: Religion, Politics, and Society in the Holy Land*, Melisende, London, 1999, 11.

[13] Faraj al-Sarraf, 'Christianity in Gaza', *Christians in the Holy Land*, Michael Prior and William Taylor (eds.), The World of Islam Festival Trust, London, 1994, 58.

[14] William Dalrymple, *From the Holy Mountain*, London, 1998, 284-5

This once powerful movement in Palestinian Christianity is today on the verge of extinction, as chronicled recently by *From the Holy Mountain*, by the British travel writer, William Dalrymple. Today Palestine offers the visitor, and the residents, a tragic skeletal remnant of the once powerful monastic movement. Dalrymple describes his journey east out of Jerusalem, passing the largest Israeli settlement of Ma'ale Adumin, a ring of concrete apartments, built on top of the remains of the once great monastery of St Martyrius. New emigrants from Russia, Canada, and the United States fill this growing apartment complex. As he journeyed toward Jericho, the road forks and he took the potholed and neglected road to the south, where he found an abandoned Greek Orthodox Church of St Theodosius. The church is constructed over what is believed to be the cave where the three Magi found shelter after departing secretly from Herod, who was probably wintering in his winter palace at Jericho. By the 5th and 6th century the church had become a centre of Christian activity, as it came to be associated with the famous Mar Saba monastery. Mar Saba was the most celebrated monastery in Palestine from the 5th-7th centuries, hosting over 700 monks who came from Greece to eastern Turkey, to settle there. The Persian invasion of 614 slaughtered most of them. Like the adventurous Dalrymple, visitors to Palestine and Israel can today see the skulls of the great St John Moschos and others as they lie in the *lavra* of St Theodosius, near the road to Jericho.[15]

Palestine was theologically diverse through its first five hundred years, an atmosphere of tolerance that began after the Judaising question was resolved around the year 50, and increased with the influence of Origen, Eusebius, and other theologians. Undoubtedly, the influx of pilgrims and monks from various Christian traditions assisted the tolerance. Among them were Armenian, Assyrian and Syriac Christians who found a home in Palestine (small Armenian and Syriac communities remain in Jerusalem and Bethlehem until today). In should be noted that the Syriac Christians spoke Aramaic and have preserved the language until today in their liturgy and in some Middle Eastern communities. The Syriac Christians (Syrian and Assyrian Orthodox) remained close to various Jewish traditions, reflected in their communities across Syria, northern Iraq and Iran.

The range of theologies is reflected in the fact that Cyril was exiled for a period in the 350s because he rejected Arianism and was viewed as too conservative by his community. Increasingly during the 4th and 5th centuries the diversity was eroded, particularly following the Council of Chalcedon (451) and the bitter rejection of Monophysitism, Arianism and Nestorianism. The rejection of Egyptian Monophysite Christianity and the Syriac tradition,

---

[15] For a useful analysis of the various Christian communities, church construction, and predominantly Christian villages during the 550-900 period, see Colbi, *op. cit.*

erroneously known today as Nestorianism, was motivated more by Byzantium's attempts to control the Egyptian and eastern Christians, neither of whom would submit to the emperor and the ecumenical patriarch in Constantinople. However, the strong influence that Constantinople exercised over Byzantine Orthodoxy on the bishops of Jerusalem and Caesarea, became the prevailing theology of Chalcedon, influenced by the schools of Antioch and Cappadocia. Until 451, Christianity in Palestine and throughout most of the Middle East had been united, but now a more imperial ecclesial form of politics brought the curse of division into Christendom.

The forced unity by imperial Christianity may have been more damaging to Christian presence and continuity in Palestine than the political pressure brought by Islam and Judaism. Colbi notes that Byzantine suppression on all local religions during the 5th-6th centuries led to revolts by the Samaritans. The initial revolt led to murderous attacks on churches in Neapolis (Nablus today). Energized by their initial success, the Samaritans travelled to Caesarea where they continued to burn churches and execute leaders.[16]

The next significant event for the Christian community in Palestine occurred in 614 when the Persian Sasanians invaded. On the eve of the Persian and the later Islamic invasion, the majority of the population, perhaps over two million, was Orthodox Christian and followed the Chalcedonian creedal formula. Archaeological investigations reveal that only Greek inscriptions are found in the churches of Palestine up to the 760s, when Arabic begins to appear. Non-Chalcedonians, such as the Armenians, a tiny Syrian Orthodox community and Coptic Orthodox Christians were allowed to remain in Jerusalem or in their respective monasteries. Among the Orthodox Chalcedonians, there was significant church construction throughout Palestine and the territories east of the Jordan River between 550-614.[17]

Pilgrimage and the growth of Palestinian Christianity continued to be steady until the Islamic invaders arrived in 636. There are, however, no accurate statistical breakdowns on the religious orientation of the population. The population was mostly Semitic and spoke a form of Aramaic in public and Greek for academic and liturgical practices. Schick estimates the population of Palestine to have been as many as three million on the eve of the Islamic invasion, of whom the majority were Christian. By now there were over 400 monasteries scattered throughout the various wildernesses from Samaria down through Judea, the Negev, and Gaza. There was also a small

---

[16] Colbi, *op. cit.*, 26.

[17] Robert Schick, *The Christian Communities of Palestine From Byzantium to Islamic Rule*, Darwin Press Inc., Princeton, New Jersey, 1995, 9-19.

pagan community and a Jewish minority of approximately 10 percent in Galilee and around the Tiberias district.[18]

In 614 the Sasanian Persians under Khosrau II (591-628) invaded Palestine and took several Christian hostages. He also carried off the 'True Cross' from the Church of the Holy Sepulchre as a gift for his Christian wife. This was the first blow to the Palestinian Christian community since the Roman persecutions that ended with Diocletian. Schick documents how the Jewish inhabitants in Galilee, perhaps embittered by Byzantine rule, joined the invading Sasanians to attack Christian communities throughout Galilee, along the Mediterranean coast including Caesarea, and inland to Lod, Jerusalem, Bethlehem, and Jericho. Schick speculates that the Sasanians advanced quickly so as to bring the region under their control, but they had a pattern of destroying churches. The Church of St Stephen, which was built north of Damascus Gate (on the present grounds of the École Biblique) was destroyed during the siege.

Schick also refers to several accounts that verify the Sasanian-Jewish alliance against Christians, such as the writings of Eutychius and Sophronius. There seemed to have been a significant amount of destruction of churches and killing Christians by Jews in northern Galilee and the Mediterranean coast up to Acre and Tyre.[19]

Reports on the capture of Jerusalem include one account of Jews offering a type of amnesty to several thousand Christians who had been rounded up at the Pool of Mamilla. The Jewish militias offered to pay their ransom fee to the Sasanian army but only if the Christians would convert to Judaism. Apparently the Christians rejected the proposal, and the Jews purchased the rights to the Christians, and killed the whole lot except for a few that were exiled to Persia.[20]

The suffering that the Palestinian Christian community experienced was significant, and as Schick notes,[21] they never fully recovered from the setbacks of the joint Sasanian-Jewish persecution. The above may be the first illustration of a modern pattern in the Middle East whereby the policies and actions of a Western government, that is associated with Christianity, had once mistreated Jews or Muslims, and the indigenous Christians are

---

[18] Schick, *ibid;* 12-13.

[19] For a detailed account of the period with documentation of destroyed churches see Schick, *ibid,* 21-30.

[20] Robert Schick, 'Christians in Jerusalem in the Early 7th Century AD, in Thomas Hummel, Kevork Hintlian, and Ulf Carmesund (eds.), *Patterns of the Past Prospects for the Future*, Melisende, London, 1999, 224.

[21] *Loc. cit.,* 225.

forced to pay the price with their blood and destruction of churches and community.

The Byzantine Emperor Heraclius (610-40) entered Palestine and defeated the Sasanians in 628. The Byzantines negotiated the return of the 'True Cross' and numerous Christian hostages at a considerable economic cost. An by-product of the continuous hostilities between Byzantium and the Persia led to the weakening of both armies of these rival powers, creating a political vacuum that left the region open to a new power. Additionally, the residents of these lands had grown fearful and increasingly resentful of the brutalities they had suffered. Palestinian Christians were among those who awaited a deliverer.

The contemporary Armenian historian, Kevork Hintlian offers the following observation concerning the resilience and durability of Christianity during this period:

> The Church in the Holy Land survived because of its extraordinary perseverance, sense of mission and diplomatic skill. In the Byzantine period up to 636 the Church besides dealing with spiritual matters was also the custodian of immense properties and had acquired a status in public life. Some emperors or governors were accommodating; others were more interested in restraining the power and the authority of the patriarch. In three centuries of ebb and flow in the Byzantine rule of Palestine (311-637) the Church was endowed with a number of earthly possessions in addition to negotiating experience.[22]

With the coming of the Persians everything changed concerning property and authority, and now further change was about to come in terms of status and authority. Once could say that the local Christians would never return to the same sense of control over their destiny as they had known during the Byzantine era. Now they would begin to understand the 'Via Dolorosa' of their Lord and search for new concepts of meaning and power as a minority community.

---

[22] Kevork Hintlian, 'Western Christians and their Diplomatic Role in the Protection and Preservation of the Holy Places', Thomas Hummel, Kevork Hintlian, and Ulf Carmesund (eds), *Patterns of the Past, Prospects for the Future*, Melisende, London, 1999, 54.

## Summary

The following points are among the many important elements of the present chapter:

1. 1st-century Palestine was more diverse than initially realized, with largely pagan Roman and Greek communities in such cities as Jerusalem and Caesarea, Samaritans in Samaria, and Arabs in Judea, all in addition to the Hebrew majority. The Book of Acts mentions pilgrims from throughout the Mediterranean world and Middle East, some of whom may have remained in Palestine as part of the first Christian community.

2. During the initial phase of Christianity, the community moved from obscurity under Rome to become the dominant religion in the new incarnation of the Roman empire, now called Byzantium, and became dominant in Palestine itself.

3. The Constantinian empire's adoption of Christianity as its 'religion of choice' accelerated the growth of the faith throughout the empire, Palestine included, while the new faith suddenly discovered that attached to it was the baggage of political power, plus the inevitable moral and spiritual compromises that come with power.

4. With the Constantinian era another historical process began, one that returns repeatedly in the history of Palestine: the primary political and economic decisions would be made in Europe.

5. The economic boost that came with Byzantine rule and its attachment to the Holy Land saw the construction of several churches, most notable being the Church of the Holy Sepulchre in Jerusalem and the Church of the Nativity in Bethlehem, both encouraged by Constantine's mother, Helena.

6. With the sudden boom in church construction came Christian pilgrims from every corner of Christianity, including Asia, Europe (including the British Isles), and Africa.

7. Monasticism flourished during this period with approximately 3,000 monks and over 60 monasteries in Judea alone, plus others in Gaza and Galilee. Eventually, there would be over 400 monasteries operating throughout Palestine by the 6th century.

8. Lively theological debate and a variety of theological traditions characterized Palestine in the 3rd-4th centuries, as scholars such as Origen, Eusebius of Caesarea, Theodosius, and Jerome drew large followings and established theological academies.

9. Christianity had essentially one ecclesiastical rule, that of the Orthodox (Greek) Church, yet there were various traditions of Christianity in Palestine giving it a pluralistic character. Included are Nestorian, Arab,

Armenian, Syriac, and Latin traditions that lived in relative harmony under Byzantine rule.

10. The Byzantine empire was weakened by military campaigns against the Persians, who invaded and occupied Jerusalem for a short period (614-628), but the empire and its rule in Palestine was significantly weakened. This prepared the way for the coming of Islam which conquered Palestine in 638 and then expanded further into the Middle East and North Africa.

# Chapter 3
# PALESTINIAN CHRISTIANS UNDER ISLAM

In 636 Byzantine forces, undoubtedly weakened by battles with the Persians, were defeated by the upstart Arab armies at Yarmuk, east of the Jordan River. Byzantium surrendered its southern provinces and after that date Palestine came under Arab Islamic rule. In Jerusalem, Patriarch Sophronius surrendered peacefully to Caliph 'Umar when he handed over the keys to the city at the Church of the Holy Sepulchre. The caliph refused to enter the great church and instead prostrated himself in prayer outside it, both as a sign of respect and to protect the church as his more zealous followers might have turned it into a mosque. The 'Umariyya mosque is built on the site to commemrate the event. 'Umar and Sophronius are said to have negotiated a covenant *(al-'Uhda al-'Umariyya)* which gave Christians full access and control of their holy sites, freedom of religion, and freedom of worship, but under Islamic rule. The patriarch pleaded with the caliph to grant the same rights to Jews, who had been banned from Jerusalem since 135 CE, but this would have to wait.

Bishop Kenneth Cragg, an insightful observer of Christian-Muslim relations with over 45 years of teaching and ministry in the Middle East, notes in his book *The Arab Christian*, that both the surrender and the construction of the magnificent Dome of the Rock some fifty years later, had both symbolic and *Realpolitik* values. Cragg recalls the comment by the first Umayyad Caliph Mu'awiya, who moved the centre of Islam to Damascus and told his followers: 'Damascus is full of Greeks ... no one would believe in my power if I did not behave, and look, like an emperor.' Dr Cragg comments:

> One of the readiest ways of being imperial was to build magnificently. The Dome of the Rock was an index to such approximation by conquerors to the conquered taking place in all the spheres to which architecture belonged—art, prestige, identity, faith, and perpetuity. Perhaps the Dome of the Rock lay in serving notice on Christianity that a supercession was under way. Its splendour would certainly outshine the Church of the Resurrection hard by. The choice of Jerusalem for its site could hardly be misread nor the import of its quality. The calligraphy moreover, from the Qur'an, had largely to do with passages incriminating Christology and the doctrine of the

Trinity and underlying the role of Jesus as prophet and as an exemplary 'Muslim'. The scribes and ceramists of Christendom were thus employed to join the issues between Caliph and Patriarch, between the heirs of Muhammad and the legacies of Chalcedon.[1]

The submission of the patriarch to the caliph was peaceful and the pact evolved out of a process of negotiations, but there was no question of where the power would now reside. The new Umayyad caliphate (661-750) certainly felt the need to assert itself in the midst of a Christian majority and no doubt the new rulers in Damascus saw Jerusalem as the most important symbol to make its statement among the other two Abrahamic religions. With the construction of the Dome of the Rock and al-Aqsa Mosque on the former site of the Jewish Temple, rising above the adjacent Church of the Holy Sepulchre, served notice that the supercession had begun.

Considerable tolerance was granted to Christians, demonstrated immediately after the Islamic conquest by a nation-wide collection for the reconstruction of the Church of the Resurrection, destroyed a few years earlier by the Persian invasion. The collection was initiated by Modestus, abbot of the monastery of St Theodosius in Palestine. Modestus visited major Christian areas throughout the region, including Ramle, Lydda, Jaffa, Tiberius, Tyre, Damascus and parts of what is today Jordan. The Bishop of Alexandria, John the Almsgiver, lived up to his name by giving Modestus '1000 sacks of wheat, 1000 of legumes, 1000 donkeys, which were exchanged for materials and labour in the reconstruction.'[2] The Church was rebuilt with encouragement from the Umayyad rulers, but with the provision that its dome would not rise above the Dome of the Rock.

The Franciscan archaeologist of Jerusalem's Studium Franciscanum, Michele Piccirillo (OFM), provides evidence that the tolerance continued under the 'Abbasid caliphs (750-1258), who moved the centre of Islam to Baghdad. Fr Piccirillo turns to a biography written in 807 by Leontius of Damascus which depicts the new political realities and the new opportunities under the 'Abbasids. The biography notes that monks frequently travelled from monastery to monastery in search of an improved spiritual climate, a better abbot, or in the case of the author, 'the ideal monk'. Travellers were allowed to negotiate their routes with full security and protection.

In the second half of the 8th century two theological developments

[1] Kenneth Cragg, *The Arab Christian*, Westminster/John Knox Press, Louisville, Kentucky: 1991, 53-54.
[2] Michele Piccirillo, 'Christians in Palestine during a Time of Transition: 7th-9th Centuries,' in O'Mahony, Gunner, and Hintlian (eds.), *op. cit.*, 50.

occurred in Palestinian Christianity. First, the interreligious dialogue that began under the Umayyads continued at a deeper level among Muslim and Christian theologians. In the early phases of the Arab conquest of Palestine, theologian-monks like Anastasius of Sinai (*c.* 700) and the famous John of Damascus (*c.* 750) wrote challenging essays to their Muslim compatriots. John's work was particularly engaging for Muslims as was that of Ibrahim of Tiberias, who debated with the Grand Mufti in Jerusalem. Ibrahim questioned the biographic details of Muhammad's life, arguing that he was not a prophet in the biblical sense. Ibrahim also argued that Muhammad's monotheism was not original and hence was not a revelation from God.[3] Of course, such Christian doctrines as the Trinity, the divinity of Jesus, the crucifixion and resurrection, as well as various New Testament texts and competing ecclesiastical authorities made Christianity vulnerable to the critique of Islam. A second development was the increased use of Arabic in theological exchanges, but Greek remained the dominant language of discourse and liturgical practice in Christianity. By the late 8th century, the Palestinian monasteries of Mar Saba, Mar Chariton, and St Catherine of Mt Sinai were producing the first Christian literature in Arabic.[4] However open and trusting the religious climate appeared during the initial phase of Islamic rule in Palestine, an abrupt change would come in due season.

Archaeologists have long felt that evidence of destroyed churches and abandoned Christian villages in the late 7th century indicate that Islam turned against Christians. Many of the cities on both sides of the Jordan were abandoned and not resettled until the 18th or 19th century, as is the case of Madaba. Piccirillo cites archaeological evidence that demonstrates convincingly a date of abandonment in the late 8th century. The precipitating events may have been accumulative, with the dominance of Islam being one of several factors, the most severe of which was the disastrous earthquake along the Jordan Valley fault line in 747. Excavations from Beisan (Hebrew *Beth Shean*) near the Sea of Galilee, to Aqaba on the Red Sea, confirm that a dramatic shift in climate and epidemics were also causes.[5]

Armstrong confirms this with reference to a severe plague in the 8th century that triggered tribal wars and pillaging of villages by Bedouin tribes. Thus there was an apparent destabilising of the Palestinian areas that underwent economic blight with local resentment toward the affluence of

---

[3] Karen Armstrong, *Jerusalem: One City, Three Faiths*, Alfred A Knopf New York, 1996, 251.

[4] Anthony O'Mahony, 'Palestinian Christians: Religion, Politics, and Society, c. 1800-1948' *op. cit.*, 13.

[5] Piccirillo, *op. cit.*, 54-55.

the clergy. Armstrong reports that churches and monasteries were attacked and for the first time Christian-Muslim relations broke down:

> A plague also wiped out large numbers of the population and the Bedouin began to invade the countryside, pillaging the towns and villages and fighting their own tribal wars on Palestinian territory. In Umayyad times, the Bedouin had fought for the caliphate; now, increasingly, they became the scourge of the country. The unrest led to the first signs of overt tension between the local Muslims and Christians in Jerusalem. Bedouin attacked the Judean monasteries and the Christians on the Western Hill became aware that the economically deprived Muslims were beginning to resent their affluence. Their churches seemed to represent vast wealth, and in times of hardship Muslims would become enraged by stories of Christian treasure.[6]

The 'Abbasid caliphate became the 'Golden Age' of Islam as there was a flowering of the sciences, medicine, and learning in the great Islamic universities. Christian scholars and physicians were highly respected and a central part of the renaissance across the Middle East, while Europe was in relative darkness. Christian translators brought the Greek classics and Hellenic philosophy to Baghdad and other universities where they were translated into Arabic often via Syriac. Christian architects were known for their skills making Baghdad under Caliph Harun al-Rashid (786-809) a capital whose splendour was unparalleled anywhere in the world. Christians were often appointed to key governmental positions, including financial posts, a function still seen today in predominantly Islamic countries.

However, by the late 9th century, the climate was beginning to change. Palestine became less important to the 'Abbasid rulers, and increasingly one hears reports of pressure to pay various Islamic taxes, such as the *kharaj* for property and the annual personal tax (*jizya*). Local administrators would add significant percentages for their 'service' and the taxation became oppressive.

Colbi refers to several atrocities towards Christians that occurred during al-Rashid's rule, including the torching of several churches and the defilement of monasteries but al-Mutawakkil was the severest of the 'Abassids, refusing to allow pubic worship and instituted several humiliating measures.

---

[6] Armstrong, *op. cit.*, page 254.

In 935 'Abbasid rule in Palestine came to an end as Muhammad ibn Tugh, a Turk from Central Asia, controlled the Egypt-Syria-Palestine sector of the region and in due course the Fatimids (909-1171), whom Baghdad regarded as heretical, expanded their rule to control the area. Palestine would become for the next three centuries a battleground among three religious and political points of tension: first, between eastern and Western Christians; second, between competing Muslim regimes; and third, between the eastern Islamic world and Western (Latin) Christians. The religious and political tension between Constantinople and Rome goes back to the early centuries of Christianity but began to manifest itself more explicitly once Constantine shifted the centre of power to Byzantium (Constantinople). When Byzantium lost considerable territory to the Sasanians and then the Muslims in the 7th century, the empire was significantly weakened. Early in the 8th century, various Byzantine emperors began to recover lost territory in what is known today as eastern Turkey and Cyprus. They also announced they would recover additional lands from Rome and from the Muslims which would include a campaign to recover Palestine and Jerusalem. During this period there was still a large Christian minority which was under no particular threat from Islam.

When Constantinople announced the desire to recover Palestine, tension increased. In 938, Jerusalem Christians were attacked by Muslim bands during their Palm Sunday procession from the Mount of Olives. The gates of the Church of the Holy Sepulchre were set on fire. Such incidents had previously been unheard of but can be attributed to foreign interference in local affairs. Incidents occurred again in 966 that led to Muslim marauders attacking church property in Jerusalem, killing several Christians, and burning the patriarch at the stake. Muslim authorities attempted to resolve the difficulties, and announcements from Constantinople or victories by Byzantine forces increased tension in parts of Palestine, which was felt by the Christian community.[7] The reign of Caliph al-Mutawakkil (847-86) ordered Christians to wear the same clothing including a patch of identification on their front and back. These practices may have been among many contributing factors to the deliberations among popes, papal advisors, and European leaders to desire a holy war to liberate the Holy Land from the Muslims.

When the Shi'ite Fatimids of Tunisia seized Ramle and much of the Holy Land in May, 970, Christian-Jewish-Muslim relations seemed to be more harmonious for a short period. Armstrong reports that when the local

---

[7] See Sidney Griffith, *Arabic Christianity in the Monasteries of Ninth Century Palestine*, Variorum, London, 1992, 120; and Armstrong, *op. cit.*, 257.

geographer Muqaddasi wrote his description of Jerusalem in 985, he saw it as a city of *dhimmis*, but with the Christians being a privileged class:

> The Christians were the most privileged people in Jerusalem: they were much richer than the Jews and more literate than the Muslims. Muqaddasi was intensely proud of his city. There was no building to rival the Dome of the Rock anywhere in the Muslim world; the climate was perfect, the markets clean and beautifully appointed, the grapes enormous, and the inhabitants paragons of virtue. Not a single brothel could be found in Jerusalem, and there was no drunkenness.[8]

But the reign of the Fatimid Caliph al-Hakim (996-1021) brought a period of significant persecution. Most scholars believe Hakim was suffering from dementia. In September, 1009, Hakim ordered the Church of the Holy Sepulchre to be razed. Once this devastating blow had been accomplished, Christians were forced to convert to Islam or wear heavy crosses around their necks. In 1021, al-Hakim went off the deep end when he declared that he was an incarnation of Allah, something clearly heretical and intolerable to Muslims. When he ordered imams to substitute the name al-Hakim for Allah in the Friday prayers, the Muslim community rebelled. Riots broke out throughout the region. One night in 1021, al-Hakim rode out of Cairo into the desert and was never seen again.[9] Periods of persecution were not uncommon among the Fatimid caliphs.

## Palestine during the Crusades (1099-1187)

When Charlemagne was crowned 'King and Emperor' in Rome on Christmas Day, 800, the rift between east and West deepened. The eastern populations under Constantinople viewed Charlemagne's actions with suspicion, weighing the evidence of implied superiority and competition. This was combined with renewed claims of authority by the papacy which saw itself as superior to all ecclesiastical rivals, particularly the patriarch in Constantinople. Greeks and many in the Arab world despised Charlemagne as 'the emperor who could neither read nor write.'

There had developed in Western Europe considerable fear of Islam and the sense that war was justifiable for the eradication of the Muslim

---

[8]  Armstrong, *op. cit.*, 259.
[9]  *Ibid.*, 260.

'infidels'. The presence of the (Muslim) Moors of North Africa ruling Spain, succeeding the Umayyads in Andalusia with frequent incursions into southern France, were reason enough to spread fear of possible Muslim domination of Europe. The Vatican and various insecure feudal European rulers seized on the Islamic threat as an opportunity to unite Europe under 'Holy Roman' rule. When Pope Urban II called for the First Crusade at the Council of Cleremont in 1095, the message found a receptive audience. There was also a residue of apocalyptic fear concerning the end of the world, as a new century was about to turn. Pilgrims and soldiers were convinced that the place to be for Jesus' Second Coming was Jerusalem.

The official Papal Bull that launched the First Crusade was issued in 1096 with four contingents from various parts of Europe departing for Constantinople. However, many of the Crusaders died on the difficult journey, some from shipwreck, others from epidemics. One force of German Crusaders attacked and massacred several Jewish communities along the Rhine Valley. A contingent composed primarily of Frankish Crusaders later conquered Antioch and having removed the Orthodox patriarch from Constantinople, restored him to Antioch as an affront to the Byzantine leadership. Eventually they reached Jerusalem which was now under the control of the Fatimid Muslims of Egypt. Following a sermon by Peter the Hermit on the Mount of Olives, the Crusaders attacked Jerusalem and conquered the city in mid-July. Every Muslim and Jew in the city was slaughtered and many Palestinian Christians with them, as the European Crusaders could not distinguish by appearance or language who was Muslim, Jew or Christian. Baldwin was enthroned as king of the Crusader feudal kingdom on 11 November 1100. Latin Christianity was imposed on the city and the Orthodox patriarch was expelled. Arab and other eastern Christians were banished from Jerusalem's churches and Jews and Muslims were denied residency there throughout the Crusader's reign.

The bloodletting that occurred in Jerusalem at the hands of the Crusaders is a matter still felt deeply in the Arab collective subconscious throughout the Middle East. In his remarkable book *Jerusalem, The Endless Crusade*, Andrew Sinclair allows an eyewitness, Raymond d'Aguliers, to describe the conquest of Jerusalem in 1099:

> Some of our men cut off the heads of their enemies ... others tortured them longer by casting them into flames. Piles of heads, hands, and feet were to be seen in the streets of the city. It was necessary to pick one's way over the bodies of men and horses. But these were small matters compared to what happened to the Temple of Solomon ... If I tell the truth it

would exceed your belief. So let it be enough to say this much, at least, that in the Temple and Porch of Solomon, men rode in blood up to their knees and bridle reins. Indeed it was just and a splendid judgement of God that this place should be filled with the blood of the unbelievers since it has suffered so long from their blasphemies.[10]

During the Crusader kingdom's rule in Palestine, the Jewish community was nearly obliterated with tiny communities remaining in Galilee. Most Muslims were executed, escaped, deported, or became slaves to the Crusaders. Palestinian Christians were allowed to live within their national groups but under Frankish Crusader rule. In addition to Palestinian Orthodox, who were generally allowed to return to their liturgical practices outside the walls of Jerusalem, there were Syriac and Armenian communities that were allowed semi-autonomy.

In 1187, Salah al-Din (hereafter Saladin), a Kurd by origin who had come to a position of power in Egypt, declared *jihad* against the Crusaders and organised a military expedition. In two swift battles, Saladin's army defeated the Crusaders and broke their control of Jerusalem, which surrendered on 2 November 1187. In Jerusalem and Bethlehem, the remaining Palestinian Christians were either Orthodox or Syriac. The Franks were expelled, as were the Armenians, who were accused of being aligned with the Franks. On the contrary, the Orthodox were granted full protection and their churches returned, although some Latin or Frankish churches were converted into mosques. Saladin did invite the Jews to return to live in Jerusalem, thus breaking the Roman ban from the year 135.

Baha al-Din, a Muslim historian of the period, stated that there were approximately 60,000 residents of Jerusalem at the time of Saladin's conquest, the majority being Christian. Another Muslim chronicler, Ibn al-Athir, added that the figure was inflated due to refugees from other cities in Palestine that had fled to Jerusalem during the hostilities.[11] Saladin continued to pursue the Crusaders and by early 1189 he controlled most of the Crusader kingdom from Gaza to Tyre. Saladin died in 1191, but his successors granted local Christians considerable tolerance and allowed them to rebuild their churches and homes as well as to build new churches. During the next two centuries,

---

[10] Andrew Sinclair, *Jerusalem, The Endless Crusade*, Corwn Publishers, New York, 1995, 56.

[11] A T Jotischky, 'The Fate of the Orthodox Church in Jerusalem at the End of the 12th Century', *Patterns of the Past, Prospects for the Future*, Hummel, Hintlian, Carmesund (eds.), Melisende, London, 1999, 189.

additional Christian communities were officially recognised in Jerusalem and Bethlehem, including Copts, Armenians, Nubians, Ethiopians and Syrian Orthodox.[12] Egyptian Ayyubid rule was replaced by the Mamluk dynasty in 1260. Mamluk rule continued from Egypt until 1517. In 1250, the Orthodox patriarch returned to Jerusalem to resume his role as the major Christian authority in the community. The supremacy of the Latin Church faded and the Latin patriarch took up residence in Rome.

## Ottoman Rule (1517-1918)

In the early 14th century, Osman (1280-1324) established a small kingdom in western Turkey and gained independence from the ruling Mongols, who had conquered the Seljuk Turks. Gradually he expanded his territory and in 1453 the Ottoman (Osmani) Turks captured Constantinople, which they called Istanbul, thus bringing to an end to the now distant glories of Byzantium. Gradually, the Ottoman forces incorporated into their rule provinces in the Balkans, Greece, Cyprus, and most of the former 'Abbasid territories west of Iran. Slowly they made their way to Palestine and captured Jerusalem and the surrounding areas in late 1516. The Ottoman ruler assumed the title of caliph, thus giving him the political and religious power necessary to resurrect images of the golden era of Islam. The reigns of Salim (1512-1520) and Sulaiman the Magnificent (1520-1566) were marked by the rapid expansion of Ottoman jurisdiction.

The Turkish Muslim rulers enforced an administrative organisation on the non-Muslim citizens of their provinces called *millets*. O'Mahony defines the *millet* as an Ottoman concept involving three dimensions: religion, religious community, and national identity.[13] The *millet* was a series of negotiated arrangements between the religious hierarchies and the Ottoman Islamic government. The Christian and Jewish 'Heads' (usually the patriarch and chief rabbi) were viewed by the Ottomans as functionaries of the state. Christian and Jewish communities were separated into their respective quarters and allowed to elect their own religious and administrative leader who would represent the community before the caliph. The Orthodox and

---

[12] Anthony O'Mahony, 'The Religious, Political and Social Status of the Christian Communities in Palestine, c. 1800-1939, *The Christian Heritage in the Holy Land*, Scorpion Cavendish, London, 1995, 238-9.

[13] *Ibid.*, 240-241; Peretz defines the *millet* as all Ottoman citizens who were divided in '*millets (nations) on the basis of religion*'; Don Peretz, *The Middle East Today*, Praeger Publishers, Westport, Connecticut, 1994, 59.

Armenian Christians were the first *dhimmis* to be recognised by the new rulers and in most cases their respective patriarch represented them in all vital decisions for their community.

Under Ottoman rule, Palestine was considered the southern province of Syria (al-Sham) with Damascus as the capital. The province was divided into five districts called *sanjaks*: Jerusalem, Nablus, Gaza, Safad, and Lajun. Each *sanjak* had a governor, called the *Sanjak Beg*, a position that could only be held by an Ottoman Turk. The *Sanjak Beg* was primarily a military position that had jurisdiction over the Ottoman occupation army and taxation (the *jizyah* or poll tax). Additionally, the *Beg* would be responsible for the armed forces of that district should a larger military force be needed by the empire.

Christians and Jews had a fair amount of freedom, but that freedom was limited by the boundaries of the *dhimmi* system. They could worship freely within their designated religious structures and conduct their religious affairs, including having their own officials administer baptisms, marriage, divorce, funerals, and all other liturgical functions. The average person was free to pursue most careers, except for high level posts in the military and political governance. We should be cognisant of the fact that Jews and Muslims had considerably fewer privileges in the Christian countries of Europe during this same period.

The Ottoman leaders introduced another dimension that especially affected the male Christian population, the *janissaries*. Highly able and intelligent young men of Christian birth were identified as potential recruits who would be sent to separate schools, usually in Istanbul, which created extremely loyal and militant Ottoman 'loyalists'. They were required to convert to Islam and underwent a rigorous military training that moulded them into an elite force. Violations were prosecuted severely. While on the active list they could not marry until retirement. The janissaries constituted between 10,000-15,000 officers and soldiers during the 15th-16th centuries. They became the leading officers in the middle level of military administration but were considered a loyal and vital community of leaders.

In Middle Eastern countries where there is a Christian minority, some version of the *millet* system remains today, including Israel. Each Christian community has its leader, a patriarch or bishop, who negotiates with the host government or Muslim religious authorities in matters of state. Religious judicial bodies would oversee matters dealing with church property, cemeteries, death certificates and burial, marriage, divorce, religious education, and other domestic ecclesiastical legal problems. They had separate courts and religious judges who were usually appointed by the patriarch, later to be ratified by the state or a representative of the caliph. In Jerusalem, the Greek

Orthodox patriarch of Jerusalem is understood as the 'leader' but Israel has chosen to play a careful game of competition between the Orthodox Patriarch Diodoros and the Latin patriarch, Michel Sabbah, given its desire to win recognition from the Vatican. However, the new Latin patriarch is a Palestinian and his close advisors are native Palestinian priests and professionals, many having grown up under Israeli occupation and are not only critical of Israel's policies but are able to develop counter-strategies. Thus a political 'tug of war' exists between the Orthodox and Latin patriarch in the pursuit of privileges and favours from Israel

During the 17th and 18th centuries, the central authority of the Ottomans began to weaken which enabled various European governments to negotiate directly for economic and pilgrimage purposes. Much earlier, France was among the first to negotiate with Sulaiman the Magnificent, followed by the Hapsburg empire. Agreements were called the *Capitulations*, which gave the respective European government limited jurisdiction over its citizens and property in Ottoman territories. Through this process several European governments developed close ties with particular communities, such as Russia with the Orthodox community of Palestine, France with the Maronites of Lebanon, and later Germany with Lutherans in Palestine or Jordan, and England with Anglicans throughout the Middle East. At times there was bitter competition, such as that of Greece with the Russians for influence over the Orthodox. The *Capitulations* became important when economic relief or protection were needed by the Middle Eastern Christian communities.

During the decline of the Ottoman empire, several countries were eager to capitalise on the opportunity this decline offered to their respective missionary movements, in particular the European Catholic and Protestant nations. Catholic presence had already seen its day during the Crusades, but now a significant period of Roman Catholic missions from France, Italy, Spain, and other nations began to find their locus in the Middle East. A separate matter was the historic competition between Rome and Constantinople for control over the holy sites in Palestine. France was able to negotiate with the Ottoman leaders and gain *Capitulations* for the Franciscans in 1604 and again in 1673, thus granting the Franciscans a dominant position in oversight of the Holy Places, which remains in effect today.

Catholic missions in the 15th-18th centuries had a significant effect on the Orthodox Churches of the entire Middle East There are five church families in the Middle East that are called 'Uniate', which adhere to the primacy of the pope and the essential church doctrines taught by the Roman Catholic Church. The earliest of the Uniate churches to emerge was the

Chaldean Catholic Church, which broke away from the Assyrian Church of the East in 1522, establishing its own diocese and patriarchate in Baghdad. The Syrian Catholic Patriarchate of Antioch broke away from the Syrian Orthodox Church in 1622, and in 1724 the Melkite (Greek) Catholic patriarchates were established in Antioch. The Melkites have become one of the largest Christian communies in Israel and Palestine, and essentially follow the Orthodox liturgy but use the Arabic language, and they maintain allegiance to the Vatican. A fourth Uniate Church is the Armenian Catholic, which has churches in Palestine but is centred in Lebanon. The fifth Uniate family to emerge was the Coptic Catholic Church with a patriarchate in Alexandria, arriving in 1824. All of these churches are products of the Latin (Roman) Catholic missionary movements of this era and while having Orthodox liturgical practices and many doctrines and spiritual traditions in common with Orthodoxy, they are clearly Catholic in polity and doctrine. The Maronite Catholic Church, which originated in Syria in the 4th century, has a different history from the others but it too united with Rome in the 16th century. There are several Maronite communities in northern Galilee but their strength lies in Lebanon, where they are the largest and wealthiest Christian community. The result of the Catholic mission enterprise were threefold: a) new churches under Rome's authority; b) significant educational and medical institutions and training centres were established throughout the region; c) but the Orthodox Church was weakened and splintered as a result. From this period forward many of the future leaders of the Palestinian community came from the strong educational background and training that can be attributed to the Protestant and Roman Catholic educational missions.[14]

German and Prussian influence sponsored Lutheran missions in the 19th century which led to churches and bishoprics in Jerusalem. First, Anglican missions sponsored by England (later the United States) initially concentrated on the conversion of Jews, which was viewed by the Anglican Mission to the Jews as a fulfilment of biblical prophecies concerning the return of Jesus to the Holy Land. The great British social reformer Lord Shaftesbury, himself an ardent evangelical Christian Zionist, was the prime mover in lobbying the British parliament and gaining popular support for the bishopric which was established in 1843, and was actually a joint-Bishop in cooperation with the Prussian Lutheran Church. The first bishop was a converted Jew. The Orthodox patriarch welcomed the Anglican bishop to Jerusalem which was a political trade-off as requested by the new Orthodox bishop in London.

---

[14] Sotiris Roussos, 'The Greek Orthodox Patriarchate and Commuity of Jerusalem,' *The Christian Heritage in the Holy Land*, O'Mahony, Gunner, and Hintlian, Scorpion Cavendish, London, 1995, 214.

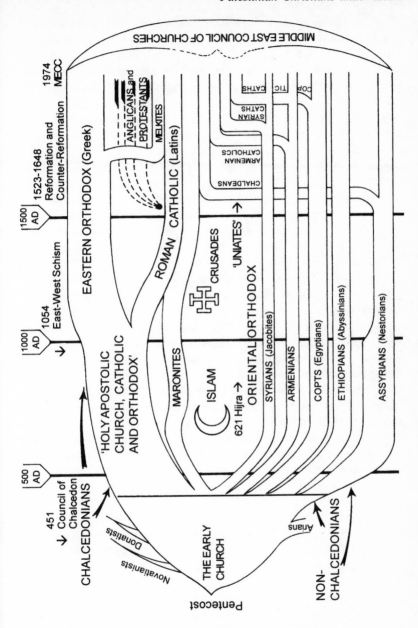

*Middle Eastern Christianity from Pentecost to 2000*
(after Revd L Humphrey Walz)

73

Following the French Revolution in 1789 several French intellectuals developed considerable interest in Egypt and the Holy Land. These interests were combined with Napoleon's colonialist ventures in 1798-99 when he invaded Egypt. Napoleon issued a statement that demonstrated remarkable insensitivity to the Muslim and Christian Palestinians and the Ottoman overlords, but reflected his grandiose visions of liberation and French power. Napoleon undoubtedly triggered a significant British colonial response once he conquered Egypt and issued his proclamation to the Jews of the world. One hears in his words not only the French colonial visions but his embryonic support for the Zionist programme that would emerge in less than a century:

> Israelites arise! Ye exiled, arise! Hasten! Now is the moment, which may not return for thousands of years, to claim your political existence as a nation among nations, and the unlimited natural right to worship Jehovah in accordance with your faith publicly and most probably forever.[15]

While the proclamation was essentially an instrument of propaganda for Napoleon in order to solicit support for his invasions from European Christian nations, it did reflect terrible insensitivity to the more than 95 percent Palestinian Christian and Muslim majority. Perhaps it was a foreshadowing of what was already emerging in England and the United States, an underlying Christian support of a Jewish state that would be the fulfilment of prophetic scriptures. These developments would converge with the Zionist movement in the Jewish community which emerged in Russia and Eastern Europe as a reaction to rising Western antisemitism.

Napoleon's incursion into the Middle East exposed the weaknesses of the Ottoman empire as he easily occupied Egypt and then moved through the Sinai peninsula and up the coast of Palestine. He captured Jaffa on 7 March 1799, and then moved toward Acre. There he issued another grandiose vision:

> The fate of the East is in the fate of Acre. Then I will overthrow the Turkish empire and found a great new empire in the East which will preserve my place in posterity.[16]

Napoleon's Middle East campaign met its end at Acre at the hands of the British, but he never got over his colonial vision. Historian Barbara Tuchman

---

[15] Quoted by Barbara Tuchman, *Bible and Sword*, Ballantine Books, New York, 1984, 163.
[16] *Ibid.*, 165.

notes that twenty years later he sat in exile on St Helena and dictated in his memoirs: 'Acre once taken, I would have reached Constantinople and India. I would have changed the face of the world.'[17]

In the 19th century, the Ottoman empire became the 'Sick Man of Europe' and was fraught with desperate attempts to revive its control over its subjects and the glory it once knew. European colonial aspirations grew with covetous competition as Britain now outpaced France in its power and influence in the region, with newly emerging Russia close behind. Speculation grew as to how these powers would divide the region. The prize for strategic as well as religious sentiment was Palestine.

O'Mahony helps us understand the nature of the Palestinian Christian community during the Ottoman era. It was predominantly an Arabic-speaking Greek Orthodox community, but with the increase of Roman Catholic and Protestant missions, the Orthodox churches were weakened. Whereas the vast majority of the Palestinian Christians had been located in towns and rural villages throughout Palestine, a trend toward urbanisation developed late in the Ottoman period. By the 19th century there were 50 percent fewer Christian villages than there were in the 16th century.[18] Jerusalem, Bethlehem, Nazareth and Jaffa were the beneficiaries of this internal migration. Most of the churches in these villages ceased to function. This shift may have been motivated by four factors: economic changes, increased education among the Christians, desire to be close to the Holy Places and religious centres, and security.

As the century drew to a close, competing European colonial powers vied for control in various parts of the world and Palestine did not escape their designs. In many instances, the colonial powers carried out their political manoeuvres through the church communities, much to the frustration of the indigenous Palestinian Christians and Muslims. One incident which reflects the delicate lines of influence was the visit of the German Emperor (Kaiser) Wilhelm to Palestine in 1898. Both the French and the British were extremely troubled by the announcement that the German emperor would visit Jerusalem. Interestingly, the politics were exercised through the Protestant and Catholic communities, with the Germans extending their influence through the Lutheran churches and the French through the Latin Catholics.

In a surprising subplot, the Germans supported the Zionists during this period, as Herzl had met with the Kaiser and many German politicians viewed the Zionists as politically useful, despite a growing climate of antisemitism. By contrast, the French had no use for the Zionists, as they

---

[17] *Ibid.*, 165.
[18] O'Mahony, *ibid.*, 243.

were still stung by the Dreyfus controversy and strong currents of antisemitism. To show their public interest in the local Christians, the Kaiser claimed that Germany would offer security for the local Christian community. Meanwhile, the Kaiser was not that interested in the Palestinian Christians as he saw no political pay-offs but seemed to be committed to establishing a German Lutheran Church (the Church of the Redeemer), which he dedicated in the heart of the Old City of Jerusalem.

This example demonstrates how the Western colonial powers used the divisions among Palestinian Christians to their political advantage, but further, how little the local Christians controlled their destiny. They were unable to prevent outside interference in their affairs let alone prevent the further fragmentation of their community. Such a situation enabled the Germans to extend their influence in the Holy Land through the Lutherans, as did the French with the Catholics, England with the Anglicans, and Russia (competing with Greece) with the Orthodox. These initiatives by the major European powers caused friction within the Christian community and caused both Palestinian Christians and Muslims to ask: 'Are these Protestants simply a "fifth column" in our midst?'

## Summary

With this rather abbreviated overview of this period, I have tried to provide the non-specialist in Middle Eastern history with a sense of the Palestinian Christian experience from the entry of Islam in 636 until the emergence of the Zionist movement in 1897. While neither exhaustive nor expansive in terms of the historical narrative, I have sought to demonstrate six major points:

1.  Christianity in the region named by the Romans as *Palestina* continued to develop its own unique history and identity with the land area between the Jordan River and Mediterranean and hence it can rightly be called Palestinian Christianity.
2.  Palestinian Christians have a distinct history which gives them an identification with the events that have taken place in their land as well as sense of being rooted and bonding to the land itself. Gradually the majority of the residents of Palestine, be they initially Jewish, pagan, or other, adopted Christianity as the religion of the majority. Although there were some Arab tribes in Palestine (some of whom were Christian), Arab political control and use of the Arabic language in churches began after the arrival of Islam.
3.  Palestinian Christians have had a historical continuity and physical

presence in the land of Palestine that has been unbroken since the first Christian Pentecost. There has never been a time when there were no Palestinian Christians in historic Palestine from the year 30 AD until today.

4.  Palestinian Christians have always been dominated by outside empires, religions, and political powers, foreign ecclesiastical power, and as a result have never fully gained control over their churches, lands, resources, political institutions and processes, nor have they gained political self-determination. This thousand-year plague of external control of Palestinian Christians has been the primary factor in the gradual erosion of the Christian population in Palestine and remains a factor with the State of Israel's continuing occupation of the majority of historic Palestine.

5.  Palestinian Christians have lived in relative harmony with Muslims and Jews throughout their history, with only occasional periods of persecution or oppression. Simultaneous attacks by Sasanian Persians and Jews before the coming of Islam to Palestine constituted the first major attack on the Palestinian Christian community since the persecution of the Roman Emperor Diocletian. Periodic persecution under Muslim rulers followed but did not significantly alter the Christian population. Persecution by Muslims and Jews was the secondary cause of destabilising Palestinian Christians.

6.  The entrance of such European imperial ventures as that of Napoleon and various Protestant and Roman Catholic missionary movements from Europe had three effects on the local Christians: a) missionaries were not effective in converting Muslims or Jews so they turned to convert Orthodox Christians; b) the indigenous Palestinian Orthodox churches were splintered and several key leaders were taken into the new Western churches; c) significant advances in education and medicine were brought by the missionaries. However, the net effect was a fragmentation of Christianity in Palestine and a weaker overall presence and witness of the Christian community. Further, several Western powers used the new mission churches to gain colonial 'beachheads' in Palestine.

# Chapter 4
# FOUNDATIONS OF INJUSTICE: 1880-1922

'Here I am,' cried the old man. Startled and somewhat incredulous, the great 'Father' of modern Zionism, Theodor Herzl, responded to the bearded old Englishman: 'That I can see, but who are you?' The Revd William Hechler, chaplain to the British Embassy in Vienna, stepped forward and responded: 'You are puzzled, but, you see, as long ago as 1882 I predicted your coming to the Grand Duke of Baden. Now I am going to help you.' Thus did the Anglican chaplain in Vienna interpret his 'prophetic' role to the very person that he saw leading the Chosen People to the Promised Land. Hechler was a dispensationalist Christian and as such believed in the literal fulfilment of certain prophetic biblical texts such as Daniel 7-9, and understood that the hour of the Jews had come. He explained these matters to Herzl, who recorded the encounter with Hechler in his diary entry of 10 March 1896:

> The Reverend William Hechler, Chaplain of the English Embassy here, came to see me. A sympathetic, gentle fellow, with a long gray beard of a prophet. He is enthusiastic about my solution of the Jewish Question. He also considers my movement a 'prophetic turning-point'—which he had foretold two years before. From a prophecy in the time of Omar (637AD) he had reckoned that at the end of forty-two prophetic months (total 1260 years) the Jews would get Palestine back. This figure he arrived at was 1897-8.[1]

Hechler impressed Herzl, who was neither religious nor acquainted with these Christian approaches to the Bible.

Far more impressive to Herzl were the political connections of the old Englishman. Herzl had been trying without success to meet with Kaiser Wilhelm, but Hechler opened the door quite easily. Contacts with the British political elite came next and many of the initial meetings were also arranged by Hechler. The secular Herzl and religiously evangelical Hechler became friends and the chaplain did everything in his power to advance the Zionist movement in its initial stages. Historians and political scientists have either

---

[1]  Theodor Herzl, *The Diaries of Theodor Herzl* (ed. Patai), New York, 1956; 71.

ignored or grossly underestimated the political role played by Christian Zionists such as Revd Hechler and Lord Shaftesbury in preparing the way for Herzl's movement.

Jewish Zionism was but one of the political and religious forces that would collide in Palestine during the next fifty years. The path leading to its acceptance was prepared in part by a Christian form of Zionism that was already at work in Western Europe and North America. As we will see, Zionism would be undergirded by British colonialism and the empire's dream to dominate the Near East while simultaneously protecting its access to the newly discovered petroleum riches of the region and to its 'Jewel in the Crown', India. On the eve of the 20th century, several European colonial powers were poised like vultures to make their move on the 'Sick Man of Europe', the Ottoman empire.

In this chapter I will set forth the political context out of which the modern Palestinian Christian emigration began, leading to the eventual dispossession of the Palestinian people. In order for this task to be achieved, we must first review the rise of Zionism in Europe and the toxic climate of European antisemitism that provoked it. Further, we will examine two types of Zionism and indicate the model followed by the mainstream of the Zionist movement, which remains the dominant perspective today in Israel and world Jewry. The emergence of Great Britain as the imperial sponsor of Zionism became important during World War I, undermining the quest by Palestinians for political legitimacy and self-determination. The political intrigue and manoeuvres of this period, while fascinating to behold, established the lethal mixture of two competing nationalisms in pursuit of the small land of Palestine.

## European antisemitism

Another major force that contributed to events in Palestine was European antisemitism, already well-advanced in Russia, Germany, Poland, the Austro-Hungarian empire, and Western Europe. The increase of Judeophobia and violent attacks on Jewish communities, called pogroms, led Jews like Herzl to conclude that they would never be secure in European gentile societies. They must find a home of their own. The most logical choice, Palestine, was already home to another people, over half a million Christian and Muslim Palestinian Arabs and only 25,000 Jews at the end of the 19th century. The failure of the world powers and local actors to resolve this problem is the story before us, a seemingly never-ending slide into violence and injustice.

Jews lived uneasily in Europe following the Spanish Inquisition, with some countries offering more freedom than others. By the early 19th century more than half of the world's Jews lived in Eastern Europe with large communities in the regional ghetto of Poland, Germany, Austria-Hungary, and Russia. There were 900,000 Jews under the Czar's rule by the early 18th century when persecution became acute. Gradually, laws were passed to further repress and confine the Jewish community including economic, vocational, and severe social restrictions. When Czar Alexander II was assassinated, the Jews were blamed, a matter his successor Nicholas II allowed to ferment despite knowing the accusation was a lie. Symptomatic of the antisemitic fervour was the infamous *Protocols of the Elders of Zion,* a racist Russian forgery that blamed Jews for most social ills. Czar Alexander knew the *Protocols* were fictitious yet like Nicholas II, he allowed Judeophobia to flourish by failing to expose such works as false.

One of the dominant political themes in 19th century Europe was nationalism. To oversimplify the matter for the sake of brevity, there were essentially two types of nationalism that developed in the West. First, and most dominant, was the French and American model, characterised by their emphasis on the equality of all persons, whatever their religion, ethnicity, or national identity. The French theme of *liberté, équalité, fraternité*, was matched by the American by-line: 'all people (men) are created equal.' The types of nations produced by each model and the basis for civil and human rights are very different in each case. The organising principle of Germany is German birth or bloodlines. Germany is a nation for the Germans, 'the Fatherland'. At its core, Germany is a nation that has favoured persons of German birth, with the accompanying mythologies and political theories that promote organising principles that justify German identity as privileged and superior.

By the 1850s, Teutonic mythology was a powerful tool of anti-Jewish sentiment in Germany, underscored in no small measure by artists of considerable stature such as Richard Wagner and philosophical giants such as Friederich Nietzsche. Deeply imbedded in German consciousness are certain theological and moral justifications for antisemitism found in leaders that gave the views a high degree of legitimacy, including Martin Luther. One of the tragic lessons of European antisemitism is that it developed its most vicious expression not in a Muslim society such as Iran or Saudi Arabia, but in the heart of sophisticated European society and the very land that gave the world the Protestant Reformation. Across German society there were respected leaders from a wide variety of professions including religion, academia, journalism and the arts, who had pushed back the prohibitions of polite society and made antisemitism an acceptable mainstream issue. In 1853, Gobineau's *Essai sur l'inégalité des races humaines* could argue quite openly in academic circles that the Aryan race was inherently superior. Before long, von Schoenerer's theories of Pan-Germanism had translated Gobineau's thesis into German nationalist ideology.[2]

Until the 1880s, most Jews had opted for assimilation in their European societies. However, the horror of frequent Russian pogroms, the most severe of which began in 1881, eroded Jewish confidence in European societies. This is clearly seen in the writings of the early Zionist Leo Pinsker (1821-91). Pinsker was a thoroughly assimilated Russian Jew. A leading physician in Odessa who wrote for Russian Jewish weeklies, Pinsker like most of the Jews believed they were fully part of Russian society. Even the pogroms of Easter 1871 in Odessa itself did not dissuade him. But the pogroms increased with frightening intensity and spread across Russia. The extensive violence of March, 1881, that followed the assassination of Czar Alexander II, spread to over one hundred and sixty Russian cities. Hundreds of Jews died and countless others were wounded. These events shook Pinsker who turned away from assimilation to the theories articulated in his important pamphlet of 1882: *Autoemancipation: an Appeal to his People by a Russian Jew*. Here Pinsker argued that Jews would always be victimised by antisemitism and would never be secure until they had their own Jewish state.

Pinsker's efforts led to the establishment of the modest movement of the 1880s, *Hibbat Zion,* which began to settle Jews in Palestine. Its success was very marginal, suffering from a lack of funding and malaria in the few sites that were settled. While the movement would be judged at most as a qualified success, it was Pinsker's vision and theory articulated in *Autoemancipation* that had lasting influence. It was the most important 'Zionist' literature to date, and as the contemporary interpreter of Zionism, Rabbi Arthur Hertzberg writes: 'Autoemancipation is the first great statement of the torment of the Jew driven to assert his own nationalism because the wider world had rejected him.'[3]

## Palestine in the 1800s

All told, there were only 25,000 (Palestinian) Jews in all of Palestine in 1881, compared to nearly half a million Arabs. Prior to the Ottoman era, the majority of the Palestinian Christians lived in small villages and towns. Beginning in the mid-15th century and continuing for the next 300 years, the Christian population moved into the major cities. The Muslims and a smaller number

---

[2]  Arthur Hertzberg, *The Zionist Idea*, Atheneum Press, New York, 1959, 38.
[3]  *Ibid.*, 181.

of Christians living in rural areas and villagers were able to sustain a modest life as farmers with cash crops like wheat, cotton, olives, oranges, and grapes. Small industries provided olive oil, textiles, bread, soap, and various food products for local export. Increasingly in the 19th century, Christians tended to be shopkeepers, teachers, government administrators, and other professionals. According to Ottoman census figures in 1880, most of the population in Palestine (approximately two-thirds) lived in six hundred and fifty-seven villages, and the remainder in four major cities and their suburbs.

The major cities were built on hills and became the economic and political hubs: Nazareth in al-Jaleel (Galilee), Jabal-Nablus (the biblical Samaria or Mount Nablus) in the northeast, Jabal al-Quds (Mount Jerusalem) in the centre, and Jabal al-Khalil (Mount Hebron) in the south. Each regional centre was surrounded by forty to fifty villages that used the cities as their economic and political centres, as they had done for centuries. Nazareth and Jerusalem had Christian majorities while Nablus and Hebron were overwhelmingly Muslim. Bethlehem and the adjacent villages of Beit Sahour and Beit Jala were situated just six miles to the south of Jerusalem and were entirely Christian, as were Ramallah and Bir Zeit to the north. The same Ottoman census estimated the population to be 11-12 percent Christian, a figure that is undoubtedly low due to the Ottoman tendency to reflect a higher Muslim population. Christians still constituted 15-16 percent of the total which can be verified by a post-World War I census conducted in 1922 by the British and League of Nations which used more sophisticated methods and stated the Christian population was 16 percent.[4]

Following the severe reign of the Ottoman governor of Palestine Ahmad al-Jazzar (1775-1804), this southern district of Syria was gradually neglected, except for the taxes required by the empire. Christians and Jews had to pay their regular 'poll tax' to the Ottoman overlords according to the Islamic *dhimmi* system. But as the Ottoman empire continued to decline in the post-1800 period, there was a simultaneous decentralisation of Ottoman controls and a gradual demand of reform from the leading families and Palestinian intellectuals. Perhaps most significant for the decades to come, the *dhimmi* system combined with the inherent weaknesses in the Ottoman empire to create a situation whereby certain religious communities became vehicles for European colonial intervention in the Middle East.[5]

Following Napoleon's Middle Eastern interlude (1798-1799) the Ottomans were challenged by the great Muhammad Ali, who was able to control Egypt, Palestine, and Syria in 1831. In an effort to gain European

---

[4] *Abstracts of the Census of 1922*, Jerusalem: Government of Palestine, 1923, 3.
[5] *Ibid*.

support for his rule, Ali liberalised the society to a degree and granted unprecedented religious freedom. Many Western Churches took note of the opportunity and sent missionaries to the region. A variety of political and economic reforms were introduced between 1830-40 that gave the Palestinians a short-lived 'taste' of self-development and empowerment. Perhaps more important, the Egyptians brought an embryonic spirit of secular democracy, proposing total equality and pointing up the errors of the *dhimmi* system. These concepts were of particular interest to the Christian community, many of whose leading sons had studied in Europe and caught the flavour of democracy and nationalism. However, after 1840 a short-lived tax revolt broke out in Palestine, and the forces of Muhammad Ali's son, Ibrahim Pasha, crushed it ruthlessly. An important by-product of this period was the dramatic increase of British political and economic influence in Egypt, particularly after the failure of Pasha's excessive building campaign and economic reforms. The British also increased their influence in Palestine after the 1840s.

European political involvement and Western Christian interests in general received an additional boost of energy from the Crimean War (1853-6). One of the causes of that war was the status and security of non-Muslims in the Ottoman territories, thus stimulating the political powers to adopt mostly Christian communities for protection. The British Anglicans and German Lutherans increased their influence in Palestine and Jordan by introducing a small number of Protestant churches plus new missionaries, to an already crowded field. Churches, schools, nurseries, hospitals, clinics, and convents were built to demonstrate their respective concern for the disadvantaged in Palestine. The unstated agenda was to weaken Russian assertions that they were protecting the Greek Orthodox majority. During this period, Jaffa and Haifa became increasingly important port cities and their facilities were upgraded for the new European tourists. When the French and Russians observed the British and German entry into Palestine, the competitive nature of their respective colonial interests encouraged the French to expand their role as the 'protectors' of the Catholics, which dated back to the Crusades.

The increase in Christian tourism during the 19th century merits an additional comment, as it became a factor in Europe's renewed interest in the Holy Land. Catholics in France, Italy, and Spain held to a 'sacramental' view of pilgrimage to the Holy Land, as did Eastern Orthodox from countries like Greece and Cyprus, believing that by a spiritual journey to the important sites of Jesus' life one could derive certain spiritual blessings. Protestants tended to focus more on the centrality of the Bible and a tradition emerged whereby they wished to see the actual sites where Jesus once walked. By 1869, tourism became a small industry as companies like Thomas Cook and

Sons organised popular tours to Palestine and Egypt. As more and more successful Holy Land tourists returned to England, the interest began to spread, making the Holy Land tour a coveted experience.

It was during this period that Palestinian Christians began to show the first signs of emigration to Europe, and North and South America. The growth of mission schools and Western influences from Catholic and Protestant missionaries, mission agencies, and clergy may have been the source of this gradual 'turning toward the West'. Through their education in mission schools, Palestinian and Syrian Christians began to learn French, English, and Spanish as well as familiarity with Western culture and the manifold attractions of the great cities in the West. The fact that the European and American countries were Christian became an attraction for the Arab Christians. Another factor was the Philadelphia Centennial Exhibition of 1876 which employed several Syrian craftsman and artists who brought back reports of the economic opportunities in the New World. For another hundred years the majority of the Palestinian emigrants would be Christians.

The continued economic decline of the Ottoman empire coupled with violence between Maronite Christians and the Druze in Lebanon were additional factors. This 'first wave' of Christian exodus from Palestine occurred during the years 1890-1917, when there was considerable movement of Arab Christians from Palestine, Lebanon, and Syria. At this time the number of Christian emigrants was not significant. These Arab Christian emigrants were often registered as Syrians or 'Syrian Turks' in the New World, as they were still considered to be residents of the Ottoman empire or the province of Syria. There were no such categories as Arabs or Palestinians in the West. Bernard Sabella, the foremost analyst of Palestinian emigration, has noted that by 1914, approximately 350,000 'Syrian Turks' had left the region, with two-thirds of them in the United States and most of the others in Latin America.[6]

Sabella adds the important point that by the early 1890s the port of Beirut was expanded and transportation was then available to most of Europe and on toward North America and South America. The pressures felt by the Maronite Catholics in Lebanon during the civil war of the 1860s led to small Lebanese communities in Paris, Brazil, and New York and Detroit. Word of the new opportunities reached the largely Catholic Palestinians of Bethlehem and the surrounding suburbs, leading to families leaving via Jaffa to the Beirut passage to the West. While there is little analysis of this routing procedure there are sufficient records and oral traditions of contemporary

---

[6] Bernard Sabella, 'The Emigration of Christian Arabs: Dimensions and Causes of the Phenomenon,' from Andrea Pacini, *Christian Communities in the Arab Middle East: The Challenge of the Future*, Clarendon Press, Oxford, 1998, 131.

families in Bethlehem to raise this as a valid possibility and worthy of further research.[7] By 1890, Palestinian Christians had dropped slightly to approximately 14 percent of the total population of Palestine, which was 94 percent Arab, 5 percent Jewish, and 1 percent foreign. The ratio of Palestinian Christians to Muslims was roughly 16-18 percent Christian, 82 percent Muslim.[8]

As the century drew to a close, Palestine was a neglected province in the decaying Ottoman empire, but European interests had been stimulated by religious, economic, and territorial motives. Ironically, the absence of Ottoman scrutiny and the European allegiances with particular religious communities had opened the door for expressions of political opposition to both the Turkish overlords and to the rapidly increasing Zionist settlements. One of the major influences on the Palestinian population during this period was the relatively recent growth of education, a matter that was a high priority of many Catholic religious orders since the 17th century. Interest in education expanded in the 19th century with the arrival of Protestant churches and mission agencies, which dramatically increased the literacy rate as well as the acquaintance of the population with European literary and political thought.

It was also the churches that brought an independent press to the Palestinian Arabs. The first three printing presses in Palestine were related to churches or mission societies: the Armenian Press, founded in 1833, the French-Fransciscan Matba'at al-Aba al-Fransisiyyin (1846), and the Holy Tomb Society (1849). The Anglican Press of 1848 and the British Missionary Church Society Press of 1879 were other early examples. By the turn of the century there were several private presses that led to a new tradition of independent Palestinian publishing. One of the first was Jurji Habib Hanania in Jerusalem (1892), followed by Basilia Jada in 1908 and Najib Nassar's Matba'at al-Karmil in 1909. They were followed by Elias Zaka's Matba'at al-Nafir in 1913.[9] All were Christians and were part of the increasing literary renaissance called *al-Nahdah*. The publishing houses were augmented by

---

[7]   Sabella, *op. cit.*, 132.

[8]   Sabella places the Christian Palestinians at 13 percent of the total population of Palestine in the early 1890s, slightly lower than others who may include Syrian and Lebanese Christian guest workers. See 'Bernard Sabella, 'A Century Apart: Palestinian Christians and Their Churches from Awakening to Nation Building', *Christian Voices from the Holy Land*, The Palestinian General Delegation in the United Kingdom, London, 1998, 9.

[9]   For a fuller discussion of the literary revival or *al-Nahdah*, see Qustandi Shomali, 'Arab Cultural Revival in Palestine', Thomas Hummel, Kevork Hintlian, and Ulf Carmesund (eds.), *Patterns of the Past, Prospects for the Future*, 283-307; and Rashid Khalidi, *Palestinian Identity: the Construction of Modern National Consciousness*, Columbia University Press, New York, 1997.

literary societies and political discussion groups that became centres of independent Palestinian political consciousness. Books and pamphlets from Syria and Egypt, centres of Arab nationalism, were reprinted in Palestine and circulated widely.

Between 1880 and World War I, the winds of Arab nationalism were blowing, first in Syria (which included Lebanon) and Egypt, but also in Palestine. Inspired initially by nationalism in Syria and Western ideas of nationalism and democracy, there were a significant number of Christian intellectuals involved in the leadership of Arab nationalism in Syria, and later in Lebanon and Palestine. Among Palestinians, some like Butros al-Bustani used the dual vehicles of nationalist literature and literary discussion groups to advance his opinions. In 1905, an important work was published in French by the Palestinian Christian intellectual, Najib Azouri, titled *La Reveille de la nation arabe* ('The Awakening of the Arab Nation'). Azouri called for Arabs to separate themselves from 'the decaying Ottoman tree' and form one independent Arab state. It is likely that the emergence of Arab nationalism in Syria, Lebanon, Egypt, and Palestine had a side effect of slowing down the Arab Christian emigration that had developed between 1880-1900. There was now hope for independence, for economic development, and for newly democratic societies. Arab Christian and Muslim communities worked in true equality and as partners in the inception and continuing struggle for independence.

By 1908 there were strong voices through the embryonic Palestinian press calling for an end to the Ottoman rule. Among their central themes were the following: a cessation of Zionist settlement, fear of the Zionist's agenda, and a call for political independence. Interestingly, the Palestinians are still making the same plea to the Western powers some ninety years later. Najib Nassar's Haifa-based *al-Karmil* was the most important Palestinian nationalist journal that helped awaken national consciousness in the masses. Nassar, a Christian, was a strong advocate of the concept of secular democracy and Arab nationalism that was filtering down from such great Syrian nationalist thinkers as Michel Aflaq, also a Christian. It was followed by the nationalist paper *Falastin*, which was founded in 1911 and lasted until 1967.

Perhaps the most influential work of Arab nationalist literature was *The Arab Awakening* by George Antonius. Antonius was a Palestinian Christian intellectual who had spent most of his life in Egypt, Lebanon, and France. Sorbonne educated and perhaps more at home in French than Arabic, Antonius nevertheless articulated the aspirations of not only Palestinians but of every Arab community, urging them to take their lives into their own hands and create Arab nationalist institutions, states and economic enterprises.

Dr Manuel Hassassian, the contemporary Armenian Palestinian scholar from Bethlehem University, has noted that during the 1917-22 period of British military occupation (but prior to the official issuing of the British Mandate), there were a number of political groups and unions that met regularly to discuss and act upon nationalist ideals. They were modelled after similar groups and unions in Syria and actually developed a close affinity with the Syrian nationalist political parties, whose political goals included the 'Greater Syria' solution or one Arab democratic state in Syria, Lebanon, Palestine and Jordan. One of the interesting groups was the Muslim-Christian society which had several cells across Palestine. It was an early example of Palestinian nationalist expression among the educated elite and was based on equality, political organisation, and opposition to the Zionist programme. Other organisations such as the Arab Club and *Al-Muntada al-Arabi* actually were in competition with each other and were dominated by the two large Jerusalem Muslim families, the Husseinis and Nashashibis.[10]

The Arab Orthodox movement was an early attempt by Palestinian clergy and laity to gain control of the Greek Orthodox Church. Now nearly one hundred years later, their cause has achieved very little. The earliest accounts of this initiative go back to the 1860s, and while they were successful in Lebanon and Syria, Greek domination of the Orthodox Church in Palestine remains until today. The Arab Orthodox movement attempted to introduce the Arabic language into the Orthodox liturgy and also to gain local control over the church properties, which were rather extensive. The highly regarded Palestinian educator, Khalil Sakakini, a Greek Orthodox layman from Jerusalem, challenged the churches hierarchy in 1908 by calling for,

> expelling these Greek priests, brethren of the Holy Sepulchre from the country and rid the Jerusalem See of corruption. I shall work for liberating ourselves from the Greek influence ... Nobody should blame us if we got rid of them and worked for their expulsion.[11]

In 1914, Sakakini left the Greek Orthodox Church and urged others to follow, claiming the church had fallen to its lowest level and it is better to leave it than try to reform it. George Antonius, also a Greek Orthodox, made a similar point, calling for the liturgy to be in Arabic and for the Greek hierarchy to stop selling

---

[10] Manuel Hassassian, 'The Influence of Christian Arabs in the National Movement', Hummel, Hintlian, and Carmesund, (eds.), *op. cit.,* 323.

[11] Yehuda Litani, 'The Harsh Summer of the Patriarch', *Ha'aretz*, September 25 1992.

property to the Zionists. We shall return to this matter in Chapter 8-9.

During the period immediately following World War I (1919-1929) there were a series of political conferences in Palestine and Damascus that embraced several of the divergent trends in Palestinian society concerning a possible political solution. Like the political clubs, these conferences were reflections of the Damascus conference of 1919, which was an attempt by Arab nationalists to avert French imperial rule over Syria (and Palestine) according to the secret Sykes-Picot agreement. The Damascus conference proposed the 'greater Syria' formula, which essentially called for one independent Arab state that included present day Syria, Lebanon, Palestine, and a portion of Jordan. It was understood that Faisal, son of the Sharif of Mecca, would serve as king. The debate was carried on across Syria, Lebanon, Egypt, and to a degree in Iraq.

In Palestine it was widely articulated for a brief period (1908-1918) in the press and by newly formed political organisations. Conferences were held in Haifa (December 1919 and again in December 1920), and Jerusalem (May 1921). The leadership included Syrians and Palestinians, but thereafter the Palestinian leadership formed their separate organisation, indicating the independence of the Palestinian nationalist movement. It was also decided to send a delegation to London to better represent the Palestinian position, but it was too late. The commitment to the Zionist movement and the Sykes-Picot agreement were too deeply entrenched in British politics and in the committees formulating the final treaties in the League of Nations. As Hassassian points out, the committee was so marginalized that they were only able to talk with the Colonial Secretary for the Near East, Winston Churchill, who was committed to Zionism.[12] These and many others developed a tradition of Palestinian national expression that called for full equality of citizenship as the basis of a new society and independent statehood. Christians became politicised virtually overnight as many saw this as their opportunity in their minority status to build a society based neither on the Islamic *dhimmi* system nor the Zionist view of Jewish superiority. Unfortunately, the winds of opposition were far greater than were the hopes for independence or secular democracy.

## *Jewish settlement in Palestine: an answer to European antisemitism*

The Jewish community in all Palestine numbered approximately 25,000 in

---

[12] Hummel, Hintlian, and Carmesund, *op. cit..*, 327-8.

1870, but as various European Jewish settlers arrived it grew to 75,000 by the 1922 census, still only 9 percent of the population. During the Ottoman period and up until the 1890s, there was no visible tension between Jews and Palestinian Arabs. As the settlement of Jews increased in the 1880s with the *Habbat Zion* movement, the great Jewish philosopher Asher Ginzberg, also called *Ahad Ha'am* ('One of the People'), sensed tension in the air. His commentary on new dynamics brought by Jewish settlement gave this prophetic warning in 1891:

> Palestine is not an uninhabited land and can offer a home only to a very small portion of the Jews scattered throughout the world. Those who settle in Palestine must above all seek to win the friendship of the Palestinians, by approaching them courteously and with respect. But what do our brothers do? Precisely the opposite. They were slaves in the land of their exile, and suddenly they find themselves with unlimited freedom. This sudden change has aroused in them a tendency to despotism, which is what always happens when slaves come to power. They treat the Arabs with hostility and cruelty, rob them of their rights in a dishonest way, hurt them without reason and then pride themselves on such actions; and no one attacks this despicable and dangerous tendency.[13]

The Zionism of Ha'am, a more humanistic and conciliatory form, was eclipsed by the harder line of Herzl and Weizmann. The latter followed the Germanic ethnocentric model of nationalism while the other was oriented toward the French and American versions. This becomes clear in Ha'am's response to Herzl after listening to his speech at the first World Zionist Congress in 1897:

> Judaism is, therefore, in a quandry: it can no longer tolerate the *Galut* [diaspora] form which it had to take on, in obedience to its will to live. When it was exiled from its own country; but, without that form, its life is in danger. So it seeks to return to its historic center, where it will be able to live a life developing in a natural way, to bring its powers into play in every department of human culture, to broaden and perfect those national possessions which it has acquired up to now, and thus to contribute to the common stock of humanity, in the

---

[13] Ahad Ha'am, quoted in D L Bender and R Bruno Leone, *Israel: Opposing Viewpoint*, Greenhaven Press, San Diego, 1989, 29-30

future as it has in the past, a great national culture, the fruit of the unhampered activity of a people living by the light of its own spirit. For this purpose Judaism can, for the present, content itself with little. It does not need an independent state, but only the creation in its native land of conditions favourable to its development; a good sized settlement for Jews working without hindrance in every kind of civilization ... This Jewish settlement, which will be a gradual growth, will become in course of time the center of the nation, wherein its spirit will find pure expression and develop in all its aspects to the highest degree of perfection of which it is capable. Then, from this center, the spirit of Judaism will radiate to the great circumference, to all the communities of the Diaspora, to inspire them with new life and to preserve the overall unity of our people. When our national culture in Palestine has attained that level, we may be confident that it will produce men in the Land of Israel itself who will be able, at a favourable moment, to establish a state there—one which will be not merely a State of Jews but a really Jewish State ... And so political Zionism cannot satisfy those Jews who care for Judaism; its growth seems to them to be fraught with danger to the object of their own aspiration.[14]

This important distinction between a 'state for Jews' and Jewish state recognizes that the former carried the ethnic particularism of the more restrictive forms of nationalism, and would breed conflict because of this exclusivity or tribalism. The Jewish State that interested Ha'am and others was mature, based upon justice, and would deal with Palestinian Arabs as equal citizens of the state. The humanistic model, while somewhat utopian, also flowered in the philosopher Martin Buber, the scientist Albert Einstein, and the first president of Hebrew University, Judah Magnes. However, it was never a major force in the Jewish community, whether in Palestine or in the diaspora. Moreover, the decisions about Palestine would not be made by Jews or Palestinian Arabs who were living in the land of Palestine, at least not until 1948. The primary decision-makers and the major political developments that determined the fate of the Holy Land and its people would take place in Europe and the United States between 1897 and 1947.

Undoubtedly, the most important event of the first half of this phase was the severe antisemitism of Europe. In this regard, Theodor Herzl (1860-

---

[14] *Ibid.*

1904) is an instructive case study. He was born in Budapest during 1860 of wealthy, assimilated Jewish parents, who moved to Vienna when he was a teenager. The family did not identify with the Jewish community nor did young Theodor receive a Jewish religious education. In fact, at the age of thirteen he chose not to take the Bar Mitzvah but instead was received into the Roman Catholic Church.

Herzl received a doctorate in 1884 and spent several years developing his skills as a playwright and essayist. In 1892, he took a position with the *Neue Freie Presse*, one of Vienna's leading newspapers, and soon was assigned to Paris. Within two years he found himself covering an event that would change his life, the trial of Alfred Dreyfus. Captain Dreyfus was a prominent Jew from Alsace-Lorraine and was accused of selling military secrets to Germany. The evidence was minimal and many were convinced the captain was framed. In December 1894, he was found guilty, was court-marshalled, and then deported to Devil's Island for a life in penal exile.

But it was not the actual conviction of Dreyfus that startled Herzl. Rather, it was the frightening collective expressions of antisemitism that emerged in 'polite' French society that shook him to the core of his being. Hertzberg's account reflects the impact that the Dreyfus case had on the young journalist:

> It was Herzl's duty as correspondent to provide his paper in Vienna with an account of the trial of Dreyfus and its effect on the public life of France. He was present at the *École Militaire* at the famous dramatic scene when Dreyfus was stripped of his epaulets and drummed out the gate in disgrace. For Herzl this moment was a hammer blow, and the howling of the mob outside the gates of the parade ground, shouting *à bas les juifs*, transformed him into the Zionist that he was to be.[15]

The deep psychological impact of the hostile crowd moved Herzl to action. Less than a year later he met with the wealthy Jewish philanthropist, Baron de Hirsch, discussing Jewish colonisation in Argentina. Within a few weeks he began drafting his Zionist classic *Der Judenstaat*. That work appeared in February 1896, and was undoubtedly the most influential written work on behalf of the Zionist movement in history. It served as a clarion call to all Jews reminding them that they would not find security in the antisemitic climate of Europe. Instead, they must reject the illusion of assimilation and develop their own state. Initially, *Der Judenstaat* was not well received by

---

[15] Hertzberg, *ibid.*, 202.

the mainstream Jewish community, neither in Europe nor the United States.

Following the publication of *Der Judenstaat*, Herzl worked incessantly for the Zionist cause. He convened the first World Zionist Congress in Basel during August 1897. Its stated purpose was simple yet profound: 'Zionism seeks to procure for the Jewish people a publicly recognised, legally secured, home in Palestine.'[16] At the Zionist Congress the leaders were able to facilitate certain goals: 1) they were able to project a nationalist ideology for Jewish statehood that could capture the imagination and will of the Jews worldwide; 2) they were able to advocate a programme of Jewish settlement in Palestine; 3) they created an organisation that could advance their programme; 4) their goals were clear and attainable. Within a few years the essential institutions, procedures, and anticipated international legitimacy would be in place. With remarkable confidence, Herzl would write in his diary after the first Zionist Congress:

> If I were to sum up the Congress in a word—which I shall guard against pronouncing publicly—it would be this:
> 'At Basle I founded the Jewish state. If I said this aloud today, I would be greeted by universal laughter. Perhaps in five years, and certainly in fifty, everyone will know it.'[17]

The entry was dated 3 September 1897, and the United Nations vote to partition Palestine was 29 November 1947, or fifty years and two months later.

## Prelude to the Mandate (Zionism and Britain: 1905-1917)

Herzl and his colleagues still lacked an international power that would grant the necessary land and political legitimacy for the envisioned Zionist state. Herzl was a pragmatist as much as he was a visionary so he deliberately left the issue of location ambiguous, despite the fact that he and most of the Zionists leaders favoured Palestine. They approached the Ottoman rulers with considerable funding from European and American donors but met with a series of delays.

An interesting development occurred shortly before the First Zionist Congress convened when a group of American Christian Zionists heard that Herzl was wavering on the Palestine option. Herzl received a Bible in which

---

[16] *Ibid*.

[17] Quoted in Benny Morris, *Righteous Victims*, Alfred A Knopf, New York, 1999, 21.

every reference to 'Israel or Zion' was marked in red with a letter encouraging the Zionists to settle only in Palestine, which was the will of God and faithful to the prophetic scriptures. The source of the Bible and letter was William E Blackstone, an American fundamentalist lay-evangelist and author, who had organised the first Zionist lobbying effort in the United States in 1891. The effort primarily initiated by Christians was committed to support the establishment of a Jewish state in Palestine in order to fulfil the prophetic scriptures.[18]

The ambiguity within early Zionism as to whether the location of their state should be in Palestine or elsewhere is instructive on another level. The vast majority of those in the Zionist leadership did not even consider the fact that over 90 percent of the population in Palestine was non-Jewish. Herzl made a trip to Palestine in 1898 but there is no record that he was interested in the Arab majority, numbering approximately 500,000, compared to less than 30,000 Jews. This blindness toward the indigenous peoples was a factor that would haunt other settler colonial ventures such as South Africa, the United States, Canada, and Australia.

Bishop Cragg offers insightful comments as to why Zionism has had this remarkable lack of awareness toward the indigenous Arab population. Cragg notes the complexity of this question and points to three related dimensions. First, he notes that Zionism viewed Palestine as 'a hinterland' which was to undergo a 'pure colonisation.' Clearly, the indigenous Palestinian Arabs were not to be consulted. As for the decision-making process, the indigenous people were a non-issue. Second, what the Zionist enterprise proposed was to leap over thirteen centuries of Arab Muslim control over Palestine and an additional 1900 years of Christian presence in the land. On one level, this may have been unrealistic and romantic, but it was entirely workable at this particular juncture of history. In this era of colonialism the European powers were often able to dominate and manage the desires of the less powerful. There was no international body nor was there international law and corresponding institutions that could challenge the European powers and hold them accountable. It seems as if in the minds of the British and the Zionists, Palestine had been placed in a type of 'limbo' or time capsule from the previous Jewish 'nation' under the Hasmoneans (161-70 BCE) until 1948, when the state was 'reborn.' Third, the Zionist use of the concept of the gentile or the 'foreigner' enabled those who adhered to

---

[18] William E Blackstone was the author of the best-selling volume *Jesus is Coming*, which is a classic in the field of 19th century American Protestant prophecy literature. Blackstone is credited with organizing the first Zionist lobbying effort in the United States in 1891, a mass appeal to the President of the United States in support of a Jewish State in Palestine.

the Zionist vision to see everyone as their enemy. While this was understandable with the violence of European antisemitism, it was not necessary for the Zionists to negate their Palestinian 'cousins' who had identified with the land for two millennia.[19]

During 1901, Herzl had grown frustrated because the enterprise had not secured an agreement on land or political legitimacy from one of the major powers. After failed meetings with the Ottoman caliph and Kaiser, Herzl pursued options with Russia and France. These also proved fruitless. In 1902 the Zionist leaders decided to concentrate their efforts on the British. Initially, they discussed Palestine and Cyprus but the British offered Uganda. Many of Herzl's own leadership were still divided as to whether the homeland should be in Palestine or if in their desperation, they should take the best available land they were offered.

The decision to shift their quest for international sponsorship to England was perceptive and politically strategic for several reasons. First, from the earliest recorded British historical documents (the 6th-century 'Epistle of Gildas') the British had a fascination with Israel and the Holy Land. The Venerable Bede's *Ecclesiastical History*, written in the 8th century, suggests that the early Britons saw themselves as the newly constituted 'Chosen People' and interpreted their conflicts with the pagan Scandinavian raiders similarly to Israel's struggles against the Moabites, Amonites, and Philistines. These symbols and references continued in such literary giants as Chaucer, Milton, Bunyan, Dryden, and others. Deep in British consciousness was at least a thousand years of attachment to and sympathy with the idea of Israel, the Jewish people and the Holy Land.

A second rationale, whose moment arrived in a timely manner for the Zionists' interests, was British imperial competition with France, Germany, and Russia. Suddenly, all four European colonial states had embarked on campaigns and political or economic support of projects in Palestine. In 1898, the German Kaiser visited Palestine and consecrated the Lutheran Church of the Redeemer, (sometimes called cynically the Kaiser Wilhelm Cathedral) in the Old City of Jerusalem. Russian support of the Greek Orthodox Patriarch and the establishment of Russian churches had developed only the previous decade. France sent high level governmental officials to Palestine in support of Latin Catholic interests and viewed itself as the co-protectors (with the Vatican) of the Catholic holy sites in the Holy Land. British colonial strategies became more focused at the turn of the century in maintaining a land bridge from the eastern Mediterranean to the Persian

---

[19] Kenneth Cragg, *Palestine: The Prize and Price of Zion*, Cassell Publications, London, 1997, 28.

Gulf, and access to the 'Jewel in the Crown,' India.

For Lord Shaftesbury, the 'restoration' was rooted in his particular view of biblical prophecy and by interpretation, of England's unique role in God's plan for the ages. Shaftesbury's dedication to the project of a Jewish state in Palestine manifested itself in political lobbying and educating the public. Others who influenced by this view were Lord Oliphant and the conservative Tory leader after the turn of the century, Lord Arthur Balfour. Throughout the previous decade, there had been several Jewish survivors of the pogroms in Russia who had settled in Britain. There was considerable sympathy for their cause, but not to the extent that the average Englishman would wish to see them settle in Great Britain. They would, however, support a settlement of the Jews in Palestine. There remained a strong tradition of Christian dispensational or pre-millennialist thought, that is, that the return of the Jews to Palestine and the establishment of a Jewish state would fulfil the prophetic scriptures. Some even thought that God would bless the British empire if they were to be the facilitating factor in settling the 'Chosen People'. Finally, there had been a variety of political efforts in parliament in support of a Jewish state, particularly through the efforts of the Christian Evangelical philanthropist and social reformer, Lord Shaftesbury. The way had been prepared by Christians and various writers who had planted the idea that Britain should support Jewish restoration in Palestine.

But the question of location was still lacking resolution as late as the Zionist Congress of 1903, which would be Herzl's last. The most viable option before them was the British offer of Uganda, with Cyprus and the Sinai still under discussion. The latter two were viewed more positively as possible stepping stones to their real goal: Palestine. The Congress voted in favour of the Uganda proposal by a unanimous count of 295 to 175. However, the young Russian Zionist, Dr Chaim Weizmann protested, pointing out that a majority of the Russians were vehemently opposed to the Uganda plan and it must be reconsidered. The decision on Uganda was tabled.

## Promises to Arabs, promises to Jews

Theodor Herzl died on 3 July 1904, only 43 years of age, and the mantle of leadership fell to Dr Weizmann, a chemist and Russian Zionist leader from Motol, near Pinsk. Weizmann had grown up in Russia's pogroms of the 1880s and distinguished himself as a scientist by the time he emigrated to England in 1905, having pioneered dyestuffs in chemistry and invented aniline blue. On 9 January 1906, Weizmann was able to arrange a meeting with Lord Balfour in London, then a prominent leader of the Conservative

Party, which was for the moment not in control of parliament. Much to his surprise, Weizmann discovered that the statesman was already predisposed to Zionism and very enthusiastic about the Palestine proposal. Weizmann sensed that the goals of the Zionist movement would eventually appeal to Britain's colonial interests, but until now the matching of interests had not occurred. He wondered how Balfour would respond to his vision and programme. Balfour's sentiments are seen in a letter to his wife after meeting Weizmann, stating that he saw 'no political difficulty about obtaining Palestine, only economic ones'.[20] Apparently, Weizmann convinced Balfour that a Jewish state could only be located in Palestine, but at this stage the British government was still inclined to offer Uganda. Balfour later told his niece, Blanche Dugdale:

> It was from that talk with Weizmann that I saw that the Jewish form of patriotism was unique. Their love of their country refused to be satisfied with the Uganda scheme. It was Weizmann's absolute refusal even to look at it that impressed me.[21]

Why was Balfour so willing to support the Zionist programme, especially at a time when British policy was oriented toward the Uganda option? There are three possible answers. First, Balfour and the Conservative Party had been voted out of office in 1905. He was free from the influence of the Foreign Office, dominated by the Liberal Party, and saw a political vehicle in having the Tories advocate the Palestine proposal. Perhaps more instructive is the second motive, his Evangelical Christian orientation, which gave Balfour the theological basis for the Palestine proposal. These views were based on his reading of biblical prophecy with a restored 'Israel' playing a vital role at the end of history. Again, his niece and biographer, Blanche Dugdale, provides the answer:

> Balfour's interest in the Jews and their history was lifelong. It originated in the Old Testament training of his mother, and in his Scottish upbringing. As he grew up, his intellectual admiration and sympathy for certain aspects of Jewish philosophy and culture grew also, and the problem of the Jews in the modern world seemed to him of immense importance. He always talked eagerly on this, and I remember

---

[20] See Donald Wagner, *Anxious for Armageddon*, Herald Press, 1995, 93.

[21] Kenneth Young, *Arthur James Balfour*, J Bell and Sons, London, 1963, 25.

in childhood imbibing from him the idea that Christian religion and civilisation owes to Judaism an immeasurable debt, shamefully ill repaid.[22]

The third motive combined the goals of the Zionists with British colonial aspirations (a shortcut to the 'Jewel in the Crown'). It was also vital that England maintain access to the Suez Canal and the vital trade routes it opened to the east. Having a people who were indebted to them while still being somewhat Western in orientation, the British viewed the Zionists as a willing partner in Palestine.

Following the World Zionist Congress of 1905, the organisation set up the mechanism for land purchase in Palestine through the Jewish National Fund, which functioned as a trust that would purchase land exclusively for Jews. Wealthy American and European Jews began to contribute generously and large tracts of land were purchased. In 1908, there were violent clashes between Palestinians and Zionist settlers in the Jaffa region, when questions were raised about the loss of Palestinian land. A series of petitions and letters were signed, collected, and sent to the Ottoman authorities, demanding that land sales and Zionist settlement activities be stopped. Najib Nassar, a leading journalist and a Christian from Nazareth, wrote extensive editorials and accounts of the problem in the Haifa newspaper, *Al-Karmil*, where he served as editor-in-chief. He was arrested for 'disturbing the peace' but released after a few days imprisonment.

When World War I broke out in 1914, Weizmann met with one of his major donors, Baron Rothschild, to discuss the significant implications of the war spreading to the Middle East. Rothschild urged Weizmann to return to England and meet with leading British politicians to secure support for the Zionist cause. Shortly after returning to his home in Manchester, Weizmann became friends with C P Scott, who was well known for his political connections and as editor of the influential *Manchester Guardian*. This friendship would benefit Weizmann for many years. Scott told him: 'I would like to do something for you,' and offered to put him in touch with the leading Tory politician David Lloyd George. He also reminded Weizmann, 'You have a Jew in the Cabinet, Mr Herbert Samuel.' Weizmann is reported to have dismissed this suggestion because in his eyes, Samuel was too much of an assimilated Jew and was opposed to the Palestine proposal. Weizmann was able to contact Samuel and Lloyd George, the latter who was about whom to play important roles in support of the Zionist cause.[23]

---

[22] *Ibid.*
[23] Dugdale, from Wilson, 34.

In 1915, Weizmann was employed part-time with the Royal Navy on an urgent project that was designed to increase the British supply of powerful explosives to be employed against Germany's deadly U-boats. Weizmann's invention of a new explosive using acetone and fermented maize proved to be a vital contribution to the British war effort. Lloyd George would state in his *War Memoirs* that the Jewish state was a reward to Weizmann for his contributions to the British war efforts in the field of explosives. In 1915, these contributions gained him respect at the highest levels of the British Navy as well as new *entrées* to the political elite. By now Balfour had returned to power, not as a member of Parliament but was appointed by Prime Minister Asquith as a member of the important Royal Committee of Imperial Defence. Balfour requested another meeting with the Zionists, their first since the conversation in Manchester back in 1906. Weizmann recalls Balfour telling him:

> You know, I was thinking of that conversation of ours, and I believe that when the guns stop firing you may get your Jerusalem.[24]

In 1915, the British accelerated efforts that would encourage various Arab leaders to join the war against the Ottoman Turks in the Mediterranean and Near East theatres. Sir Henry McMahon, British High Commissioner for Egypt was designated by the Foreign Office to conduct policy with the Arabs, and in this regard he dispatched the famous Lawrence of Arabia to befriend the Sharif of Mecca. As part of the wooing of the Arabs, McMahon wrote a series of letters to the Sharif, who was the central character of the Lawrence drama. In his second letter, dated 24 October 1915, Sir Henry wrote:

> I am empowered in the name of the Government of Great Britain to give the following assurances and make the following reply to your letter:
>
> 1. Subject to the above modifications, Great Britain is prepared to recognise and support the independence of the Arabs in all the regions within the limits demanded by the Sharif of Mecca.
> 2. Great Britain will guarantee the Holy Places against all external aggression and will guarantee their inviolability.
> 3. When the situation admits, Great Britain will give to the Arabs her advice and will assist them to establish what may

---

[24] Quoted in Wilson, 40.

appear to be the most suitable forms of government in those various territories.[25]

The letter was deliberately ambiguous about independence for the Arabs yet specific concerning regions to be excluded. McMahon had been precise about the excluded areas: Mersin and Alexandretta (on the Turkey-Syria border); a district of Syria west of Damascus and Homs (Beka'a and coastal Lebanon); Aden, and Kuwait. The Arabs were led to understand that the remainder of the eastern Mediterranean to the Gulf would become independent and thus became vigorously involved in the fight against their occupiers, the Turks. It was in this aspect of the Great War that the famed T E Lawrence ('Lawrence of Arabia') became involved. The first promise, therefore, was to the Arabs and gained a new ally for the British but with the promise of independence to those who would remain loyal to the Allied cause in the war effort.

The ink was barely dry on the second McMahon letter when the British negotiated an entirely different arrangement with the French that would divide the Middle East between them. Sir Mark Sykes, an MP with previous Middle Eastern experience, was appointed to conduct secret negotiations with France concerning the disposition of the Ottoman empire. His counterpart from France was François Georges Picot, also a diplomat with extensive experience in the Middle East. Both colonial powers were eager to strengthen their foothold in the Middle East, with the French eyeing the territory where they had extensive holdings and influence since the Crusades: Lebanon, Syria, and Palestine. The British wanted a land bridge from the eastern Mediterranean to the Gulf, so as to secure their oil interests while maintaining direct access to India. On 16 March 1916, the Sykes-Picot Agreement was signed in total secrecy between France and Britain, certainly without the knowledge of the Arabs, whose interests Sykes-Picot betrayed.

Palestine was still desired by both the French and the British, not to mention the Russians, Germany, the Turks, the Zionists, various Arab nations, and by the indigenous Palestinian Arab majority. The British wished to see leadership in Palestine that would remain under their control. With the emergence of Arab nationalism and the Arab majority being an unknown quantity, the British believed that the Zionists were the better known and safer 'horse' to ride. Moreover, the argument can be made that two of the key decision-makers in this case, Lord Balfour and David Lloyd George were predisposed to Zionism from their Evangelical Christian backgrounds, with the influential Winston Churchill supporting Zionism for political reasons.

---

[25] Thomas and Sally Mallison, *The Palestine Problem in International Law*, Longman, Harlow, England, 1986, 72

Weizmann was aware of the Zionist Christian religious support and its potential value for the Jewish political Zionists. In his autobiography, *Trial and Error,* Weizmann wrote:

> ... men like Balfour, Churchill, Lloyd George, were deeply religious and believed in the Bible, that to them the return of the Jewish people to Palestine was a reality, so that we Zionists represented to them a great tradition for which they had enormous respect.[26]

Thus a dramatic convergence occurs in the World War I era bringing together Christian Zionism, Jewish Zionism, and British colonial interests.

His Majesty's Government was not finished offering the 'much promised land' to others. Ironically, at the point in which England's offers were made they had no official claims to Palestine and the majority of the population was opposed to their intents. But morality and legality would not override the empire's colonial vision and they had immediate political needs due to World War I. By late 1916 the British War Cabinet concluded that they needed the United States to assist their campaigns against Germany. With extensive connections with the political elite in Washington, DC, the Zionists claimed they could deliver the very people who might advance such a decision. In addition, Dr Weizmann's formula for explosives had given the British an advantage on the battlefield. Thus with these two important points of leverage with the War Cabinet the Zionists began to find support for the Jewish state proposal for Palestine. The political agenda was augmented by Balfour's eye on the prophetic interpretation of the Bible, which according to his reading indicated that God's sovereign plan for history included the Jews returning to Palestine and the divine blessing would fall upon England for facilitating the plan.

During 1917, a series of draft documents were exchanged between the Zionist leadership in England and His Majesty's War Cabinet. There was to be no consultation with the ninety percent majority population in Palestine. The Zionists still lacked international standing and political legitimacy for their platform. They had requested of the British authorities a clear statement of support for the right to establish a Jewish state in Palestine, but several Cabinet members had misgivings. Some Jewish leaders, such as the MP Philip Magnus, preferred that Jews remain a moral and religious people as opposed to a political nation like every other state. Magnus and others

---

[26] Chaim Weizmann, *Trial and Error*, quoted in Wilson, 46.

believed the 'calling' of the Jews was to be a conscience and model for the world and feared the Zionist political vision as a compromise. The majority of the Jewish leadership in the world were opposed to the Zionist programme well into the 1930s. Further, the highest ranking Jewish member of the British Government, the Secretary of the Foreign Office for India, Lord Edwin Montague, was vehemently outspoken in opposition to Zionism and the Palestine proposal. Montague stated at one point:

> I assume that it means that Mohammadans and Christians are to make way for the Jews ... you will find a population in Palestine driving out its present inhabitants, taking all the best country ... Palestine will become the world's Ghetto.[27]

Nevertheless, on 2 November 1917, Lord Balfour issued the following letter after gaining approval from the War Cabinet:

> His Majesty's Government view with favour the establishment in Palestine of a national home for the Jewish people, and will use their best endeavours to facilitate the achievement of this object, it being understood that nothing shall be done which may prejudice the civil and religious rights of existing non-Jewish communities in Palestine, or the rights and political status enjoyed by Jews in any other country.[28]

Not by accident, the letter names the Jewish people as recipients of Palestine as their 'national home,' but neither names nor indicates the right of a national home for the overwhelming majority, the Palestinian Arabs, the Jews constituting slightly less than 10 percent of the population and the Palestinian Arabs over 90 percent. As the Jewish historian Arthur Kessler so succinctly summarised the exchange: 'one nation solemnly promised to a second nation the country of a third.' Perhaps more to the point, in this case the second nation was neither a nation nor did it possess political legitimacy before the League of Nations or any other body of international or regional authority. But legitimacy was precisely what the Zionist leaders seized in this case, and it marked the most important victory at the international level in their quest for statehood.

---

[27] W T Mallison, 'The Balfour Declaration: An Appraisal in International Law', in Ibrahim Abu-Lughod, *The Transformation of Palestine,* Northwestern University Press, Evanston, 1971, 74.

[28] *Ibid.*, 47.

The Balfour Declaration granted a dubious form of legitimacy to the harder line Zionist belief that Jesus possessed a divine right to the land whereas Palestinians did not have the same promise. Balfour's commitment to the Zionist programme and his advancement of their proposal for recognition by England was rooted in his dual commitment to Britain's colonial politics and his Christian Zionist ideology. Balfour had no interest in consulting the indigenous majority about his proposal to the Zionists, nor did he seem to deem them a people. A memorandum to Lord Curzon in 1919 makes his views clear:

> In Palestine we do not propose even to go through the form of consulting the wishes of the present inhabitants of the country ... the Four Powers are committed to Zionism, and Zionism, be it right or wrong, good or bad, is rooted in age-long traditions, in present needs, in future hopes, of far profounder import than the desires and prejudices of the 700,000 Arabs who now inhabit that ancient land ...[29]

Balfour's candid remarks point to biblical imagery: 'that ancient land', 'age-long traditions.' Moreover, the colonial strategies of the British with the French (Sykes-Picot Agreement) and the additional promises to the Zionists inherent in the post-World War I treaties, were anchored in his view of enlarging Britain's colonial reach in competition with the French and others.

One could legitimately question whether Balfour and others intended to support an actual state for the Jews in Palestine. The reference in the Balfour Declaration is to a 'homeland,' a rather nebulous term. Later statements by Balfour and the leader of the Tory Party, David Lloyd George, indicate that they fully intended for the Zionists to have a Jewish state in Palestine. Lloyd George was very specific in an answer to Weizmann: 'We meant a Jewish state.' Or as Michael Prior summarised the strategy of the Foreign Office: 'It is clear that homeland was a mere circumlocution for state.' Dr Prior quotes from Herbert Young, an official in the Foreign Office during these years, one of tactics, not strategy, the general strategic idea being the gradual immigration of Jews into Palestine until that country becomes a predominantly Jewish state ... But it is questionable whether we are in a position to tell the Arabs what our policy really means.[30]

---

[29] Doreen Igrams, *Palestine Papers, 1917-22, Seeds of Conflict*, John Murray, London, 1972, 73.

[30] Michael Prior, *The Bible and Colonialism*, Sheffield Academic Press, Sheffield, 1997, 127.

## *The post-war settlement in Palestine*

Both the Balfour Declaration and the Sykes-Picot Agreement were negotiated without the knowledge of the Arabs. The Sykes-Picot secret agreement came to light in late 1917 when the Bolsheviks gained access to it and released the document for public consumption. Once the Balfour Declaration came to light, the Arabs noted the dual betrayal. Both the French and British tried to pacify the Arabs and underscore previous promises made in the McMahon correspondence. A British diplomat, D G Hogarth was sent to the Sharif of Mecca to allay the Arabs' fears. The British were fully aware of their duplicitous tactics but believed there was still a path by which they could maintain control and out-manoeuvre the Arabs. They decided to deal with Faisal, son of Hussein, and encourage him to welcome the Jews to Palestine provided they do not undermine the rights of Arabs. Faisal was more willing to do so once the British and French promised him the kingship over Syria. Indeed, Faisal was granted Syria, against the wishes of Syrian and Palestinian Arab nationalists. In order to pacify the other son, Abdullah, the British carved out the territory east of the Jordan River and called it Transjordan. Both territories, like Iraq, were placed under British tutelage, or semi-autonomous local management, called 'Mandates'.

Still unresolved was the 'much-promised' Palestine. The Palestinian Arab majority expected full independence while the Zionists believed the British War Cabinet had made a commitment to implement a Jewish state. US President Woodrow Wilson, a champion of self-determination and human rights for indigenous people, sent an investigative body called the King-Crane Commission. The essence of their findings are as follows:

> It is to be remembered that the non-Jewish population of Palestine—nearly nine-tenths of the whole, are emphatically against the entire Zionist programme. To subject a people so minded to unlimited immigration and to steady financial and social pressure to surrender the land, it would be a gross violation of the Principle just quoted (self-determination), and the people's rights, though it be kept within the forms of law.[31]

Among the conclusions in the Report were the following:

> It can hardly be doubted that the extreme Zionist program

---

[31] Mallison and Mallison, *op. cit.,* 76.

must be greatly modified. For a 'national home for the Jewish people' is not equivalent to making Palestine into a Jewish State; nor can the erection of such a Jewish State be accomplished without the gravest trespass upon the civil and religious rights of existing non-Jewish communities in Palestine. The fact came out repeatedly in the Commission's conference with Jewish representatives, that the Zionists look forward to a practically complete dispossession of the present non-Jewish inhabitants of Palestine, by various forms of purchase.[32]

Unfortunately, the wisdom of the King-Crane Commission brought neither wisdom nor influence to the treaties and various formulas passed by the League of Nations following World War I. The Palestinian Arabs were not represented in any negotiations in advance of the treaties so it is no surprise that the formulas and language favours the British and French colonial interests and the Zionist movement. Despite the fact that the Wilson Doctrine of upholding the rights of indigenous people, with the principles of 'self-determination' and independence being fundamental, these principles were not followed in Palestine. Instead, the French and British patterns of dominance would continue with inevitable patterns of injustice falling upon the indigenous majority. The San Remo Peace conference of 1920 was the initial formula that would implement the colonial designs resolve on the former Ottoman territories, utilising the concept of 'Mandates'. The Arabs were generally opposed to the mandatory system from the moment it was proposed, sensing that it violated the hope of the Wilson principles and the promises of the McMahon letters. The British and French were able to gain some limited Arab support for their formulas, but only in so far as they would be promised kingdoms and limited independence. Naturally, the Zionists favoured San Remo and the agreements that would follow, as their desires were safeguarded in the very language of the proposals. For example, the Zionist's opposed the principle of democracy for Palestine because more than 90 percent of the population was Palestinian Arab. Instead, the language chosen by the British and Zionists proposed a 'Jewish homeland', the very controversial section included in the Balfour Declaration of 1917. Thus the Zionist formulas were maintained in tact while the interests of the Palestinians and other Arabs were either reduced or overridden by the language of Balfour. The alliance of the Zionist 'fathers' with British colonialism would pay dividends for the Zionists, with the

---

[32] *Ibid.*, 77.

rights and needs of the majority population placed at the margins. The seeds of conflict were sown and ratified by the settlements emerging out of World War I. They have yet to be reconciled nor is there hope that they will be resolved in the near future.

## *Summary*

1.  The Zionism of Herzl and Weizmann is essentially a 19th-20th century European form of nationalism with its roots in the 'tribal model', sometimes called Romantic German or ethnocentic nationalism. It places the dominant ethnic group (the 'tribe' or bloodlines) as the organising principle of the nation with commensurate privileges, rights, and political favours granted first to them. The belief that only the Jewish people had a divine right to historic Palestine characterises both the harder line Romantic Zionism and Christian Zionism, whereas the more secular humanistic Zionism of Ha'am, Albert Einstein and Judah Magnes rejected the divine right argument.

2.  As the early Zionist fathers, principally Herzl and Weizmann, searched for political legitimacy and sponsorship by a major colonial power, they received numerous rejections but eventually found support from Great Britain.

3.  The pathway leading to British support was paved in part by a form of evangelical Christian Zionism, which greatly influenced humanitarians such as Lord Shaftesbury and a generation of politicians such as Lord Oliphant, Lord Balfour, and Prime Minister David Lloyd George.

4.  The 'first wave' of Palestinian Christian emigration began in the 1880-90 period, stimulated by four factors: Western Christian education in the missionary schools which offered European languages and familiarity with Western culture; reports of economic advantages stemming from Syrian participation in the 1876 Philadelphia Exhibition; declining fortunes under the Ottoman empire and Christian-Druze violence in Lebanon; new transportation to the West through the new port of Beirut.

5.  European antisemitism was the major social illness that led to the emergence of Zionism. There is little if no evidence of political or social tension in Palestine between Palestinians and Jews prior to the arrival of Zionism from Europe and the ensuing exclusively Jewish settlements.

6.  British colonial efforts, represented in part by the Foreign Office, matched various needs expressed by the Zionist movement, as the British leadership found Zionism more to their liking than Arab interests.

7. Palestine was a remote and often forgotten corner of the Ottoman empire in the 1800s, with a tiny Jewish community (under 25,000) and a dominant Palestinian majority (over 425,000), of which approximately 16 percent were Christian, the balance Muslim. The Christian-Muslim ratio was roughly 20 percent Christian to 82 percent Muslim. These ratios would begin to drop in the 1880s with the rise of Jewish settlement and the first wave of Christian emigration.

8. Napoleon's failed campaign in Palestine coincided with European Protestant missionary activity. Protestant missions stimulated the growth of literacy in Palestine and the study of European ideas, especially nationalism. Arab nationalism grew after 1900 with Arab Christians in the forefront of its leadership. The British made conflicting promises to the three parties during the World War I years. She promised independence to all Arabs who would fight against the Ottomans; she promised the French a control over half of the region; and she promised to weaken or reduce Russian influence.

# Chapter 5
# THE AMBIVALENCE OF HAND AND VOICE: PALESTINE UNDER BRITAIN (1920-1948)

Middle East scholar and theologian, Bishop Kenneth Cragg, characterises the period this chapter will undertake as 'The Prey of Ambivalence'. He takes the imagery from the familiar story of Jacob and Esau when the Patriarch Isaac, while on his deathbed, sensed deceit within his family: 'The voice is the voice of Jacob but the hands are of Esau' (Genesis 27:22). Bishop Cragg makes the following point:

> In the history of the conflict over Palestine-Israel the ambivalence of hand and voice has sometimes been the other way round, what has been done being more telling than what has been said. There has been deep ambiguity in both spheres, ambiguity which has kindled misgivings, caused these to deepen into entire distrust and so tangled positive purposes in crippling enmity.[1]

While the Jacob and Esau symbolism may not be precise, there are certain parallels that apply to both the Palestinians and the Zionist movement. Jacob as Zionism is clever, pragmatic, and opportunistic. He has the wisdom and encouragement of his 'guarantor' mother Rachel, initially Britain and later the United States, who labours behind the scenes to insure that Jacob (Zion) would receive the 'birthright' (political legitimacy, colonisation, claim to the land). Esau is unwise and naïve concerning the odds against him, and is perhaps falsely confident in his historic claim to the 'birthright'. The bumbling Esau, like the Palestinian leadership, fails to recognise his predicament until it is too late and options for a just and peaceful resolution have been foreclosed.

The predicament of Jacob and Esau describes in part the complex state of affairs in Palestine during the troubled decades of the 1920s, 30s and 40s, and the subject of the present chapter. Zionism has always been adept at establishing 'facts on the ground', as Prime Minister Menachem Begin described the massive construction programme and land confiscations in the late 1970s and mid-1980s. In this chapter, I will rely on the most complete,

---

[1] Kenneth Cragg, *Palestine: The Prize and Price of Zion*, Cassell, London, 1997, 51.

highly objective, and least known account of the period under study: *The Chariot of Israel* by the former Prime Minister of Great Britain, Harold Wilson.[2] Strangely, this important volume literally disappeared after its publication in 1981 and remains unknown and out of print. The events of the 1920-48 period in Palestine's history set in motion the political dynamics that led to the triumph of Zionism and the Palestinian catastrophe (*al-Nakba*), including the loss of land, population, and the envisioned independent state of Palestine. Palestinian Christianity began its steady decline during this period with its most significant losses occurring during the 1948-49 *Nakba* ('Catastrophe').

## The Roaring Twenties: the situation in Palestine from 1920-29

The collapse of the Ottoman empire resulted in a temporary political vacuum in Palestine that was quickly filled by Great Britain and the newly emerging Zionist institutions and organisations. The Balfour Declaration granted the Zionists their first expression of legitimacy by a major political power. The language of the Balfour Declaration was inserted into the treaties negotiated by the League of Nations following World War I. The Declaration and its successive expressions in the treaties can be credited in part with accelerating a three-way power struggle in Palestine during the 1920-1948 period among the British colonial government, the Zionist movement, and the Palestinians.

Unlike the biblical account of Jacob and Esau, where there was a single birthright promised to Esau, the British had made conflicting promises to each son: one to the Zionist movement and the other to the Palestinian Arabs. Each promise was made independently of the other but the motives were similar: to gain assistance from each party in the war effort against the Germans and Ottomans. We recall the McMahon correspondence of 1915-16 promised independence to the Arabs if they would join the war against the Ottoman empire, while the Balfour Declaration (2 November 1917) promised a Jewish homeland in Palestine for the Zionists. Whether the promise implied in the McMahon documents was to include Palestine is ambiguous, but two matters are clear: Palestine was not excluded from independence (as were such territories as Aden, Alexandretta, and Lebanon). Moreover, the Palestinian leadership interpreted the McMahon letters as a promise of independence and raised this issue on numerous occasions, particularly in the 1930-47 negotiations, a point the Foreign Office did not deny. As we shall observe at the end of the chapter, the British officially adopted the Palestinian

---

[2] Harold Wilson, *The Chariot of Israel,* W W Norton, London, 1981, 44.

right of political independence by late 1947 and unofficially rejected the Balfour Declaration.

To complicate matters, in the spring of 1916, the British concluded the secret Sykes-Picot Agreement that proposed to divide the Ottoman territories between England and France. These conflicting promises would prove to be a lethal mixture as the Zionist and Palestinian national aspirations were placed on a collision course. Like the blind Jacob, Britain naively assumed that through its status as a dominant world power with considerable influence, the two warring clans could be brought into peaceful compliance under Britain's 'benevolent rule'. Such a peace would never come.

British rule in Palestine began unofficially when General Allenby, Commander of British Forces in the Near East, arrived in Jerusalem in November 1917. In a technical sense, the British military administration, known then as the Occupied Enemy Territory Administration, was placed in charge of Palestine until 30 June 1920, when a British civil administration assumed control. The political official appointed to head the mission was the little known Winston Churchill.

Harold Wilson notes that Churchill was a committed Zionist. He refers to a letter Churchill wrote in 1908 to a Manchester constituent who opposed the Uganda solution for the Zionists. Churchill wrote:

> Jerusalem must be the only ultimate goal. When it will be achieved it is vain to prophesy: but that it will some day be achieved is one of the few certainties of the future.'[3]

Churchill was passionately committed to the Balfour Declaration and to the Zionist programme as advanced by Chaim Weizmann and the harder-line leadership. Churchill also played an important role in negotiations with Palestinians and the new Transjordan Arabs. He apparently saw his role as one of neutralising Arab opposition to Zionist interests, promising the Arabs there was 'nothing to fear' even if there was massive Jewish settlement: 'the rights of the existing non-Jewish population would be strongly preserved.'[4] Churchill's words would prove to be empty as nothing would be done by the British or anyone else to provide political rights and legal protection for the Palestinian majority during Churchill's 'watch'. By the early 1920s the two parties were on a road to violence that would occur between 1923-1948 in ever increasing doses.

A warning about the consequences of the British-Zionist policies came in 1919 when President Wilson appointed the King-Crane Commission.

---

[3] *Ibid.*, 54.
[4] *Ibid.*

The Commission was comprised of two impartial American scholars whose purpose was to listen to the desires of the indigenous Arab and Jewish populations in Palestine and report back to the League. One of the strongest conclusions issued by the Commission was the following:

> If that principle (self-determination) is to rule, and so the wishes of Palestine's population are to be decisive as to what is to be done with Palestine, then it is to be remembered that the non-Jewish population of Palestine—nearly nine-tenths of the whole—are emphatically against the entire Zionist programme. To subject a people so minded to unlimited immigration and to steady financial and social pressure to surrender the land, would be a gross violation of the principle just quoted and of the peoples' rights, though it kept within the forms of the law.[5]

The King-Crane Report was suppressed until 1947, a matter that still merits further investigation. Had the conclusions of the King-Crane Commission Report been made public and more importantly had they been heeded in 1921, both Great Britain and the international community might have corrected the disastrous path upon which they were about to embark. The concluding warning of the King-Crane Report could not have been clearer:

> It can hardly be doubted that the extreme Zionist program must be greatly modified. For a national home for the Jewish people is not equivalent to making Palestine into a Jewish State, nor can the erection of such a Jewish State be accomplished without the gravest trespass upon the 'civil and religious rights of the existing non-Jewish communities of Palestine'. The fact came out repeatedly in the Commission's conference with Jewish representatives that the Zionists look forward to a practically complete dispossession of the present-not-Jewish inhabitants of Palestine, by various forms of purchase.[6]

These words have a tragically prophetic ring and sadly, they would be fulfilled.

---

[5] Samih Farsoun with Christina Zacharia, *Palestine and the Palestinians*, Westview Press, Boulder, Colorado, 1997, 325.

[6] Farsoun, *ibid.*, 325.

The San Remo Peace Conference of April 1920 officially granted Britain the Mandate over Palestine, commencing rule of the British Mandatory Government in the Palestinian territories. The Charter for the British Mandatory Government included the Balfour Declaration, which committed British policy to support aspirations of the Zionist movement while simultaneously supporting Arab independence. The Mandate also included a clause permitting the Jewish National Fund to become a landholding company in Palestine for property purchased exclusively for Jews.

The concept of 'Mandates' was developed by the League of Nations with considerable support from the United States' President Woodrow Wilson. Wilson was a champion of democracy and the right of indigenous peoples to be granted their freedom through the application of self-determination for the majority population. The more developed nations or peoples were classified as Mandate 'A,' or nations that needed a few years of 'guidance' before being granted full independence. Palestine was classified under the 'A' Mandates, which were deemed the most advanced and worthy of independence after a brief tutelage.

The League of Nations' Covenant stated the principle of independence in this manner:

> Certain communities formerly belonging to the Turkish empire have reached a stage of development where their existence as independent nations can be provisionally recognised subject to the rendering of administrative advice and assistance by a Mandatory until such time as they are able to stand-alone. The wishes of these communities must be a principle consideration in the collection of the Mandatory.[7]

The League of Nations through its various conferences and treaties was able to provide for the independence of most nations in the Middle East and significant people groups with two exceptions: the Kurds and the Palestinians. Not only were the Palestinian Arabs denied political sovereignty, but the documents ratified by the League granted the Zionists a right to sovereignty. Perhaps more problematic was the fact that the nation that had brokered the Zionists initial political legitimacy and had acted repeatedly as their advocates rather than impartial party, Britain, was granted the Mandate over Palestine. It was little wonder that the Palestinian leadership was pleading for any other nation to serve as the Mandatory power, even the United States.

---

[7] Quoted in Thomas and Sally Mallison, *The Palestine Problem in International Law*, Longman Group, Harlow, England, 1986, 64.

The Paris Peace Conference (1922) ratified the basic framework of the San Remo meetings but it gave full legitimacy to the Zionist movement. England received the Mandate over Palestine and the final text of the Paris meetings included the language of the Balfour Declaration. Actually, Weizmann and the Zionists had argued for a more forceful expression of the Zionist agenda. Wilson, cites the following evidence by quoting Weizmann's summary of the San Remo and Paris Peace Conference:

> Palestine to be recognised as the Jewish National Home with liberty of immigration to Jews of all countries, who are to enjoy full national, political and civic rights; a charter to be granted to a Jewish Company, local Government to be accorded to the Jewish population.[8]

Thus it was clear by 1922 that the Zionist leadership viewed Palestine as their Jewish National Home, whether partitioned or not, with no regard for the rights of the Palestinian majority. The Jewish homeland was, in Weizmann's mind, imbued with the right of political self-determination, and thus would become a Jewish state, rather than a state for all of its citizens. Weizmann summarised his intentions in an often quoted line, that came in response to Home Secretary Joynson-Hicks, who had challenged the Zionist control of the British Mandatory rule, that 'Palestine would be Jewish as America is American and England is English.' Joynson-Hicks was one of the few voices in the British leadership who demonstrated the courage and political foresight to warn what would happen if the rights of over ninety percent of the population were ignored.

However, according to Wilson, Churchill rather than Joynson-Hicks had the last word, both in the parliamentary hearings and on the ground in Palestine. Churchill's intentions could not have been more clear, as declared in the following statement: 'I will do all in my power to forward the views of the Zionists, in order to enable the Jews once more to take possession of their own land.'[9]

Many experts in international law, such as the late Thomas and Sally Mallision of the George Washington School of Law, have argued that the San Remo and Paris Accords were in violation with the Covenant of the League of Nations. Further, the Covenant should supercede these later agreements:

---

[8]  Wilson, *op. cit.*, 44.
[9]  *Ibid.*, 60.

... sovereignty, of economic arrangement, or of political relationship, upon the basis of the free acceptance of that settlement by the people immediately concerned, and not upon the basis of material interest or advantage of any other nation or people which may desire a different settlement for the sake of its own exterior influence or mastery.[10]

The effects of the pro-Zionist British Mandatory rule would prove devastating to the Palestinian Arab population. At the time the Mandate assumed *de jure* administration of Palestine, the population was 743,000 according to the British census of 1922. For the first time, due to Jewish immigration, the Jews had overtaken the Palestinian Christian population by a ratio of 83,000 to 71,000. The Jewish population actually doubled from 7 percent of the population in 1916 to 14 percent in 1922. By 1936, the Jewish population would grow to an astounding 400,000. To cite an example of the growth, Tel Aviv was a village of 2,000 Jewish settlers in 1916 but had grown to a city of 30,000 by 1925, without a single gentile in its environs. The Jewish Agency was given full control over the lands purchased, which stipulated that non-Jews were refused the opportunity to own land. Further, the Histradut or Jewish Labour Agency was established to promote Jewish business, of course, hiring only Jews.

Of the population, 589,000 were Muslim Palestinians, meaning the Christian-Muslim ratio now dropped to approximately 15 percent. However, Christian emigration did not seem to affect Jerusalem and large cities in Palestine, perhaps because the British did improve the economy in the urban areas and Christians like Muslims reaped the economic benefits. However, the small Christian villages and towns such as Bethlehem began to show increased emigration during the Mandatory period. Jerusalem's population remained a 52 percent Palestinian Christian majority in 1922, and the community was stable until the hostilities of 1948.

O'Mahony gives significantly lower figures for the Palestininian Christians in relation to the total population. He cites a figure of aproximately 10 percent (9.6) in the 1922 British census, with a note that the Christian community lost 13 percent of its population during World War I, with most leaving due to emigration but a 4 percent mortality rate. The majority went to South America, particularly from the Bethlehem district. Brazil, Chile, and parts of Central America became destinations during this period. The turn of political events in favour of the Zionists

---

[10] Mallisons, *ibid*.74.

and the increase of tension during the 1920s were certainly factors in the accelerated emigration.[11]

During this period a new phenomenon occurred in Palestine: frequent violent attacks between Palestinian Arabs and Jews. Palestinians began to react to Zionist settlement and British policies out of frustration and desperation, sensing the situation was out of control. Violent clashes occurred at the Wailing Wall and near the Haram al-Sharif (the Noble Sanctuary which includes the Dome of the Rock and Western Wall) in 1923, and more frequent clashes took place through the decade. In 1929, a vicious massacre took place in Hebron, with 67 Jews murdered and scores wounded. The decade ended with the lines drawn more rigidly than ever but with the British now caught in the midst of a possible civil war that they had arranged.

Harold Wilson points to a 1929-30 report on these incidents by the Colonial Office Governor, Sir Walter Shaw, who demonstrated unusual insight into the Palestinian predicament:

> There can, in our view, be no doubt that racial animosity on the part of the Arabs, consequent upon the disappointment of their political and national aspirations and fear for their economic future, was the fundamental cause of the outbreaks of August last ... To the Arabs it must appear improbable that such competitors (Zionist immigrants) will in years to come be content to share the country with them. These fears have been intensified by the more extreme statements of Zionist policy and the Arabs have come to see in the Jewish immigrant not only a menace to their livelihood, but a possible overlord of the future.[12]

Shaw understood the roots of the violence which included not only loss of land and livelihood, but a British tilt in favour of Zionism and the possibility that there might be a Zionist 'overlord' occupying the Arab majority.

## Settler colonisation and revolt: Palestine 1930-1939

There was no way of reversing the political dynamics and pragmatic realities that had now been unleashed in Palestine. During the 1930s-40s the Zionists

---

[11] O'Mahony, *ibid.*, 34-35.

[12] Wilson, *ibid.*, 69.

and the Palestinians found their positions hardening and becoming more violent. The option of creating a bi-national state in Palestine had long passed. The British quickly realised that their advocacy of the Balfour programme had brought irreconcilable differences and a recipe for perpetual violence. Any decision to curb Jewish colonisation would now trigger a violent reaction from the Zionist militias and the Revisionists. Could the British now try to balance two different demands for justice and independence in this tiny land?

The thirties brought another crisis to the fore. While much of the initial Zionist colonisation in Palestine was in part a reaction to the pogroms of Russia, Poland, and Austria, there was now the reality of Nazi Germany and its threats to destroy the German Jewish community. How could the British set limits on Zionist colonisation when hundreds of thousands of Jews were at risk? The British continued to allow a liberal immigration policy toward European Jews coming to Palestine, allowing 217,000 between 1932-1937. The increase in Zionist settlers was dramatic, a fact not lost on the Palestinians, who began to request Britain, the United States, France, and others to lift their quotas and take in the European Jews.

In 1931, the British census showed the population of Palestine to be slightly over one million (1,040,000) with 84 percent Palestinian Arab and 16 percent Jewish residents. That year the Jewish immigrants totalled 3,409 but the figure nearly tripled in 1932 to 9,553. In 1933 the figure more than tripled again, skyrocketing to 30,327. The 1931-32 figures did not include illegal immigrants, while the 1933 figures were inclusive, so there may have been higher numbers in the earlier years. In 1934, the immigrants rose to 42,359 and jumped to 61,854.[13] To underscore how significant the population ratios had changed since the issuing of the Balfour Declaration, in 1918 the Jewish population in Palestine was 8 percent with a Palestinian Arab population of 92 percent. By 1931 the Jewish population had reached 17 percent of the total, but by 1939, the ratio had shifted dramatically with the Jewish population representing 33 percent of the total.

With the ratio of Jews to Palestinians escalating by 12 percent within a five-year period, the Palestinian reaction was angry and increasingly confrontational. Political leadership in the Jerusalem Palestinian community fell to the traditional Muslim families, and Hajj Amin al-Husseini was selected by the community and appointed Grand Mufti by the British. Hajj Amin and the circle of leadership around him advocated categorical opposition to the Zionists and initially did not reject the British, but maintained a critical stance toward their support of Zionist colonisation.

---

[13] Wilson, *op. cit.*, 73.

Until the 1929 Hebron massacre, Palestinian protests had been relatively non-violent, but the tripling of Jewish settlement and other factors led them to turn violent. In 1935, an underground band of guerrilla fighters abandoned the political process and took matters into their own hands in the Galilean hills under the leadership of Sheikh Izzedin al-Qassem. When they were captured and the sheikh killed, Palestinian demonstrations became larger and more militant. Inspired by the martyrdom of al-Qassem, in mid-1936 a full-scale Palestinian revolt was underway. Palestinian businesses and professional organisations organised a national strike.

At this point the British appointed a Royal Commission under the leadership of Earl Peel to investigate the violence in Palestine. The Commission issued its report in July 1937 and concluded that the Mandate was unworkable. It recommended that Palestine be partitioned into two separate states: one Jewish and one Arab, with a corridor from Tel Aviv-Jaffa to an enlarged Jerusalem that would remain under British control. The Jewish state would be comprised of Galilee and the Mediterranean coast (from the Lebanon border to Gaza). The proposed Palestinian state would cover the West Bank (slightly larger than today), the Negev, and the Gaza Strip. The proposal was filled with problems, including: the Zionists would receive the best land; the Palestinian minority was nearly equal to the Jewish majority (roughly 238,000 to 250,000) in the proposed Jewish state and their future would be in jeopardy; the Jewish state would have a smaller land base than would the Arabs.

The Peel Commission Report was debated in the House of Commons and unanimously adopted. While the implementation phase of the report was underway, the government proposed a prohibition on further land transactions that would effect the partition, and Jewish immigration would be capped at 8,000 per year. The Zionist leadership accepted the principle of partition but opposed any limitations on immigration. The Palestinians rejected the partition proposal completely, finding it unjust in terms of land given to Jews, of placing a significant number of Palestinians in jeopardy, and a gross violation of the principle of self-determination for the majority population, the foundation of which rested in the McMahon letters and the League of Nations Covenant. Most Palestinians held onto the vision of a single independent state in Palestine.

The British then backed away from the commitment to partition Palestine, giving the measure further study. In January 1939, the Foreign Office convened Palestinian and Zionist leadership in London and proposed to them a single, bi-national state for Palestine. The Zionists vehemently rejected the proposal and the Palestinians, while not rejecting it out of hand, were lukewarm.

The Palestinian revolt was brutally crushed in 1939 by military campaigns that included various Zionist militias alongside the British forces. Many of Israel's future military leaders, including Moshe Dayan, received their training during this period under one of the leading British military strategists, Col. Orde Wingate. Wingate was an ardent Christian Zionist, known for his passionate commitment to a restored Jewish state in Palestine that would be necessary to fulfil biblical prophecy. In a feature story on Wingate in the *Chicago Tribune* honouring Israel's fiftieth anniversary, staff writer Ron Grossman summarised Wingate's legacy:

> Nowadays Wingate is probably little more than a name to most Israelis. He spent scarcely three years in the land that was then part of British empire and known as Palestine. Yet he developed tactics that remain the combat philosophy of Israel's armed forces today. He also tutored many who became its famed commanders, Including (Moshe) Dayan and Yigal Allon, whose elite strike force, the Palmach, utilised Wingate's trademark aggressively mobile tactics to win the 1948 War of Independence.[14]

Grossman goes on to show the considerable influence that Wingate's particular brand of Christian Zionism played in his commitment to Zionism's triumph:

> Wingate also had a special feeling for the Bible, keeping his own well worn copy always at hand. When stumped by a strategic problem, he would turn to the Book of Judges. There he would find inspiration in the account of Gideon, the great general of ancient Israel and, like Wingate, a master of hit-and-run guerrilla tactics. That attachment to the Scriptures inspired Wingate with a feeling for Palestine's Jewish inhabitants that set him apart from other British military officers.[15]

Wingate preferred to remain in Palestine but was transferred to Ethiopia where he helped free the country from Mussolini, and then was sent to Burma where he led a guerrilla force that was credited with saving India from a Japanese invasion. He was killed in a plane crash in 1944 and never realised his dream of returning to Jerusalem under Israeli Jewish control.

---

[14] Ron Grossman, 'Remembering One of Israel's Founding Fathers—A Protestant Scotsman', The *Chicago Tribune,* 29 April 1998, Section 5, l.

[15] Grossman, *ibid.,* 1.

His remains were buried in Arlington National Cemetery in Arlington, Virginia, but both Israel and Ethiopia negotiated to have Wingate's remains transferred to their respective countries. The Israel burial was at a settlement for Yemeni Jewish orphans named Yemin Orde, which was surrounded by Arab forces during the 1948 War of Independence. Wingate's wife Laura had coincidentally returned to Israel during this period and learning of the battle for Yemin Orde, she insisted on being flown over the settlement where she dropped Wingate's famous Bible from the aircraft with this message:

> To the defenders of Yemin Orde. Since the spirit of Wingate is with you, even if he cannot command you in person, I am sending you the Bible that he carried with him on his war travels and from which he drew the inspiration of his victories. Let this be a mark of the pact between you and him, in victory or defeat, from now to eternity.[16]

A few days later the Zionist forces were victorious at Yemin Orde.

## The Hitler factor

By early 1939, Europe was beginning to feel the immediate threat of Nazi aggression. When Hitler invaded Czechoslovakia on 17 March 1939, the fears became reality and Britain, like other European nations, shifted their priorities to preparations for war. The Nazi threat effected British policy in three ways. First, increasing pressures from Hitler would demand most of the resources of the treasury and of troops to wage war against Germany. These shifting priorities would affect most of England's colonial holdings during the 1940s. Second, the British desperately needed oil for the war effort, which meant improved conditions with the Arab nations in the Middle East. In order to gain the support of the Arab world, British policy in Palestine would need to demonstrate a greater sensitivity to Palestinian Arab demands, particularly after the devastating manner in which the Palestinian rebellion of 1936-9 had been crushed. Third, reports of genocide by Hitler against European Jews would challenge limits proposed on Jewish immigration into Palestine.

When Hitler invaded Czechoslovakia, the Palestine Committee of the Cabinet was holding discussions in London with a small Palestinian delegation concerning the proposals to curb Jewish settlement and to explore

---

[16] *Op. cit.,* 4.

a political solution. The Zionists under Dr Weizmann's influence decided that they could no longer work with the British. According to Wilson, Weizmann told the US Consul in Jerusalem that he must declare himself irrevocably in opposition and commit the Zionist movement to 'a policy of non-co-operation with Great Britain.'[17]

The Cabinet was at this time preparing its White Paper on Palestine, which was submitted to the Mandates Commission of the League of Nations on 17 May 1939. In an effort to meet the Arab agenda, the White Paper proposed: firstly, a Palestinian state would be established within ten years. While this did not rule out partition, it demonstrated to the Arabs that Britain would honour the promises inherent in the McMahon correspondence and the League of Nations' principles. Second, Jewish immigration would be limited to 75,000 over the next five years. Third, the British would carefully regulate land sales in order that the proposed Palestinian state would not be negatively affected. The White Paper also made a significant statement concerning the protection of the holy sites of all three religions. The British also released to the public the McMahon papers, which clarified their promised independence to the Arabs during the 1915-6 period. These steps greatly assisted the British goal of gaining access to Arab oil reserves for the war effort. The shift in British policy also countered Nazi promises to various Arab countries of future independence, should they side with Germany during the war.

The Zionist leadership issued a strong rejection of the White Paper, insisting that England was betraying them and the proposal was simply a means of appeasing the Arabs. The extreme wings of the Zionists in Palestine, such as the Revisionists under the leadership of Ze'ev Jabotinsky (1880-1940) called for military resistance against the British forces. There was also significant pressure on the British to grant the Jewish Agency the right to field an independent Jewish army that would fight under its own flag in Palestine. By the early 1940s, there were over 40,000 British-trained Zionist troops in Palestine. They had been armed initially by the British but by the 1940s had developed several sources of weapons including the United States, Czechoslovakia and other European countries. The proposal for an independent Zionist army was rejected by the British, thereby stimulating the rise of independent Zionist militias.

As an increasing number of Jews were fleeing from Hitler's genocidal policies, the British responded by maintaining the limits established under the White Paper. Britain and the United States, both of whom might have received the desperate refugees, maintained their quotas. Many of the

---

[17] Wilson, *ibid*., 104.

quotas were based on rather primitive psychological testing designed to impose 'quality control' and restrict certain populations. During World War I, the United States Public Health Service at Ellis Island administered various psychological performance tests that focused especially on Eastern Europeans, Italians, and African immigrants. Test results established that 83 percent of Jews, 80 percent of Hungarians, 79 percent of the Italians, and 87 percent of the Russians were declared 'feebleminded' and thus 'inadmissible'. These same attitudes prevailed during the 1920s-World War II era. These ethnic restrictions based on what would now be judged as racist regulations were still influential with the need for Jewish immigration into the United States was greatest, 1935-48. On the other hand, the Scandinavian and English speaking countries were favoured.[18] The Zionist organisations, including the militias, embarked upon a strategy to by-pass the restrictions on immigration while they mounted terrorist activities against the British and the Palestinians. By the early 1940s, the British were so consumed with the demands of the European theatre of the war with the Axis powers that they were not able to give Palestine the attention it commanded.

In May 1942, the Zionist leadership held a conference at the Biltmore Hotel in New York City. By this time they and the world were aware of Hitler's genocidal policies. The 'final solution' principle of Nazi policy had been widely circulated in Europe and North America. The international community had been slow to respond to Hitler's genocide, so one understands why the Zionist organisations and world Jewry decided to take matters into their own hands. However, the political implications of the Biltmore policies and the injustice this would bring to Palestine are a separate matter that needs analysis.

Over six hundred Zionist Jews gathered at the Biltmore Hotel in New York City in an attempt to solidify their strategies. Meeting in New York gave the Zionists the potential to gather the largest, most influential, and wealthiest Jewish community in the world, the North American Jews. As a result, the Biltmore Program was a maximalist policy demanding 'the immediate establishment of a Jewish commonwealth over all of Palestine with full control over immigration.' The policy was adopted by the World Zionist Organization at the Biltmore Hotel. From this point there was no possible means of reconciling the Zionists' demands with those of the Palestinians.

---

[18] Leon A Kamin, *The Science and Politics of I.Q.*, John Wiley and Sons, New York, 1974, 16-17.

## The Spiral of Violence in Palestine: 1940-48

In Palestine the Revisionist Zionists followed the militant ideology of Ze'ev Jabotinsky and were gaining momentum and influence within the larger Zionist leadership. During the late 1930s-1940s, there was a marked increase in Jewish terrorist operations. One of the early Revisionist organisations, the Irgun Tzvai Leumi, was taken over by the Stern Gang, led by one whom Harold Wilson labels 'the murderous Menachem Begin'.[19] Begin rejected the gradualist approach of Weizmann and despised the compromising Ben-Gurion, described aptly by the British historian Christopher Sykes: 'his denunciations of Ben-Gurion and his colleagues of the agency could hardly be exceeded by a rabid anti-Semite.'[20]

In November 1945, a close friend of Churchill, British Colonial Secretary, Lord Moyne, was murdered on a Cairo street by two Stern Gang terrorists. One of the two was a young man named Yitzhak Shamir, who was destined like Begin to become Prime Minister of Israel. Weizmann hastened to Palestine in order to counsel the Jewish community against terrorism and to be patient. He also assured them of an emigration rate of at least 100,000. This number had been assured by American Zionists who had a direct line to the new President, Harry S Truman, who in turn brought pressure on the British government to accept that figure in the spring of 1945. It was clear that Weizmann had the majority behind him but no leaders were able to control the Irgun and Stern Gang operations.[21]

Not only did the British find themselves economically, spiritually, and physically drained by World War II, but now they were trapped by American pressure in favour of the Zionists while British forces faced a steady increase in Jewish terrorist operations in Palestine. Further, many British political leaders were aware of how they had sold-out the Palestinian majority. Thus the British rejected the Truman pressure to admit 100,000 Jews into Palestine until the Jewish Agency stop Jewish terrorism. By now there were reports of collusion between the main British-trained militia, the

---

[19] *Ibid.*, 121.

[20] Christopher Sykes, *Crossroads to Israel*, World Publishing, Cleveland, 1965, 194.

[21] Wilson provides the exact quotation from Bevin: 'I came to the conclusion that the mere wiping out of the White Paper would not lead us very far. There has been agitation in the United States, and particularly in New York, for 100,000 Jews to be put in Palestine. I hope I will not be misunderstood in America if I say that this was proposed with the purest of motives. They did not want too many Jews in New York. ... If we put 100,000 Jews into Palestine tomorrow, I would have to put another division of British troops out there. I am not prepared to do it.' In his footnote on the same page, Wilson adds: 'He (Bevin) was not "misunderstood in America." Truman understood perfectly and never forgave Bevin.' *Op. cit*, 153.

*Haganah*, with the Stern Gang and LEHI. The British then imposed martial law (Emergency Regulations) which enabled the British military to apprehend and imprison residents of Palestine without trial. These same regulations were later used by the State of Israel during their occupation of the West Bank, Gaza Strip, and East Jerusalem.

The violence only escalated in Palestine. LEHI attacked a series of British military posts and oil refineries. Police stations, railroads, and public utilities also became targets. Palestinian civilians were murdered on a regular basis by the Jewish terrorists with no hope of capturing the killers. Palestine was a cauldron of terrorism and murder, clearly a police state, with a three-way war among the British, Zionists and the largely disarmed and vulnerable Palestinians.

In 1946, the Zionist terrorist organisations stepped up their activities, took British officers hostage and blew up Acre Prison while attempting to free convicted terrorists. The Irgun with *Haganah* support retaliated against the British on 22 July by blowing up the wing in the King David Hotel (Jerusalem) that was used by British officers, killing 91 soldiers, officers and non-British military. The attack was cleverly planned so that at 11.00 am, milk churns containing explosives were routinely delivered to the hotel service entrance and later triggered by a timing device. The operation was led by Menachem Begin. By the end of the year, the Zionist terrorist organisations had killed a total of 373 persons, 300 of whom were Palestinian civilians. There were Palestinian terrorist movements during this period but they were numerically and politically insignificant, exercising most of their activities against Palestinians who were selling land to Zionists or collaborating with the Zionists and British.

The violent cauldron swirling in Palestine begged for a just and humane solution for the Jews who had fled Hitler's genocide, but also for the Palestinian majority, who were steadily witnessing a decline in their quality of life and security in the land of their birth. At this point, war in Palestine seemed to be inevitable. The British and Americans made one last-ditch effort to rescue the situation in late 1946. The new Foreign Secretary, Ernest Bevin, was not a Zionist and was in fact critical of the failure of the one-sided policies that could be traced back through Churchill and David Lloyd George to Lord Balfour's Declaration. Further, Bevin had a tough-minded, independent streak that caused him to challenge political pressures when they appeared to be manipulative. For example, in 1945 a controversy was brewing between the British Foreign Office and the Truman Cabinet, quite possibly provoked when the Truman Administration leaked word to the New York *Herald Tribune* on 30 September 1945, that Truman was requesting of the British that 100,000 Jews should be settled in Palestine. By implication the political message was that the Foreign Office was stalling. Bevin's reply to Truman came at the Labour Party Conference a few months later, when he caustically retorted that President Truman was insistent on settling 100,000 Jews in Palestine because 'he didn't want too many Jews in New York.' [22]

One of the 'New' Jewish historians, Professor Ilan Pappe of Haifa University (Israel), observes that Bevin had to 'navigate between the two contradictory opinions' in the British Foreign Office and parliament, as well as the violent opposition of Zionist militias, the major Zionist organisations, and the various Palestinian tendencies.[23] Additional factors were pressure from the United States in favour of the Zionists and international pressure through the newly established United Nations. In early 1947, Bevin introduced the final British proposal that attempted to avoid a crisis in Palestine. Bevin's proposal was a compromise that would grant provincial autonomy to Palestine under British supervision. He accepted the United States-Zionist formula to admit 100,000 Jewish refugees in Palestine but added the caveat that the settlement should occur in stages (4,000 Jews per month for two years). The formula for settlement was open to negotiation as the Zionists and United States had not agreed on that portion of the plan.

Bevin's proposal was rejected by the Zionists and Palestinians. The Zionists would now settle for nothing less than partition with a Jewish state in the larger portion, while the Palestinians wanted an independent state in all of Palestine. The gap and explosive trajectory of events could not be bridged. Pappe summarises the situation:

> The inability to find an acceptable solution, the increase in Jewish operations against British personnel and installations in Palestine, a particularly cold winter in the British Isles coupled with shortages of coal and bread, an economic crisis brought about by the American demand for a return with high interest of the funds transferred to Britain as financial assistance during the Second World War—all these developments contributed to the realisation that the Palestine problem was insoluble, and led the British cabinet to submit it into other hands.[24]

---

[22] Ilan Pappe, *The Making of the Arab-Israeli Conflict*, 1947-51, St. Martins Press, New York, 1994, 14.

[23] Harold Wilson was part of the Labour government during this period and shares several personal insights in Wilson, *ibid.*, 128.

[24] *Ibid.* The Zionist Organization of America (ZOA) voted in October 1946, for a Jewish state over all of Palestine. Ben-Gurion's diaries indicate the Zionist fathers had desired a single Jewish state since the late 1930s but counselled each other not to make it public for it could result in the loss of British and American support.

During the February-September 1947 period, the British Foreign Office continued to be intimately involved in negotiations with the Americans and United Nations Committees, as well as with the Palestinians and Zionists. Future British Prime Minister Wilson again provides intimate details of the decisions and discussions from the British side, as he was personally involved. After surveying the American pressures and varying opinions in the Foreign Office, Wilson makes a striking observation:

> What is surprising in this catalogue of events, as is clear from our earlier chapters, is the fact that every Cabinet decision, every approach to Washington, Cairo or Tel Aviv recorded in this chapter, every Foreign Office manoeuvre, seems to have been taken without reference to the Balfour Declaration— almost as if it had never been made—and successive commitments made on Britain's behalf, to say nothing of the firm pledges made time and again by the Labour Party in the years leading up to 1945, indeed by leaders who were to occupy high positions in the Cabinet. It was as though Balfour, Lloyd George—and Churchill—had never lived.[25]

This stunning insight by someone of Wilson's stature and first hand knowledge of the British Foreign Office deliberations is in itself sufficient commentary on the disastrous Declaration. The Balfour formula, granting political legitimacy to the Zionists and tilting British and Western foreign policy in their favour, became the fundamental reason for the failure of the Mandate. According to Wilson and certainly in my opinion, it seems to be the case, as events during the succeeding two years would demonstrate. Sadly, the destructive political trajectory of Balfour and the Zionist Fathers could not be corrected, as the British politicians were attempting. The British leadership felt itself increasingly pressured by the United States who had no military forces in Palestine, at a time the British were under siege while carrying the financial burden. Wilson notes; 'London and Washington could hardly have been further apart, on objectives, methods, or timing.'[26]

Winston Churchill, took the floor of Parliament on 23 July, and began by giving a short chronicle of his support for Zionism and the Zionist interpretation of British policy in the Middle East. Later in the same speech, Churchill's comments reflected the resentment British officials were

---

[25] Wilson, *op. cit.*, 153.
[26] *Ibid*, 153.

developing in reaction to pressure but no financial or military support from the United States. He recommended the following:

> Here is the action—action this day. I think the Government should say that if the United States will not come and share the burden of the Zionist cause, as defined or as agreed, we should now give notice that we will return our Mandate to the UNO (United Nations Organization) and we will evacuate Palestine within a specified period.[27]

Wilson reports on the confidential meeting of the British Cabinet on 15 January 1947, which he describes as 'a full-dress strategic discussion on what Britain's approach to the problem of Palestine should be.' The Colonial Secretary and the Foreign Secretary had prepared papers, which were set before the Cabinet and are filed still today with each page headed in large red letters, 'TOP SECRET'. The memorandum by the Foreign Secretary stated that there were three choices before them: a) provincial autonomy for Palestine; b) a unitary independent state, which the Arabs supported; c) partition, which the Zionists supported.

When the Cabinet met on 14 February, Wilson notes 'there was every reason for finding a means for reducing the commitment in the Middle East.' He adds that the economic crisis in 1947 had become severe with the balance of payments deficit elevating far above the support received from the United States and others. England was enduring its coldest winter in decades with coal shortages and cuts in electricity. BBC programming was cut during 9-12 am and 1.30-3.30 pm. Lord Mountbatten was about to go to India to negotiate the end of British rule. It was not the time to increase the British commitment and in fact, the mood was swinging toward surrendering the Mandate and having the United Nations take on the matter.[28]

The Cabinet decided to refer the problem to the United Nations General Assembly and make a statement to this effect to the government of the United States and both Houses of Parliament within one week. However, the Cabinet did not surrender the Mandate, as Bevin would say, Britain was merely inviting various opinions from the world community on how the Mandate could best be exercised. On 18 February the Foreign Secretary heard from US Secretary of State George Marshall, that the United States supported the referral of the Palestine problem to the UN, where it would be processed by the Trusteeship Council. Marshall asked if the rate of Jewish

---

[27] Wilson, *op. cit.*, 175.
[28] *Ibid.*, 190.

immigration could be increased during the interim period, but the Foreign Secretary rejected the suggestion and referred it for study by the Cabinet.

The United Nations formed a special investigative body called the United Nations Special Committee on Palestine (UNSCOP). UNSCOP sent a delegation to Palestine in June, whose task was to make local inquiries into the grievances and desires of the Jewish and Palestinian communities. In brief, the Palestinian Arab community was vehemently opposed to partition, arguing that it was the majority population (66 percent), owned over 97 percent of the land, plus the significant political facts that they had a legitimate claim to the land and sovereignty. Further, the Palestinians owned 80 percent of the land proposed for the Jewish state, and it was the best agricultural coastal land. The Zionists, while a recent political entity, had the arguments of religious-historical claims, the need for a state of their own for the refugees of European antisemitism, and that they alone had a political claim through the Balfour Declaration. The Zionists were prepared to accept partition while the Palestinians were not, claiming the partition scheme was merely a fig leaf covering the Zionist's true intentions to dominate the entirety of Palestine.

On 25 November 1947, the UN Ad Hoc Committee approved the UNSCOP report, which recommended partition, but only by a vote of 22 to 15 with 20 abstentions, thus lacking the two-thirds majority necessary for adoption. The Zionists conducted a filibuster and gained a four-day delay due to the Thanksgiving Day holiday. The holiday enabled the United States to lobby several smaller nations in favour of partition. On 29 November 1947, the resolution was adopted narrowly but did meet the required two-thirds majority.

Jewish towns and kibbutzim throughout Palestine celebrated by dancing in the streets long into the night. Golda Meir records the joy that Jews felt that evening:

> For two thousand years we have waited for our deliverance. Now that it is here it is so great and wonderful that its surpasses human words.[29]

On the other side of Palestine there was neither joy nor hope. The worst case scenario was now unfolding and the Arab population was left unprotected and ripe for exploitation. The Palestinians had been betrayed by the international community and a cloud of darkness fell over them. Violence broke out at once. The Palestinians knew they were outgunned and virtually

---

[29] Larry Collins and Dominique Lapierre, *O Jerusalem*, Pocket Books, New York, 1973, 33

would stand alone, despite rhetoric from some of their Arab neighbours concerning the overstated threat to 'drive the Zionists into the sea'. Their worst days would be ahead and the life they once enjoyed in historic Palestine would turn into a living hell on earth, which they would call to this day *al-Nakba*, 'the catastrophe'.

## Summary

1. 'The Ambivalence of Hand and Voice', title and thesis of Chapter 5, alludes to the biblical account of Jacob usurping the birthright from Esau (Genesis 27), with parallels to the Zionist movement's questionable political legitimacy in Palestine at the expense of the naïve Palestinian Arab majority.

2. The collapse of the Ottoman empire led to a political vacuum in Palestine and a three-way power struggle among the British Mandatory forces, the Zionist movement, and the Palestinian Arabs.

3. Palestinian Christianity began its steady decline during the 1920-48 period.

4. Great Britain made conflicting promises to three parties: the Arabs (through the McMahon Correspondence of 1915-6); the Zionists (the Balfour Declaration of November 1917); and to the French through the secret Sykes-Picot Agreement (1916). The latter became the prevailing basis for the treaties settling World War I and effectively established the British rule.

5. Key British political leaders had Zionist sympathies, which advanced the Zionist agenda. Among the British sympathisers were Lord Arthur Balfour, Prime Minister David Lloyd George, and Winston Churchill, the Colonial Secretary who oversaw the Mandatory administration in Palestine.

6. The American-led King-Crane Commission's Report of 1919 was critical of the Zionist agenda and predicted that violence would follow if the desires of the 90 percent Palestinian Arab majority would be overridden. The report was suppressed until 1947.

7. Careful lobbying by the Zionist leadership and British politicians inserted the Zionist agenda and the Balfour Declaration into the San Remo and Paris Peace Treaty (1922), thus giving the Zionists their entrée for increased colonisation, institution building, with British support. These political developments undermined the Wilson principles of self-determination for the majority populations in former Ottoman territories, which were enshrined in the League of Nations Covenant.

8. Jewish immigration, land purchase and confiscation began to create tension between the new Zionist immigrants and Palestinians. There was little conflict between Arabs and indigenous Palestinian Jews prior to this period. Also, the Jewish population began to outpace the Palestinian Christians for the first time since the year 135.

9. Zionist settlement exploded between 1918-1939, reducing the Palestinian Arab-Jewish ration from 92-8 percent to 67-33 percent in 1939. In 1936, the Palestinians revolted and were eventually crushed by British military and Zionist militias, eliminating many Palestinian nationalist leaders. The Peel Commission recommended quotas on the Jewish immigrants and a partition of Palestine. The White Paper (1939) set the quotas at more restrictive levels, causing the Zionist militias to increase terrorism against British installations and the Palestinian population. The Biltmore Platform of 1942 adopted a harder line position including a Jewish state, negating the single state solution.

10. The Nazi Holocaust led to massive Jewish refugees from Europe, but several Western nations set quotas on Jewish populations which forced most of the refugees to Palestine.

11. Successive American Administrations adopted the Zionist agendas and brought considerable pressure on the British Foreign Office, which was showing signs of support for the Palestinian Arab positions outlined in the King-Crane Report. However, the devastating economic, political, and emotional effects of World War II, plus Zionist terrorism, led the British to decide to withdraw from Palestine.

12. The situation in Palestine was ripe for a Zionist victory by November 1947. The vulnerable Palestinian community, still the majority of the population, were fearful for their future.

# Chapter 6
# ZION'S TRIUMPH,
# PALESTINE'S *NAKBA*/CATASTROPHE

When Itzhak Rabin issued his memoirs in 1979, he triggered significant controversy throughout Israel and the American Jewish establishment. Rabin, who was destined to become the first Israeli Prime Minister to greet Yasser Arafat and negotiate directly with the Palestine Liberation Organization in 1993, was a decorated war hero and had been a commander of the *Haganah* ['the standing army'] during the 1948 War. When the long-anticipated memoirs were published a taboo subject was opened as Rabin recalled how David Ben-Gurion ordered residents of the largely Christian Palestinian towns of Lydda and Ramle to be evacuated. Rabin wrote the following:

> We walked outside, Ben-Gurion accompanying us. Allon repeated his question: 'What is to be done with the population?'
> B G waved his hand in a gesture which said:'Drive them out.'
> The population of Lod (Hebrew for Lydda) did not leave willingly. There was no way of avoiding the use of force and warning shots in order to make the inhabitants march the ten to fifteen miles where they met up with the Legion.[1]

Caught off guard by Rabin's announcement were the Israeli government, military, and the always efficient Israeli public relations mechanisms in the Europe and North America. For more than twenty years, the official Zionist interpretation of the Lydda-Ramle events was to either justify them as necessary defensive military measures or simply to deny that they occurred. As for the large number of Palestinian refugees from the 1948-51 events, Israel generally reduced the numbers by one half or created other explanations as to why approximately three quarters of a million Palestinians suddenly became refugees.

Rabin's public revelations were initially released to the Israeli public in a Hebrew edition but when it came to the English edition the section on Lydda-Ramle was censored. If the volume's English translator had not leaked

---

[1]  Itzhak Rabin as quoted in Ian and David Gilmour, 'Pseudo-Travellers', *London Review of Books*, 7 February 1985, 10.

the story to the *New York Times* it might have escaped the attention of Europe and the United States. One of those who was expelled by the Ben-Gurion order and lived to describe it was a young boy by the name of Audeh Rantisi, now a retired Anglican priest and former Deputy Mayor of Ramallah. Revd Rantisi's family can trace their roots back to the 4th century in Lydda, but they lost their homes and land in a single day, 12 July 1948. They were not compensated for their losses nor have they been able to return to their homes and property. Rantisi's account was retold in his autobiography *Blessed Are the Peacemakers*, but on several occasions I have heard him share the story with Christian tour groups:

> I walked hand in hand with my grandfather, who carried our only remaining food—a small tin of sugar and some milk for my aunt's two-year old son, sick with typhoid. I remember many terrible signs. Mothers lying exhausted on the roadside with their children. I will never forget one mother who died from exhaustion. The daytime heat often was well over one hundred degrees. Her tiny baby was crying, trying to nurse at the dead mother's breast.[2]

Until the Rabin revelations, only a handful of Israeli and Palestinian scholars would question the official Israeli government interpretation of the 1948 war. The handbook of the Israel Information Service of 1967 reflects the 'official' position:

> If the Arab states had not waged open war on Israel on the morrow of its re-establishment in May 1948, the Arab refugee issue would never have arisen.[3]

Gradually, the 'official' Zionist-Israeli story has lost credibility among most Israelis and in much of Europe. Once the 'New Israeli historians' gained access to declassified Israeli military documents, the historical and political discourse of the period took on new scholarly investigation. Now after twelve major volumes by Israeli historians and an Israeli State Television series aired during the fiftieth anniversary of Israel (1998), a new level of debate has followed, except in the United States where several of the old myths still have currency.

---

[2]  Audeh Rantisi, *Blessed Are the Peacemakers*, Zondervan Publishing House, Grand Rapids, 1990, 26.

[3]  Government of Israel, *Refugees in the Middle East*, Israel Information Service, 1967.

Included in the 'new' historical information is evidence of the following: a) the Zionist movement was following a carefully devised military strategy that had been prepared well in advance of the events of 1948. It was carefully implemented in December 1947, and continued until the Armistice in the fall of 1949; b) the centrepiece of the comprehensive military strategy was Plan Dalet (or Plan D, for the corresponding letter in the Hebrew alphabet), which was designed to depopulate major concentrations of Palestinians while expanding the borders of the new State of Israel; c) the initial phase of the strategy (December 1947-early April 1948) took place prior to the attacks from neighbouring Arab countries and saw nearly 300,000 Palestinians expelled as refugees, thus dispelling the myth that the Zionist military actions were in response to Arab aggression; d) by the time of the September 1949 Armistice, between 726,000-775,000 Palestinians had been forcibly expelled from their homes and land, thereby giving birth to the Palestine refugee problem.

In this chapter we will examine these and other dimensions of the 1947-49 period. The entire chapter will be devoted to this two-year period as it marks both the culmination of the previous fifty years of European colonial policies, the triumph of the Zionist movement, and the impending catastrophe (*Nakba*) that would befall the Palestinian Arabs. Additionally, this period sets in motion a series of political, economic, demographic, and regional crises and dynamics. Finally, the Catastrophe of 1948-9 had tragic effects on the Palestinian Christian community, marking the largest single numerical loss for that community in history.

## *The other side of Israel's creation and War of Independence*

On 29 November 1947, an international radio audience listened to the United Nations vote on the partition of Palestine. Nowhere was the audience more intense than inside Palestine. The Palestinian Arab majority, approximately two-thirds of Palestine's population in 1947, listened with apprehension as they would have the most to lose if the partition vote were to be adopted. Jews who supported the Zionist movement, whether inside Palestine or among the diaspora, listened intently to see if their dreams for a Jewish state would now come true.

In order for the partition vote to be adopted, it was necessary for a two-thirds majority to vote in its favour in the newly formed United Nations' General Assembly, which was undertaking its first major international issue. Slowly, the votes were recorded and by a slim majority (and after weeks of intense lobbying of smaller nations by the big powers, the United States and the Soviet Union) the vote was approved. Three votes less than the required 33 majority and the partition proposal would have been defeated. Ten nations decided to abstain, including England, Mexico, Chile, and China, all of whom were inclined to oppose the partition proposal but were persuaded by the big powers to refrain from casting a negative vote. Later the Soviet Union would reverse its position after seeing the results of the partition plan.

The Zionists in Palestine and Jews throughout the world celebrated the vote long into the night. Palestinians were devastated. Who would protect them now? Clearly the Arab nations were too divided and weak to come to their assistance. Palestinians had seen their 94-percent population majority steadily decline after thirty years of Zionist colonization. Now they wondered how such an injustice could have been committed by a supposedly impartial international body designed to alleviate suffering and war. Still, the Jews were only 34 percent of the population and they owned less than 7 percent of the land. Even in the proposed Jewish state, Palestinians were a near majority of the population (48 percent) and owned approximately 75 percent of the land. More problematic is the fact that the partition plan would give to the Zionists 55 percent of the land of Palestine including the prime agricultural and coastal land.

Once the United Nations voted in favour of partitioning Palestine, hostilities erupted between the Zionist militias and the Palestinians. The first phase of the struggle, December 1947-early April 1948, is typically called the Civil War. Phase II (April 1948-September 1949) has been named by Israeli and Zionist writers as the 'War of Independence'. Palestinians find the terminology misleading for two reasons: first, both titles come from the Zionist point of view and reflect their perspective of 'dominance'. For example, the 'Civil War' was not a military struggle between two armies or communities of relatively equal resources but the humiliating and predictable defeat of a rather small Palestinian militia, which even Zionist writers have called 'ragtag', out-manned and out-gunned. The Palestinians had been virtually destroyed as a resistance force during the 1936-8 'revolt' when the British with Zionist support killed approximately 15,000 Palestinians, imprisoning or executing most political leaders and dismantling their political and military infrastructure. Neither the British Mandatory forces nor the Zionists allowed the Palestinians to rebuild what had been lost just nine years previous.

Many arguments hinge on who initiated the hostilities in December 1947. Zionists have offered evidence that points toward the Palestinians, such as mass demonstrations on 30 November-1 December, against the partition vote. The demonstrations were followed by a 2 December attack on a Jewish bus by Arab youths near the airport in Lydda, followed by another attack on Jews in the Jerusalem market. British accounts state that while there were injuries in these attacks no Jews were killed. On the other side of the ledger, British sources point out that the Zionist militias, the Stern Gang and Irgun, attacked and killed two Palestinians during the demonstrations of 30 November. Palestinians claim the Lydda attacks were in response to these killings by the militias, termed by British and Arab sources as 'terrorist organizations'. Morris and Zionist historians argue that the Palestinian demonstrations constituted the initial blow, but now other Israeli 'New Historians', such as Ilan Pappe and Avi Shlaim, claim the Zionists struck the first blow. They point to Stern Gang and Irgun attacks that killed Palestinians and escalated the tension to a higher level than did the spontaneous demonstrations in response to the partition vote.

It may be that the debate over the first demonstration versus the first killings as the initial provocation will be left to future historians. Perhaps a more important discussion is that which new Israeli historians Ilan Pappe and Avi Shlaim have raised concerning whether the Zionist militias were seeking to provoke a violent confrontation with Palestinian demonstrators. These 'New Historians' offer evidence that the Zionist leadership was well aware of their military advantages and essentially had the Palestinians out-manned, outgunned, and out-trained. Statistics demonstrate that the Palestinians had limited military potential in 1947, having been under close scrutiny by the British Mandatory Government since their decimation in the 1936-39 revolt. In December 1947, the Palestinians had a fighting force of only 2,500 men, the majority of whom were not trained and lightly armed. They did not receive support from the neighbouring Arab armies, international forces or suppliers until January 1948, which amounted to a total of 4,000 men, volunteers included, also poorly armed and ill-equipped.

These figures compare poorly with the Zionist forces, many of whom had been trained by the British during the Palestinian Revolt of 1936-39. One of the organizers of the Zionist militias, Moshe Shertog, claimed that during World War II, the *Yeshuv* had mobilized 26,000 recruits for active service plus 7,000 for local defence. They also recruited over 5,000 men of fighting age who came as volunteers from across the globe. Significant weaponry came into their hands from Eastern and Western Europe, Czechoslovakia in particular. By April 1948, the *Yeshuv's* standing army (*Haganah*) had 32,000 trained forces plus 30,000 in reserve. The militias claimed an additional 6-7,000, with the Irgun claiming 5,000 alone. By June the newly formed Israeli Defence Forces had 42,000 men and women under arms and by mid-July the IDF was fielding nearly 65,000 troops. By early spring 1949 their numbers jumped to 115,000. The combined armies of the Arab Legion at their peak reached no more than 40,000 troops in Palestine.[4]

---

[4]  Morris, *Righteous Victims*, 217.

Thus the Zionists knew they could destroy the Arabs if they gained strategic military posts and attacked them early and often. The opportunity to seize strategic military posts and weaken the Palestinian resistance came during the weeks following the partition announcement of 29 November 1947, when the British announced their intent to leave Palestine within six months (15 May 1948).

Second and more important, Israeli and Palestinian historians with access to recently declassified Israeli military documents now know that the so-called 'Civil War' was but one stage in a larger and more comprehensive Zionist military strategy. As previously mentioned, the most important aspect of the comprehensive plan was the strategy called Plan Dalet. It was designed to defeat the Palestinian resistance during the first stage and then to gain additional territory that would enlarge the Zionist state. Plan Dalet had been in the discussion stage for approximately ten years. Its final design emerged in stages, but as we shall see, many of these elements were in place by 1944. Perhaps the most significant aspect of Plan Dalet to emerge from the 'New Historians' is confirmation that one of its central goals was to forcibly transfer the majority of the Palestinian population out of prime agricultural and urban areas. If they were able to achieve such a manoeuvre, the new Jewish state could expand its borders while reducing its Palestinian population. This dimension of Plan D dated back to the 'founding fathers of Zionism', Theodor Herzl included. Palestinians call this phase *al-Nakba*, 'the Catastrophe', not the War of Independence.

To understand the Zionist's motives during the initial phase of fighting from December 1947 until the spring of 1948, we need to examine the Zionist idea of 'transfer', or expulsion of the Palestinian population. There are several theories concerning this controversial subject, but today few deny that the 'transfer' policy was at the centre of the Zionist military strategies concerning the large Palestinian population in their midst. Israel's 'New Historians' like Benny Morris support the idea that 'transfer' had been under discussion among leading Zionists since the mid-1930s but he is the least critical of the 'transfer' policy, both by his uncritical acceptance of IDF and Zionist documents and by his tendency to justify the policies of the Zionists as 'necessary' due to security issues and the uncertainties facing the *Yeshuv.*

Nevertheless, Morris does quote a portion of David Ben-Gurion's letter to his son Amos in October 1937, which stated that if the Palestinians will not leave voluntarily (when the Zionists assume power), 'we must expel the Arabs and take their places ... and if we have the means to use force ... to guarantee our own right to settle in those places, then we have to force them out at our disposal.'[5] Ben-Gurion and the Zionist leaders were careful not to discuss the 'transfer' concept in public as it would betray their true intentions and undermine the public perception that they were willing to accept the boundaries of the UN partition proposals and offer safeguards to the large (48 percent) Palestinian minority.

Palestinian analysts of the period, particularly Harvard's Walid Khalidi and the historian Nur Masalha argue that the concept of 'transfer' was a long term Zionist policy calculated to accomplish three objectives: a) to humiliate and conquer the Palestinian population both inside the proposed Jewish state and in the areas proposed for the Arab state; b) 'purify' or 'cleanse' a large section of land within the proposed Jewish state of its large minority (48 percent) Palestinian population thus allowing the Jewish state to expand and 'Judaise' these lands, towns and cities; c) to expand the boundaries of the Jewish state proposed by the United Nations to include strategic military, agricultural, and economic sectors of the Palestinian regions.

Those who question whether these were long-term Zionist goals they can refer to the 'founding fathers' of the movement, including Theodor Herzl, who wrote the following in his diaries some fifty years prior to the events:

> We shall have to spirit the penniless population across the border by procuring employment for it in the transit countries, while denying it any employment in our own country ... Both the process of expropriation and the removal of the poor must be carried out discreetly and circumspectly.[6]

Herzl's policies were being put into practice by the Zionist militias during Plan Dalet and then by the newly formed government of Israel after May 1948. The person in charge of the land purchases for the Jewish National Fund, and later for the government of Israel, was Joseph Weitz, who revealed his policy concerning the Palestinians as early as December 1940:

> It must be clear that there is no room for both peoples in this country. With Arab transfer the country will be wide-open for us. And with the Arabs staying the country will be narrow and restricted ... the only solution is the Land of Israel, or at least the Western Land of Israel (i.e. the whole of Palestine from the

---

[5]  Tom Segev, 1949: *The First Israelis*, The Free Press, New York, 1986, 4, 6.

[6]  Theodor Herzl, *Complete Diaries*, Herzl Press and Thomas Yoseloff, New York, 1960.

Mediterranean to the Jordan River) without Arabs ... the only way is to transfer the Arabs from here to neighbouring countries, all of them, except perhaps Bethlehem, Nazareth, and old Jerusalem. Not a single village or a single tribe must be left. And the transfer must be done through their absorption in Iraq and Syria and even in Transjordan. For that goal money will be found and even a lot of money. And only then will the country be able to absorb millions of Jews ... There is no other solution.[7]

The Palestinian-Israeli historian Nur Musalha argues that the concept of transfer is 'embedded in the Zionist perception that *Eretz Israel* (the Land of Israel) or Palestine is a Jewish birthright and belongs exclusively to the Jewish people.'[8] One can find various apologies for the idea of 'transfer' in most contemporary Zionist thinkers and Israeli political leaders from the harder line Ze'ev Jabotinsky, Menachem Begin, and Benyamin Netanyahu of the Likud Party or Revisionist Zionists, to the Labour oriented Ben-Gurion, Moshe Sharett, Moshe Dayan, Golda Meir, Itzhak Rabin, to the present prime minister. In his book *Expulsion of the Palestinians: The Concept of Transfer in Zionist Political Thought 1882-1948* (1992) and the recent *A Land Without a People: Israel, Transfer, and the Palestinians 1949-96* (1997), Musalha convincingly demonstrates how the concept was formulated and implemented from the pre-Israel state period until the present moment. Using the diaries and correspondence of Israeli political leaders, as well as Israeli military archives, he argues that whether the policy was massively imposed (as in the 1947-49 period), or in a gradual manner as it is today, it is nothing less than an intentional strategy of ethnic purification.

The first stage of the planned depopulation of Palestine was in fact a military campaign designed to defeat the weak Palestinian resistance and secure strategic military areas in advance of the anticipated Arab invasion. The initial phase of the larger military strategy was called Plan C (Plan Gimmel in Hebrew) and the Zionist militias executed it to near perfection. Morris defends the tactic, arguing that when hostilities broke out in December 1947, the Zionist leadership was not certain they could defeat the combined forces of the Arab countries.

The Palestinians did fight successfully against the Zionists during the initial months, particularly in the strategic Jerusalem-Tel Aviv corridor.

---

[7] Diary of Joseph Weitz, Central Zionist Archives (Jerusalem), A246/7; entry of 20 December 1940, 1090-91; quoted in Nur Masalha, *A Land Without a People*, Faber and Faber, London, 1997, 78.

[8] *Ibid.*, ix.

During this initial phase, the undermanned Palestinian resistance had little or no support from the Arab countries but were led by the courageous Abdel Khadir al-Husseini in several military campaigns in this vital Tel Aviv-Jerusalem corridor, as well as in the Jerusalem and Ramallah hill country where they fought the Zionists to a standstill. In March 1948 the Palestinian militias attacked Zionist caravans and killed several civilians, physicians, and nurses. Morris notes that Jerusalem's Jewish residents were fearful for several weeks thinking the Palestinian militias might gain control of the corridor and stop food and medical supplies from reaching Jerusalem.

To most analysts, including Benny Morris, the turning point in the so called 'Civil War' phase came on 8 April 1948, when Husseini was killed in the battle for al-Kastil in the Jerusalem-Tel Aviv corridor. Morris comments: 'The death of the most prominent Palestinian military figure and commander of the militias in the Judean Hills-Jerusalem area proved to be a turning point in the "civil war." '[9] From that date forward there would be no Palestinian victories in the war, as Husseini's death combined with successive Arab defeats constituted a dramatic change in the struggle. Thus the first phase, Plan Gimmel, of the war of 1948 ended after the first week of April 1948.

## Plan Dalet and the Palestinian flight (April 1948-September 1949)

If the Palestinians did not leave of their own volition nor were they ordered to leave by their leaders, then why would approximately three-quarters of a million (out of 900,000) depart within eighteen months? The answer seems to lie in the Zionist concept of mass 'transfer', which found its initial expression in Plan Dalet. One of the major strategists behind the plan was the archaeologist turned politician, Dr Yigal Yadin, who wrote:

> I prepared the nucleus of Plan D in 1944 when I was head of planning in the underground and I worked on it further in the summer of 1947 when the Chief of Staff, Yaacov Dori, fell ill. The Plan was to take control of the key points in the country and on the roads before the British left.[10]

The timing of Plan D was to coincide with the withdrawal of the British forces (15 May 1948) but technically Israel declared its independence a month earlier. Yadin added that his planning for the *Haganah* included compiling a

---

[9] Morris, *op. cit.*, 206.
[10] Michael Palumbo, *The Palestinian Catastrophe*, Faber and Faber, London, 1987, 54.

complete list of Arab villages and major population centres in Palestine, noting the population figures, location, notable leaders, and then setting priorities for implementation. Palumbo refers to an interview published after Yadin's death, in which he noted the Palestinian areas that lay outside the proposed Jewish state that were slated for expulsion. Ben-Gurion ordered the *Haganah* to begin its aggressive assaults on 19 December 1947, just three weeks after the United Nations partition announcement: 'In each attack, a decisive blow should be struck, resulting in the destruction of homes and the expulsion of the population.'[11]

The initial assaults were effective in Jerusalem and Haifa plus surrounding villages, causing an estimated 30,000 Palestinians to flee to Arab countries. Many were well-to-do Christian families. The relatively easy success of the militias in taking Kolonia, a Palestinian village in the Jerusalem hills, apparently encouraged two extreme Zionist militias to propose to the *Haganah* leadership that they (the Irgun and Stern Gang) attack another village, Deir Yassin. This small Palestinian village just to the west of the present site of the Knesset (Israeli Parliament) had a non-aggression pact with neighbouring Israeli towns and had even offered the *Haganah* reports on Palestinian military operations in the region, so the *Haganah* commander opposed the plan. Nevertheless, the village of Deir Yassin was destroyed on 9 April, with most of the residents murdered or fleeing as refugees. One day after the massacre, a Swiss physician working for the International Red Cross, Dr Jacques de Reynier, was informed of the incident and decided to investigate. He was particularly well-suited for the mission as he had rescued Jews from Nazis in Germany and Greece. When he arrived, the militias were still in the 'mopping up phase'.[12] 'One militiaman began to intimidate him so as to force him away from the killing, which was still in process, however another militiaman recognized de Reynier as the same physician who had saved his life on three occasions when he was a prisoner in a Nazi concentration camp. Dr de Reynier was struck by the coldness of the operation and commented: 'All I could think of was the SS troops I had seen in Athens.'[13] At the end of the day his team reported that they counted over 250 dead bodies in Deir Yassin, most women and children, who had been stuffed down a well after being killed. The actual numbers continue to be disputed with various Palestinian and Israeli historians debating figures between 110-254, but Deir Yassin's impact would have far larger ramifications.

On 14 April a British team of investigators interviewed the few women who survived the massacre and learned that multiple sexual atrocities

---

[11] *Ibid.*, 40.

[12] *Ibid.*, 53.

[13] *Ibid.*, 54-55.

were committed by the Zionist militias. Rape became an additional weapon against the Palestinian residents, which in the conservative Muslim and Christian Arab culture is a taboo that marks a woman for life and is scarcely discussed. Only those who had nothing else to lose would admit to it, which seemed to be the case for the survivors of Deir Yassin. The heightened Arab sensitivity concerning rape was turned into a weapon by the Zionist militias and used to terrorize villagers as Plan D was implemented. This was also a feature of Serb attacks on Muslims in Kosovo.

The massacre at Deir Yassin became a *cause célèbre* for the Irgun and Stern Gang. Menachem Begin's autobiography, *The Revolt*, refers to it as a strategic military victory which the *Haganah* approved and to which the Jewish state owes significant praise. Begin's initial autobiography sang praises for the victory at Deir Yassin but the Dell paperback version released in the United States after his 1977 election as prime minister, softens the rhetoric and justifies the killing, without dealing with the irrefutable evidence of a massacre.

A 1972 report in the largest circulation Israeli newspaper, *Yediot Aharonot*, printed the account of one of the Irgun militamen who was involved with Begin in Deir Yassin: '[They] shot everyone they saw in the houses, including women and children—indeed the commanders made no attempt to check the disgraceful acts of slaughter.'[14] Unfortunately, the 1972 Israeli account gained little if any attention in the Western press.

The military uses of the Deir Yassin massacre complemented the goals of Plan D and in effect made its implementation much easier. The shocking news of Deir Yassin spread like wildfire across Palestine, carried by the Palestinian community and by various Zionist militias. Palestinians realized that if a village like Deir Yassin, which had a non-aggression pact with the Zionists, was destined for massacre, rape, and destruction, then the same was possible for everyone else.

Zionist militias took to the roads with military vehicles equipped with loudspeakers to proclaim the coming terror of Deir Yassin. For decades, Israeli sources denied the intimidation campaign while they downplayed the significance of the massacre (many denied that it was in fact a massacre). There are numerous independent sources that verify the massacre at Deir Yassin, and others that refer to the intimidation campaign with the now infamous 'lorries with loudspeakers'.

One independent account was nearly erased from history. The account in question was recorded by the missionary Bertha Spafford Vester, daughter of the Spafford family who founded the American Colony in Jerusalem. The famous radio news commentator of the 1940s-50s, Lowell

---

[14] *Yediot Aharonot*, 4 April 1972, as quoted in Gilmour and Gilmour, *ibid.*, 10.

Thomas, called Bertha Vester 'a modern Florence Nightingale'. With the family and staff, Bertha served nearly three generations of Jews, Christians, and Muslims in Jerusalem while she observed events such as the end of the Ottoman empire, the British Mandatory phase, and then the proclamation of modern Israel. The story of the Vester family coming to Palestine merits additional comment.

The Spafford family had come to Palestine in the 1880s as missionaries from Chicago. Her father was a successful lawyer who was significantly involved in the ministry of evangelist Dwight L Moody, her mother a beautiful Norwegian immigrant. In November 1873, Vester put his young wife and four daughters on the French luxury liner *Ville du Havre,* for a vacation in Europe. He planned to join them in a couple of weeks, after finishing business in Chicago. On 22 November at approximately 2:00 am, the luxury liner collided with a British vessel, split in two, and sank within twenty minutes. The mother was knocked unconscious as she clutched the four girls, and woke up rescued in a small boat but all of the daughters perished. When word of the tragedy reached Horatio Vester, he was devastated but booked passage immediately for France, to be with his wife. During the long trip to Paris he wrote the hymn 'It Is Well With My Soul', still a classic in Evangelical churches.

Ten years later Anna and Horatio Vester, blessed with three new daughters, decided to leave Chicago and become missionaries in Jerusalem. Their efforts later became the American Colony, initially a medical mission to Jerusalem's poor but today an elite hotel and restaurant in East Jerusalem. Bertha Spafford Vester lived from 1878-1968, and observed the dramatic changes taking place around her in Palestine from the 1890s until her death. Most of her observations are recorded in the original text of a volume entitled *Our Jerusalem.*

In 1949, Bertha Vester completed her memoirs (actually begun by her mother Anna), and tried to find a publisher in Jerusalem, to no avail. Later she travelled to New York City and was told that until the paragraphs about Deir Yassin were deleted, the book would not reach the publication stage. She relented, and the 'clean' volume of *Our Jerusalem is* still distributed by the *Jerusalem Post*, Jewish bookstores, and the American Colony, but minus the Deir Yassin account. However, Vester took the original manuscript to Lebanon and the full account was published by a small Beirut company, Middle East Export Press, Inc. The latter account contains a chapter 32 with the following paragraph:

> The Zionists took the opportunity and made an example of the
> Village of Deir Yaseen, where Arab men, women, and children

were massacred. A repetition of the taking of Jericho by Joshua, it wrought the same result, and a reign of terror swept the country. Loud speakers mounted on jeeps or armoured cars paraded the Arab sections of Western Jerusalem warning the inhabitants that if they did not leave, the Deir Yaseen treatment would be their fate. Many Muslims and Christians fled for their lives. In my Children's Hospital, 1 took in fifty babies under two years old from the village of Deir Yaseen.[15]

On 12 May 1948, Zionist militias entered Beisan, a strategic city in the Jordan Valley. The day marked an end to life as the residents of Beisan once knew it. Two days later, perhaps with a touch of tragic irony, the Zionist militias rounded up all the male citizens of Beisan and brought them to the centre of town. The men of Beisan were given exactly two hours to evacuate their families and belongings from their homes or be killed. It was the day before David Ben-Gurion and the Zionist 'fathers' officially proclaimed Israel a nation. Thus Beisan is perhaps a unique symbol of the Palestinian *Nakba* as the catastrophe faced by its citizens occurred simultaneously with the triumph of Zionism. Its poignancy is especially pronounced as its citizens were trucked out of their homes while Zionist militias were preparing these very homes and gardens for an exclusively Jewish town to be called Beit Shean, cleansed of its Palestinian residents, its Arab identity, and history.

Young Naim Ateek had just turned eleven when the fateful day occurred. He still remembers it vividly. His father and older brother returned from the town centre and announced to the family that they must leave their home immediately. Panic set in as they quickly pulled their most important possessions into a variety of suitcases and sacks, carrying only what each person could manage. They were forced to board a bus designated for Christian families that headed north out of Beisan and eventually dropped them on the outskirts of Nazareth. Muslim families were placed on a bus that travelled east out of Beisan, dumping them at the Jordan River and forcing them to walk to the east. Ateek summarises: 'We had no army to protect us. There was no battle, no resistance, no killing; we were simply taken over, occupied, on Wednesday 12 May 1948,' and expelled two days later.[16] Within a day the Palestinian Arabs were expelled from Beisan and the city was repopulated with Jews, making the transfer complete. Beisan was 'cleansed' of its Arab population and remains so today.

[15] Bertha Spafford Vester, *Our Jerusalem*, Middle East Export Press, Beirut, 1950, 375.
[16] Naim Ateek, *Justice and Only Justice*, Orbis Press, Maryknoll, New York, 1989, 7.

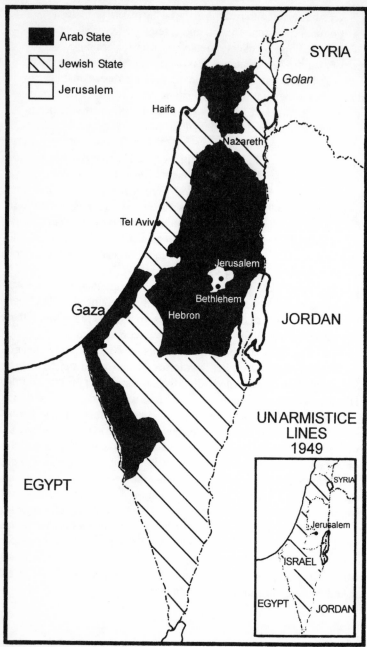

*The UN Partition Plan 1947 and, inset, the Armistice Lines, 1949 (after UN map 3063 rev 1, 1983)*

The tragedy of Beisan is illustrative of three strategies of Plan Dalet. Beisan was targeted early in the Dalet campaign because it was in the strategic Jordan Valley region and thus had vital military significance for the Zionist militias. Morris notes that the *Haganah* and other Zionist militias had successfully taken Haifa, swept across northern Galilee while depopulating all Palestinian villages in that region, taking Tiberias and eastern Galilee by 21 April 1948. Thus they demoralized the weak Palestinian resistance and gained control of most of Galilee and critical parts of the Jordan Valley prior to the invasion of Arab armies. The Arabs sought a truce at this point which the Zionists rejected because they knew that they could meet the expectations of the Dalet strategy and possibly expand upon it.[17]

The Lydda-Ramle expulsions constituted the third round of the Dalet strategy. In this phase, the Israeli armies and militias concentrated on the coastal region south of Tel Aviv, including Jaffa and areas inland running south to Gaza. Within a week they had pushed the Arab Legion back and shifted their focus to completing the work begun in Galilee. Nazareth fell on 16-17 July, the last Arab majority city to fall. Haifa had already been defeated and most of its Palestinian population was forcibly marched out and pushed into Lebanon. Nazareth did not receive the 'cleansing' effect, which seems to be attributed to the Israeli commander who refused on moral grounds to comply with Plan Dalet.

The final phase of Dalet occurred in the autumn, with the remaining elements of the Arab Legion forces being pushed back to Egypt in October 1948. Egyptian troops, who reached Latrun and threatened to advance to Tel Aviv and Jerusalem, were now so weakened that they were easily pushed into Gaza, where the majority of the Palestinian residents in this corridor had settled. By the end of 1948, Syria, Lebanon, Iraq and Transjordan had abandoned their military plans and the beleaguered Egyptian army was huddled in Gaza. By the Armistice agreement of 1949, the Israelis had expanded their territory from 54 percent to 77 percent of historic Palestine. The proposed Palestinian territory was cut in half, from 46 percent to 23 percent. Approximately 425 Palestinian villages and towns were destroyed within the next three years. Roughly 75 percent of the Palestinian population, or 756,000 out of nearly 900,000, had been forcibly expelled from their homeland, the majority becoming refugees.[18] The important corridor between Tel Aviv and Jerusalem was now in Israel's possession as was the whole of Galilee and northern Samaria. The weakened Palestinian region, called thereafter the West Bank, was annexed by Jordan, and the Gaza Strip was administered by

---

[17] Morris, *loc. cit.*
[18] *Ibid.*, 211-212.

Egypt. Both districts were filled with the majority of the 756,000 Palestinian refugees, homeless and mostly penniless, the majority now dependencies of the United Nations.

Israeli historian Dr Ilan Pappe, argues in his recent book *The Making of the Arab-Israeli Conflict 1947-51* that the overall Zionist goal was much larger than Plan Dalet or its various components. Pappe notes that the Zionist leadership had a goal that gradually developed, beginning with Herzl's early formulations concerning a Jewish state in part of Palestine to a more ambitious goal of turning all of Palestine into a Jewish state. The remarkable success of Zionist colonization in the 1920s-late 1940s, combined with the tragedy of the Holocaust and readiness of the international powers to support Zionism, created a climate by the mid-1940s for the strategy to shift from sharing the land to seizing all of Palestine.

The maximalist strategy became operative in May 1942 at the famous meeting in New York City at the Biltmore Hotel, but the plan had been emerging for several years. Pappe writes:

> Throughout the mandatory period the Jewish leadership in Palestine on various occasions declared its goal of turning Palestine as a whole into a Jewish state. A very clear reference to such determination was made by the Jewish leadership in May 1942, in the Hotel Biltmore in New York, and this became known as the 'Biltmore Programme'.[19]

According to Pappe's analysis, there was no timetable and the practical steps were not fully developed in this regard, but the goals were clear. The Zionist leadership had rejected the bi-nationalist state concept and now was rejecting the partition or 'two state' proposal, but could not state as much publicly as it would lose the amazing political gains that were in place by the time of the Biltmore meeting. In a formal sense, one cannot claim that Plan Dalet became an aspect of this larger goal of a Zionist state in all of Palestine until the spring of 1948. At that time, the strategies for 'mass transfer' were combined with other military and territorial goals, and brought into conformity with Plan Dalet.

Again, Pappe writes:

> An important part of Plan D, overlooked by most of those who have discussed it, is the reference it contains to a takeover of governmental institutions as well as the safeguarding of a

---

[19] Ilan Pappe, *The Making of the Arab Israeli Conflict 1947-1951,* I B Tauris, London: 1994, 4.

continued normal functioning of services vital for the community. It was in fact meant to complete the process, begun in 1937, of creating an embryo state in Palestine. That is, it was not merely 'geared to achieve military ends', but rather intended as the final state in the transition between the Jewish community under the mandate and the Jewish state as it was to emerge on 15 May 1948.[20]

Thus the goals were much broader than the depopulation of selected regions of the proposed Jewish state or even the expansion of the state to include strategic and economically desired sectors of the Arab state. These dimensions were important components of the larger strategy which was in essence to take gradually but steadily all of Palestine, even if it would take an additional fifty years, and to Judaise it sufficiently so that whether in name or in function, it would be incorporated into *Eretz Israel*.

## Palestinian dispossession and its interpreters

Since the mid-1980s, several Israeli and Palestinian historians and political scientists have gained access to CIA and BBC radio archives and Israeli military documents of the December 1947-September 1949 period. In Zionist terminology the December-May phase is known as 'the Civil War' with the April 1948-September 1949 period named 'Israel's War of Independence'. Until now the popular interpretations of these events have followed a 'Zionist friendly' view, such as that put forth in the popular *O Jerusalem* by Collins and LaPierre or Leon Uris' *Exodus*, which argued: 'the absolutely documented fact that the Arab leaders wanted the civilian population to leave Palestine as a political issue and a military weapon.'[21] Many of us in Europe and the United States were brought up on the Uris imagery or the graphic film portrayal of *Exodus* featuring a courageous Paul Newman leading the highly moral and significantly outgunned Jewish forces to victory in Israel's 'War of Independence'. The film even has radio broadcasts (no less in English) ordering the Arabs to leave their homes. The suggestion is made that Arab leaders were making the broadcasts under advice from their Nazi advisors. Two myths were thereby combined: first, that Israel represented the underdog 'David' against the gigantic Palestinian and Arab opposition (the Philistines), who were evil and even had pro-Nazi tendencies. Further, we were told that

---

[20] *Ibid.*, 55.
[21] Leon Uris, *Exodus*, Simon and Schuster, New York, 1963, 553.

the Palestinians essentially left their homes of their own volition or at the request of their own leaders. In other words, they only have themselves to blame today for the abandonment of their homes and villages, plus the fact that they have had to spend fifty years in refugee camps far from their native lands.

Another Zionist myth that frequently reappears in various forms throughout Europe and North America claims that Palestinian Arabs were not the majority of the population in the land of Palestine and, as a result, have no claim to the land. A more extreme version of this argument was that of Israeli Prime Minister Golda Meir, who could state emphatically in 1969 that 'there are no Palestinians.'

In early 1984 a massive volume of 601 pages appeared in England and the United States by Joan Peters titled *From Time Immemorial: The Origins of the Arab-Jewish Conflict Over Palestine.* The book appeared to be based on extensive scholarship with hundreds of footnotes and the endorsement of highly credible literary, scholarly, and political figures. Pulitzer Prize winning historian Barbara Tuchman wrote: 'This book is a historical event in itself, a discovery that has lain in the dark all along until its revelation by Joan Peters unrelenting research. It could well change the course of events in the Middle East.' Adding to Tuchman's endorsement are similar pronouncements by the novelist Saul Bellow, holocaust survivor and best-selling author Elie Wiesel, and former US Supreme Court Justice Arthur J Goldberg.

During the first half of 1984, Peters was treated to a series of positive reviews in major US newspapers and journals, plus television appearances. The positive reviews came early, no doubt well organized by a skilled Madison Avenue publicity office that delivered a review by Ronald Sanders in the neo-conservative, pro-Israel *New Republic* on 23 April 1984. *The New York Times* followed on 12 May with a glowing review by Bernard Gwertzman, followed by the pro-Likud oriented Daniel Pipes in the American Jewish Committee literary journal *Commentary* issue of July 1984. Most of the reviews were remarkably uncritical which gave an aura of absolute credibility to Peters' arguments. The major reviews were buttressed by a national media tour that was co-ordinated by the government of Israel and several American Zionist organizations that included appearances by Joan Peters on national and local television and radio talk shows.

The thrust of Peter's argument was the dual case that Palestine (Israel) was lightly populated by Arabs at the turn of the century (1900), most of whom were 'recent arrivals' and not native Palestinians, and thus the Jews have the true historic claim to all of Palestine. She argued that the lightly enforced British emigration regulations allowed a large number of

Arabs to settle in Palestine for economic purposes after World War I, thus enlarging the number of Arabs but they were not indigenous to the land. They were 'itinerant workers' who had no historic claims. She added that the actual number of Palestinians displaced in 1947-49 was much smaller than reported by the United Nations (750,000) and others.[22]

Several scholars began to check Peters' sources and analyse her arguments. Gradually, more critical reviews of her work appeared but without national recognition. Jewish researcher Norman Finkelstein discovered that Peters' statistics actually contradicted themselves at several stages plus the fact that they did not correspond to British mandatory demographic studies of the period. Finkelstein then demonstrated how her statistics were inflated and falsified throughout the book. He also offered several examples where Peters selectively quoted brief sections of documents (i.e., the Hope-Simpson Report and the Peel Commission Report) to justify her arguments, whereas if she had quoted the primary conclusions of the report her very argument would have been refuted.[23]

When Peters arrived in London in February 1985, for her publicity tour, a devastating critique by the highly regarded journalists and authors Ian and David Gilmour awaited her in the *London Review of Books*. The Gilmour's concentrated on the familiar Theodor Herzl-Max Nordau slogan (borrowed and adapted from the Christian Zionist Lord Shaftesbury) 'A land of no people for a people with no land', which was resurfacing in new form in Peters. They proceeded to dismantle the core of *From Time Immemorial*. Peters' case was essentially that the Jews had significant numbers in Palestine before 1948 and the Palestinians did not, nor were the refugee figures of significance (nor was there an exchange of populations), and hence the violence in the Middle East over the claims of the Arabs was entirely their own fault. They added that Peters described Palestine as 'virtually empty' at the turn of the century.

The Gilmours' review exposed Peters' arguments on a case-by-case, argument-by-argument, and statistic-by-statistic basis and concluded that the book was totally fraudulent. Among the sources used by the Gilmours

---

[22] Joan Peters, *From Time Immemorial*, Harper and Row, New York, 1984, 377-381. There are various estimates given for the actual number of Palestinian Arabs forcibly evicted by the *Nakba*, with independent sources giving a conservative 714,000 up to a higher number of 800,000. United Nations estimates claim 750,000 but sociologist Janet Abu-Lughod sets the range at 770,000-800,000 in 'The Demographic Transformation of Palestine', in I Abu-Lughod, *The Transformation of Palestine*, Northwestern University Press, Evanston, 1987, 139-63. I will use the United Nations figure of 750,000. Israeli sources downsize the number to 520,000.

[23] Norman Finkelstein, *Image and Reality of the Israel-Palestine Conflict*, Verso, New York, 1995, 21-50.

were highly regarded Jewish sources such as the British politician Sir Moses Montefiore, who visited Palestine in the 1830s, and the Zionist Ahad Ha'am, who wrote enthusiastically about the large Arab population and the flourishing olive and orange groves, etc. For later years they point to official Zionist and British sources which amply refute her attempts to reduce the Palestinian population and inflate the Jewish population. They cite the fears of David Ben-Gurion and others who felt the Arab population was too large, so it needed to be reduced by 'transfer'.

A critical aspect of Peters' argument lies in the demographics of Jews in Palestine during the post-World War I-1948 era. Here she cites the Hope-Simpson Report and later the Peel Commission Report of 1937 to justify her case. The Gilmours conclude that the large figures cited by Peters concerning the 'pseudo-travellers' (Arabs) from other Arab countries were actually the statistics for Jews who had settled in Palestine, thus rendering her central argument false:

> So the thousands of illegal immigrants and the British activity in their favour, on which Ms Peters lavishes much frenzied censure, were Jews, not Arabs. It is difficult to convey adequately the importance that Peters attaches to this point. She comes back to it some twenty times and denounces the 'injustice' to the Jews at least seven times. Yet the alleged 'injustice' to the Jews was in fact a concession. Instead of bolstering Peter's case, the Hope Simpson report destroys it. Ms Peter's treatment of the report shows that her handling of such evidence cannot be trusted even when she seems to be quoting it.[24]

Finally, Peters cites the often repeated myth that in 1948, the Palestinians were told to leave by their own leaders, or 'broadcasts from Arab countries compelled the Palestinians to leave.' Beginning in 1949, these claims were made by Zionist authors and generally accepted as fact in Europe and the United States for decades. In 1958, the Irish researcher and journalist, Dr Erskine Childers, travelled to Israel as a guest of that government to research these claims. The Israelis were unable to produce a single verification of the broadcasts or pronouncements by Arab leaders. Childers then turned to examine CIA and BBC archives that monitored all broadcasts of the entire Middle East covering the 1948-49 hostilities. After several years of careful

---

[24] Ian and David Gilmour, 'Pseudo-Travellers', *London Review of Books*, 7 February 1985, 10.

research Dr Childers concluded: 'there was not a single order, or appeal, or suggestion about evacuation from Palestine from any Arab radio station, inside or outside of Palestine in 1948. There is a consistently monitored record of Arab appeals, even flat orders, to the civilians of Palestine to stay put.'[25] The Gilmours then quote Count Bernadotte, the UN Mediator, as having stated just before his assassination: 'The exodus of Palestinian Arabs resulted from panic created by fighting in their communities, by rumours concerning real or alleged acts of terrorism, or expulsion.'[26]

After the humiliating exposure by the Gilmours and others in the British press, Peters was scheduled to travel to Israel for a promotional tour. Word reached the Israeli press concerning the treatment the book received in England, and then a devastating review by the Israeli scholar Yehoshua Porath appeared. Porath not only confirmed the critiques levelled by the Gilmours and Finkelstein, but went further. Porath rightly critiqued the Arab myths that rejected Jewish claims to Palestine, but was more harsh on Peters and others who attempted to reject Palestinian claims and, like Peters, simply replace them with Zionist claims. Porath stated:

> Like most myths these generally contain some element of plausibility, some grain of historical truth, which through terminological ambiguity is then twisted into a false and grotesque shape. The unfortunate thing about Joan Peter's *From Time Immemorial* is that from a position of apparently great learning and research, she attempts to refute the Arab myths merely by substituting the Jewish myths for them.[27]

Not wanting to risk further embarrassment in Israel, where Peters and her publicists had expected 'royal carpet' treatment, the visit was cancelled. Sadly, the myths continued to be proclaimed in the United States for several years but the scholarly community had at least raised critical issues concerning the falsification of data and erroneous conclusions. The Joan Peters book illustrates the dangers of high-priced propaganda in the disguise of scholarship and 'historical breakthroughs' on any question, but it would appear that the Middle East and the Israeli-Palestinian case are particularly vulnerable to misinformation, and Americans quite vulnerable to consume it.

---

[25] Erskine Childers, 'The Other Exodus', *The Spectator*, 12 May 1961.

[26] Gilmour and Gilmour, *ibid.*, 10.

[27] 'Mrs Peter's Palestine', Yehoshua Porath, as reprinted in *The New York Review of Books*, 16 January 1985, 36.

## Effects of 1948 on the Palestinian Christian community

It is important to state at this point that the entire Palestinian community, both Christian and Muslim, suffered the devastating effects of the *Nakba* equally. An enormous number of Palestinian Muslims became refugees during 1948-49, perhaps as many as 675,000. In other ways, Christians suffered as much as the Muslim population. In terms of economic and property losses, Palestinian Christians may have lost more in Jerusalem. Proportionately, they owned more property and had higher income levels in pre-1948 Jerusalem than their Muslim compatriots, so overall losses in economic terms were more severe on a *per capita* basis.

According to a study by demographer Daphne Tsimhoni, Christians numbered 28,000 in 1945, constituting 37 percent of the total population of Jerusalem, which was down from 51.6 percent in the British census of 1922. By comparison, the Palestinian Christian population of today's Jerusalem is less than 7,000, or 37 percent of the population of the 1945 figure. By natural increase the Christians today would number close to 100,000 in Jerusalem but instead they have been reduced to less than 2 percent of the population.[28] When the events of 1948 came, Jews owned slightly less than 2 percent of the land in Jerusalem with 84 percent owned by Palestinians and the Christian and Muslim religious communities, with the remainder being public land.

The events of 1948 forced out approximately 40 percent of Jerusalem's Christians who fled to Jordan or the Jordanian-controlled East Jerusalem or West Bank. Further, the Armistice lines of 1949 were drawn in such a way that major Christian areas, including Palestinian Christian residents and church property, became part of West Jerusalem, now under the control of Israel. Major tracts of land belonging to the Armenian, Greek Orthodox, and Latin Patriarchate were suddenly under Israeli control. The Pontifical Biblical Institute, the Ratisbon, Terra Sancta College, the Monastery of the Cross, and the Russian Compound were now on what would soon become the Jewish side of Jerusalem, while most of the Christians had either been pushed out or fled to the other side of the line. Sadly, the Greek Orthodox Patriarchate chose to sell much of this land or leased it to the government of Israel at very low costs. Palestinian Orthodox have reinvigorated organized efforts to regain these lands and in some cases have introduced law-suites against Israel or the Patriarchate.[29]

---

[28] Daphne Tsimhoni, *Christian Communities in Jerusalem and the West Bank Since 1948*, Praeger Press Westport, Connecticut, 1991, 22-23.

[29] Christian Palestinian nationalists had sought to gain control over their properties, economics, and liturgy during the brief phase of nationalism in pre-World War I

In terms of residential property, a Palestinian Christian scholar who had been in charge of land taxation under the British Mandate over Palestine and later served as the 'Land Specialist' for the government of Jordan, estimated that over 13 percent of the residential property lost in 'West' Jerusalem was from Christian individuals or families. Approximately 25 percent of the land lost was owned by Churches or Christian institutions.[30] This included the properties and surrounding land mentioned above, plus villages in the environs of West Jerusalem that were then annexed to an enlarged Israeli Jerusalem. These included Ein Karem, Lifta, and Beit Safafa, all with significant Christian institutional and family land holdings. These were all lost to the Israelis without compensation to their rightful owners. Gradually all of the Palestinian Christian residents of the wealthy western side of the city were either forced out or simply left so that by 1968, following the 'Six Day War', none were left. This once wealthy Christian community with its extensive land holdings became impoverished and were now refugees, not having been compensated for their losses. A census conducted in 1967 by the government of Israel showed that while 15.6 percent of the Muslim Jerusalemites were refugees after 1948, 37 percent of the Christians were refugees, a far higher percentage.[31] The figure is an indicator of the enormous economic and property losses that began the devastating downward spiral of that community.

Until now, not a single Palestinian refugee from 1948 nor their families have received a cent of compensation nor have they been allowed to return to their homes and land. Israel annexed West Jerusalem in 1959 and seized the property of the former Palestinian residents, the majority of whom were Christians. Many of the West Jerusalem homes were large and rested on valuable property. Of continuing concern is the significant amount of church property throughout Palestine that was either seized outright or minimal compensation was offered to church authorities. Among the properties is land owned by the Greek Orthodox Church, such as that upon which the Knesset (Israeli Parliament) and Dome of the Book are built. The Russian Compound was turned into a notorious prison, called Muscobiyyeh by the

---

Palestine. Similar efforts have continued but have not taken on a strategic legal and economic dimension until the mid-1990s. The Arab Orthodox Congress of Israel, headquartered in Nazareth, has organized an International Task Force in support of Christianity in the Holy Land during 1999 that has filed six legal suites against the Greek Orthodox Patriarchate in efforts to recover church property leased or sold to the government of Israel without the knowledge of the Palestinian Christian community. These issues will be discussed in more detail in Chapter 7.

[30] Sami Hadawi, *Palestinian Rights and Losses in 1948*, Saqi Books, Amman, Jordan, 1988, xvii and 117-137.

[31] O'Mahony, *loc. cit.,* 59-60.

Palestinians, known today for its torture and abusive treatment of Palestinians from the Occupied Territories.

Consider the village of Ein Karem, birthplace of John the Baptist, that was a Christian village with 4,500 citizens, 90 percent of whom were Roman Catholic in 1948. All of its citizens were forced to leave after the Deir Yassin massacre, losing their houses, land, and churches. Today, the churches have been turned into museums and in one of the great ironies of history, the Yad Vashem Holocaust Museum and memorial sits on Palestinian land, which has now been 'cleansed' of Palestinians. The original residents were never compensated for their losses. Every international dignitary and many Western tourists pass through Yad Vashem every week, unaware of the irony that they are standing on land that rightfully belongs to another people.

Accurate statistics are not available for property and banking seizures by Israel from Palestinians as a whole, but one can draw interim conclusions from the work of Dr Sami Hadawi, a researcher and former tax official in Palestine under the British Mandate. Hadawi estimates that approximately 13.4 percent of the land in the old city of Jerusalem was owned by Christians and was entirely taken over by the State of Israel. However, this figure includes only land owned by individuals and Christian families. An additional 34 percent of the land in East Jerusalem was owned by churches or by Christian institutions. Virtually all of this land was lost to Israel, either through force or by a lease agreement. Much of the land belonged to Arab or Armenian Church communities, Christian organizations, or the property deeds were held by Palestinian Christian families. Hadawi's study *Palestinian Rights and Losses in 1948* carefully enumerates the property losses and calculates them at $169,000 million according to their value in 1948.[32] If these claims, which do not account for many of the institutional losses nor the psychological damages, were to be given a dollar value in the year 2000, they would amount to tens of billions of dollars. As Palestinians reopen the question of reparations, they will certainly follow the model utilised by Israel and the World Zionist Organization in seeking compensation from Germany, Austria, Switzerland, etc.

As a result of the war and Zionist Plan Dalet, the Palestinians lost between 726,00-770,00 out of a population that was 1.4 million in 1949. It has been documented that a minimum of 425 and possibly 440 villages were destroyed between 1948 and 1955. The United Nations, which created the State of Israel, passed UN Resolution 194, which addressed the refugee problem in paragraph 11 as early as 1948.

---

[32] Hadawi, *loc. cit.*, 136.

Resolved that the refugees wishing to return to their homes and live in peace with their neighbours should be permitted to do so at the earliest practicable date, and that compensation should be paid for the property of those choosing not to return and for the loss of or damage to property which, under principles of international law or in equity, should be made good by the government or authorities responsible.[33]

Israel's membership of the United Nations was in part contingent upon its enforcement of Resolution 194, which had been passed prior to Israel's admission. A United Nations mediator, Count Folke Bernadotte of Sweden was sent to Jerusalem to meet with the Israelis and seek their implementation of the resolution. He saw the desperate situation facing the overwhelming numbers of refugees, mostly in tents, and proposed that Jerusalem must revert to be an international city, with the Negev, Lydda and Ramle returned to a Palestinian state. He allowed the entire Galilee to be granted to Israel. Bernadotte added, however, that the first order of business must be the return of the Palestinian refugees. He laid the blame for their departure squarely with the Israeli leadership, and issued a seven-point demand, one of which was virtually the same wording as appeared above in Resolution 194.

Bernadotte was not popular in Zionist circles after these pronouncements. On 17 September he arrived in the Katamon section of Jerusalem, now almost exclusively Jewish, and his vehicle was stopped by an Israeli jeep. One of the soldiers placed a machine gun through the left rear window and sprayed bullets point-blank at Bernadotte and assassinated him. It was generally understood that the man who pulled the trigger was Yitzhak Shamir, who became Israeli Foreign Minister in 1977 alongside Prime Minster Menachem Begin, and eventually succeeded Begin as the Prime Minister.

Israel essentially violated the UN Resolution of May 1948 that established Israel when it passed the Law of Return in 1950 granting every Jew in the world (born of a Jewish mother) the right of returning to Israel and receiving citizenship and compensation. This law of racial exclusivity was a direct response to the claims of Palestinians for compensation or the right of return. This was actually preceded by another, the Absentee Property Regulations of 1948, which allowed Israel to seize property vacated by the Palestinian refugees. In 1950, Israel passed the Absentee Property Law, which actually allowed it to seize the property and sell it at the value established by

---

[33] United Nations Resolution 194, paragraph 11.

its Knesset. Only Jews were allowed to purchase the property, which excluded Arabs and any persons outside the state of Israel. These laws effectively transferred their property to the State of Israel through legal mechanisms designed for Jews only. Moreover, the property was stolen through these means from Palestinians and handed over to the Jewish National Fund, who sold it only to Jews. Palestinians were eliminated from the process and their land was Judaised which brought additional revenue to the government of Israel.

## Summary

1.  Between December 1947-September 1949, 726,000-775,000 Palestinian Arabs were driven from their homes and land as a result of a carefully planned military strategy by the Zionist movement. The overall theory behind the strategy had been discussed among Zionist leadership from the days of Herzl and can be summarized by the term 'transfer'. The significant military components were Plan Gimmel which was enforced from December 1947-early April 1948, followed by Plan Dalet.
2.  For several decades Zionist writers and Israel promoted the theories as to why Palestinians 'left' including broadcasts from neighbouring Arab governments, the Joan Peters' myth that there were few indigenous Palestinians in the land (Golda Meir's 'there are no Palestinians'), or orders from their own leaders told them to leave. Gradually, Israeli Arab, and other historians have convincingly demonstrated that these theories have no basis in historical fact and confirmed what the United Nations envoy Count Folke Bernadotte stated prior to his assassination by Zionists in 1949, that 'the Palestinians left out of intimidation.' It is now known that the driving force behind their forced exodus was the implementation of Plan Dalet and various aspects of transfer proposals in what can properly be called today an 'ethnic cleansing' operation, known by Palestinians as *al-Nakba*. The 'transfer' mechanisms and strategies would change but remain in place until today.
3.  The Palestinians rejected the United Nations partition plan due to its inequities as it gave the Jewish state 54 percent of the prime land and left a large (48 percent) Palestinian majority under their control. Palestinians were still 66 percent of the entire population of Palestine and owned 98 percent of the land. As a result of the 'transfer' campaign, Israel gained an additional 23 percent of historic Palestine and reduced its Palestinian population to 18 percent.

4.   In brief, the thesis of the Zionist leadership was as Palestinian historian Nur Masalha observes, 'more land, less Arabs'. The weak resistance from overmatched and out-gunned Palestinian and Arab Legion armies encouraged this strategy to be implemented in the 1947-49 period and continue the execution of it in Galilee and later the West Bank, Jerusalem, and the Gaza Strip.

5.   The Palestinian Christian community was particularly hard hit during the 1947-49 period, suffering its greatest losses in its history during this brief period. The relatively wealthy Jerusalem community was particularly affected. The Christians would never recover from the losses of the *Nakba*.

# Chapter 7
## PALESTINE UNDER ZION:
## IT'S ALL ABOUT LAND (1949-93)

On Friday 25 February 2000, I was present at Chicago's Orchestra Hall as the brilliant Israeli Conductor of the Chicago Symphony Orchestra, Daniel Barenboim, delivered the US premier of the unusual modern opera, 'What Next?' by the American composer, Elliot Carter. As Maestro Barenboim opened the evening with a ten-minute verbal introduction to 'What Next?', one could hear murmuring in the audience, such as the person beside me stating: 'Why is he doing this? Let's get on with it!'

Immediately we understood why 'What Next?' necessitated the conductor's interpretation as the strange lyrics and dissident chords took us into another dimension. If Maestro Barenboim had not prepared us, I dare say 90 percent of the audience (myself included) would not have known that the opera took place immediately after an automobile crash, as a bride and groom were rushing to their wedding and collided with another car that was carrying a mother, a young boy, a bizarre astronomer, and a philosophy professor.

The collision left all passengers in a state of unconsciousness so the opera moved into a mysterious dream world as they begin to act out negative aspects of their personalities, manifesting a marked inability to communicate with each other. It quickly became clear that the young couple should not get married as the groom demonstrated extreme immaturity. Only the twelve-year-old boy seemed to be in touch with reality, which for him was to repeatedly articulate his urgent need for a cheeseburger and fries.

As the unusual opera moved toward its final movement I became more and more fascinated with how the piece was a commentary on the shocking effects that our secular culture have on people and relationships, but also how this might apply to the after-effects of crisis that faced Palestinians in 1949. Not only had they collided with the powerfully, but they were dealt a devastating blow that rendered them temporarily unconscious in the political, spiritual, and psychological realms. Their plight was one of collective shock and angst. Would they ever pull out of this utterly desperate catastrophe—or *al-Nakba*? Could they survive as a people with more than half of their community expelled from their homes and land, destined to live in abject poverty, struggling to simply live to see another day?

For a variety of reasons, the plight of the Palestinians never seemed to tap the conscience of the Western world, perhaps because of its guilt over not responding to the Jewish Holocaust a few years earlier. Israel and the Zionist movement were remarkably effective in mobilizing support at the highest levels of strategically important Western governments, the international media, as well as from synagogues and churches. They were also able to make effective use of the biblical symbolism and linkage between the modern Zionist state and ancient Israel. In short, Israel and the Zionists gained sympathy and legitimacy in the hearts and minds of Europe and North America; Palestine and the Arabs did not.

Professor Keith Whitelam, Chair of Religious Studies at Stirling University (Scotland), summarizes the point: 'The land termed Palestine has no intrinsic value of its own but becomes the arena for "the real and authentic history" of Israel.'[1] Whitelam develops the thesis that the Zionist movement was amazingly effective in making the linkage between the Bible and the Zionist agenda which helped mobilize political support in 'Christian' Europe and the United States. By accepting the Zionist interpretations, however, it meant the negation of Palestine and Palestinians and in some cases even granted legitimacy for their destruction and dismemberment.

Why is it that the Palestinian Arabs were never able to mount a successful public relations campaign in the West? For example, why is it that Palestinian Catholics did not enlist support from Catholic Europe, the influential archdioceses of the United States, and the Catholic majority in South America? The Vatican position on the Israeli-Palestinian conflict has been consistent with United Nations resolutions with a hint of support for the Palestinian case. Or why did not the Palestinian Lutherans generate more sympathy in Germany and Scandinavia or the Palestinian Anglicans find immediate sympathy in Britain and the United States?

The answer is quite simple. Prior to 1948 there was little contact between Palestinian Christians and the churches of Europe and North America. Until recently most Christians throughout the world were not aware that there were Christians in Palestine, let alone have an awareness of their continuity in the land since the day of Pentecost. It is still true that few Western Christians know that the survival of Palestinian Christians in the Holy Land is at stake. In fact, the Western churches tended to favour the Zionist cause and have shown little interest or sympathy to their Christian sisters and brothers.

Throughout this text I have followed a loose chronological method of telling the story of the Palestinian Christians, and through them, we have

---

[1]  Keith Whitelam, *The Invention of Ancient Israel*, Routledge, New York, 1996, 43.

157

examined the Palestinians as a whole. In Chapters 7 and 8, I will modify the historical approach and turn to more thematic interpretations of the 1949-93 period. The present chapter will begin with the effects of 1948 on the Palestinian Christian community and then turn to the central political issues: land and political sovereignty.

## *The* Nakba *and the Palestinian Christian Community*

In an otherwise important and valuable study on Palestinian Christianity, Ben Gurion University professor Daphne Tsimhoni barely mentions the *Nakba* as a significant factor in the sudden reduction of Palestinian Christians after 1947. Instead, her 1993 volume *Christian Communities in Jerusalem and the West Bank Since 1948*, gives a subtle nod toward Islam and 'Muslim Jordan' as the culprits:

> For hundreds of years Christians lived under Ottoman Muslim rule as *dhimmis* (protected believers in inferior religions) ... Although it introduced some changes, the British mandatory government accepted the millet system as the basis for its relations with the various religious communities. When, after thirty years of rule by a Christian power under the British mandate, authority reverted to the Muslim Jordanian government, the Palestinian Christian communities were understandably anxious.[2]

One is always struck by the historical moment in which an author decides to begin his or her narrative. Tsimhoni, like many traditional Zionist historians, begins her volume in 1948 which does not provide the reader with the political context of the rise of Zionism, colonization, and the manoeuvres that eroded Palestinian national aspirations. She makes a brief reference to 'Christian' Britain, as if the Mandate treated Palestinian Christians favourably. On the one hand, she does not analyse the character of the British rule, which as we have seen in the previous chapters, allowed the Zionists to triumph politically and militarily over the Palestinians. The British Mandate commenced on the heels of the Balfour Declaration and the treaties ending World War I, which granted the Zionists their first political legitimacy and the opportunity to accelerate the colonization of Palestine. Palestinian

---

[2] Daphne Tsimhoni, *Christian Communities in Jerusalem and the West Bank Since 1948*, Praeger Publishers, Westport, Connecticut, 1993, 11.

Christians were in the forefront of political opposition with their Muslim compatriots in opposing both the Mandate and the Zionist enterprise. Theirs was not a minority position but represented the views of the majority of the Christians in Palestine. Thus Tsimhoni has established a questionable basis for her initial chapter by introducing presuppositions that are anti-Muslim, pro-British mandate, and subtle pro-Zionist orientations.

By beginning her study in 1948, she nuances the argument toward a critique of Islam and sympathy toward British mandatory rule. She is establishing the premise that 'Israel will save the Christians.' Her discussion attempts to demonstrate various anti-Christian policies of the Jordanian government, such as allowing religious broadcasts through the year but not during Ramadan. This argument actually undermines her case, for Jordan did allow church services and Christian prayers to be broadcast for approximately 48 weekends, but not during Ramadan. By comparison, Israel has not allowed Christian worship and prayers to be broadcast on Israeli television, aside from a portion of the Christmas Eve service in Bethlehem. Nevertheless, the author states in her conclusion to chapter one: 'The Israeli occupation of Jerusalem and the West Bank was welcomed by many Christians as a balancing force against the growing influence of Islam.'[3] Few Christians would state this, as they shared the harshness of the Israeli occupation after 1967 in equal measure with the Palestinian Muslims.

Perhaps more confounding is the near absence of any critical reference to Israeli hostilities toward Christians during the *Nakba*. Her valuable research, with otherwise fine analysis and statistics, carefully avoids the material I have referred to in Chapters 5 and 6. After establishing the above premise in the initial chapter, the author writes expansively about the 'Transformation to Israeli Rule' in the West Bank and East Jerusalem after June, 1967. She claims that restrictions on the purchase of property were eased by the Israelis, and there was no interference with Christian educational and mission agencies. Tsimhoni mentions that 'restrictions on property were stopped,' grants in aid were offered to the communal clubs and charitable institutions by the Israeli government, and the Israelis 'restrained from interfering in the operation of the Christian schools.'[4] One could conclude that Palestinian Christians were treated to a rather benevolent rule once Israel occupied them in 1967, but as we shall see, this was not the case. Instead, the enormously tragic population and property losses of 1948-51, would only continue until 2000 and beyond, at a slower pace, and their political rights and fundamental freedoms would be denied.

---

[3]  *Ibid.*, 11.

[4]  *Ibid.*, 9.

We cannot help but ask why Palestinian Christians emigrated in large numbers to Amman, Jordan, after the *Nakba* of 1948-9 and again after hostilities in 1967. If Israeli rule had been so benign and the Jordanian rule so oppressive between 1949-67, one would think that the Christians would have opted for Israel in the 1967 emigration. Certainly eighteen years would have given them sufficient time to evaluate the two regimes. However, the Palestinian Christians chose Jordan, because they had seen Israel's policies in the *Nakba* as well as the abuses placed on the Christians of Galilee. Further, they believed that Israel initiated the 1967 War which led to additional losses for the Palestinian community, including another refugee crisis. One wonders how Tsimhoni could overlook these matters and write her narrative so positively toward Israeli policies.

She continues:

> Shortly after 1967, the State of Israel declared the sanctity and inviolability of the holy places, and undertook measures to guarantee this. The churches were indemnified for damage caused during the 1948 and 1967 wars.[5]

However, there is no mention of the enormous property losses suffered by the churches, monasteries, and private citizens during the 1948-49 hostilities, and the fact that the land and homes or institutions have not been returned. Whether we consider the vast lands of West Jerusalem or the near suburbs such as Ein Karem and Lifta, or the property of Lydda and Ramle or Beisan, there is no discussion of these. The uncritical reader will be impressed by the compassionate generosity of the Israelis in helping to rebuild the Church of the Holy Sepulchre and the Maronite vicarage, which is true, but these are veritable 'drops in the bucket' in comparison to the land and population losses suffered by Christians alone in 1948-9 and 1967.

Another negative development that Tsimhoni ascribes to the Palestinian Christians is 'Arabization'. She implies that some Palestinian Christian leaders were influenced more by Arabization or Palesitnian nationalism, and hence were not cooperative with Israel. Here she mentions how the previous Anglican bishop, an Englishman by name of George Appleton was so cooperative with Israeli authorities that he received the 'Distinguished Citizen of Jerusalem' award from the government in 1970. However, the selection of a Palestinian as Anglican bishop in 1976 is judged by Tsimhoni as 'causing an erosion of the friendly relations that had developed with the former Anglican archbishop.'[6] The present Latin Patriarch,

---

[5] Tsimhoni, *ibid.*, 9-10.
[6] Tsimhoni, *op. cit.*, 10.

Michel Sabbah, the first Palestinian in the post, is given negative reviews by the author as 'the only church head who has persistently absented himself from Israeli official ceremonies and receptions at the presidents residence on the grounds that the Vatican does not recognize the State of Israel and Jerusalem as its capital.'[7]

The negative overtones of the author toward 'Arabization' are directed most harshly toward Melkite Catholic Vicar Hilarian Cappucci, who was allegedly caught transporting weapons between Lebanon and Israel. There remain aspects of the case that are inconclusive concerning the guilt and questionable evidence concerning Vicar Cappucci, as some believe the weapons were planted in the car, as Cappucci claimed. For Tsimhoni, the Cappucci case merely underscores her point on the dangers of 'Arabization'.

The Christians of Palestine did not fare well in the 1949-93 period, as is indicated by the accelerated patterns of emigration that we will discuss later in the chapter. Had the situation improved under Israeli rule, the emigration certainly would have decreased. The reality is that the Palestinian Christians were victims of the same policies that were directed toward the Muslims, as the Palestinians were one community struggling for their political and national rights.

## What land?

As Bishop Cragg states: 'The land is competitively loved ... "Land", then, and land-love are the theme of all else.'[8] The Israeli-Palestinian question is fundamentally one of who possesses political sovereignty over the land of Palestine (also called Israel, ancient Canaan, the Holy Land, *Eretz Yisrael*, or *Filistin*), and who has gained political and economic support for their claim from the dominant international powers. The Palestinians have by and large lost repeatedly in the political and demographic struggles for the land. Their loss became the gain and was undoubtedly the goal of political Zionism from the time the early Zionist fathers met in Basle in August 1897.

At this point it may be useful to review the exact parameters of the land we are discussing. The international borders of Palestine were defined during the treaties following World War I and a form of colonial control was eventually granted to the British (1922-1948) in what was called a Mandate. The partition plan of the United Nations defined the land area as 10,162 square miles, or 26,320 square kilometres lying on the eastern end of the

---

[7] *Ibid.*, 10.

[8] Cragg, *Palestine: The Prize and Price of Zion*, xii.

Mediterranean and extending east to the Jordan River, following the western side of the Dead Sea and continuing south to the Red Sea. In the north, it is bound by the southern border of Lebanon and the Syrian Golan Heights and the Sinai peninsula in the south. Palestine is approximately the size of the state of New Jersey or one third the size of the United Kingdom.

This map would undergo a series of political changes once the partition plan was confirmed by the United Nations in 1947. Israel's land would expand by 23 percent due to its success in the *Nakba*/War of Independence of 1948-49. In 1967, Israel's rapid military victory brought the Golan Heights, West Bank, East Jerusalem, the Gaza Strip, and the Sinai under its authority. In 1978, Israel seized what it called a 'security Zone' at its northern border with Lebanon. Egypt received back the Sinai through the Camp David Accords of 1978, and Israel in late May-June 2000 withdrew from Southern Lebanon. Still unresolved are the Golan Heights, West Bank. East Jerusalem, and Gaza Strip. Palestinians have received approximately 9 percent of their territories and negotiations continue under the Oslo framework. It is anticipated that Israel will retain the majority (over 60 percent) of the Palestinian areas.

## The core of the conflict

Had there been an international legal instrument enabling the Palestinians to challenge the legality of the Balfour Declaration or the legality of the Zionist movement establishing exclusively Jewish colonies in Palestine, the history of these critical years might have been written differently. The fact that Britain in the years 1918-22, had not as yet received the Mandate for Palestine from the League of Nations should have prevented them from disposing the land to another party. Nevertheless, the Balfour Declaration effectively granted the Zionists a form of political legitimacy that only the Arabs seemed to have challenged, but the Zionists effectively gained what they had been seeking since their founding meeting in Basle.

Zionists seized the opportunity offered by the British, as had many others in different times and places (the British and Americans included) because there were no courts of appeal nor mechanisms that might have curbed such massive colonization. Meanwhile, the British occupation and Zionist colonization weakened the Palestinian majority and eroded both their claims and their political organization, the latter having always been weak and dominated by the Ottoman overlords.

Still, when the decisive moment arrived in November 1947, the actual population statistics favoured the Palestinians. Even with the Jewish settlers (most European Ashkenazi Jews) increasing from a mere 6 percent in 1900 to 34 percent in 1947, the Palestinians still owned approximately 93 percent of the land and constituted a clear majority (66 percent) of the population. However, the partition vote granted the Zionists a decisive political, economic and strategic advantage, as they would receive 54 percent of Palestine including the prime coastal and agricultural areas. The partition also gave the Zionist leadership the political opportunity they had been awaiting, enabling them to implement the first stage of a goal affirmed at New York's Biltmore Hotel in 1942: the entire land of Palestine would eventually become the Jewish state.

## Zionist strategies in Galilee after 1949

After the Armistice of 1949, Israel concentrated on three strategies in Galilee, patterns that would also be pursued after 1967 in the remainder of Palestine. In order to insure military control, Israel imposed martial law on Galilee's Palestinian minority (reduced from 48 percent to 20 percent of the population inside Israel). The public rationale for the policy was 'security' but Israel's real designs were demographic factors, as they wished to insure Jewish dominance by removing the Palestinians who were now citizens of Israel.

Several civilian laws were passed by the Knesset in the early years of Israel's existence that formed the basis of land confiscation, allowing it to appear legal while providing a 'legal' defence whenever challenged. 'The Law of Acquisition of Absentee Property', the 'Emergency Articles for the Exploitation of Uncultivated Lands', the 'Law for the Requisition of Land in Times of Emergency', and the 'Law for the Acquisition of Land' became the foundation for the Israeli government's seizure of massive amounts of Palestinian land, under the guise of legality. The latter law was particularly far reaching as it allowed the government to seize any Palestinian property in which the owner could not prove legally that his or her name was on the deed.

As a result of the new laws, Palestinians, unable to prove they were in their houses between 15 May 1948-September 1949, were liable to lose their house and land. The military was instructed to seize land of partially evacuated Arab villages and others that were fully abandoned in the military operations of 1948-49. The unspoken motive driving the decisions was the fact that only 7 percent of the land of Palestine belonged to Jews when the State of Israel was declared. Israel wished to create mechanisms by which it could increase Zionist ownership of the land so these laws provided a form of 'legal' procedures to justify land seizures of massive proportions.

Before 1948 there were 485 Palestinian villages in the territory that became the State of Israel. The vast majority of the villages were destroyed and their population expelled. Only 60 of these villages remain. After 1949 there were many attempts by separated family members who had fled into Lebanon, Syria, or Jordan (and the West Bank) to return to their homes. Still others simply returned to farm the land they loved or worked due to economic desperation. The Israeli Defence Forces were especially alert to prevent such occurrences, which led to a series of skirmishes along the Egyptian, Lebanese and Jordanian borders during 1950-67.

## The case of Bir'am

The case of the northern Galilee village of Bir'am has become well known in some circles due to the remarkable ministry of Fr Elias Chacour, the Melkite Catholic priest, who has built schools and a university in Ibillin, a small Palestinian village between Haifa and Nazareth. Fr Chacour tells in his autobiography *Blood Brothers,* how his family took in Jews during the events of 1948 because they had arrived homeless from Hitler's aggression in Europe. In November 1948, his village was told that due to security problems along the Lebanon border, all the residents of Palestinian villages would need to temporarily evacuate their homes and leave. Some were sent over the border into Lebanon, never to return, and the majority were sent to another Christian village named Jish, some 6-7 miles away. They carried some of their belongings to Jish but not all of them as they were told they would return to Bir'am within a few weeks.

The weeks turned into months, and the months into years. Four years later the residents of Bir'am took the matter to Israel's High Court of Justice (there is no Supreme Court in Israel as the military is the final authority in judicial decisions). The High Court decided that the villagers could return to Bir'am in December 1953. The residents joyfully packed their suitcases and made the return trip, mostly by foot. They planned to be back in their homes for Christmas Day. Fr Chacour recalls that as they came to the top of the hill overlooking their beloved village, their spirits dropped for the Israeli Government's Christmas gift to them was the bombing of the entire village, thus preventing their return. In fact, every house in Bir'am was bombed and destroyed with the only remaining structure being the tower and a wing of the Melkite Church. The land of Bir'am and hundreds of acres surrounding it were declared 'abandoned property', confiscated, and turned over to the new Kibbutz Bara'am. There were 10,000 residents of Bir'am displaced, becoming refugees inside their own country.

Fr Chacour recalled the scene to me as he had experienced it as a twelve year old: 'Sometime before Christmas Day, the village of Bir'am was destroyed, all of it. The poor families stood numbed by the horrors of the spectacle. You can not imagine the pain that we felt, the anger, the hopelessness as we turned and made the long journey back to Jish.'

Several years later the Dean of the Law Faculty at Tel Aviv University, Prof Amnon Rubenstein, wrote the following article about the Bir'am case in *Ha'aretz,* the leading Israeli daily, in which he concluded:

> There is no doubt that their expulsion was committed without authorization, without confirmation of the commander in chief, without the confirmation of the government, and without legal basis. The whole thing was done according to the disputed tradition of establishing facts (on the ground), a tradition which reached its epitome in the illegal blowing up of a whole Arab village.[9]

Until today, the residents of Bir'am, like those of neighbouring Ikrit, Mansarah, and the majority of the northern Galilee corridor were forced out and as Professor Rubenstein rightly characterized the case, they have become refugees within their own country. These were Israeli citizens, who according to the founding principles ('The Charter') of the State of Israel, were entitled to have full protection and rights under the law. The Charter states: '[the Jewish State] shall uphold the full social and political equality of all its citizens, without distinction of religion, race, and sex.' The Palestinian residents of Israel from these villages lost everything, including their homes and property, despite a ruling in their favour in the highest court of Israel. Why they have not returned after 52 years is not so much a mystery as it is illustrative of Israel's commitment to control 'more land and less Arabs'.

Between 1948 and the mid-1960s, Israel seized the land of several Arab villages or large tracts of land from families and religious institutions while incorporating them into Israeli state land. In the vast majority of cases there was no compensation given in return, as in the cases if Ikrit and Bir'am. As was the fate of Bir'am, Israel gave the Palestinian land to various Jewish groups who established a *kibbutz* or forest over destroyed Palestinian villages. Often one can find a cactus and rubble from old structures in Israel's numerous forests and parks; such a Canada Park near West Jerusalem. Most of these sites are former Palestinian villages, now numbering 425 in pre-1948 Israel, Gaza, and the West Bank.

---

[9]  Quoted in Joseph L Ryan, 'Refugees Within Israel', *Journal of Palestine Studies*, Vol. II, no. 4, 1973, 9.

## Removing Palestinian Christians from Galilee

Following the 'cleansing' of Galilee's northern border and the replacement of most of the Palestinian Arab population with Jews, Israel considered a new experiment with the Christians of Galilee. The new strategy toward the Christian community was known as 'Operation Yohanan,' a pet-project of the previously discussed Josef Weitz, Director of the Jewish National Fund's Land Settlement Department. 'Operation Yohanan' was a plan that originated in Weitz's office in 1950 and gained support from Prime Minister Ben-Gurion and high-ranking Israeli officials. Many were awaiting the development of such a manoeuvre as a way of reducing the Palestinian Arab population. Of interest is the fact that it was the Palestinian Christian population that was targeted by the scheme.

The plan was very simple. Israel would transfer a number of Palestinian Christian families to Argentina as a trial case to see if the project might work for the remainder of the Christians in Northern Galilee, and perhaps elsewhere. Brazil was also a possible destination. Weitz described it in the following memorandum to Ya'acov Tzur, Israel's ambassador to Argentina:

> The chief purpose of this matter (Operation Yohanan) is the 'transfer' of the Arab population from Israel. I have always, and already before the establishment of the state, feared the Arab minority in our midst, and those fears are still existing, not in theory but in practice. In addition to this, we lack land, and if not now, we will feel its shortage after a short time, when the objective of 'curtailing the exiles' is realized. By the transfer of the Arab minority from Israel through mutual agreement (between Israel and Argentina) the better it will be for the state. From this viewpoint I see the wish for one group from the village of Gush Halav (Jish in Galilee) as the beginning of the way to realize the idea.[10]

According to the Palestinian historian Nur Masalha, 'Operation Yohanan' was kept in strictest confidence. Weitz continued to work on the arrangements in absolute secrecy as he made a trip to Argentina in 1951 in order to confirm its feasibility. On his return, he met with Foreign Minister Moshe Sharett on February 1952, and with Prime Minister Ben-Gurion the next day. In both meetings, he reported on the transfer of Christians scheme, and received the

---

[10] Yusef Weitz, JNF, to Ya'acov Tazur, Ambassador to Argentina, letter dated 15 June 1951, Israel Archives, Foreign Ministry, #2402.16; quoted in Nur Masalha, 'A Galilee Without Christians?', O'Mahony, *op. cit.*, 194.

affirmative, with Ben-Gurion commenting: 'the Christian church would certainly oppose; but it must be carried out.'[11] Eventually, the Christian residents of Jish rejected the plan, noting the unfair compensation and the difficulty that may lie ahead in adjusting to the situation in Argentina or Brazil. The scheme was eventually dropped, perhaps more due to potential public relations ramifications.

## *The Church hierarchy and Israel: whose land?*

One of the tragic aspects of the church's legacy in Palestine since the arrival of Zionism has been the numerous cases in which the Greek Orthodox Patriarchate has leased, granted, or sold land to the Government of Israel and its various Israeli land companies. In the previous chapter I discussed several of the land leases or grants made by the Greek Patriarch to Israel in the greater Jerusalem district. Similar arrangements were made throughout Israel proper with significant losses to the Christian community in Galilee. Land grants and sales have continued to the present day and are now being challenged in the courts by a revived organization of Palestinian priests and laity called the Palestinian Orthodox Congress. The group convened in 1993 after realizing that their various appeals and requests to the Greek Orthodox Patriarch were falling on deaf ears.

Among the goals of the Congress are: 1) to call the Greek Orthodox Patriarchate to accountability for church properties sold or leased to the Government of Israel and its various land companies; 2) to create a joint commission including Palestinian Orthodox lawyers, priests, and experts to be part of all future decisions on the disposition of church land and property; 3) to insure that past and future land sales are returned to the local churches; 4) to encourage Palestinian priests to prepare for becoming Bishops, which necessitates the vow of celibacy; 5) to have an account of the millions of dollars received by the Patriarchate from tourism and rentals; 6) to insist that the Patriarch advocate the feelings of the Palestinian Christian community on such matters as the peace process, Israel's settlement policy, the future of Jerusalem, the right of refugees to return or receive compensation; 7) schools and education in general have been low priorities within the Jerusalem Patriarchate, a matter which must be reversed as the community is losing its youth; 8) there has been a complete failure of the Patriarchate to encourage Palestinian men to become priests and women to become deacons, a matter which must be corrected so as to develop indigenous leadership; 9) there must be a total freeze on land and property sales to Israel.

---

[11] Masalha, *op. cit.*, 208.

A disturbing example of the Palestinian Orthodox Congress' scores of grievances over land is a case dating back to 1973, when the Greek Orthodox Patriarchate sold church property which included a cemetery in Tiberias to an Israeli development company. The Patriarchate received the money and did not account for it. Soon the Kinneret Hotel, complete with a swimming pool and parking lot were built over the cemetery, but without removing the bodies or providing for their reburial. By 1973, the Christians of Tiberias had long been driven out of Palestine with the majority forced into Lebanon and Jordan as refugees, unable to return to their homes. However, a small number of Christians had found haven in Nazareth and Haifa and would periodically return to the graves. When they attempted to revisit the cemetery in 1973, to pray and pay respect for their loved ones, they discovered the hotel and swimming pool crudely built over the cemetery. Appeals to the Patriarchate had been ignored until recently when the Orthodox Committee initiated legal challenges against the Patriarchate, which sold the land to a development company.[12]

Similar cases exist throughout Israel and Palestine with disenfranchised Palestinian Christians challenging not only the Greek Orthodox Patriarchate, perhaps the most serious offender, but also the Melkite Catholic Bishop for Galilee and the Armenian Orthodox Patriarchate. It is important to note that there are two components of the tension that now exists between Palestinian Christians and their foreign hierarchy. First, most Orthodox patriarchs and the overwhelming majority of bishops have traditionally been foreign (Greeks have controlled the Orthodox Patriarchate since the 15th century with Lebanese and Syrians dominating the Armenian and Melkite bishoprics). Second, Israel has been able to influence the elections of several patriarchs and selection of bishops since 1948. Various 'favours' such as travel immunities, tax credits, and visas for church staff have been given to encourage the hierarchy to pursue Israel's desires.

During an extensive interview with Dr Fuad Farah in his Nazareth home, I was given a large file of documents and legal briefs that demonstrated the seriousness of their grievances. Dr Farah, Executive Director of the Arab Orthodox Congress, reminded me that their initiative was not new, as it stood on the programme and principles of the early Palestinian Christian nationalists of the 1905-15 era, the majority of whom were from Galilee. Palestinian nationalist leaders like Khalil Sakakini, George Antonius, Najib Nasser, and Najib Azouri, were all Greek Orthodox Christians and passionate nationalists who opposed the Zionist movement, then in its infancy. They also challenged Ottoman and later British rule in

---

[12] Author's interview with Dr Fuad Farah, Nazareth, Israel, 9 January 2000.

their pursuit of a Palestinian state. Their desire for the church was the creation of indigenous Palestinian Christian leadership that had control of its worship, local polity, property, and assets. They wished to reform the church from within as it was out of touch with the peoples' needs. They challenged the Greek domination of their church and sought to bring the leadership into compliance with the Palestinian Orthodox congregations by a series of ecclesiastical procedures, legal measures, and through non-violent advocacy strategies (sit-ins, demonstrations, etc.).

A memorandum by the Executive Committee of the (Palestinian Christian) Orthodox Congress in Israel views itself as standing in the tradition of the great nationalists from the pre-World War I era. The Memorandum reflects the anger and alienation that the Palestinian laity have felt for centuries toward the Greek hierarchy:

> There is a general feeling among our church members that if the present conditions within the Jerusalem Patriarchate do not change for the better, and if its disregard for the basic needs and rights of the church members remains as it is now, a bitter conflict at all levels between the church hierarchy and the Orthodox community is imminent. The total neglect of the basic needs of the parish churches against the extravagant wasteful spending and lavish living at the summit, the scandalous, corrupt, immoral and unbecoming conduct of many of our holy fathers, and the insulting remarks of the Patriarch to the press against his own congregation, have thrown a dark image on the noble heritage of Orthodoxy in this land, and has marred our relationship with our religious leadership.[13]

The memorandum goes on to challenge the enormous wealth of the Patriarchate, most of which has been gained at the expense of land and property sales of local Palestinian Orthodox families and churches. They make particular reference to Orthodox churches, cemeteries, and large tracts of land that were left unguarded and not maintained after the events of 1948. Due to the Patriarchate's negligence of land and church buildings abandoned

---

[13] 'Memorandum' of the 'Arab Orthodox Initiative Committee,' 26 June 1998. Attached to the memorandum are eight documents obtained from the Central Zionist Archives and other official Israeli sources concerning land dealings between the Greek Orthodox Patriarchate and the Government of Israel. The documents are available for a small fee from Dr George Madanat, Chair of the International Task Force to Save Orthodoxy in the Patriarchate of Jerusalem, 2300 West Third Street; Los Angeles, California 90057.

in 1948, they were confiscated by the new Government of Israel under the new 'absentee property laws', designed for precisely such opportunities, or land was leased and sold by the Greek Patriarchate.

The memorandum goes on to note that while over 99 percent of the congregations are comprised of Palestinian Arabs, there are no 'mixed' councils authorized to make decisions concerning the distribution of property, despite repeated requests since the turn of the last century. References to '100-year lease agreements' with the government of Israel or Israeli land investors, all at minimal financial or no remuneration to the church, have been signed at the expense of the Palestinian Orthodox Christians. The memorandum adds: 'The Patriarchate's blunt refusal to disclose details of such secretly drawn transactions and contracts that are never made public, or explain how their proceeds, estimated at millions of dollars, are spent, arouses in us deep feelings of suspicion.' They add that this collaboration between the Patriarchate and the Israeli Government is in part to blame for the 'systematic decline of Orthodoxy in the Holy Land, threatening to a great extent its survival and destiny.'[14]

On 9 September 1992, the respected *Ha'aretz* newspaper carried an interview that reporter Yehuda Litani conducted with the Patriarch, The Patriarch claimed that his authority over the land and the church affairs is a historical one:

> When did the Arabs come here?' he asked, 'The Greeks have been here for over 2000 years. They came with Alexander of Macedonia in the year 322 BC ... The Arabs arrived only during the 7th century. This is our Church, the church of the Greeks. If they do not accept our laws, they have one alternative—choose another church, or establish one of their own.[15]

The Patriarch went on to condemn the Palestinian Orthodox Congress as 'people who never attend church nor do they have any faith in God,' and they 'should be driven to a mental hospital.' He added: 'What right do these people have to be our partners in the property which is all ours? What do they need the money for? To continue using drugs?'[16] Litani's article ends with this pointed comment: 'There is no hope for basic changes soon.' This is all high politics, says Daoud from Beit Jala, 'Rabin, Kollek, King Hussein and King Fahad all smile for them and as usual it is the Palestinians who lose at the

---

[14] Interview with Dr Fuad Farah, and *ibid.*
[15] Yehuda Litani, 'The Harsh Summer of the Patriarch,' *Ha'aretz*, 25 September 1992.
[16] *Ibid.*

end.'[17] Daoud's attitude reflects why many Palestinian Orthodox Christians have grown cynical and alienated from their church.

The efforts of Dr Farah are impressive for their organizational achievements since resurrecting the Palestinian Orthodox Congress in 1993, but they have little political and legal leverage. The Congress has over a dozen cases pending in the Israeli courts, some of which may be taken to the High Court of Justice in Israel. Also, they have raised the issue of a 1941 law passed under the British Mandate, which would give Palestinian Orthodox Christians more power in decision-making concerning the distribution of church property and related matters. However, both cases have little potential for success as the traditional Israeli military rationale, 'security,' can override even the decisions of the High Court of Justice. On the practical level, they have little money and no staff. All of the Congress' leaders are volunteers who have other jobs. The expectation remains that these cases will be buried in legal manoeuvres or eventually thrown out of the courts and the Knesset under 'security' arguments. Unless there is a dramatic infusion of funding and full-time legal staff to carry on the work, the primary function of the Congress may be a moral one. If the vast numbers of Palestinian Orthodox Christians in the diaspora can organize and finance a significant legal campaign and mount an international public relations effort, they may be able to raise the case for reparations or the return of the property to the local Palestinian Christians.

## *Israel conquers the remainder of Palestine: facts on the ground*

Israel's easy victory over Jordan, Syria, and Egypt in June 1967 gave it dominance over its most immediate enemies, strategic sections of each nation's land, and a new problem: what will it do with twice as many Palestinians? One land issue that Israel acted upon immediately (June 27 1967) was Jerusalem, with Arab East Jerusalem and over 100,000 residents annexed by the State of Israel. Jerusalem was declared the 'eternal' capital of Israel.

While leaving the status of the West Bank and Gaza Strip 'open' to future negotiations, Israel conducted a quiet pattern of settlement and land confiscation in these territories, similar to that which was followed in Galilee. The entire region was placed under a military occupation and controlled with a combination of military forces, border guards, many of whom were Arabic

---

[17] *Ibid.*

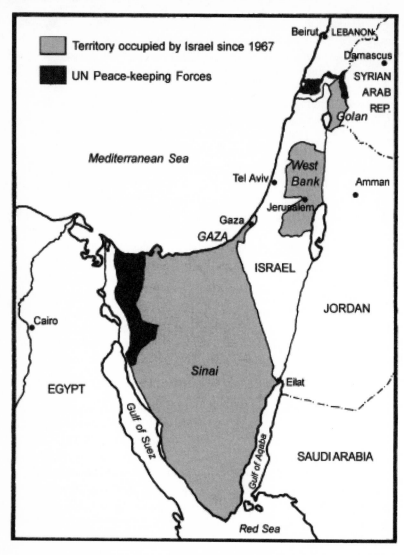

*Territory occupied in the 1967 War and UN Peace-keeping Forces (after UN map, 3014, November 1978)*

speaking Druze (citizens of Israel of an Islamic sect that cooperated with Israel), and military intelligence units (Shin Beit) who generally operated in street clothes. Within a short time there was an extensive network of paid Palestinian informants in place, many recruited after periods of imprisonment. Soon Israeli and Palestinian political analysts began to suspect that the military occupation was permanent. As for the United Nations resolution (UN 242) calling for Israel to withdraw from the territories seized in 1967, there were indications that Israel was simply insincerely acknowledging the discussion, primarily for Western consumption.

In the months and years immediately following the June 1967 War, Israel concentrated on Arab East Jerusalem and expropriated some 30 acres of buildings within the Old City and turned them over to Jews, driving out the Palestinians without compensation or alternative housing. On 11 June, the Maghribi (Muslim) Quarter, just outside the Wailing Wall, was bulldozed and 650 persons were evicted without compensation to make way for a new plaza for Jews visiting the Wall. Outside the Old City the East Jerusalem region suffered more, with over 4000 acres of Palestinian land confiscated by 1971. By 1978 the total land confiscated in greater Jerusalem would reach 23,640 acres with 76,000 Jewish settlers now living on stolen Palestinian land. Israel always offered a legal justification for the land thefts, claiming the land had been declared 'state' or 'public' land, and thus the confiscations were 'legal'. However, over 90 percent of these lands were privately held by families or by Christian and Muslim trusts.

The controversial cases of the Greek Orthodox Church selling or leasing Christian property continued in the 1960s-1990s, and became a prime source of settlement land. For example, the Patriarchate sold the large land holdings of Mar Elias Monastery on the Jerusalem-Jericho Road. Today the largest Israeli settlement in the West Bank, Maale Adumin, sits on the Orthodox property, sold by the Patriarch at a bargain price to the Israeli Government. Most recently, the Patriarchate sold significant tracts of land in the last major tract of land between Bethlehem and Jerusalem, Abu-Ghnaim (Har Homa). As a result Israel has the possibility of completely encircling Jerusalem's Arab community while cutting off the northern and southern districts of the West Bank from Jerusalem.

Within a few months of the War of 1967, the Israeli Labour Party initiated a policy of seizing Palestinian land through a variety of pseudo-legal manoeuvres. The first settlements began in Jerusalem as exclusively Jewish apartment buildings called French Hill, just to the north of the city. These were followed by a string of agricultural and paramilitary settlements along the Jordan Valley. They were followed by a secondary line of settlements that were both military and residential along the Jordan rift, or the mountainous region north of Jerusalem and west of the Jordan River.

The latter blocs of settlements were conceived by the Labour Party as lines of defence in case of Arab attacks from the east. They were also designed to encircle Palestinian population centres, so as to engulf and contain them. The pattern prevented the growth of Palestinian areas while Israel built military strongholds that would dominate the Palestinian cities. The lines of settlements were connected by super-highways and electrical and water grids. By 1987, 52 percent of the West Bank had been taken for settlement purposes whereas 30 percent of the Gaza Strip had been seized. By 2000 over 60 percent of the West Bank and 42 percent of the Gaza Strip remain under full Israeli sovereignty.

Civilian populations that are occupied by a foreign military power are protected by various legal instruments that have evolved over time, such as the Hague Conventions of 1899 and 1907. These Conventions state in essence that private property cannot be confiscated or unilaterally declared state property and transferred or annexed by the occupying power. The Hague Convention of 1907 added:

> The property of municipalities, that of institutions dedicated to religion, charity and education, the arts and sciences, even when State property, shall be treated as private property. All seizure or destruction of, or wilful damage to, institutions of this character, historic monuments, works of art and science, is forbidden, and should be made subject of legal proceedings.[18]

It is ironic that the Nazis virtually ignored these legal prohibitions when they annexed European territories and imposed martial law or created puppet regimes to rule them. Lands were annexed, in several cases populations were transferred, religious and private property was stolen, and numerous crimes were committed against the civilian populations of Europe. The issue of land confiscation, illegal settlement, and annexation of land to Germany became significant issues at the International Military Tribunal at Nuremberg (otherwise known simply as Nuremberg). One of the Nazi's routine practices was the establishment of exclusively 'Aryan' (German) settlements either to displace the indigenous population or to place them in the midst of the conquered civilians, but on their lands. The Nazi actions were declared illegal and the legal provisions of the Hague Conventions were upheld. In an effort to prevent such practices and to protect civilian populations and their lands, the Geneva Conventions of 1949 were issued. Article 49, paragraph 6 of the Geneva Convention IV, strictly prohibits the establishment of civilian

---

[18] Thomas and Sally Mallison, *op. cit.*, 242.

settlements on conquered territories. Israel was a signatory to the Geneva Conventions. Once having been a victim of Nazi aggression and genocide, it remains a mystery how Israel consistently violates legal instruments designed to prevent the very atrocities committed against Jews by the Nazis.

Most member states of the United Nations signed the Geneva Conventions and have pledged to uphold them in practice. The official policy of the United States which was adopted in 1967 (and reiterated in April 1978 in an explicit legal document) relative to Israel's settlements, states clearly that settlements are illegal.[19] Through the years, successive US administrations and both houses of Congress have ignored or manipulated this policy so as to avoid public criticism of Israel. As a result, the settlements have accelerated, particularly during the Reagan and Clinton Administrations.

When the Likud Government of Menachem Begin was elected to lead Israel in 1977, their declared policy was to expand existing settlements and develop new colonies. The policy that would be followed for several years was drafted by M Drobles, head of the World Zionist Organization's Department for Rural Settlement. The plan declared the intent of the Likud Government to increase the settlement process during the next five years (stage I). They simply ignored international law and justified their actions with this statement:

> Settlement throughout the entire Land of Israel (*Eretz Yisrael*, which to Likud included the West Bank, E Jerusalem, Golan Heights, and Gaza Strip) is for security and by right. A strip of settlements at strategic sites enhances both internal and external security alike, as well as making concrete and realizing our right to *Eretz-Yisrael*.[20]

The Likud Cabinet member selected to implement the Drobles strategy was the aggressive Ariel Sharon who, with Begin and other Likud legislators, sought to 'create facts on the ground.' Likud saw the settlements as tactical measures to prepare for future annexation or incorporation of all of *Eretz Yisrael* under Israeli sovereignty, declaring a planned demographic shift that would be buttressed by the exclusively Jewish colonies in the Palestinian territories. Significant financial incentives were adopted by the government to encourage Israelis to move to the settlements, which in 1980 were lightly populated. In fact, in 1982 there were only 20,000 to 25,000 Jews living in the settlements but Sharon's declared goal was to reach 300,000 by the end of

---

[19] Memorandum, Department of State, 'Concerning the Legality of Settlements in the Occupied Territories', Washington, DC, 21 April 1976.

[20] 'The Drobles Plan', reprinted an Mallison and Mallison, *op. cit.*, 446.

the 1980s. The timing was perfect as far as the United States political leadership was concerned. President Jimmy Carter had viewed the settlements as illegal, as did the official policy of the United States State Department. However, the newly elected Ronald Reagan, possibly the most pro-Israel president in US history, would issue no statement against them. During the Reagan period the Likud-oriented Israeli lobby (AIPAC, etc.) was able to have legislation adopted that would both increase foreign assistance and military aid to Israel, and deliver grants in the initial quarter of the fiscal year enabling Israel to earn money from the interest. The grants were issued without conditions or the necessity of accounting for expenditures, unique for any recipient of US aid.

The large amounts of US aid (possibly over $6 billion annually) enabled Israel to divert funds to expand settlements, road construction to connect the settlements and bypass Palestinian cities, while confiscating additional land for these purposes. Nor has the United States, Israel's largest source of financial and military assistance, done anything of substance to curb the relentless march of illegal settlements.

## A resource more valuable than oil

In the Middle East, there is one resource that is more important than oil. It is water, a truly precious commodity in this region of increasing populations and diminishing resources. Dr Thomas Stauffer, internationally recognized authority on energy and water and for twelve years professor of economic geography at Harvard University, notes:

> There is a painful paradox: oil is abundant, water is not. The analyst concerned with resource politics or resource economics in the Middle East cannot fail to note that the depletable resource—oil—is amply available ... Ironically, it is the renewable resource, water, that is in desperately short supply. The consequences are profound. Scarcity, obviously means conflict; oil wars are less likely than water wars.[21]

Professor Stauffer reminds us that there are three ancient rivers involved in the Arab-Israeli struggle for water, which he calls 'Canaanite Water: The Tale of Three Rivers'. They are the Jordan, the Yarmuk , and the

---

[21] Thomas R Stauffer, 'Water and War in the Middle East', Center for Policy Analysis on Palestine; Washington, DC, July 1996, 1.

Litani in Lebanon. There are other potential crises among Turkey, Iraq, and Syria over the Euphrates River and Egypt and Sudan over the Nile, but for our purposes we will concentrate on the 'Canaanite Waters'.

Israel began to plan the diversion of the Jordan River in the late 1940s, shortly after statehood. Stauffer notes that they did divert part of the upper Jordan in the 1950s and completed the project when its National Water Carrier system was completed in the late 1960s. However, this provided only one-fourth of the water necessary for Israeli consumers, who have been undisciplined until recently, in agricultural, industrial, tourist, and ordinary civilian uses. The search for new sources did not take long for in 1967, Israel gained control of the West Bank and gradually integrated its rich water sources into Israel's national water system. Israel then restricted the use of water for Palestinians to pre-1967 standards and introduced meters to ration the water consumption. At the same time, the increase of settlements drew West Bank water for their agricultural and entertainment use (swimming pools) plus normal civilian uses. Few restrictions have been placed on the settlements, but most Palestinian areas are now facing water rationing, such as Bethlehem, which had water approximately 50 percent during the hot summer months of 1999.

Stauffer summarizes the water issue surrounding Israel and the West Bank which makes the case why Israel's thirst for Palestinian water is the unspoken reason why it will not surrender all of that area in upcoming peace negotiations.

> Hegemony over the West Bank is therefore doubly critical...
> for Israel's water supply. First, control of the National Water
> Carrier is rooted in the West Bank and, second, Israelis must
> preempt local use of the Mountain Aquifer so that the water
> will flow down to the coastal wells and springs (built by Israel
> to seize the West Bank water), rather than being available
> 'upgrade' for consumption by the local Palestinian population.
> Thus, control of the West Bank is inextricably linked to Israel's
> ability to capture and divert a total of 800-900 million cubic
> meters per year—400-500 from the Upper Jordan River itself,
> plus 400 mcm/y from the West Bank aquifers. The flow of
> these two sources together is equivalent to 50 percent of
> Israel's total present water consumption.[22]

In the Gaza Strip the water situation is more acute. There are now over one

---

[22] *Ibid.*, 8.

million Palestinians living in Gaza, 70 percent of whom are refugees according to the United Nations. Gaza is the second most densely populated area on the planet, and if one removes the 40 percent of Gaza controlled by Israel, it becomes the most dense. Much of the population lives in impoverished refugee camps such as Jabaliya, where over 100,000 people are contained in less than two square kilometres.

The water crisis in Gaza is severe. Palestinians receive 30 percent of the available water, much of which is now highly salinised and often contaminated. Israeli settlers, who number less than 4,000, have 40 percent of the land and use of 70 percent of the water.[23] One sees water freely pumped into the settlements agricultural areas or the swimming pools while Jabaliya refugees face strict water rationing. Open sewers run down the streets of Jabaliya. Harvard University researcher Sara Roy, perhaps the foremost academic specialist on Gaza's economy and land situation, claims that Israel's policy has been one of de-development, including a deliberate destruction of Gaza's economy and infrastructure.

The central issue here is the West Bank water , which Stauffer notes is the key to 50 percent of Israel's water. Control of the source of the water and of the West Bank, which is the source of the productive Palestinian Mountain Aquifer and the waters from the Yarmuk and Jordan Rivers, remains unresolved. There is also a hydraulic importance to the Golan Heights, although Israel may be able to negotiate control of the source of the Jordan so as to return most of the Golan if its access to the Jordan River source is under Israeli sovereignty. However, it is unlikely Israel will surrender any sections of the West Bank that are vital to its control of the aquifers.

The other source for Israel's water needs is the Litani River in south Lebanon. Most independent Israeli and international experts, such as Stauffer, believe Israel has been diverting water from the Litani since its invasion of Lebanon in 1978. Since the Litani riverbed is higher than that of the Sea of Galilee (Lake Tiberias), it is believed Israel has tried to drill tunnels that allow the gravity to take Litani water down to the Israeli National Water Carrier system at the Sea of Galilee. It is possible, however, that the Hizbullah resistance has made this plan unworkable, and Israel's May-June 2000 withdrawal from Lebanon ended this tactic, at least for the time being. Thus the West Bank and control of the Jordan River system will be even more vital in the years to come if Israel is to maintain its present (or increased) levels of consumption. With Israel's water needs so high and the sources dropping (the Sea of Galilee dropped significantly in 1998-99 due to drought conditions), Israel will need to either curb its appetite for water consumption or find new

---

[23] Sara Roy, *Journal of Palestine Studies*, Vol. xxviii, no. 3, Spring 1999, 64-79.

sources. For the immediate future, surrender of the West Bank sources will not be an option for Israel.

## *Two wars, no peace (The October War of 1973 and the Lebanon War of 1982)*

Many of the Middle East wars since the creation of modern Israel have come about after the failure of intense peace negotiations. This was the case in 1948, as the international community failed to reach a settlement with the Arabs and war followed, as we documented in Chapter 4. Similarly, when peace might have been reached with Egypt in 1953-54, Israel joined the British and French plot that created the Suez Crisis marking the last time the United States took a strong position in the prevention of war in the Middle East. The 1967 War emerged as regional and international parties failed to resolve the growing tension between Israel and Syria on the northern border and with Egypt to the south. Israel's pre-emptive attack destroyed the Egyptian air force before a single plane lifted-off the runway, making the remainder of this abbreviated 'six day war' not so much a miracle as the success of Israel's first strike ability.

Again, the failure of the Arabs and Israel to reach an agreement based on what is still the international consensus on Israel and Palestine, United Nations Resolution 242 (Israeli withdrawal from territories captured in June 1967 in exchange for peace) and another war was within sight. An additional factor was the deep sense of humiliation felt by the Arabs following successive losses to Israel (1948 and 1967). Reversing the political alignments of his predecessor, Gamal Abdel Nasser, Egyptian President Anwar Sadat expelled Soviet advisors from Egypt in July 1972. Soviet influence remained with Egypt and Syria, but a new political dynamic was beginning. Then the Egyptians and Syrians caught Israel by surprise in the October War of 1973, and had Israel trapped during the initial week. Suddenly everything shifted in Israel's favour as the United States entered the arena on Israel's behalf, particularly when Israel was close to using nuclear weapons in its defence. The battles turned in Israel's favour and despite taking serious losses, Israel was the victor.

Cold War politics played a major role in the United States' support of the Israeli position in opposition to the formula of a United Nations Middle East peace conference, based on UN Resolution #242 (and #338 adopted after the War of 1973). Many in Europe and the Middle East were optimistic that a Geneva based peace conference would bring the major parties to the table under United Nations auspices, but opposition by the United States and Israel delayed it.

The new political alignment now came into play as Anwar Sadat made a surprising move flying to Israel in November 1977, and proclaiming in the Israeli Knesset Egypt's readiness to accept a peace treaty with Israel. Egypt was assailed by its Arab 'brothers' and a boycott was officially imposed on it by the Arab League of States. Egypt however pursued the bi-lateral Israeli-Egyptian peace process known as the Camp David Accords, which brought an Israeli withdrawal from the Sinai Peninsula and economic and political treaty between Egypt and Israel. It was signed on 17 September 1978, at Camp David, Maryland, by Israeli Prime Minister Menachem Begin, Anwar Sadat, and US President Jimmy Carter.

In theory, the Camp David Accords accepted UN Resolution 242 as the basis for a comprehensive peace between Israel and its neighbours, however the Accords had two major flaws. Israel interpreted UN 242 differently than did the rest of the international community, claiming it needed only to withdraw from 'territories', not all of the territories it had occupied since 1967. These differences of interpretation were allowed to stand without resolution, thus enabling the Israeli occupation over East Jerusalem, the West Bank, Gaza Strip, Golan Heights, and southern Lebanon to continue. The second flaw was the issue of the Palestinians which was left open-ended, and in fact, was never officially addressed.

On 6 October 1981, Anwar Sadat was assassinated by military officers thought to be involved with an Islamic political opposition movement. Egypt and Israel continued what has remained a 'cold peace', with no aggression between the two but with little positive benefits following from the Camp David accords other than increased US military assistance for both parties. However, the major Arab military power was 'sealed off' in a treaty with Israel, thus paving the way for Israel to deal with the question of Palestinian nationalism, 'once and for all'. The more militant Likud Government, led by Revisionist Zionists such as former Stern Gang operative Begin and the hawkish Ariel Sharon, now Defence Minister, were eager to attack Lebanon. With the country destabilized by six years of civil war, it was an opportune time to destroy the PLO leadership and its various resources in Beirut.

The Israeli invasion of Lebanon began on 4 June 1982, not 6 June as is generally reported. I was in Beirut with a team of Christian relief and development executives and recall vividly the massive bombardment of West Beirut's Fakhani district and the Citi Sportive, near our hotel. There were two air bombardments that day, each lasting twenty to thirty minutes, with US supplied F-16 aircraft committing significant damage with approximately 40 deaths and over 200 wounded. The rationale given by Israel was that of securing its northern border, however the incident given as justification for the attack was the attempted assassination of Israeli Ambassador Shlomo

Argov in London on 3 June. Scotland Yard issued a statement immediately after the incident that an anti-PLO movement led by the terrorist Abu-Nidal was responsible for the attack, and the PLO's ambassador in London was also on his hit-list. Despite the PLO denouncing the attack and having maintained a treaty on the Lebanon border that dated back to July 1981, Israel nevertheless used the opportunity to invade Lebanon.

The actual ground invasion began on 6 June 1982, and the war that followed lasted until the end of August of the same year. The Israeli's hoped to achieve a number of goals: to humiliate Syria; to destroy the PLO's headquarters and fighting forces in Lebanon; to crush Palestinian nationalism both inside Israel and also outside; and to place their Lebanese ally and Lebanon military strongman, Bashir Gemayel, on the throne as head of Lebanon. The scenario was in place by September 1982, however a number of problems occurred. The PLO was expelled from Lebanon and took up residence in eight other Arab countries, thus decentralizing the movement. Bashir Gemayel was elected President of Lebanon in early September, but died in an explosion two weeks later, possibly at the hands of Syria or pro-Syrian organizations in Lebanon. On 16-18 September, the tragic massacre at the Palestinian refugee camps of Sabra and Shatila in Beirut's southern suburbs left between 1000-4000 dead, an event that is still remembered by Palestinians.

## *The effects of political instability on Palestinian Christians*

With the most severe numerical decline of the Christian population in Palestine coming as a result of the 1948-49 *Nakba* period, the remaining fifty years have been witness to a steady decline in Christian numbers, influence, and vitality in Palestine. Most Israeli and Western analysts of the decline have pointed to factors other than the *Nakba*, Israeli occupation, and the political turmoil of the post-World War I/British Mandate period. Tsimhoni consistently downplays the above factors and although she makes occasional references to the 'great exodus of Christians' from Jerusalem, she fails to mention the Dalet Plan, the forced expulsions from Ramle, Haifa, Lydda and hundreds of other towns and villages that constituted the *Nakba*. Instead she establishes early in her narrative on 'demographic issues' that Israel 'staved off the Arab armies,' thus repeating the Zionist mythology discussed in the previous chapter. With no references to the Dalet Plan's intent to 'empty' or 'transfer' Palestinians from these population areas, the average reader assumes that the Israeli strategies were fully justified and were mere actions of self-defence. The framework is established for several explanations for the Christian exodus, but not the *Nakba*, not political decisions that undermined the Palestinian nationalist cause, and certainly not the Israeli occupation.

The proportion of Palestinian Christians to Muslims has decreased steadily since World War I due to three factors: the accelerated Christian emigration, the higher Muslim birth-rates, and the fact that Muslims are less likely to emigrate. It is striking to note that in 1922, the British census recorded 13,413 Muslims in Jerusalem as opposed to 14,699 Christians, thus Christians constituted 51.4 percent of the Palestinian population. By the second British census the Muslims had passed the Christians, with 19,894 Muslims to 19,335 Christians. The striking difference comes in 1961, when the Muslim population was 49,504 and the Christians had dropped to 10,982. The major cause for the drop was the *Nakba*, with emigration the second factor. Normal population growth for the Christians would have placed them in the 25,000-30,000 range or more. By 1989, official Israeli government figures placed the Muslims at 130,733 and Christians had grown to only 11,767.[24]

What Tsimhoni fails to mention is the acceleration of the Jewish population in Jerusalem, which was the equivalent of the Muslim population in 1922, but by 1990 had exceeded the Muslim population. The settlement of Jews in exclusive Jewish colonies (settlements) targeted the Jerusalem area with the goal of altering the demographics of not only the Western part of the city, but also of the formerly Arab East Jerusalem. By 2001 the Jewish population will surpass the combined Muslim and Christian population due to the focus by succeeding Israeli governments, both Labour and Likud, to solve the future status of Jerusalem by Judaizing the city.

Tsimhoni is correct in noting that there was a significant internal migration of Muslims from Hebron to Jerusalem, but she does not explain why so many jobs and shops in the Old City were suddenly available. Many of the vacated shops were owned by Christians who were forced to leave in 1948 or by their own volition decided to emigrate. Hebronites began to see the economic opportunity and took over many of the shops, which is understandable. Tsimhoni, however, is trying to create a case of Muslim 'takeover' of the jobs and forcing the Christians to emigrate. For example, she makes a rather trivial argument that since 1978, the mosques in the Old City have installed loudspeakers that broadcast sermons and commentary for long periods on Friday, which apparently have an intimidating effect on the local Christians. She draws this conclusion: '[The loudspeakers] though initiated by the Supreme Muslim Council in order to demonstrate the Islamic nature of Jerusalem in opposition to Israeli rule, this has hurt the Arab Christians first and foremost.'[25]

---

[24] Tsimhoni, *ibid.*, 20.

[25] *Ibid.*, 21.

It seems rather diversionary to base one's argument on the Muslim loudspeakers on Fridays as the main illustration of the Muslim power in the city which 'has hurt the Arab Christians.' Again, Tsimhoni fails to indicate how the Judaization has taken significant land from the Christian Quarter, and that outside the Old City, the situation is worse. Palestinian Christians (and Muslims) find it difficult to attain building permits when their families increase, thus forcing emigration. Colonies are built for exclusively Jewish settlement, but Palestinian Muslims and Christians have a housing shortage. Thus, the argument is somewhat minor with regard to the 'Muslim loudspeakers', when the Israeli government and local settlement organizations are seizing land at every opportunity, which is the single most serious factor in the emigration.

Many of the Palestinian Christians who emigrated after 1948 settled in Amman, Jordan, a matter that Tsimhoni views with suspicion. She cites a 1964 Jordanian census that lists 42,800 Christians (overwhelming majority are Palestinians), whereas in 1948 there were virtually none. While Tsimhoni generally renders negative comments concerning the plight of Christians in 'Muslim Jordan', the case is the opposite. Palestinian Christians have thrived in Jordan, particularly in Amman. They have succeeded in all professional fields and in business, and they have considerable influence. Their churches are generally large with schools and various Christian institutions that show tremendous vitality. The Orthodox Club is a highly desireable location for weddings and social events in Amman. Thus the Palestinian Christians in Amman have done very well in the social, material, and quality of life questions, but many still long for their original homes.

## Conclusion

To Tsimhoni's credit, her section on 'Trends Since 1967' is quite accurate in listing four basic reasons for the continued emigration of Christians. The list includes: 1) the lack of a political solution in the Arab-Israeli conflict; 2) the deterioration of the economy for Palestinians, especially for the urban middle class, which is the majority of Palestinian Christians; 3) the lack of affordable housing, particularly in Jerusalem; 4) the resurgence of Islam. While we can question her analysis and 'resurgence of Islam' argument, given more than a hint of an anti-Islamic bias, the other reasons are accurate. She fails to mention in each case that these negative developments build on the devastating losses during the *Nakba*, and all have been initiated by the Government of Israel, aside from those supported by internal divisions within the Palestinian Christian churches, whether of their own making or imposed by external political and ecclesiastical powers.

## Summary

1. The land of Palestine 'is competitively loved,' states Bishop Cragg, which points to the land being the core issue in the Israeli-Palestinian conflict. This rather small land, approximately the size of the state of Delaware or New Jersey in the United States, is only 10,162 square miles, but its strategic location and religious significance to the three Abrahamic religions makes it of central importance.

2. It can be argued from a position of international law that Britain did not have a legal right to advocate the Zionist cause and ignore the Palestinian case, nor did the Zionists have a claim enabling them to settle the land of Palestine.

3. Following the *Nakba*, the new Government of Israel concentrated on creating legal prohibitions against the refugees returning while simultaneously redrawing the demographics of Galilee. The expulsions from the Christian villages of Ikrit and Bir'am illustrate the case as does 'Operation Yohanan' which is an experiment to expel more Palestinians from Galilee.

4. The Greek Orthodox hierarchy has controlled the largest Church in Palestine in terms of its hierarchy being Greek; but the most devastating aspect is in its land arrangements with the 'government of Israel'. The Palestine Orthodox Congress has mounted a campaign to take back a portion of the land lost since 1948 and allow priests to become bishops. To date there has been no progress.

5. The rapid decline of Christians in Palestine since World War I has been due to several factors, the most serious of which are: Israel's continuing confiscation of Palestinian land and construction of exclusive Jewish settlements in their place, the lack of a political settlement, the forced expulsions during *al-Nakba*; and the lack of housing and jobs.

6. Gaining access and control of new sources of water has been a political goal of Israel since its creation in the 1940s, but it was realized with the territories conquered in 1967. Control of waters feeding the Sea of Galilee, the Jordan River, and Israel's sovereignty over the West Bank aquifers will be the unspoken factor underlying what territory Israel does and does not return in upcoming negotiations with Syria, Lebanon, and the Palestinian Authority.

7. The situation for Palestinian Christians continued to decline during the 1967-1993 period, with the number of Christians in Jerusalem and the West Bank falling to approximately 4 percent by the early 1990s. The primary political reasons for the emigration of Christians since 1967

include the following: severe political and economic instability, massive land confiscation, unemployment, severe shortages in housing.

# Chapter 8
## PALESTINE UNDER ZION:
## THE NEGATION OF TIME AND SPACE (1949-93)

One of the many profound scenes in Stephen Spielberg's *Schindler's List* occurs when the Nazi military commander brings his troops together on the eve of their attack on the Cracow Ghetto (1944). His speech recalls how Jews had fled Spain and other countries in order to find safe haven in cities such as Cracow some 700 years ago. He went on to recite the heights of scholarship and civic life that they reached. The pre-attack speech ended: 'Tomorrow we will make history. It will be as if those 700 years never happened.'

The conquest of weaker nations and ethnic or religious minorities by powerful nations and empires is a pattern repeated throughout history. The Ancient Egyptian, Assyrian, Babylonian, Greek, and Roman empires conquered ancient Israel and most of the Middle East, imposing their military regimes, culture, and political control upon the residents of these lands. Often the local population was 'transferred' (expelled) to the empire itself, usually accompanied with a significant loss of life and destruction of property. At other times the local population was brought under control through a severe military occupation, such as that which occurred during the 'Second Temple' period in Palestine during the time of Jesus. The Roman destruction of Jerusalem and expulsion of Jews in 66-70 and again in 132-5 AD represent a savage destruction of the Jewish community. It also involved a rewriting of history and the renaming of Jerusalem, which became Aelia Capitolina. An edict was issued by the Romans in 135 banishing Jews from the city. Similar patterns of conquest and control have been conducted in the modern colonial period by such empires as the British, French, German, Japanese, Spanish, the United States, Russia/Soviet, and many others, all of which used various methods of conquest, population transfers, and resettlement.

The conquering power generally embarked upon the rewriting of history after its perceived success, which includes its own narratives on the process of conquest and the history of the conquered, such as that proposed by the Nazi commander in *Schindler's List*. Common themes in 'conqueror histories' are such elements as the uncivilized nature of the indigenous people and the new opportunities now available, thanks to the new regime. The conquered land is often depicted as previously empty, undeveloped, or in need of 'civilized' people to give it value and unleash its potential. There are generally partial truths in these claims but the consequences of the new policies on the indigenous people are of little importance. The work of Edward Said (*Orientalism* and *Culture and Imperialism*) and many other literary critics have examined Western literature to demonstrate how it articulates the imagery and political ideology of the conquerors while simultaneously denigrating the indigenous Middle Eastern peoples. The work of pro-regime Western historians, novelists, the media, and often various components of academia are enlisted to provide a degree of respect and perceived objectivity to the 'history'. These views generally complement the ideology of the conquering powers.

The new State of Israel and the world Zionist movement embarked upon a similar campaign quite early in the history of Zionism, but accelerated the project following the events of 1948-49. The land of Palestine and Palestinians had been represented as a 'land of no people' by the early Zionists. The Jewish people were represented as the 'underdog' against the Arab nations who were Goliath the giant. Jewish refugees from Hitler would now come and 'make the desert bloom,' as if there were no civilized people, no agriculture, nor a culture of any value in the land prior to the birth of Israel. The wicked Philistines of biblical lore became the Palestinians who were enemies of 'God's people' and needed to be defeated.

The remarkably easy victory of Zionist forces over the Palestinians and Arab armies could then be represented to Western (predominantly Christian) nations and to Jews as a 'miracle', but the means of achieving that victory were never fully disclosed. The narratives of the indigenous ('conquered') people could always be denigrated as radical and far-fetched, especially if the conqueror had been the first to project their version of 'history'. In the case of the Palestinians much was ignored after 1948, including the 425 plus Palestinian villages destroyed and the 726,000 refugees created in the process. Professor Whitelam summarizes the project:

> ... it is the nation state, Israel, which has replaced Canaanite culture characterized as merely a loose conglomeration of city-states. Israel represents the ultimate in political evolution, the European nation state, and the pinnacle of civilization which surpasses and replaces that which is primitive and incapable of transformation. Thus Israel has replaced Palestine, and Israelite history thereby silences any Palestinian past ... The existence of the modern state and its claims to continuity with some earlier state of the Iron Age is the determining factor in the choice of terminology. The claim to continuity means that other claims to existence, other perceptions of the past, are effectively silenced. We are left with the history of Israel, past

and present. There is no Palestine and therefore cannot be a history of Palestine.[1]

The means by which Palestine was divested of meaning as a historical reality and Palestinians rendered invisible as a people are in part the tasks of this chapter. It will take a similar thematic approach as did the previous chapter and again focus on the events of 1948-1993. Whereas chapter 7 concentrated exclusively on Zionism's control of the land, here we examine three strategies of negation that were employed by the State of Israel in order to take total control of the land and people of Palestine while Israel began the long but steady process of Judaising the whole of Palestine. The three strategies to be examined in this chapter are: 1) the negation of Palestinian history including the negation of Palestinians as a distinct people; 2) the negation of Palestinian national identity and national consciousness (nationalism), including the right to an independent Palestinian state on Palestinian soil with representation by their own leadership; 3) the negation of peace (peace proposals that would in any manner compromise the ultimate Zionist goal of bringing all of Palestine under Jewish sovereignty). The overarching argument of the chapter is that the negation of the land (Chapter 7), of Palestinian nationalism, national identity as the Palestinian people, and the negation of a just peace, provide the context by which we can understand the rapid decline of Christians in the Holy Land during the past fifty years.

## The negation of history

Because the categories of history and land (or 'place') overlap it is necessary to review some of the conclusions of the previous chapter. Chapter 7 developed the Zionist's goal of complete control over historic Palestine which was achieved in two stages, December 1947-48 and the War of 1967. In the latter, Israel conquered not only the remainder of Palestine (East Jerusalem, the West Bank, and Gaza Strip) but also portions of Syria (the Golan Heights) and Egypt (the Sinai). In that East Jerusalem and the West Bank had been occupied and administered by Jordan since 1949, Israel effectively occupied portions of three Arab countries as well as the entirety of Palestine. By the end of 1978, Israel invaded and occupied a significant section of southern Lebanon, which was consolidated during the Lebanon War of 1982, including

---

[1] Keith W Whitelam, *The Invention of Ancient Israel*, Routledge Books, New York, 1996, 56.

the placement of a pro-Israel President in Lebanon and the expulsion of the PLO at the end of the War.

However, Israel's primary focus was historic Palestine and control of the resources, economy, and the military occupation of the Palestinian people in East Jerusalem, West Bank, and Gaza Strip. The Judaisation of Galilee provided the working model for what Israel began to implement in the Territories. Important is the fact that in 1967, there were virtually no Jews in the West Bank and Gaza Strip, with East Jerusalem (including the Old City) having only 5,000 (against 70-75,000 Palestinian Christian and Muslim Arabs). Thus there would need to be an implanting of Jews in these territories, a programme that began immediately after the War of 1967 with the Labour Party's settlements, or exclusive Jewish communities, on what was formerly Palestinian land.

Through this sophisticated and persistent programme of creating 'facts on the ground', Israel would be able to claim sovereignty (not recognized by most nations nor by the United Nations) in over 60 percent of the West Bank and 40 percent of the Gaza Strip, and approximately 98 percent of Jerusalem. The Jewish population in previously 'Arab' East Jerusalem will soon surpass the Arab population if the Jewish-'only' settlements continue to be built. Palestinians need only learn the lessons of 1948, when the Palestinian population of all of Jerusalem (including the sub-districts) was 110,000 and Jews nearly 100,000. Palestinians owned 84 percent of the property (14 percent was public and 2 percent owned by Jews). During the *Nakba*, 70,000 Palestinians were forced out of what became West Jerusalem and became refugees, with Israel seizing their property.

On the eve of the 1967 War, East Jerusalem had a population of 70-75,000, 95 percent of whom were Palestinian Arabs. By the year 2000, Jewish settlers reached 176,000, with 200,100 Palestinian Arabs.[2] By 2005 it is projected that the settlers will surpass the Palestinians, thus enabling a long-term Zionist goal to be achieved.

Complementing the Israeli occupation and colonization of Palestine has been a denial and replacement of Palestinian history. From Herzl to Netanyahu, Israeli leaders and their spokespersons in the West have generally articulated a view that Palestinians were of little no value ('A land of no people for a people with no land'), with no legitimate claims to Palestine. Mainstream Zionist ideologues re-mythologized issues of land, places, human and national rights, and even questions of who initiated hostilities in the wars of 1948, 1956, 1967, 1973, and 1982. One of the consistent themes in Zionist mythology that still has currency in the West is 'The Jews shall make

2 Martha Wenger, 'Jerusalem', *Middle East Report*, May-June 1993, 10.

the desert bloom,' despite independent accounts of Palestinian success in agriculture The underlying message was always that Zionism has a right to the land and Palestinian Christians and Muslims do not. The 'make the desert bloom' myth contains at least three vital elements that would benefit the Zionist cause: Jews have a right to the land, Palestine was only desert before Jews returned, and now Israel will bring a miracle to this desert and create a 'real' nation. 'Real' history commences, according to this view, when the Jews return to the land and particularly when they become a state. The myth has been wrapped in biblical imagery that has increased its marketing value in the European and North American nations who have familiarity with biblical themes.

How does Zionism make its historical claim if there were so few Jews in Palestine after the Roman expulsion of 135 AD? Do the Palestinians have a stronger claim in as much as they have had a continuous presence since the 1st century and perhaps back to the Canaanites? Were they not the ancient ancestors of today's Palestinians and therein have their own claim to the land?

Zionists wrestled with these issues in the early years of the *Yeshuv* (pre-1948 Israel). One of the most influential of the early Zionist ideologues from this era was Aaron David Gordon (1856-1922), who is generally accepted as the most influential thinker of the 'second *Aliya*' (1897-1920). Gordon arrived in Palestine in 1904 to do physical labour and serve as one of the pioneers in the *Yeshuv*. His uncompromising principles, ideals, simple lifestyle, and his probing analysis gained respect among the early Zionists. Gordon was an interesting blend of the socialism he had learned as a youth in Russia and Jewish mysticism.

Zionism in this early phase of its development was still open to a variety of perspectives with a significant number of 'liberal' thinkers whose Zionism was influenced more by Marxist concepts and European democratic socialism than by the tribal nationalism of Germany that came to dominate the ideology of Herzl, Weizmann, and Ben-Gurion. When asked about the Palestine question, Gordon was clearly torn, according to the Hebrew University political philosopher Zeev Sternhell. Gordon recognized that the Arabs had a historical right to Palestine, but he immediately added: 'but our historical right is undoubtedly greater.' He justified it on two grounds: first, the sweat and blood of those who worked the land; and second, the historical linkage back to the Bible. Even as a secular thinker, Gordon accepted a type of biblical argument:

> It all came from us; it was created among us. And what did the
> Arabs produce in all the years they lived in the country? Such

creations or even the creation of the Bible alone give us a perpetual right over the land in which we were so creative, especially since the people that came after us did not create such works in this country, or did not create anything at all.[3]

As Sternhell's important book demonstrates in early Zionism, significantly influenced by a blend of Marxism and the secular liberal European tradition, one sees the tribal ('Germanic') form of nationalism gaining a foothold in Zionist ideology. Here the biblical particularism overrides natural (inalienable) rights and universal doctrines of human and civil rights are overridden by the 'clan' (a community among communities). Tribal Zionism is what dominated the mainstream of Zionist ideology from Herzl and Gordon to Chaim Weizmann and David Ben-Gurion, and remains in effect with the Labour and Likud parties in Israel. The humanist and social democratic traditions were in fact transformed by tribal Zionism so they too reflect varying degrees of a 'tribalism of the left', which one still finds in Israel in the Meritz and the left of centre Labour Party Shimon Peres.

Keith Whitelam, although commenting on the state of biblical archaeology, might be discussing tribal Zionist versions of the history of Israel and Palestine when he writes: 'The land that might be termed "Palestine" has no intrinsic value of its own but becomes the arena for the "real and authentic history" of Israel.'[4] The operational assumption in much of contemporary biblical archaeology is that nothing of significance occurred in the Holy Land before Abraham's arrival nor after the Second Temple period (70 AD), and became meaningless again until the 'return' of the Jews in 1948. Pre-Abrahamic Palestine is of little interest to Western biblical archaeology and most other forms of scholarship. Further, what occurred among Palestinian Christians and later Muslims between 70 AD and the present day is little significance. Thus ancient Canaan and contemporary Palestinians have been effectively silenced. Until the early to mid-1980s Palestine and Palestinian history either did not exist or it awaited the few shreds of legitimacy granted by scholars approved by mainstream Zionists. In this regard, it remains an astounding fact that Golda Meir, Prime Minister of Israel, could boldly state as late as 1969:

There was no such thing as Palestinians ... It was not as though there was a Palestinian people in Palestine considering itself

---

[3] A Gordon as quoted in Zeev Sternhell, *The Foundling Myths of Israel*, Princeton University Press, Princeton, New Jersey, 1998, 71-2.

[4] Whitelam, *ibid*, 43.

as a Palestinian people and we came and threw them out and took their country away from them. They did not exist.[5]

The fact that she was addressing a journalist with one of London's major newspapers indicates that Golda Meir's working assumption was that Palestinians were essentially invisible and could now be folded into the Arab masses somewhere in the Middle East, but clearly not in Palestine.

Meir was simply restating what Herzl once wrote in his diary: 'We shall spirit the penniless population into the neighbouring countries.' Just as the population was unnamed and unknown to Herzl, in a similar fashion Lord Balfour did not name the 90 percent majority population in his infamous declaration which called Palestinians 'the existing non-Jewish communities in Palestine'. Balfour was more precise when he later elaborated on his views:

For in Palestine we do not propose even to go through the form of consulting the wishes of the present inhabitants of the country; though the American Commission has been going through the forms of asking what they are. The four great powers are committed to Zionism and Zionism, be it right or wrong, good or bad, is rooted in age-long traditions, in present needs, in future hopes, of far profounder import than the desire of the 700,000 Arabs who now inhabit the land. In my opinion that is right.[6]

Perhaps Golda Meir assumed the project of replacing Palestine and Palestinian history had been completed by 1969 and it was time to test her assumptions. Or one could argue that the Israeli Prime Minister believed the Palestinians were non-entities, and was simply careless in revealing in public what she really believed. After all, with the quick and devastating defeat of the Arabs in 1967 having just been completed, the Israelis were feeling very much in control, perhaps bordering on arrogance. Finally, all of Jerusalem and historic Palestine were theirs, and it was time to complete the task of replacing or at least marginalizing the Palestinians in various parts of the land.

In like manner, biblical archaeology became an important instrument of advancing the overlapping political and religious case of Zionism. Whitelam

---

[5] *The Sunday Times*, 15 June 1969; quoted in David Gilmour, *The Dispossessed*, Sphere Books, London, 1980, 12.

[6] Lord Arthur Balfour as quoted in Colin Chapman, *Whose Promised Land?*, Lion Publishing Company, Batavia, Illinois, 1992, 61.

points out that biblical archaeology has intentionally concentrated on the late Bronze Age and early Iron Age with a near exclusive focus on areas within the State of Israel today. Little serious scholarship ventures outside these parameters to examine earlier periods of archaeological interest, such as pre-Abrahamic Canaan.

Whitelam describes how research on ancient Israel has been shaped by the modern nation-state Israel and the ideology of tribal Zionism.

> The dominant model for the presentation of Israelite history has been, and continues to be, that of a unified national entity in search of national territory struggling to maintain its national identity and land through the crises of history. It is a concept of the past which mirrors the presentation of the present. Zionism, with its roots in nineteenth-century European nationalist movements, has invariably presented its 'historic mission' in terms of a return to an empty, desert wasteland awaiting European technology ... in order to make it habitable and prosperous.[7]

Whitelam continues his analysis: 'It is also a "master story" that creates ancient Israel in its own image, the image of Western nation states, and at the same time silences other possible accounts of ancient Palestine's past.'[8] Therefore, by emphasizing a particular interpretation of ancient Israel concerning the land, the covenant with the Jews, the conquest of the Holy Land, etc., while ignoring the archaeology of ancient Canaan or early Palestinian Christianity, the case for Palestine has been obliterated. The message of ancient Israel without the broader context of Canaan or early Christianity, let alone Islam, provides ample justification for modern Israel and Zionism to eclipse Palestine, whether ancient or modern. In fact, most scholars, clergy, and laity never consider the case for Palestine.

Perhaps more challenging to the usual fare offered by Western biblical archaeology is the work of Professor Ze'ev Herzog and a number of Israeli and international scholars who, like Whitelam, are challenging the core assumptions of the field. Herzog is Professor of Archaeology and Ancient Oriental Cultures at Tel Aviv University in Israel and one of the most highly regarded Israeli archaeologist. His recent revelations are not new as they have been discussed among scholars for at least a generation, but recently the following views have gained international attention thanks to Herzog:

---

[7] Whitelam, *ibid.*, 21.
[8] *Ibid.*, 28.

1.  There was no sudden military conquest of ancient Canaan by Joshua but the cities declined gradually over hundreds of years.
2.  There is no evidence for the Exodus from Egypt, nor for the Wilderness Wanderings, nor proof that the Hebrew people were in Egypt during the time of the Patriarch Joseph through the time of Moses.
3.  There were hundreds of small villages and clusters of farms throughout Palestine in the Early Bronze Age (around 1200 BC), but not an ancient kingdom of Israel nor a loose tribal confederation. Ancient Canaan or Palestine may have been filled with a variety of tribes and ethnic groups but scholars are uncertain of the origins of the Jews.
4.  The name Israel was given to one of these rural population groups who lived in ancient Canaan. The earliest reference is 1208 BC according to an Egyptian document from the period of Merenptah, king of Egypt in this period.[9]

Putting aside the more radical thesis of the new Israeli archaeologists, let us return to Professor Whitelam. If his analysis of biblical scholarship is even 'half' correct, then biblical scholars and archaeologists in particular have to re-examine their operational assumptions as they have serious geopolitical consequences. Whitelam is harsh when he states:

> Biblical scholarship ... has collaborated in an act of dispossession, or at the very least, to use [Edward] Said's phrase, 'passive collaboration' in that act of dispossession. The construction of the literary entity 'ancient Israel' ... has silenced the history of the indigenous people of Palestine in the early Iron Age ... the failure to acknowledge the constructions of the past which have dominated the discourse of biblical studies for the past century or more are shaped by political and social locations, has ensured the silencing of Palestinian history.[10]

Just as Zionism and the mainstream of biblical archaeology have found historical (and political) linkage between ancient Israel and present-day Zionist Israel, so too has there been a negation of ancient Palestine

---

[9] Ze'ev Herzog, 'Deconstructing the Walls of Jericho', *Ha'aretz*, 29 October 1999; reprinted in *News from Within*, Vol. XV, No. 11, December 1999.

[10] Whitelam, *ibid.*, 222.

(Canaan), Christian and Muslim Palestine, and modern Palestinian history. The task of both biblical archaeology and modern Middle Eastern historians, be they church historians or secular, is to recover that silenced history and continuity from the present, back 2,000 years to Palestinian Christianity, and even to ancient pre-Abrahamic Canaan. Only if biblical, archaeological and secular, historical scholarship become intellectually free to research and articulate a Palestinian history that retains what is known of ancient Israel and Palestinian Judaism while affirming the Palestinian dimension, from the pre-Abrahamic period until the present, will there be any hope of saving Palestinian Christianity from extinction; we will also be on the road to justice for Jews and Arabs alike. This quest has barely begun but it is essential if we are to outgrow the damaging myths that have led us back to tribalism, which has a habit of revisiting the Promised Land.

Must we leave this discussion in an 'either/or' dimension? Cannot the Holy Land be shared with three religions and two nations having equal legitimacy? Why must one dominate at the expense of eclipsing the other? The maximalist Christian position is represented by the Crusades, the maximalist Islamist perspective by Islamic Jihad or the Muslim Brotherhood in Egypt, and the maximalist Jewish perspective articulated by revisionist Zionists and elements of the ultra-orthodox parties whose power is steadily increasing in Israel.

Bishop Cragg has commented on Zionism's moral dilemma in this regard:

> There is in Zionism an exilic necessity for the other party, the paradox of gathering from out of diaspora and an exodus into one.[11]

Certainly, most Zionist readers will take exception to the bishop's analysis, but it is a challenge they must hear and offer a thoughtful reply. Does mainstream Zionism carry 'an exilic necessity for the other party?' Are there not voices in Israel and the American Jewish community that are challenging the policies of the contemporary state? Aside from the humanist school of Zionists like Buber, Judah Magnes, Ahad Ha'am and others, and the 'New Historians' of today, Zionism has not been able to see the Palestinian as equal. Most tributaries of Zionism have rejected principles of universal and inalienable human rights for Palestinians (including national rights) and hence our dilemma. The history of Palestine and of Palestinians has been an exercise that necessitated ratification by the State of Israel, until recently.

---

[11] Cragg, *Palestine: The Prize and Price of Zion*, 18.

The arrival of the 'new' Israeli historians such as Benny Morris, Ilan Pappe, Avi Shlaim, Tom Segev, Meron Benvenisti, are changing the parameters of the debate, offering hope, a re-examination of past deeds, and the beginning of a sincere quest for truth and justice. As they and others gain influence on the body politic, as is slowly beginning to happen, the seeds of hope for a truly just peace take on an element of realism. However, the forces arguing for maintaining the status quo remain strong and in control.

## The negation of Palestinian nationalism

We have noted the significant role that Palestinian Christians played in the rise of Palestinian national consciousness in the post-1900 period leading up to World War I. Palestinian Christians such as Khalil al-Sakakini, George Antonius, Khalis Iskandar al-Qubrusi and Najib Nassar, all in Galilee, were committed to a non-sectarian nation-state that would be democratic while respecting the three Abrahamic religious communities. Jerusalem-based nationalists had Christian involvement but the leadership tended to be Muslim, with several of the traditional families at the centre of the movement, including Said al-Husseini, Ruhi al-Khalidi, Muhammad al-Budairi, and the great resistance fighter of the *Nakba*, Abdel Khadir al-Husseini.[12] Whether in Galilee, Nablus, or Jerusalem, all Palestinian nationalists were concerned about the emergence of any ethno-religious nationalism whether it be Muslim, Jewish, or Christian as it would inevitably relegate minorities to a second class status.

In the initial phase of the Palestinian national struggle, the leaders were opposed by Ottoman officials and later the Zionist-British alliance of the post-World War I era. The University of Chicago Middle East historian and political scientist, Rashid Khalidi, has argued convincingly in *Palestinian Identity* that Palestinian nationalism was not a mere reaction to Zionism:

> ... the argument that Zionism was the main factor in provoking the emergence of Palestinian identity ignores one key fact: a universal process was unfolding in the Middle East during this period, involving an increasing identification with the new states created by the post-World War I partitions ... As part of this universal process, moreover, Lebanese, Syrians, Egyptians,

---

[12] Rashid Khalidi, *Palestinian Identity*, Columbia University Press, New York, 1997, 19 and 223. Khalidi gives a useful history of the emergence of Palestinian national consciousness with attention to the early Palestinian press in Galilee and Jerusalem.

Iraqis and Jordanians all managed to develop their respective nation-state nationalisms during the same period without the dubious benefit of a Zionist challenge.[13]

The influences were more the Arab nationalist thinkers in Syria (Michel Aflak) and European nationalism, as well as the Palestinian desire for independence from foreign occupation, which at that period was Ottoman.

It must be reiterated that Palestinian nationalism was not derived from Jewish nationalism nor was it a mere reaction to Zionism, as many Zionist analysts are inclined to argue. Christian nationalists were ideologically motivated by the Western forms of nationalism to which they had been exposed but also through the wisdom that that comes from their experience as a religious minority, Christians would only survive in Middle Eastern societies if they were democratic, secular, and accepted universal norms for human rights.

The national movement was broken by the Ottoman overlords before World War I and then by the British whose designs for Palestine had no place for an independent Palestinian state. After Britain facilitated rapid Zionist settlement in the 1920-mid-1930s, the Palestinian national struggle continued, and there was no division between Muslims and Christians. As Hajj Amin al-Husseini emerged as the dominant figure in the Palestinian national struggle, he had several Christian advisors at the core of the leadership, including Christian nationalist George Antonius. British allowances for high levels of Jewish settlement in the 1930s exploded in frustration during the Palestinian revolt of 1936-39. The crushing of the revolt combined with the destruction of the Palestinian community in 1948, leaving more than half of community as refugees, led to nearly two decades of struggling for mere survival. National consciousness became secondary to survival, relief for the needy refugees, and reconstruction, with the international community carrying much of the burden through the United Nations Relief and Refugee Works Association (UNRWA), with help from the Arab League. Christian and Muslim relief efforts were also significant. The national struggle for liberation would be postponed.

Palestinian theologian Cedar Duaybis has observed that Zionist leaders had a secondary goal in Plan Dalet, the destruction of Palestinian nationalism. 'They [the Zionists] targeted the urban areas, particularly Haifa and Jerusalem for two reasons: to depopulate Palestinians from these areas and seize them for the new Jewish state, but also to eliminate nationalism.' She added: 'As a native of Haifa we had a tradition of independent nationalist

---

[13] *Ibid.*, 20.

thought which was passed on by our families, churches, and teachers. After the *Nakba* this was disrupted until the mid-1960s.'[14]

The 1950s witnessed the revival of Arab nationalism throughout the Middle East with Beirut, Damascus, Cairo, and Baghdad being centres. The most prominent movements and parties were secular pan-Arab types such as the *Ba'ath* (Renaissance) party, initially in Syria and later in Iraq, which had from the beginning both Muslims and Christians at the centre of leadership. Egyptian president Gamal Abdel Nasser inspired pan-Arab unity and liberation during this period, calling for Arabs to seek independence from European domination and from Zionism.

During the late 1950s-60s, the American University of Beirut became a major centre for Arab nationalism. One of the first Palestinian organizations to emerge was the Movement of Arab Nationalists (MAN), founded by a Palestinian refugee of the *Nakba* Greek Orthodox Palestinian Christian and paediatrician Dr George Habash. MAN and its successor, the Popular Front for the Liberation of Palestine were Marxist and called for the destruction of Zionism and the creation of one secular democratic state in Palestine. Christians and Muslims in the diaspora as well as inside historic Palestine were drawn to Habash and the movement, many remaining loyal until today. Nevertheless, the Christians and Muslims were fully united in the national struggle, with no signs of attacks on the other.

In the late 1950s-early 60s, another Palestinian nationalist movement emerged from the slums and refugee camps of the Gaza Strip and Cairo, fully independent of the Beirut and West Bank Palestinians. Ideologically, it was grounded in a blend of the Muslim Brotherhood movement and Nasser's pan-Arabism. *Fateh* (Arabic for the 'opening' or 'victory') began as a student movement in Cairo and took the name, the Arabic acronym for the Palestine National Liberation Movement. Most of the founding members were sons of Palestinian refugees who settled in the impoverished refugee camps of the Gaza Strip in 1948.[15] Among them were Salah Khalif (later Abu Iyad), Khalil al-Wazir (Abu Jihad, later head of the PLO's military wing), Farouk Khaddoumi (Abu Lutof, head of the PLO's political department), and Yasser Arafat (Abu Ammar), who became chair in 1969. Farsoun observes:

> What distinguished *Fateh* from the start was that its ideology went against the grain of the pan-Arabism of the times. The group believed that the cause of Palestine would be advanced and won only by Palestinians, not by the Arab states,

---

[14] Cedar Duaybis in an interview with the author, Jerusalem, 8 January 2000.
[15] Alain Gresh, *The PLO: The Struggle Within*, Zed Books Ltd., London: 1985, 251-1.

reversing the conventional discourse of pan-Arabism.[16]

*Fateh* became the dominant Party of the Palestinian national movement, and while led initially by a close clique of Muslims (influenced by the Muslim Brotherhood), it developed into a secular democratic movement with a disproportionate number of Christians in the leadership by the early 1970s. Among them was perhaps the greatest spokesman, the poet and writer Kamal Nasser, who was assassinated by a hit-squad led by the current Prime Minister of Israel, Ehud Barak, in a covert terrorist act in Beirut (1972).

From the beginning, the PLO was committed to armed struggle against Israel in order to liberate Palestine, a controversial belief that was at the centre of the Palestine National Charter (adopted in 1965) until the Palestine National Council meeting of November 1988. At that meeting the PLO accepted a 'two-state solution' to the Palestine problem (which implied *de jure* recognition of the state of Israel). The Habash-led PFLP was more ideological than *Fateh* and therefore rejected the 'two-state solution'. PFLP continues to hold to the one-state resolution, or 'a secular democratic state in all of Palestine'. The PFLP maintained its commitment to armed struggle, which included such militant strategies as the hijacking of civilian aircraft, attacks on Jewish civilians (Munich Olympic games in 1972), and military resistance to Jordan, which led to the disastrous Black September of 1971-72. These initiatives brought international attention to the Palestinian cause but generally not in a sympathetic way, as governments and the general public were shocked by these tactics and most Westerners were sympathetic to Zionism.

Another Marxist group, the Democratic Front for the Liberation of Palestine (DFLP), emerged in the late 1960s but it sought a more independent line of thought and support. The group was Marxist but not aligned to the Soviet Union or any of the eager sponsors. Led by another Palestinian Christian, Naif Hawatmeh, the movement tended to emphasize grass-roots involvement. A large number of Palestinian Christians in Lebanon, Jordan, and the West Bank joined the PFLP or DFLP rather than *Fateh* and smaller groups.

Three significant developments occurred in 1974. On 12 June, the Palestine National Council, which is the PLO's Parliament, replaced its previous goal of establishing a secular democratic state in all of historic Palestine, with that of a secular democratic state in any part of liberated Palestine. This was an indirect recognition of Israel but Israel (and the United

---

[16] Farsoun, *ibid.*, 176.

States) did not acknowledge this development as significant. Then on 28 October, the Arab summit meeting in Rabat, Morocco, affirmed the PLO as the 'sole legitimate representative of the Palestinian people', which removed Jordan or Syria as representatives of Palestine in future negotiations.

In November 1974, Yasser Arafat addressed the United Nations General Assembly which was a significant advancement for the Palestinian case, as he held out a gun but also an olive branch to the world and to Zionists:

> When we speak of our common hopes for the Palestine of the future, we include in our perspective all Jews now living in Palestine who choose to live with us there in peace and without discrimination ... that we might live together in a framework of a just peace in our democratic Palestine.[17]

The General Assembly then passed UN Resolution 3236 which reaffirmed the PLO as the 'sole legitimate representative of the Palestinian people'. Instead of utilizing this historic opportunity for peace negotiations, both Israel and the United States ignored the opportunities after the 1973 war and peace fell by the wayside.

Israel shifted the focus of debate to what Arafat mean by this phrase: 'Palestine ... in our perspective all Jews who chose to live with us in peace and without discrimination.' Did he mean that Israel as they knew it had to be destroyed, which was the dominant rhetoric from the Zionist's analysis of the Palestinian Charter? Did Arafat mean that the political ideology and practice of Zionism must be dismantled, and a de-Zionised state could be constructed? Was the movement closer to saying there would be two states, one Jewish and one Palestinian? The ambiguity of language was always a characteristic of Arafat, who became sometimes a master of 'double-speak' so as to provide sufficient political manoeuvrability. This strategy was often necessary due to the many Arab states who wished to control or weaken the PLO, in addition to the Zionists and Israel. Syria always saw Palestine as part of 'Greater Syria', and Assad had Arafat and Kaddoumi imprisoned in the late 1960s, and has often tried to undercut the PLO. Thus the movement has been forced to 'play off' any one of a number of Arab leaders while maintaining its struggle against Israel. The PLO's position on accepting Israel's right to exist did not become clear until 1988 in the Algiers Declaration of an independent Palestinian state in East Jerusalem, the West Bank and Gaza Strip.

Little known is the first major movement of Christian support for

---

[17] Colin Chapman, *Whose Promised Land?*, Lion Publishing, Oxford, 1983, 97.

Palestinian nationalism, the 'Christians for Palestine' conference, held in Beirut in the summer of 1969. Among the speakers were Yasser Arafat, Dr George Habash, Kamal Nasser, and a number of Lebanese Arabists who brought the secular democratic vision for Palestine into the churches. It was primarily supported by the World Student Christian Federation and the Antiochian Orthodox Church. The architect and heart of the movement was the Director of the WSCF Office in Beirut, Gabriel Habib, a product of the Orthodox Youth Movement in Lebanon. Habib was a Lebanese Christian of the Antiochian Church and a law student at the American University in Beirut. He was heavily influenced by Arab nationalism during his student years and by Bishop Georges Khodr. Habib went on to become the founding general secretary of the Middle East Council of Churches in 1974, but never lost his vision of blending Christian support for a secular democratic movement within the Arab states.

Israel's opposition to Palestinian nationalism was severe and comprehensive. In Israel proper and in the Occupied Territories (East Jerusalem, West Bank, and Gaza Strip) it was illegal to belong to any organization affiliated with the PLO, or to talk with any member of the PLO, print or articulate PLO political material and statements, and even to display the Palestinian flag and colours (including on one's person). At any given time there were 10-15,000 Palestinians incarcerated within Israel and the Occupied Territories, Palestinians were prevented from organizing any political party in Israel that opposed Zionism, which left only the Israeli Communist Party as an option for most Palestinians (it was often led by Christians). In the Israeli Occupied Territories, PLO cells sprang up underground and virtually every Palestinian became a member, but lived with the insecurity of infiltration by the Israeli intelligence and certain imprisonment.

The Israeli victory over the Arab states in June 1967 did not dismantle Palestinian nationalism, but it did alter its trajectory. Another 245,000-300,000 Palestinian refugees were forced out, some from the West Bank becoming refugees for the second time in twenty years.[18]Again, a large number of Palestinian Christians were either forced to flee or chose to emigrate, given another war and now an Israeli occupation. But Palestinian resistance became stronger, with the locus shifting first to Jordan, and after the Black September crisis to Lebanon. By the mid-1970s there were 450,000 Palestinian refugees in Lebanon and the PLO became a major political force in the internecine struggle of Lebanese politics. Steady Palestinian raids on Israel and rocket

---

[18] David McDowall, *Palestine and Israel: The Uprising and Beyond*, University of California Press, Berkeley and Los Angeles, 1989, 84.

attacks on the northern Israeli villages brought savage Israeli bombardments and invasions. In 1978 Israel invaded Lebanon up to the Litani River, creating at least temporarily over 250,000 Lebanese and Palestinian internal refugees. Israel withdrew partially, but maintained a five-mile 'security zone' across the south of Lebanon which was patrolled jointly by Israel and an Israeli trained and sponsored Lebanese militia (the SLA or Southern Lebanese Army).

The leader of the movement, Major Saad Haddad, was a Lebanese Christian who defected from the Lebanese army with several hundred colleagues to join Israel's effort in the south of Lebanon. Haddad became a 'favourite son' of Israel, who sponsored him from his 'shoelaces to his Uzis'. Haddad became a celebrity with American Christian fundamentalist groups oriented toward the Christian Zionists. He regularly toured the United States to raise funds and serve as one of Israel's public relations models with American Christians.

However, Israel's prime concern in Lebanon was the destruction of Palestinian nationalism and establishing a pro-Israel Lebanese regime. By the late 1970s, the district along the southern coast of Lebanon, beginning with the slums of south Beirut to the Israeli border, was unaffectionately called by Israel 'Fatehland'. On 6 June 1982, Israel launched a massive invasion by air, land, and sea. I had the misfortune of being in Lebanon with a delegation of Christian relief and development leaders for the initial ten days of the war that dragged on until late August. At that point the United States under Ambassador Philip Habib and Saudi diplomats negotiated a PLO withdrawal from Lebanon, including over 10,000 Palestinian fighters, leaving the refugee camps and impoverished south-suburban areas unprotected. Our American delegation had a meeting scheduled with the US ambassador and staff on Sunday 6 June 1982, at approximately 9:00 a.m. We were sitting with the ambassador when he received word that a full-scale invasion was underway. The ambassador put his head in his hands and said something unprintable about the US administration encouraging the Israeli hawks, Prime Minister Begin, Defence Minister Sharon, military commander Rafael Eitan, and the Likud government. These three had been looking for a war with the Palestinians for over a year, and had in fact conducted a bloody three weeks of raids and counter-raids during July 1981. A treaty secretly arranged by Saudi Arabia brought Israel and the PLO to the negotiating table and both sides agreed to halt all terrorist operations and violence over the Lebanon border. The PLO abided by the accord without a single infraction until April 1982, when a few Katushya rockets were launched in response to an Israeli air-raid that killed 19 children and 14 adults. The Palestinian targets were symbolic gestures and fell far from civilian populations. However, during the July 1981-May 1982 truce period, the United Nations counted over 1,100

Israeli violations of the border and one by the Palestinians.

The Lebanese War represents one in which Israel was the clear aggressor and as in 1948, had an overwhelming advantage in the number of troops, technology, and the sheer fact that the PLO had no airforce and no navy. Sophisticated F-15 and F-16 aircraft and the latest in US military technology was field-tested on the Palestinian and Lebanese populations. The war did remove the PLO from Lebanon but did little to quench the power of Palestinian nationalism, which was perhaps the major goal.

The Sabra-Shatila massacre of 16-18 September 1982 was the chilling sign given to the Palestinians left behind in Lebanon. The massacre had high level Israeli co-ordination and military support but the actual killing was carried out by various Lebanese rightist militias. Many believe the Lebanese militias included a unit from Major Haddad's SLA, plus Phalangist units authorized by Bashir Gemayel and Samir Geaga. I interviewed eyewitnesses to the killings at the camps on the day after the massacre, when survivors were just returning to dig bodies out of the rubble with the Red Cross and Lebanese Boy Scouts. They described an outright butchering, including beheading men and cutting of fingers to take their gold rings. Estimates ranged from 800 to 4,000 for those who were murdered in the two camps. I personally witnessed mass burials by the Red Cross and Red Crescent which included over 600 body bags in one large grave at the southern edge of Shatila Camp. Preparations were underway for another grave of similar size on the opposite side of the camp. These numbers plus other factors place the total number of Palestinians massacred in this incident in the 2,000-2,500 range.

Following the Lebanon War of 1982, the PLO and Palestinian nationalism in general had been decentralized with Arafat and most of the leadership in far-away Tunis and his military forces were scattered across eight Arab countries. By 1987 the PLO was clearly suffering from a lack of co-ordination which resulted in declining international respect. Inside the West Bank and Gaza Strip, Israel was having its way with massive settlement construction, the denial of national expressions of political support for the PLO, frequent closure of universities, and a steadily growing prison population. It appeared in early November 1987, that Palestinian nationalism was at its lowest ebb since the founding of the PLO. What remains amazing is the resilience of Palestinian nationalism, which, after 100 years of various Ottoman, British, Zionist, American and fellow Arab countries' attempts to silence or destroy it, continues to be strong with a significant capacity to reinvent itself from the grass roots to the top of Palestinian society.

## The negation of peace

Before Benyamin Netanyahu became Prime Minister of Israel, he served several Israeli posts in the United States where he was known as a clever 'spin-doctor' for the Likud party. During the Gulf War and the various Middle East peace negotiations that followed, Netanyahu was fond of using the phrase 'Arafat never misses an opportunity to miss an opportunity.' The argument was convincing on the surface as Arafat and the PLO appear to be the ones opposing Israel's peaceful offers.

In the interest of space I will examine only one of the five Arab-Israeli wars of the past fifty years, that of 1948. This particular conflict is important for three reasons: 1) it established the pattern of propaganda and basic themes that are still in use, particularly among Israel's Western allies; 2) several important Israeli historians have analysed the 1948-49 period and have in effect countered the dominant Zionist narrative concerning the events of these years; 3) most important is the fact that Palestinians suffered their highest losses of land and population living in historic Palestine during 1948-9, and most grievances concerning land, political sovereignty, refugees, compensation, and a just peace must begin with 1948.

One of the first of Israel's 'New Historians' was Simha Flapan, a founder of the state in 1948. In his final years, Flapan focused his energy on researching several of the founding myths of Israel but gave particular attention to the 1948-49 period. Flapan argued that during April 1948, the United Nations set up a truce commission in an effort to prevent the impending war in Palestine with the British withdrawal scheduled to begin within a month. He notes that the Arab countries were torn about the fighting, but there was an opportunity to negotiate a cease-fire that might have prevented the *Nakba*. Egypt and Syria were prepared to support a cease-fire while Transjordan was not. He quotes the United States ambassador in Cairo who cabled the State Department to the effect that the Arabs were ready to sign any face-saving device that would allow them to back away from their overstated rhetoric.

The United States had proposed that there be a ceiling of Jewish immigrants allowed per year in exchange for a truce. To sweeten the deal, the United States pledged additional assistance to the Jews settling in Palestine. Unfortunately, Ben-Gurion and the Zionist leaders opposed the truce, and no doubt the reason was that the Zionists perceived the weakness of the Arabs and their historic opportunity to achieve the goals set forth in Plan Dalet. Further, the Zionists now knew how weak the Arab regimes were and they naturally wished to take full advantage.

US leaders such as President Truman and many in his administration had supported Zionism for several years and helped force the UN partition vote in 1949. However, with the Ben-Gurion rejection, the State Declaration fluctuated between anger and embarrassment. Truman then warned Israel that a rejection of the truce would constitute a freeze on most US aid to Israel.[19]

At this point, only Transjordan stood outside the Arab consensus of opposing Israel at all cost. Transjordan's uniqueness came due to its quest for Jerusalem and the West Bank. It is possible that a concerted diplomatic initiative would have brought Transjordan into the fold, except for Israel's rejection of the peace proposal. It is now known that with Plan Dalet in full operation and the fact that Israel knew by early April 1948 that it could fulfil the territorial goals of Dalet and the mass exodus of Palestinians. Israel was not about to make peace with the Arabs.

Another of the 'New Historians' who prefers the label 'post-Zionist scholars' is Dr Ilan Pappe, senior lecturer in political science at the University of Haifa (in Israel). The author of several important volumes on themes related to Zionism and the early years of Israeli statehood. Pappe has demonstrated how the *Yeshuv* and then Israel managed conflict with the strongest Arab force in 1948, Jordan's Arab Legion. His volume, *Collusion Across the Jordan*, has shown that the *Yeshuv* made an agreement with King Abdullah whereby the Legion would not unite with the other Arab armies in exchange for the option of annexing the West Bank:

> The *Yeshuv's* military advantage (in 1948) was significantly enhanced by an unwritten agreement signed by the Jewish Agency and Jordan's Arab Legion, prior to the war. The agreement confined the Arab Legion to the struggle over Jerusalem and its vicinity and prevented it from taking a larger part in the battle which could have linked it with the Syrian troops entering Palestine in the north and Egyptian ones entering it in the south. New evidence was found in Egypt of how Egyptian and Syrian generals were misled to believe that their forces would eventually meet with the legionaries entering Palestine from the east. In return, the Israelis accepted Jordan's *de facto* annexation of parts of Palestine (later to be known as the West Bank).[20]

---

[19] Simha Flapan, *The Birth of Israel*, Pantheon Press, New York, 1987, 174-181.
[20] Ilan Pappe, 'Fifty Years Through the Eyes of 'New Historians in Israel', *Middle East Report,* Volume 207, Number 28; Summer 1998; 14.

The strategy was successful, as it allowed Israel to defeat the invading Arab armies one by one while it has been able to use the 'myth' until today that it was the Arabs who would not make peace in 1948, and 'tiny' Israel was under attack from five invading armies. In truth, as Israeli scholars themselves are proving, Israel not only initiated the War in 1948 but it manipulated other Arab leaders into alliances that enhanced Israel's military superiority. All of this was done under the false premise that the Arabs were the initiators of the conflict, the Arabs had the military advantage, and Israel's victory was a miracle.

Pappe adds:

David was not fighting against Goliath. This is not just a statement of a historical truth. It is a message to Israeli society that Israel was not born miraculously. Nor is it because of its claimed moral uniqueness, an invincible state that can live by the sword and impose its will with military force.[21]

The twin myths of Israel being the underdog David fighting Goliath (Arab giants, Palestinian terrorists, and Islam) continue to have currency in the United States, particularly with successive US presidents and Congress. Pappe warns: 'Historical circumstances unfavourable to Israel may develop eventually. Therefore, it must seek other means in order to be accepted by its neighbours.'[22]

## Intifada

In November 1987, I was on sabbatical and living in Cyprus, doing research in Middle Eastern Christianity while working part-time for the Middle East Council of Churches. One evening I turned on the television to watch the evening English news broadcast from Jordan and was struck by the reporter's statement that the Arab Summit was about to open in Amman with the leaders arriving from around the region. Yasser Arafat had arrived at Amman Airport that afternoon and no Jordanian leader met him, which was previously unheard of, given the celebrity status that Arafat and the PLO had commanded since 1974. This was a particular insult in the Arab world where protocol mandates that the leader of a host country send a high level delegation to greet foreign

[21] Pappe, *op. cit.,* 15.
[22] *Ibid*.

dignitaries and if at all possible, to attend themselves. The commentator concluded: 'The Palestine question has dropped to agenda item #28 out of a scheduled thirty items.'

The announcer continued: 'For years the Palestine Question had been at the top of the priorities for the Arab world but at this Summit, it may not even be addressed.' Palestinians were wondering if their leadership had failed them and Israel was finally the victor. A community that had endured so much suffering since 1948 was now beginning to feel abandoned again by their Arab neighbours, by the international community, and in doubt about the direction they had been pursing in search of justice and freedom.

Three weeks later, on 7 December 1987, an Israeli military vehicle drove into a line of Gaza workers who were lined up to receive their job assignment in Israel early that morning. Eight Gazans were killed in an accident that unleashed the rage of a community that had been abused for forty years. Many felt the 'accident' was deliberate but it is still unknown whether or not it was. Now it does not matter. This was the incident that triggered the *Intifada*.

On 8 December, angry protests and demonstrations erupted throughout the Gaza Strip with mostly young people and families of the 7 December victims demanding justice. The rage grew with each town and refugee camp coming out to confront the Israeli military. Demonstrations were largely non-violent but stones and bottles began to be hurled at the Israeli army with the usual response of tear-gas, rubber coated bullets, and live ammunition. There were several Palestinian casualties taken to hospitals after the first day.

The confrontations spread to the West Bank as reports came out on the incident in Gaza with clashes occurring from the northern districts near Jenin down to Hebron, where clashes were intense. Within days all of the Palestinian territories, including East Jerusalem and several cities inside Israel, began to confront the Israeli Defence Forces. Israel responded with force, and soon there were several Palestinian youths killed, and named 'martyrs.' The movement could neither be contained nor terminated by Israel's responses, which seemed to have underestimated the fury and lack of fear demonstrated by the Palestinian youth. The uprising was called the *Intifada*, or a translation 'the shaking off' (of occupation, oppression, and injustice). Palestinian nationalism had resurrected in a new form that started with the youth at the grassroots level.

In many ways the four strategies of negation were challenged over a four-year period. Israel, for the most part, responded with predictable force. In January, 1988, Minister of Defence Itzhak Rabin ordered the breaking of bones and beatings. The Israeli Defence Forces, who were trained for warfare, were unable to harness the tactics of youths armed with stones and sling-shots. Soon the international media turned sour on Israel, and the images of David and Goliath were reversed.

In some ways, the four strategies of negation were in the process of undergoing a strategic reversal during the *Intifada*. Public opinion in Israel began to discuss a withdrawal from the 'ungovernable' Gaza Strip, where the IDF was repeatedly humiliated. The land now appeared for a time to be negotiable, and the leadership of the *Intifada* was ready to make peace, but only on the terms of a total Israeli withdrawal, based on the United Nations Resolutions #242 and 338. Likewise, peace was again possible, amidst the tension of the *Intifada* and the suffering on both sides. The international community began to pressure Israel through the United Nations and other venues to end its occupation and make peace based on the international consensus. The fury of Palestinian nationalism was being unleashed in clever but steadfast ways, but clearly Palestinian nationalism was not dead, it was stronger than ever, until the Gulf War redirected the focus on Saddam Hussein. Arafat's misguided 'embrace' of the Iraqi dictator cost the Palestinians most of the political good-will that the *Intifada* had developed and cost the PLO hundreds of millions of dollars annually in aid from the Arab Gulf. By the end of the Gulf War the *Intifada* had run out of steam and the Palestinian organizations were on the verge of bankruptcy. Israel had recovered its tarnished image and, thanks to Saddam's missile attacks during the Gulf War, the Zionist state was once again 'David' in the midst of a hostile neighbourhood. The gains of self-sacrifice and countless young lives during the *Intifada* seemed to have been in vain as talk of Middle East peace negotiations returned to centre stage in early 1991.

## The vanishing Palestinian Christians of the Holy Land

Bethlehem's mayor, Hanna Nasser, is a warm and likeable man who is also passionate about his 'little town'. The Nasser family has lived in Bethlehem for more than 400 years but is concerned about the future of his family's legacy in Bethlehem. His family is like most other Christian families throughout Israel and the Palestinian areas have seen most of their living relatives emigrate from Palestine to Europe, Australia, North or South America. Hanna's brother now lives in El Salvador, he has a first cousin in Montreal and another in Venezuela. Several relatives live in California and more in Chile.[23] Similar

---

[23] Bernard Sabella, 'Palestinian Christians: Challenges and Hopes', *Out of Jerusalem: Christian Voices from the Holy Land*, Palestine General Delegation to the United Kingdom, London, 1997, 5.

stories can be told by Palestinian Christians in Jerusalem, Ramallah, Nazareth, and other cities in Israel and the Palestinian territories where Christians have been living in significant numbers.

On the eve of the hostilities in 1948, Palestinian Christians were 15-16 percent of the total population in Palestine. By 1967 their percentage had dropped to 12-13 percent. In Jerusalem the Christians were 51.4 percent of the population of the city in 1922 and today they are less than 2 percent. As the millennium turned, Palestinian Christians were 1.9-2.0 percent of the population in Israel and Palestine. We have noted that the most significant loss came in 1948 when approximately 40 percent of Christians were forced out of what became West Jerusalem. In what is now Israel, around 35 percent of Christians were forced out during the 1948 hostilities. Overall, around 230,000 Palestinian Christians have left historic Palestine since Israel's birth in 1948. Had they remained, by natural increase alone their numbers would be well over one million today.

Of the Christians that remain, the majority live in the State of Israel and primarily in Galilee. They number between 135,000-140,000 and have Israeli citizenship although they are second class citizens in most regards with restrictions on housing (Palestinian Arabs cannot live in most kibbutzim, or Israeli settlements, nor in many housing projects and 'Jewish only' communities); quotas are imposed on them at Israeli universities, and they cannot serve in the military which becomes the basis for housing opportunities and many government supported entitlements.

Palestinian Christians belong to fifteen different denominations, the largest of which (51 percent) is the Greek Orthodox with 42,000, followed by Latin (Roman) Catholic at 36,000. The total number of Protestants is only 4,600, Melkite (Byzantine) Catholics number 2,500 and Syrian Orthodox 3,000. The Armenian Orthodox, the second oldest Christian community, has dropped drastically since 1948 to only 2,800. The Coptic Orthodox number 1,500 with only 800 Assyrian Orthodox (Church of the East), who still conduct their liturgy in Aramaic, the language of Jesus and first century Palestine.[24]

Clearly, the largest Christian emigration came in 1948-49 during the *Nakba* when approximately 60,000 Palestinian Christians were forced out of their homes and land, constituting 35 percent of the Palestinian Christians at that time. Another wave of refugees was created in 1967 during and immediately after the June War, and since then there has been a steady decline. One cannot say exactly that Christians were targeted in each case by Israel but we can say

---

[24] Lynda Brayer, 'Decimation of Palestinians in the Occupied Territories of Palestine', Catholic Information Network; <http://www.cin.org/decimpal.html>.

that among Israel's strategies in each major purge was a strategy to remove Palestinians and the Christians suffered a higher percentage loss in terms of their numbers.

Since 1967, the combination of land loss to Jewish settlements, the lack of a political resolution to the problems in Palestine, and the economic factors including the lack of good jobs have all been contributing factors. The Israeli attorney Linda Brayer states that there seems to be a strategy behind the Christian emigration: 'systematic policies and practices that are intended to wipe out the Christian community of East Jerusalem and the West Bank in occupied Palestine.'[25]

Attorney Brayer's words reflect the feelings of many Palestinian Christians but it is difficult to prove the case. It may be more accurate to state that Palestinian Christians, as a vulnerable and numerically weaker community, were victims of Israeli hostilities in higher proportions than their Muslim sisters and brothers, but the Muslim numbers were significantly higher. Many of the Palestinian Christians established themselves in East Jerusalem and Amman, Jordan, the latter becoming the centre of a rather wealthy Christian community in the 1980s-90s. A large community fled to Lebanon in 1948 and again in 1967, and many did well in business and various professions, but were forced to flee after the Israeli invasion and War of 1982, to be numbered among the 400,000 poor and nationless refugees of Lebanon today.

Many Palestinian Christians found jobs in the Gulf countries during the oil boom of the 1960s-1993, where they became wealthy but many lost everything when Iraq invaded Kuwait and most Palestinians were expelled from the Gulf countries in the wake of the war. Both Christian and Muslim Palestinians in the Gulf became refugees again, the majority going from riches to rags overnight. Most were taken in by Jordan, which has consistently been the most hospitable of the Middle Eastern countries, aside from the Black September period of the early 1970s.

Chapter 5 noted that in 1870-80, a tradition of Palestinian business people began to seek jobs, which led to large emigration patterns to South and Central America. The cities of Bethlehem, Beit Sahour, Beit Jala, and Ramallah lost the most citizens to these regions. Bethlehem Palestinians claim that there are more Palestinian Christians from Bethlehem in Chile or Brazil than live in Bethlehem today. Large Palestinian Christian communities live in France, UK, Australia-New Zealand, and North America as well. If the trends continue, most Palestinian Christians say there will be nobody left in a generation but a handful of elderly and Western Christians, giving evidence

---

[25] *Ibid.*

that Christianity is essentially a Western religion and does not belong in the Middle East.

## Summary

1. Throughout history, the conquering powers have often engaged in the transfer (expulsion) of the indigenous peoples and embarked upon a rewriting of their conquest and even the history of the conquered people to fit the political image desired by the victors. Zionist history until recently has engaged in such a historical narrative, accompanied by various myths concerning the emptiness of the land, backwardness of the Arabs, and how the Jews would 'make the desert bloom.'

2. Biblical archaeology has facilitated the mainstream Zionist mythology (rather than the humanistic Zionist view or one aware of Palestinian history) and granted simultaneous credibility for the hard-line Zionist arguments, which have had the net effect of replacing Palestinian history and negating their national struggle.

3. The historical and political context by which we can understand the dramatic losses in the Palestinian Christian population during the 1948-93 period include the loss of homes and land, forced expulsion of 35 percent of Christians, the negation of their history and of Palestinian nationalism.

4. 'Tribal' Zionism, a term suggested by Hebrew University professor Zeev Sternhell, is based on the German-'blood' nationalism. Eventually, it overshadowed the humanist and liberal European Zionism by the 1920s with the triumph of such leaders as Herzl, Weizmann, Jabotinsky, Gordon, and Ben-Gurion. Gradually a 'tribal' Zionist master story (history) was developed which made effective use of the Western media, governments, novels, biblical archaeology and the churches, film, politics, and academics. The influential *Biblical Archaeology Review* is illustrative of how the Zionist master story is packaged for Western Christian consumption.

5. Palestinian nationalism emerged independent of Zionism during a struggle with the Ottoman empire after the turn of the last century (1900). Palestinian Christians in Galilee played a major role in developing national consciousness during this early phase, which was effectively crushed by the Ottoman and then the British empires. There is no evidence of tension between Palestinian Muslims and Christians during this period as they were united in their common national struggle against the Ottoman Turks, then the British, and later the Zionist movement and the

State of Israel.

6. The PLO evolved out of the Pan-Arab movements of the late 1950-60s plus the Palestinian national consciousness emerging in Beirut, Cairo, and within the Gaza Strip and West Bank. The PLO was begun in 1965 with a variety of political ideologies and movements under its umbrella. The *Fateh* movement gained control of the PLO by the late 1960s as Yasser Arafat and his *Fateh* leadership assumed control and hold it until today. The major Palestinian factions (Fateh, the PFLP, and DFLP) involved Palestinian Christians in the central leadership of each party from the outset.

7. Middle Eastern Christian support for Palestine and Palestinian nationalism came in 1969, with the Christians for Palestine conference in Beirut, Lebanon. Most Middle East Churches and their hierarchy, with the exception of Lebanon's Maronite Catholics, supported the PLO and the Palestinian national struggle for self-determination.

8. Palestinian nationalism has consistently reinvented itself throughout the past century and has been embraced by virtually every Palestinian both inside and outside historic Palestine. It will not disappear in the near or distant future despite continuing attempts by the State of Israel, the United States and various Arab regimes to either destroy or weaken it.

9. Palestinian Christianity has been caught in a maelstrom that is spinning out of control and propelling its inhabitants outward through emigration, forced expulsions and a general erosion of the institutions of historic Christianity. If the present rate of decline continues there is concern that Palestinian Christianity will virtually disappear within 40 years.

10. Israeli 'post-Zionist' historians such as Simha Flapan, Benny Morris, Meron Benvenisti, Tom Segev, Avi Schlaim, Zeev Sternhell, and Ilan Pappe, continue to develop a new historical narrative that challenges the old body of mythology in Zionism and begin to create space for the legitimate grievances of Palestinians concerning their loss of land, national identity, and history. From this space it is assumed the Palestinian story itself will be accepted as legitimate and meritorious of implementing Palestinian human and national rights in historic Palestine. Once this project is in place, the Palestinian Christians will be encouraged to remain in the land and many return in a 'Christian *Aliya*'.

# Chapter 9
# THE OSLO PEACE PROCESS (1993-2000): *APARTHEID* IN THE HOLY LAND?

Through a number of coincidences I happened to be in Washington, DC on September 13 1993 and was able to secure a pass to the White House signing ceremony between Israel and the Palestine Authority. Having spent the previous twelve years working on human rights and peace issues in the Palestinian-Israeli conflict, I found it mind-stretching to see Israeli Prime Minister Itzhak Rabin and PLO Chairman Yasser Arafat shake hands under the watchful eye of US President Bill Clinton.

The *Washington Post* reported that Clinton was unable to sleep the night before the signing so he arose at 3:00 am, read sections of the book of Joshua, and reworked his speech. He began by saying:

> Welcome to this great occasion of history and hope. Today, we bear witness to an extraordinary act in one of history's defining dramas, a drama that began in a time of our ancestors when the Word went forth from a sliver of land between the River Jordan and the Mediterranean Sea. That hallowed piece of earth, that land of life and revelation is the home to the memories and dreams of Jews, Muslims, and Christians throughout the world.

The president went on to insert quotations from the Hebrew scriptures, the New Testament, and the Qur'an that direct their followers to seek peace. He referred to how Jews and Muslims once lived together and wrote 'brilliant chapters in the history of literature and science. All this can come to pass again,' he added.

President Clinton concluded with a strong pledge on behalf of the United States to ensure that this peace process would bear fruit:

> The United States is committed to ensuring that the people who are affected by this agreement will be made more secure by it, and to leading the world in marshalling the resources necessary to implement the difficult details that will make real the principles to which you commit yourselves today ... Mr

Prime Minister, Mr Chairman, this day belongs to you ...
Together, today, with all our hearts and all our souls, we bid
them *shalom, salaam, peace*.[1]

The optimistic part of me could not help but being caught up in the
promises of the hour, knowing that over fifty failed peace proposals and tens
of thousands of lives had been lost in wars and armed resistance during this
one hundred year conflict. As Arafat noted in a sombre sentence: 'families of
the victims of the wars, violence, terror, whose pain will never heal. For them,
this ceremony has come too late.' Rabin added a similar reference in his
speech: 'We who have fought against you, the Palestinians, we say to you
today in a loud and a clear voice: enough of blood and tears. Enough!'

But other voices in me raised a cynical and critical commentary on
the festivities. Was it all a political masquerade for the world to witness the
illusion of peace that the Israelis and Americans were orchestrating? Why all
the sudden media attention to the Palestinian case? For more than twelve
years many of us were calling for recognition of the PLO and a peace based
on United Nations resolutions 242 and 338 (land in exchange for peace).
Why all the sudden interest in recognizing the PLO and talking of 'land for
peace'? Just 24 hours ago Arafat and the PLO were considered terrorists and
he was forbidden from entering the United States? Why was the United
Nations excluded from the process? Was this a tactic to circumvent resolution
242 or would it truly be implemented? Finally, would the United States be
able to serve as an impartial and honest peace broker, holding each party
accountable to the difficult decisions and timetables needed to implement
peace? I was torn between hope and cynicism, having seen too many
opportunities for peace lead to self-destruction. I decided to give the Oslo
Accords until the end of December (1993) to determine whether the process
was for real or a charade.

In this chapter I will review the path that led to the 13 September
1993 signing ceremony and the complicated regional and international context
in which it emerged. Then I will turn to the Oslo Accords themselves, noting
that they are not a peace treaty *per se* but a framework in which a series of
confidence-building measures and implementation procedures might occur.
The Oslo Process will then be evaluated and we will ask, now seven years
after the 'handshake', if they have brought a just and lasting peace to the
Holy Land, and what the effects of Oslo have been on the Palestinian Christian
community.

---

[1]  *Washington Post*, 14 September 1993.

## *The regional and international context*

A number of international, regional, and internal (within Israel-Palestine) factors converged in the early 1990s to bring not only Israel and the PLO to the negotiating table, but most of the Arab leaders and Europe to lend their support. On the international level, the break-up of the Soviet Union left the leading opponents of the Israel-United States alliance without significant military and economic support. In this regard, Syria and various Palestinian opposition groups such as the PFLP and DFLP were without a major sponsor, and the Russian influence in the United Nations had diminished to mere symbolism. The Islamic resistance groups were not a significant factor in their opposition to Arafat in the early 1990s but this would change quickly.

The most important regional development was the Gulf War (strictly speaking the second Gulf War of January-February 1991, with the Iran-Iraq War of the 1980s being the first), which had a number of ramifications. Saddam Hussein's invasion of Kuwait immediately drew regional and international attention away from the *Intifada*, where the Palestinians had been winning the international public relations battle with Israel and for the first time had gained the sympathy of Europe and North America. The Gulf War changed everything as Israel was able to achieve two strategic gains during this brief period: first, to win back its public relations battle in the West as the victim of Arab aggression; secondly, to place the entire West Bank and Gaza Strip under a 23-hour-a-day curfew, with crippling effects on the economic, agricultural, and political life of the Palestinian residents. The severe repression crippled the political momentum built up by the *Intifada* and Arafat's foolish support of Saddam Hussein did the rest. This damaging embrace did more than anything else to reverse the public relations gains of the *Intifada*.

The coalition built by the United States through the United Nations involved most of the Arab world, including Syria. Jordan understandably stood outside the consensus, given its proximity to Iraq. In mid-August, 1990, I was in Amman and had the opportunity to meet privately with King Hussein, who described how he and Egypt's Hosni Mubarak were trying to maintain a degree of independence from the United States and the coalition, so as to provide Saddam a 'face-saving way out of Kuwait'. The king felt that Saddam would withdraw but the United States was not interested in a peaceful settlement through negotiations. Rather, it seems to have desired a war to reassert itself politically and ecomonically in the region.

Another significant loss to the Palestinians came from the Gulf states, especially Kuwait and Saudi Arabia, who had been major donors to the Palestinian cause and was home to upwards of 500,000 Palestinian professionals. Due to Arafat's support of Saddam Hussein, approximately 90 percent of these Palestinians were expelled, losing their jobs and most of their savings. The millions of dollars in remittances that the PLO received from the Gulf countries was cut off overnight. Thus Palestinians suffered on four counts: more refugees, the loss of the Gulf Palestinian salaries (significant portions of which were sent back to support relatives in Palestine), the loss of tens of millions of dollars from these donor nations, and the loss of political support regionally and internationally that had been bought with the sacrifices and struggle of the Palestinians in the West Bank and Gaza Strip during the *Intifada*. These losses cannot be measured in terms of their accumulative impact on the PLO and the Palestinian community inside Palestine and most of the losses were irreversible.

Between late 1987 and the Gulf War, Israel had been profoundly affected by the *Intifada* and even the hard-line Likud government was convinced that Israel could no longer control three million Palestinians. Further, Israel was in need of advanced weaponry and a missile defence system from the United States, and had requested $10 billion in loan guarantees, to be paid over a five-year period. It was clear to the United States Department of State that Israel would use much of the $10 billion for the construction of illegal settlements and infrastructure in the West Bank, East Jerusalem, and the Gaza Strip. For the first time since the Eisenhower administration, the US President George Bush and his Secretary of State, James Baker, had linked the loan guarantees to Israel's support of the peace process. Israel also saw the multi-layered weakness of Arafat and the PLO, and the diminishing of the *Intifada*, as opportunities to deal with the Palestinians from a position of overwhelming strength.

Palestinian Christians began to sense the fragile situation in which they found themselves. They noted the blunders that the PLO leadership had committed in the relationships with Iraq. They sensed the growing strength of Hamas and the steady erosion of the secular democratic political solution for the Palestinians. The political and public relations gains of the *Intifada* were steadily eroding. On the regional level it seemed that Israel had regained its prestige and a new United States hegemony was beginning to dominate the Middle East (and many other regions). Christians throughout the region were beginning to sense that the loss of the democratic vision based on secular rather than religious ideologies or nation states was quite possibly a sign that their best days were behind them.

With considerable fan-fare, the United States, led by Secretary of State James Baker, and an emasculated Russia under Mikhail Gorbachev, convened Israel and the major 'confrontation' states (those whose borders touched Israel) in Spain on 30 October 1993. The Palestinians were not allowed to represent themselves through the PLO, which Israel and the Israeli-influenced US Congress considered 'a terrorist organization'. Attending the Madrid Conference were Israel, Jordan, Syria, Lebanon, Egypt, and Palestinian observers who were 'attached' to the Jordanian delegation. Israel rejected Palestinians who were residents of Jerusalem (Israel's 'greater Jerusalem') as it might give indirect recognition of the Palestinians having a legitimate claim to any part of Jerusalem.

The Madrid process struggled and limped along for over eighteen months with various venues in Europe and Washington, DC, but little movement was observable on the various 'tracks' that had been agreed to in November, 1993. The Palestinian-Israeli track was the most urgent on many levels, but it became clear that Israeli Prime Minister Yitzhak Shamir and the Likud-led government were using the Madrid process for a series of delays. Palestinian spokesperson, Dr Hanan Ashrawi of Bir Zeit University, summarized the failure of the Madrid meetings as:

> Paralysis and inertia. The Israeli delegation lacked the will and the instructions to actually negotiate, keeping up a semblance of participation without addressing the real issues ... Digressions into trivia, circumvention of substance—these became the key non-moves of Israel's evasive tactics.[2]

Her observations were correct, a matter Shamir not only admitted, but boasted he had the 'power' to tie up the procedures for ten years with no results.[3]

## The Oslo Accords

By the end of 1992 the Madrid Process had collapsed and Israel had a new government led by the security-oriented leader of the Labour Party, Itzhak Rabin. William Jefferson Clinton, a Democrat with little foreign policy background, defeated George Bush for the presidency of the United States. Rabin continued Likud's policy of accelerated settlement expansion in the Jerusalem region and flexed his muscles by expelling 416 Hamas leaders to

---

[2] Quoted in Morris, *Righteous Victims*, 614-5.
[3] Morris reports that Shamir had made the statement in an interview with an Israeli (*Ma'ariv*) journalist, claiming he would like to drag out the negotiations without any results for at least ten years. The prime minister claimed later that he had been misquoted. Morris, *op. cit.,* 615.

Lebanon on 17 December 1992. The expulsions only served to give Hamas more credibility within the Palestinian community and drew international sympathy to their cause. During the next six weeks thirteen Israelis, mostly military personnel, were murdered and Rabin sealed off the occupied territories from Israel. Rabin decided to pursue a policy of total separation of Palestinians from Israel, cutting economic, social, and normal travel. It was still illegal for Israelis to meet or negotiate directly with the PLO so there were no official channels available to break the deadlock. The strategy of 'total separation' has become the dominant policy of both Likud and Labour in their relationship with the Palestinians in Jerusalem, the West Bank and the Gaza Strip. This strategy forecloses for now a policy of accommodation with the Palestinians and gives Israel a position of dominance. The 'total separation' strategy which seems to be acceptable to the United States also negates the United Nations resolutions 242 and 338, which are the international consensus for a just and durable peace.

Informal and periodic contact had been maintained all along among Jerusalem Palestinian leaders like Faisel Husseini, Hanan Ashrawi, and Dr Sari Nusseibeh with the Israeli 'left' and the peace community as well as with some left of centre Labour Party members, such as Yossi Beilin. The Israeli left had always found careful and discrete means of maintaining the contact throughout the 1980s, some facing brief prison sentences for their dialogue with the PLO. In December 1992, Professor Yael Hirshfeld of Haifa University and Yossi Beilin travelled to London to meet with Ahmed Qurai (Abu Alaa), the PLO's minister of finance. An old friend of both, Norwegian academic Terje Rod Larsen, Director of the Norwegian Institute for Applied Social Sciences in Oslo (FAFA), was brought in to the discussions. Beilin, Hirshfeld, and Abu Alaa knew Larsen and his wife Mona Juul, now a senior official in the Norwegian Foreign Ministry. The parties met covertly in London and the meetings went well, so the Norwegians offered to host a more serious and intensive session in Norway.

On 29 January 1993, the Knesset repealed the ban on talking to the PLO which gave the Israeli's additional cover should the secret meetings be revealed by the press. In a September 1999 visit to Chicago for the sixth anniversary of the Oslo Accords, Terje Larsen shared some of the nuances of the meetings with a North Park University audience. Larsen noted the importance of the human connections that were made between the Palestinians and Israelis, such as exchanging photographs of families and relaxing before a fire in a lodge in the mountains of Norway, sharing stories of each others lives. Gradually, a deeper sense of trust and respect grew between Abu Alaa and Beilin.

By February, Abu Alaa had the support of Yasser Arafat and Beilin-Hirshfeld had the support of Foreign Minister Shimon Peres, and lukewarm openness to the dialogue from Prime Minister Rabin. By May they were getting down to specific aspects that would shape documents to be exchanged in pursuit of a political settlement. Rabin and the Israelis saw that they could make a deal with the Palestinians when they were at their weakest point in 25 years. They also knew that the power of Hamas was on the rise and they might be able to 'unload' the ungovernable Gaza Strip, a centre of Hamas and mass resistance, and force Arafat to manage security there instead of Israel. The Palestinians and Arafat were desperate on every level and Palestinian insiders claimed that Arafat's declining health and a brush with death in a plane crash a few years earlier had weakened his will to resist.

Shimon Peres and Abu Alaa became the key negotiators on behalf of their respective governments as Norway's Terje Rod Larsen, with occasional intervention by the foreign minister, Johan Jergen Holst, brought matters to an agreement in mid-August. One of the key issues was to find an instrument of mutual recognition, a matter the PLO had been seeking and which had been blocked by Israel and the United States since the late-1960s. An agreement was reached on the night of 18 August after seven hours of extensive conference calls and negotiations between Oslo, Tunis, and Tel Aviv. Once they reached an agreement, Peres and Abu Alaa flew to Oslo where they initialled the agreement.[4]

Some key actors, such as Larsen, believe the United States was not informed until this point, but others believe the Israelis had been covertly leaking information to the Americans all along. Peres, Abu Alaa, Larsen and Holst then flew to a United States air base near Santa Barbara, California, where Secretary of State Warren Christopher witnessed a secret signing ceremony. Washington was brought in as Israel insisted on US backing, which would make the agreement more likely to be passed by the Knesset. Arafat had no such backing or guarantor, a matter that continues to haunt him with the pro-Israel leanings of successive US administrations.[5] Thus what Arafat was forced to do was circumvent his own executive committee and the Palestine National Council (the Palestinian Parliament), much to the resentment of many of his close officials. Palestinians had been strong advocates of democracy since the founding of the PLO (1964), but now it appeared as if Arafat was assuming the role of a military dictator (Israeli and Palestinian critics say it was always his style). The Israeli Knesset adopted the Oslo Agreement on 30 August but the PNC never voted on it.

News began to leak out of the international press that Israel and the PLO had recognized each other and 'a peace agreement' was in the offing.

---

[4] *Op. cit.,* 621.
[5] Author's interview with Terje Rod Larsen by the author in Chicago, Illinois, 12 September 1999.

The date of 13 September 1993 was set for a signing ceremony on the White House lawn. It is important to note at the outset of our discussion of the Oslo Accords that they are a set of guidelines and objectives toward a peace process, not a formal treaty or even official agreements as erroneously portrayed in the media. They were at best a set of principles or an agenda that would hopefully lead to a negotiated peace between Israel and the PLO. The Oslo process itself was projected to be relatively long with various agreements to be scheduled over the next six years with 'final status talks' scheduled to begin on 6 May 1999. The most complicated issues, such as the status of Jerusalem, settlements, refugees, final borders, the right of return and foreign policy with the neighbouring states were delayed until the 'final status talks.'

The Oslo Accords were greeted with general enthusiasm on the Israeli side, primarily from the centrist Labour Party and the left. Amos Oz, perhaps the most influential contemporary writer in Israel, told BBC radio on 3 September: 'Only one moment in history equals this for me—the creation of the Jewish state by the United Nations resolution in 1947. And that also was achieved by compromise.' Likud opposition leader Benyamin Netanyahu and chief of the Israeli Defence Forces general staff, then General Ehud Barak, opposed the Oslo Accords on security grounds.

Arafat began to see opposition not only from Hamas and the Marxist wings of the PLO (Dr George Habash of the PFLP and Naif Hawatmeh of the DFLP) but within his own Fateh Party, Foreign Minister Farouk Khadoumi and head of the Beirut office Shafik al-Hout vehemently opposed Oslo. Habbash told Monte Carlo radio on 30 August that the proposed deal was 'a trick to rob Palestinians of their legitimate rights.' Edward Said, the respected Palestinian scholar and critic of the Oslo process, added:

> The deal before us smacks of the PLO leadership's exhaustion and isolation and of Israel's shrewdness. Many Palestinians are asking themselves why, after years of concessions, we should be conceding once again to Israel and the United States in return for promises and vague improvements in the occupation that won't all occur until the 'final status' talks some three-five years hence, and perhaps not even then.[6]

The Oslo Accords came to be known as the Declaration of Principles (DOP). In them the PLO seemed to concede much more than the Israeli partner. Arafat agreed to recognize Israel's right to exist in peace and security;

---

[6]  Edward W Said, *The Nation*, 20 September 1993.

that he was willing to renounce the Palestinian Covenant; he would accept United Nations resolutions 242 and 338 (land for peace); renounce terrorism and control anti-Israeli terrorism emanating from Palestinian areas; and assume responsibility for all PLO behaviour and curb what is against the principles of the DOP. Vital issues that were conspicuously absent from the agenda were the following: refugees and their right of return or compensation; the status and future of Jerusalem; the end of Israeli settlements and land confiscations; the degree of sovereignty that the PA would have over land returned to it by Israel; water and Israel's siphoning water from West Bank aquifers; and Israel's commitment to completely withdraw from the West Bank, Gaza, and East Jerusalem.

There have been five major agreements since the 1993 initialling of the Oslo Accords:

1. *The Cairo Agreement of 4 May 1994*, in which Israel withdrew from portions of the Gaza Strip and the city of Jericho and redeployed around these areas while the Palestinian Authority assumed responsibility.
2. *The Paris Protocol of July 1994*, which dealt with trade and a variety of business and economic issues between Israel and the Palestinian areas.
3. *Oslo II Agreements at Taba, Egypt, September 1995:* Israel agreed to re-deploy its troops to other Palestinian population areas other than Gaza and Jericho, granting an additional 3 percent to the Palestinian Authority.
4. *The Hebron Agreement of 15 January, 1997:* after a long period of tension and failure to implement the DOPs under the Netanyahu government, in which Israel agreed to withdraw from the majority but not the Israeli settlements in the centre of Hebron nor Kiryat Arba on the perimeter.
5. *The Wye River Agreement of October 1998:* after an eighteen month period of terrorist attacks by Palestinians and delays by the Netanyahu government, the parties convened in the United States in an attempt to get the negotiations back on track, with some minor Israeli withdrawals in exchange for increased security provisions for the Palestinians.

Israel agreed to withdraw from two major Palestinian population centres, Jericho and the Gaza Strip, within two months. It would re-deploy troops in the region surrounding these two areas. The PLO would be responsible for policing the two autonomous areas but Israel would maintain overall security in the remaining 98 percent of the Palestinian areas. Palestinian elections would need to be conducted within nine months. Thus the PLO received its coveted recognition, particularly by the United States and Israel, but only a small percentage of its land was returned to Palestinian sovereignty. Worse, the entire arrangement, as we shall see, was leveraged in Israel's favour in a number of critical areas.

Many, but not all Palestinian Christians celebrated the DOPs. Anglican Bishop Samir Kafity issued his official statement after the signing:

> Tonight we celebrate, both Palestinian and Israeli, together with the multitude of people who care for peace and justice, the inauguration of the journey of peace. That journey, starting today from Jericho and Gaza, will undoubtedly reach all of the towns and cities in the Palestinian territories. Together with our neighbours, Israel, Jordan, Syria, and Lebanon, we look forward to a new era of justice and peace in the Middle East ... We shall continue to pray here in St George's Cathedral (Jerusalem) with our Muslim and Jewish sisters and brothers for God's blessing on this journey of peace: a prayer that all the peoples of this region might live in the perfect image of God. ... 'Blessed are the peacemakers for they shall be called the children of God.'[7]

But many asked whether the Anglican bishop's statement was perhaps somewhat romantic. Would the forces of peace win out? Palestinians had not experienced an Israeli government that treated them as a people with human rights or political rights. What kind of a peace would it be? Would it be one that was steadily interrupted by terrorism from Israeli and Palestinian opposition groups? Would it be a peace based on justice and security for all sides? Would greed and self-interest take over and undermine the good intentions? The Palestinians and Israelis would know within a matter of three months.

## Implementing the Oslo Peace Accords

The international praise for the Oslo Accords and the sudden surge of positive coverage for Arafat and Rabin were remarkable, leading many to speculate that it was the result of significant government involvement and a well-orchestrated public relations firm. Arafat and Rabin were candidates for the

---

[7] Bishop Samir Kafity, Press Release, Anglican Archdiocese of Jerusalem and the Middle East, 14 September 1993.

Nobel Peace Prize (and won), and it was rare to see a critical commentary of the peace process or even Arafat, outside of his appearance. Israeli Foreign Minister Shimon Peres and others laid claim to the 'new' Middle East with promises of massive Israeli and Arab economic cooperation. In early November (1993) I received a series of telephone calls from various Middle East experts and former advocates of Palestinian human rights who were now celebrating the new era of peace through economic co-operation. I was told that Vice President Al Gore and a coalition of Arab-American and Jewish American investors were looking for wealthy 'friends' who could facilitate peace and make significant money by joining their coalition. Having no money to invest I was not interested, but they thought I could open the door to some wealthy friends. My cynicism about the pro-Likud Al Gore and other all too familiar opponents of justice and human rights left me in an unco-operative mood and I declined after rendering my displeasure over the enterprise.

By November 1993, the DOPs began to encounter a series of frustrating delays and barriers as the 'mask of peace' began to be peeled away. Both the Israelis and Palestinians began to blame each other for the difficulties they would encounter. The initial implementation step was to be a commitment on 13 December 1993 by Israel to withdraw from the majority of Jericho and the Gaza Strip, an agreement that Israel delayed for seven months rather than the agreed upon two months.[8] Some Palestinians turned against the Oslo Accords during this period and many who had supported them just two months earlier now became angry about a possible betrayal by Arafat, the Americans, and Israel.

Various delays in implementing the first phase of Israeli withdrawal simply served to erode trust throughout the Palestinian community. Additional confidence eroding factors included the failure of the international community to deliver on the economic incentives promised to Arafat after the 13 September signing. Then came the most severe blow of the initial year of Oslo when at least 29 Palestinian Muslims were gunned down while praying at Hebron's Ibrahimi Mosque on 25 February 1994. The perpetrator, Dr Baruch Goldstein of Kiryat Arba (a fanatical settlement near Hebron) was enshrined a hero with the Israeli 'right' and many settlements.

As a result of the Hebron massacre, a strict curfew was imposed on Palestinians (but not Israelis) during which there were lively protests and an additional 30 Palestinians were shot to death with over 100 wounded. Israel then placed all of the West Bank and Gaza Strip under a strict curfew. By

---

[8] The 'Agreement on Gaza and Jericho', also known as the Cairo Agreement, was not signed until 4 May 1994, with the United States, Russia, and Egypt serving as witnesses (in Cairo).

March 1994, support of the Oslo Accords on the Palestinian side slipped from the 87 percent it enjoyed in October (1993) to approximately 45 percent as anger over the Hebron massacre and the closures shifted initial support to clear opposition.[9]

Many Palestinians had suspected that Israel was using the delays to gain stronger negotiating positions and also show the Palestinians that Israel could 'get what it wanted' from the Oslo process. The erosion of the positive spirit that had initially accompanied the Oslo Process had now turned to bitterness. The majority of Palestinians began to accept what the opposition had stated at the outset: Palestinians cannot trust Israel or the United States, as they will use the DOPs to their advantage and cheat on Palestinians.

By the time Israel withdrew from occupied Jericho and the Gaza Strip, Palestinians experienced the first taste of freedom in these small cantons, but they also saw for the first time that what Arafat had negotiated was only a partial withdrawal. When the long delayed 'maps' of Oslo became available to the public it was clear that the proposed 'autonomous' Palestinian districts were not connected to each other. What the Palestinian people anticipated had now come to reality: the Palestinians were not receiving territory back from Israel that could lead to a real independent state nor were Israel, the Palestinian Authority, and the United States negotiating on the basis of United Nations resolutions 242 and 338. Due to their weak negotiating posture and the imbalance of the process (with a pro-Israel convenor—the United States—managing the process) the Palestinian leadership had not received significant land in return for all of its concessions on security, recognition of Israel, etc. Instead, the Palestinians were about to receive several small, isolated, cantons or *bantustans* (semi-autonomous zones or districts) that had limited freedom but left Israel in charge of 98 percent of the West Bank and 40 percent of the Gaza Strip. Approximately 70 percent of the Palestinian population would need to live in these *bantustans*.

Political analysts on both the Israeli and Palestinian sides began to recall the Allon Plan, which was developed by the Labour Party following the June 1967 War. The plan became operational in June 1968 and Labour's settlement policy had been following it since the war. The Allon Plan provided for Israel to maintain control of the West Bank along the Jordan River and Dead Sea region, thus providing a long security belt along the border with Jordan. It added the Hebron region and significant sections of the Judean highlands where the major water aquifers and reserves were located. Significant settlement was planned for the Jerusalem area, especially targeting

---

[9] *Promises, Promises, The Realities of Oslo*, London: World Vision UK, 1999, 3.

the Old City of East Jerusalem, and the newly annexed areas of the West Bank that were added to Israeli-expanded Jerusalem. Through these measures Israel would control approximately 65 percent of the West Bank, including the prime agricultural and water reserves, plus the areas bordering Jordan and Syria. The Allon Plan was Israel's alternative to United Nations resolution 242, and the Oslo Accords were beginning to look like a reworking of the Allon Plan.

The basic document concerning the occupied Palestinian areas and the key formula claimed by the Oslo Accords is found in UN resolution 242, adopted in November, 1967, calling for: 'Withdrawal of Israeli armed forces from Territories occupied in the recent conflict' (the War of June, 1967). Israel wished to retain the territory, with Abba Eban going so far as to state: 'We interpreted the War not just as a victory, but as a kind of providential messianic event that changed history permanently and gave Israel the power to dictate the future.'[10] Eban's perspective reflects what most of the Labour Party believed in that era, from Ben-Gurion to Golda Meir and on to Itzhak Rabin (Peres admitted after Rabin's death that the late Prime Minister had always had the Allon Plan in mind when discussing the Oslo process).

The Israeli argument concerning UN 242 is that the language of the agreement does not bind them to withdraw from 'all' of the Territories it occupied in 1967, only part of them. In making this agreement, Israel is left in the advantageous position that it can determine how much (occupied) land it can transfer to its sovereignty through a variety of measures. Further, Israel continues to claim sovereignty over East Jerusalem and has annexed it and a large portion of the West Bank into the (Israeli) 'Greater Jerusalem', and has imposed Israeli law and municipal practices on the Arab sector. Thus, according to Israel's interpretation of UN 242 as it pertains to East Jerusalem, the West Bank, Gaza Strip (and the Golan Heights), Israel retains a *de facto* 'right' to confiscate and settle these areas, despite the fact that such practices are blatant violations of international law and both the letter and spirit of UN 242 and 338. To date no international court, national, or trans-national organization has brought a meaningful challenge to Israel despite the fact that these practices undermine peace and a future settlement based on justice and the rule of law. The Oslo Accords, by ignoring Israel's practices, have in fact encouraged additional settlement activities, and as such have threatened to undermine the prospects for a just and durable resolution of the conflict.

---

[10] Thomas Friedman, *New York Times*, June 14 1987, as quoted in Baylis Thomas, *How Israel Was Won*, Lexington Books, Boston, 2000, 190.

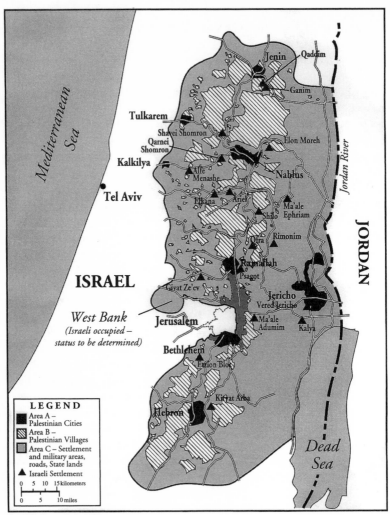

LEGEND
- ■ Area A – Palestinian Cities
- ▨ Area B – Palestinian Villages
- ▢ Area C – Settlement and military areas, roads, State lands
- ▲ Israeli Settlement

0  5  10  15 kilometers
0  5  10 miles

Source: Yediot Aharonot, October 6, 1995

## *Two major indicators of peace: land and economy*

### Issues related to the Land

The Oslo Peace Process was theoretically designed to lead to the implementation of United Nations resolutions 242 and 338 in exchange for peace with the neighbouring states. The design of the land agreements, however, have excluded the city of Jerusalem from the negotiations, which has served to facilitate Israel's project of Judaising Arab East Jerusalem plus the portions annexed from the West Bank. In addition, by dividing the West Bank into three zones (Areas A, B, and C) Israel has gained exclusive control over area C, which includes 70 percent of the West Bank. Further, another 18-20 percent known as area B, is under joint Israeli and Palestinian control, but Israel claims jurisdiction on security measures for Area B, and has taken land from this area for roads, infrastructure, and for military purposes. At the Wye River negotiations, 3 percent of area B was set aside for environmental uses, but it will remain uninhabited and Israel has the final word in security. Therefore to date, only 10 percent of the West Bank and 60 percent of the Gaza Strip and none of Jerusalem are available to the Palestinians as of mid-2000.

As has been noted above, the 9 percent of the West Bank known as Area A, is comprised of isolated districts or *bantustans*[11] that remain disconnected, are easily controlled or 'closed' by the occupying power, and are thereby deprived economically, politically, and socially. Whether an updated form of *apartheid* was in the design of Israel from the outset of the Oslo process is difficult to tell at this stage, but this is the clearest vision of what is emerging on the political, economic, and demographic aspects.

A problematic feature of *apartheid*-type regimes is that they utilize the resources of the conquered territories for their own economic advantage. Perhaps the most valuable resource in the Middle East is not

---

[11] The term *bantustan* applies to those autonomous zones that were proposed by the *apartheid* policy of the South African regime to be set aside for black and coloured South Africans, where they would have limited political and economic autonomy but still be under the sovereignty of the South African government and military. The proposal was never accepted by the blacks as it was designed to give the white minority a means of controlling the black majority, remove them from white areas, and offer limited resources for their survival. The scheme is similar to the 'reservations' on which Native Americans were placed. The comparison is parallel in that the Zone A 'Palestinian Areas' have limited autonomy and are surrounded by the Israeli Defence Forces. Also, the final destination of these zones is yet to be determined so the West Bank and Gaza *bantustans* are in the process of formation.

oil but water, an issue over which future wars will be waged. One of the most extensive water resources in the eastern Mediterranean region lies in the Palestinian Territories known as the West Bank. According to the leading Israeli human rights organization, B'tselem, Israel is siphoning between 50-60 percent of the water of the West Bank, causing the 2.4 million Palestinians to face increasing shortages, rationing, and future depletion of this vital resource.[12]

For the previous eight years the Palestinian population centres have had severe water rationing during the summer months, particularly during the near drought conditions of 1999. Also of note is the extensive industrial and military dumping of hazardous waste into the West Bank, in some localities directly over the most important aquifers. The combination of diverting water to Israeli sources, depriving Palestinians of their own water, while creating environmental hazards for the Palestinians, represents a clear image of the injustices of *apartheid*. Meanwhile, Israel continues to increase its diversion of West Bank water to the settlements, where the swimming pools are full, the lawns are green, and the water is abundant.

Another dimension of *apartheid*-like practices creating a situation of injustice for the majority by the occupying power is in the realm of travel restrictions due to military closures. Presently, Palestinians can travel freely only when inside their own Area 'A', which is surrounded by Israeli military checkpoints. Less than 10 percent of the Palestinian population has been able to receive the plastic travel cards (like the South African 'pass laws') that enable them to move to jobs, worship, visit family, or attend a university. We will examine the other aspects in a later section, but here we can illustrate this by noting the effects on universities and students.

There are six universities in the West Bank and two in the Gaza Strip. Travel between the universities is blocked for nearly all of the students, faculty, and staff. Permits may be granted by Israel but then they are frequently withdrawn. When the West Bank is placed under a total closure or when the zone in which a university resides is closed, such as Bethlehem, students cannot reach their classes. The Gaza Strip has suffered the most from the closures, as many of the students enrolled at Bir Zeit or Bethlehem University have not been able to attend classes for several years. A World Vision report cites a figure of 1,200 Gaza students being affected. When Israel declares a closure on either Gaza or the West Bank, students must return home and all permits are cancelled. Then they must re-apply for renewed permits with no guarantee they will be granted.

---

[12] B'Tselem, *Disputed Waters: Israel's Responsibility For the Water Shortage in the Occupied Territories*, B'Tselem, Jerusalem, Summer, 1998.

Bir Zeit University is the oldest and most prestigious of the Palestinian schools. Its Human Rights Action Project has studied the closures and report that some students take 9 years to complete their 4-year undergraduate degree. Several Gaza students enrolled at Bir Zeit in 1996 lost their permits after a Hamas bus bombing and have not been reinstated, thereby losing four years of their educational careers.[13]

## Economic and trade aspects of the Oslo Accords

Since Israel's military occupation of the Gaza Strip and West Bank in 1967, these areas have become increasingly dependent upon the Israeli economy, trade, and commerce. The Palestinian areas have been under a near total Israeli control in such matters as imports and exports, water usage, electricity, relief and development, and local and international communications. During this period Palestinians have been prevented from exporting their produce. The Oslo Accords promised relief to the Palestinians as these matters were to be discussed in April 1994 at the Paris Economic Protocols—the major economic, commerce, and trade component of the peace process. Various articles in the Paris Protocols provided the basis by which Palestinian and Israeli imports and exports would be granted equal trade status with a particular focus on gaining access for Palestinian agricultural and industrial exports to international markets. In the Paris meetings, the European Union offered preferential trade agreements with both sides. It was agreed that a seaport and airport would be opened in the Gaza Strip.

Through the first quarter of the year 2000 (six years into the Protocols) very few of the Paris economic reforms have become operational, or their function has been so minimal that they have not improved the rapidly deteriorating Palestinian economy. The airport in Gaza opened in November 1999, after numerous delays and with the prohibition that Israel has total control over each person and export that leaves the airport. Even Yasser Arafat must have Israel's permission before leaving the airport. Few international flights land or depart from Gaza rendering it more a symbolic victory than a truly functioning airport.

However, the most significant of all the factors effecting the Palestinian economy are the closures of the major Palestinian population centres that presently lie in Zone A. Israeli security checks and military encirclement of 70 percent of the Palestinian population residing in these zones have led to high unemployment rates, increased poverty, loss of imports and exports, and severe economic blight.

---

[13] *Promises, Promises: The Realities of Oslo*, World Vision UK, London, 1999, 20-21.

The Harvard University economist, Dr Sara Roy, has studied the economies of the Gaza Strip and West Bank for two decades and has closely monitored the effects of the Oslo Accords on both areas. Roy has summarized the interim report on the Palestinian economy as of 1999 in devastating terms:

> … a marked deterioration in Palestinian economic life and an accelerated de-development process. The key features of this process have been heightened by the effects of closure, the defining economic feature of the post-Oslo period. Among its results are enclavization, seen in the physical separation of the West Bank and Gaza; the weakening of economic relations between the Palestinian and Israeli economies; and growing division within the Palestinian labor market, with the related, emerging pattern of economic activity … the prospects for sustained economic development are nonexistent and remain so as long as closure continues.[14]

Roy's careful statistical, political, and demographic analysis confirms that Palestinians are in far worse economic shape after seven years of the Oslo Accords than they were prior to the Accords in the summer of 1993.

Roy uses the term 'de-development' to describe what has occurred to the Palestinian areas since 1967, a trend that Oslo has accelerated. 'De-development' can be defined as 'a structural relationship between a stronger (dominant) and a weaker (subordinate) economy.'[15] She compares it to underdevelopment which fails to utilize the resources and reach the potential of the people and the said economy, whereas 'de-development' is an intentional process of undermining the subordinate economy through various procedures that give political and economic benefits to the dominate party (Israel).

Among the procedures Roy points to are: 1) the expropriation and dispossession of Palestinian economic resources such as land, water, control of electricity, control of planning, etc; 2) 'integration and externalisation': restricting employment opportunities in the Israeli market for Palestinian goods while limiting the development of the Palestinian economy so as to discourage internal economic activities; 3) deinstitutionalization: the consequences of 1 and 2, the strangulation of Palestinian industries to the extent that there are few if any viable business and industrial systems and

---

[14] Sara Roy, 'De-development Revisited: Palestinian Economy and Society Since Oslo', *Journal of Palestine Studies,* Volume XXVII, Number 3, Spring, 1999, 64.

[15] *Op. cit.,* 64-65.

institutions that generate capital. Here Roy makes the stunning observation that in 1927 the average business establishment in Palestine employed 4.2 persons, and today it is the same. Thus the Palestinian business sector is not capable of providing employment let alone generate capital at a higher rate than it did more than 80 years ago.

To place this in perspective, we should bear in mind that the international economy has been in the midst of the 1990s boom and Israel itself has reaped the economic benefits of the growth, both in terms of its external markets and in terms of its own GNP. Development of new (mostly technological) industries have boomed for Israel in the 1990s , and now it has access to more international markets than at any previous time in its history.

To briefly illustrate the point, Roy looks at the effects that the military closures have had on the Palestinian areas since 1993. Roy points to March 1993 as the beginning of the closures, but they were actually 'field-tested' by Israel during the Gulf War (January-February, 1991) when total closures were imposed on the West Bank and Gaza Strip which were at times a 23-hour-a-day 'shoot on site' military enforcement. Israel learned the lessons of these severe policies and refined them for later use.

Following Oslo there were three types of closures: 'General'—restrictions on labour, goods, and production between the Palestinian areas (Gaza and West Bank) and Israel; 'Total Closure'—complete banning of any movement, usually following an attack on Israeli military or civilians by Palestinians; 'Internal Closures'—restricts movement of people and goods between the Palestinian areas inside the West Bank or Gaza Strip. Roy claims the 'closures' have:

> … almost entirely eliminated movement between the West Bank and Gaza, in effect isolating the two territories from each other, and has severely diminished economic activity between the Territories and Israel. Furthermore, by restricting Palestinian access to Jerusalem, the closure policy has bifurcated the northern and southern regions of the West Bank, whose primary road connections pass through Jerusalem. Since East Jerusalem is the commercial heart of the West Bank, closure has debilitated the city's Arab economy. In fact, by early 1998, less than 4 percent of Palestinians living in the West Bank and Gaza Strip had permission to enter Jerusalem.[16]

Roy gives several economic factors that demonstrate the severity of the closures. Unemployment fluctuates according to the type of closure

---

[16] *Op. cit.,* 69.

imposed by Israel. During the March-April 1996 total closure after Hamas bombings, unemployment rose to 66 percent of the Palestinian work force. In general, unemployment has tripled since the Oslo Accords were signed. The largest employer is now the Palestinian Authority, which restricts the development of industry, import and export systems, and kills the potential of reversing the rapidly declining GNP. Added to this is the fact that the population of the Gaza Strip is expected to double by 2010. She adds that the PA created at least 65,000 jobs between 1993-1997, which now employs more Palestinian workers (18.7 percent) than the manufacturing sector (16.6 percent) or agriculture (11.6 percent), and was virtually tied into construction (19 percent). The World Bank has noted the imbalance in the Palestinian Authority payroll by warning that the consequences will be felt in the declining resources for education, health services, and other social services.[17]

Another indicator is the decline of private investment in the Palestinian economy in relation to the GDP. Since the Oslo Accords were signed, private investment has continued to slide. In 1993 (pre-Oslo), private investment was $529, or 21 percent of the GDP. In 1995 it dropped to 8 percent of the GDP at $320 million. It increased slightly in 1996 to 12 percent but has continued to slide below 8 percent since then.[18]

Yet another factor that has damaged the Palestinian economy is the corruption and mismanagement of the Palestinian Authority itself. The World Bank and International Monetary Fund in co-operation with the CIA were made aware of significant irregularities and threatened to cut off all aid until the Authority submitted to their practices. Whether this was put into practice or not has not been made public at this point.

Finally, Roy points to the export-import ratios, which the Paris Protocols had promised to adjust so that Palestinians would have 'equal access' to Europe and other markets as does Israel. She concludes that Israel has nearly killed Gaza's ability to export products (citing a 1997 United States State Department Report), which noted that 99 percent of Gaza's goods come from Israel and 1 percent from Egypt, thus giving Israel a controlled outlet for its products.[19] While Gaza did trade with the West Bank and Egypt prior to 1993, the closures and border restrictions have nearly eliminated these markets. Thus the promises of the Paris Protocols are at this point frozen in terms of their capacity to revive the Palestinian economy. Whether they will be enacted in a manner that can save the Palestinian economy at any time soon is doubtful. The Wye River Agreements, which were touted as placing peace on track, enabled Israel to effectively control the economic

---

[17] *Op. cit.*, 70.
[18] *Op. cit.*, 71-72.
[19] *Op. cit.*, 77-78.

areas to be discussed, and the matters of closures, settlements, and decline of the Palestinian economy were matters not to be discussed.

Roy concludes that the Palestinians are in an economic *bantustan* situation, which she defines it as 'economic enclavization':

> Economic enclavization describes a process of growing economic separation or partition and bifurcation that strikingly parallels its political counterpart, Bantustanization. Economic autarky, which is linked to enclavization, refers to a turning inward of economic behavior, which is linked to enclavization, refers to a turning inward of economic behavior away from international market relations toward more traditional activities and production modes. These new dynamics, expressed in employment, trade, and income patterns, have further crippled the Palestinian economy.[20]

Roy adds: 'As long as closure remains in place—as seems likely given present circumstances—there will be no economic development or improvement in living conditions.'[21] She believes that political solutions will also fail if they do not stop the destructive effects of the closures and the other economic forms of 'de-development.'

Whether it is from a political analysis of continued Israeli colonization of the prime Palestinian land or the diversion of prime resources such as water, or the military containment of the Palestinian population in small islands surrounded by rings of settlements and the Israeli military, it is a situation that can best be summarized as *apartheid*. The above analysis by Professor Roy provides the economic data that underscores the gradual deterioration of the Palestinian economy, even to the extent of economic dependence on the occupying power and a depressed economy that will need decades to recover. The Oslo Accords and their failure to contain Israeli expansionism in the Palestinian areas, the failure to loosen the damaging and complex closures between Palestinian areas and Israel and Palestine, have created a depressed, third-world group of tiny *bantustans* that have little hope of political, economic, or social viability in the coming decades.

These are among the conditions that cause an increasing number of Palestinian Christians and Muslims to search for a way to escape. In a recent visit to Jerusalem, I dined with leading Palestinian clergy who discussed the following statement: 'Most Palestinian Christians now have emigration

---

[20] *Op. cit.*, 68.
[21] *Op. cit.*, 79.

on their mind as the primary way of coping with our depressing situation.'
As priest and pastor reflected on the thesis, one by one they all agreed. After
seven years of the Oslo Accords and no sign of any superpower (the United
States) or trans-national organization (the United Nations), nor coalition of
nations (the European Union or Arab League), nor moral arguments from
Christian, Muslim or Jewish communities, will hold Israel accountable to any
peace process. Such a situation breeds insecurity and the desire to escape,
particularly if you are a shrinking minority. Nevertheless, despite the
hopelessness on the political, economic, demographic, and social levels,
there are still those in Palestine and Israel who hope and will make sacrifices
for a just society, and will remain in their lands to pay whatever price is
necessary to work for a just peace in the Holy Land. They will never submit
to Israel's occupation of their land and the persistent infringement of their
human and religious rights.

## Summary

According to the preceding narrative and documentation by both American,
Israeli and Palestinian political and economic analysts, the Oslo Peace
Accords have led to a deterioration of the political, economic, spiritual,
demographic, and psychological dimension of life for the Palestinians inside
the West Bank, Gaza Strip, and East Jerusalem. The Oslo Peace Accords
were initially well received by Palestinians and Israelis alike with opinion
polls showing over 85 percent approval rating from Palestinians and similar
results for Israelis after the signing ceremony on 13 September 1993. The
Accords may have been the last possibility for the indigenous Christians of
Palestine to sense a reversal of the various factors that have caused their
community to emigrate in significant numbers over the previous fifty plus
years. This accelerated deterioration has affected Christians and Muslims
alike, but as the Palestinian Christians are the smallest and most vulnerable
community, their exodus is most noticeable. The following summary of the
1993-2000 period provides many but not all of their reasons for the failure of
the Oslo Accords and why the subsequent climate of injustice is likely to
facilitate the disappearance of most of the Palestinian Christians over the
next fifty years:

1.   The Oslo Peace Accords and the subsequent meetings and agreements
     have been inadequate to hold Israel accountable for a variety of practices
     that have undermined a just peace, including economic and physical
     closures of the Palestinian areas, restrictions on travel from one district

to the other including limitations on travel to worship sites and for medical emergencies.

2.  The Oslo Accords and subsequent implementation meetings, including the Paris Protocols (July 1994), the Cairo Agreement (May 1994), the Oslo II Agreements at Taba Egypt (September 1995), the Hebron Agreement (January 1997) and the Wye River Agreement (October 1998), are structurally porous and allow the stronger political power to manipulate the process. The PLO, having been weakened by political miscalculations by its leadership during the second Gulf War and by the end of the Cold War, saw the dramatic political and public relations gains of the *Intifada* disappear within a matter of weeks in 1991. As the stronger party, Israel has been able to utilize a series of delay tactics, first during the failed Madrid Peace Talks of November 1992-the summer of 1993; and then to employ more sophisticated delay and renegotiate strategies during the Oslo peace process, leading to months and years of frustration and failure. Such tactics have undermined the process and created a climate of anger and cynicism.

3.  The Oslo Accords have made the Palestinians responsible for policing the Palestinian opposition to the Oslo Accords, whether in the Gaza Strip or West Bank, both of which Israel has failed to contain and eliminate. Now most security failures are blamed on the Palestinian Authority and have often become the pretext for implementation delays and Israel's demand to renegotiate previously agreed upon principles and strategies.

4.  The United States has not served as an honest and impartial facilitator of the peace process. Internal pressure by the Israeli lobby on pro-Israel members of the US Congress, the State Department, or Clinton Administration officials have caused the Israeli agenda to dominate the terms of the negotiations, the process of implementation, and the end results.

5.  The Oslo process has neither slowed nor has it halted the illegal land confiscations and accelerated Israeli colonization of Areas B and C of the West Bank, particularly in the Jerusalem region. Thus the question of Jerusalem is being determined by Israel's creation of facts on the ground and erosion of the fragile demographic balance between Jewish and Palestinian populations in what was previously Arab East Jerusalem has now been altered in favour of the Jewish population.

6.  In addition to delaying and pre-empting negotiations on the future status of Jerusalem, other critical issues that have been removed from negotiations are the following: the right of Palestinian refugees, (approximately 55 percent of the Palestinians in the world), to return to

their homes or receive compensation, as have Jews from Germany and other European nations for property lost during the Nazi era; the cessation of various military closures in the West Bank, East Jerusalem, and Gaza Strip; the right of Palestinians to maintain sovereign control over the use of such vital natural resources as water (of which up to 60 percent of the Palestinian water resources are diverted to Israeli use); the total cessation of Israeli colonization of Palestinian land through settlements and confiscation procedures; the end of restrictions, primarily in Jerusalem, that prevent family reunification or remove Jerusalem residency rights from Palestinian citizens of Jerusalem.

7.  The Arafat-led Palestinian Authority has become increasingly dictatorial, oppressive of Palestinian human rights, and corrupt in its management of development funds received from the international community. The PA is not only mistrusted by the World Bank and much of the international community but it is increasingly unpopular, feared, and will be resisted by the local population. While it is striving to correct previous errors, the jury is still out concerning the capacity of the Authority to practise representative democracy and carve out an independent political line from its current Israeli and CIA domination. It is vital that democratic procedures be imposed with strict accountability mechanisms for compliance by the Palestinian Authority.

8.  The Oslo process has granted Palestinians complete rule over only 9 percent of the West Bank and 60 percent of the Gaza Strip and none of East Jerusalem. Under the existing provisions of the Oslo Accords with Areas A, B, and C, the Palestinians will only receive at most 40-50 percent of the West Bank and will loose much of its natural water reserves and contiguous land upon which to build a sovereign state. Closures and various restrictions on the Palestinian economy, travel, and political organizations have left the Palestinians isolated and impoverished. The only just solution to the dilemma is for the Oslo Accords to be restructured or entirely new negotiations be opened under impartial international supervision with the framework based upon the existing international consensus, United Nations resolutions 242 and 338.

9.  The best analogy that has been used to describe the present and anticipated future of the Palestinian areas is *apartheid*, or separate autonomous colonies, otherwise known as *bantustans*. These isolated, impoverished, and controlled regions have no future as a viable independent and sovereign state nor can they generate sufficient capital to provide a liveable future for the population. Further, this arrangement will breed terrorism and frequent unrest for both the Israeli and

Palestinian communities, and will undermine the long range prospects for a just and durable peace.

10. The few tangible economic and developmental advancements received by the Palestinians are in the end managed and controlled by the United States' Central Intelligence Agency (CIA) and the Israeli military and various intelligence organizations (primarily the Mossad). For example, any Palestinian individual or vehicle using the new Gaza-West Bank access road must possess a plastic security card that includes a background check. Travellers cannot stop along the road and must exit at sites indicated on entry. Likewise, any person departing or entering via the Gaza Airport may do so only with the clearance of the Israeli security forces. Even President Arafat must have Israeli clearance to enter and exit from the airport.

11. There is a serious political, economic, social, and demographic asymmetry in the structure, implementation, and results of the Oslo Peace Accords that favours Israel and is managed by the United States in an Israeli direction. It appears at this writing that the Oslo process has been used by the United States to create US-Israeli hegemonic zone in the eastern Mediterranean.

12. Given the constricted and generally hopeless quality of life in the Palestinian areas, conditions do not appear to have the potential to reverse the momentum for emigration that had been developing among Palestinian Christians since the establishment of the State of Israel. Thus the remaining 2 percent of the Palestinian Christian population is likely to emigrate as well. As Canon Naim Ateek, an Anglican priest and a leading voice in the Palestinian community, observed in January, 2000: 'Today, as never before, the majority of the remaining Christians are planning to leave, and those who are still here, have the seeds of emigration planted in their minds.'

# Chapter 10
# DEATH OR RESURRECTION?

In 1853, the Russian Czar declared Orthodox (Christian) supremacy over the Church of the Holy Sepulchre and other major Christian sites in the Holy Land. The edict came after decades of escalating tension between the two emerging imperial powers, France and Russia. French political aspirations were often expressed through the Roman (called Latin in the Middle East) Catholics, whereas Russia favoured the Eastern Orthodox Church. Illustrative of the problem in Palestine was an event that occurred during Christmas, 1847, when Latin priests and Greek and Russian Orthodox monks fought pitched battles inside the Church of the Nativity. The struggle was precipitated when the Latin priests hung a silver star over the cave believed to be the birthplace of Jesus Christ. On the surface, the star seemed to be an innocent gift from France but it was charged with political symbolism due to the growing rivalry with Russia. The decision to hang it directly over such an important Christian holy site was interpreted by Russia and all Orthodoxy as a provocative expression of Catholic and French sovereignty over this holy place. Tempers flared when monks came to blows using large crosses and candelabra as weapons as they slashed and severely beat each another. After the police restored order and carried off the wounded monks, the Ottoman governor of Palestine ordered a sentry of 'neutral' Muslim soldiers to guard the Church of the Holy Sepulchre and the Church of the Nativity from the passions of the Christian leaders.[1]

Tampering with holy sites in Jerusalem during times of heightened political tension can have far reaching consequences, as occurred on 28 September 2000. A visit to the Haram al-Sharif ('the Noble Sanctuary' known to Israelis as the Temple Mount) by the controversial Israeli Likud Party Chair, Ariel Sharon,[2] triggered a wave of angry protests by Palestinian

---

[1] Peretz, *op. cit.,* 87.

[2] Sharon's long public career included leading an October 1953 raid on Palestinian refugees in Kibya (Jordan) where 45 homes were blown up and 69 Palestinians were killed. In 1982, as Israel's Defence Minister, Sharon was the architect of the invasion of Lebanon and was implicated by an Israeli commission as 'indirectly' involved in plotting the Sabra-Shatila massacre where between 2,000-4,000 Palestinians killed. International organizations such as Amnesty International, the International Commission of Jurists, and the United Nations General Assembly condemned Israel's

Muslims that spread throughout the Holy Land and eventually to major cities around the world. In late September 2000 Sharon announced that he would compete with the previous Prime Minister, Benyamin Netanyahu, for leadership of the Likud Party as the government of Ehud Barak was on the brink of collapse. Palestinians were aware that a Sharon-led government would implement aggressive policies toward Jerusalem and further colonization of the Palestinian territories, undoubtedly placing these districts under the exclusive domain of Israel. Thus the presence of Sharon and the Likud Party leadership was sufficient to unleash a flurry of stones that drew gunfire from upwards of 1,000 police (sent by the Barak government) to protect the Sharon delegation. Four Palestinians were killed and over one hundred wounded in this initial incident By early December, the number of Palestinians who had been killed was approaching 325 with over 9,000 wounded, many maimed for life. Palestinian cities such as Bethlehem, Beit Jala, Ramallah, and Gaza were shelled by tanks and US-made Apache helicopters on a regular basis and at unprecedented levels. Both sides described the situation as a state of war.

A December 2000 delegation of 24 US Christian leaders were told by the Vatican's Apostolic Delegate in the Holy Land, Fr Pietro Sambi, that the situation for Palestinians was reaching crisis proportions. There were realistic fears of starvation in Palestinian villages and refugee camps. Concerning the fears of Palestinian Christians, he emphasized the need to keep the faith alive in the Holy land, but added: 'There is also a sense of solitude and loneliness for Christians, without a strong sense of solidarity.'[3] Increasingly, Palestinian Christians were feeling a sense of abandonment by their fellow Christians around the world as they stood under intensified Israeli bombardment and military closures. Bethlehem's Christian leadership cancelled Christmas celebrations for what had been planned as a series of gala events with tens of thousands in attendance. Instead, the Christians of Bethlehem will recall Christmas 2000 as a time of war, deprivation, and living under daily bombardment from the Israeli army.

The Sharon visit was by no means the primary cause of the violence but simply the match that lit the fire, unleashing a seven-year reservoir of pent up Palestinian anger. Palestinians understood very well that in the year 2000, after all the deadlines of the Oslo Peace Accords had passed, they were in a far worse political, economic, and demographic situation than they had been prior to the 13 September 1993 signing of the Oslo Accords. Driven by

---

disproportionate use of force against the demonstrators but the clashes continued. As October wore on both Israeli and Palestinian analysts began to interpret the Palestinian resistance as '*Al-Aqsa Intifada*' or the Palestinian War of Independence.

[3] Press release, Notre Dame Center, Jerusalem, December 10, 2000.

domestic political needs, US President Bill Clinton and Israeli Prime Minister Ehud Barak pressured Arafat and the Palestinians meet at Camp David in July 2000 in an attempt to produce a quick solution on the most complicated issues (the future status of Jerusalem, the right of return for refugees, international borders of Israel and the future Palestinian state, the cessation of Israel's illegal settlements, etc.). Arafat balked, claiming he did not have the domestic support necessary to decide on the most vital factors in the Israeli-Palestinian relationship and requested an additional three months for preparation. Under mounting pressure from the United States, Arafat went to Camp David but the negotiations ended in a stalemate. Immediately, both Clinton and Barak blamed the Palestinians for rejecting Israel's 'generous' offer. The two sides seemed far from a peace settlement by September, and Barak's political fate hung in the balance. The collapse of the Camp David meeting marked what most Palestinians already knew as 'the end of the Oslo Peace Process.' It is in this context that Sharon's visit to the third holiest site for Muslims must be understood as a provocative political statement. Israeli human rights attorney Allegra Pacheco's editorial in the *New York Times* summarized why Palestinian anger ran deeper than the Sharon event:

> Pointing the finger solely at Mr. Sharon for the violence in Israel, the West Bank and Gaza simply masks the painful truth that many supporters of the Middle East peace agreement signed in Oslo in 1993 do not want to admit: the Oslo process cannot succeed. The proponents of the agreement, including the Clinton administration, never fully informed the Palestinian people that the accord did not offer any guarantee of Palestinian self-determination, full equality and an end to the military occupation. In reality, 'Oslo' wears no clothes at all.[4]

Pacheco and other Israeli and Palestinian analysts argue convincingly that the Oslo peace process led to another form of Israel's occupying approximately 90 percent of the Palestinian areas and could never lead to real independence and political sovereignty. Actually the Oslo process became a disguise for the gradual implementation of an *apartheid* system in East Jerusalem, the West Bank and Gaza Strip that formally authorized Israel to dictate the means by which they would institute a clever form of military and economic control over the Palestinians. Pacheco summarizes the results of Oslo:

---

[4] Allegra Pacheco, 'Israel's Doomed Peace', *The New York Times*, 3 October 2000.

Since 1994, Palestinians have seen the influx of 50,000 new Jewish settlers into the West Bank and Gaza, and paving of more than 400 kilometers of roads on confiscated land, demolition of more than 800 Palestinian homes, a threefold increase in unemployment in the territories, and a 21 percent decline in their gross domestic product, and the arrest of 13,000 Palestinians, and complete curtailment of freedom of movement.[5]

Adding to the seriousness of the Israeli-Palestinian violence was an international dimension that began to manifest itself by mid-October. Anti-Israel and anti-American sentiment grew dramatically across the Middle East, Asia and the Islamic world as massive demonstrations were held in most capitals and major cities throughout the world. The London demonstration of 22 October reported 20,000 participants while marches in Cairo, Beirut, and Kuala-Lampur turned out nearly 100,000 in each city. Televised pictures of Palestinian youths being shot by Israeli soldiers and accounts of the disproportionate use of force were broadcast instantly on television and internet accounts added analysis that fuelled the anger. Soon there was concern that other 'fronts' to the conflict would open as the Lebanese militia Hizbollah captured three Israeli soldiers and Israel threatened retaliation in Syria and Lebanon. When the *Cole*, a United States navy vessel was bombed by what appeared to be a suicide mission in Yemen, killing 16 and wounding scores, the growing anti-US sentiment in the Middle East was unmistakable. Western countries closed embassies and placed their military installations on high alert and tourism, particularly Holy Land tourism, dropped by as much as 90 percent. The region was on the brink of war.

On 25 October, reports circulated in several newspapers and western Christian organizations monitoring the persecution of Christians worldwide that Palestinian Muslims had deliberately used Christian towns from which to attack Israeli settlements. The initial article, published in the *Jerusalem Post* on 25 October, claimed that Israel was helping Palestinian Christians to emigrate as a result of renewed Muslim aggression. It appears that the article was more a public relations 'cover' for Israel's military strategy of aerial and land bombardment of the large Palestinian Christian populations in Bethlehem, Beit Sahour, and Beit Jala, allegedly in response to Palestinian gunmen shooting into the nearby Israeli settlement of Gilo. Fortunately, no Israeli settlers were killed at Gilo, but several Palestinians died in the Bethlehem district. In addition, a climate of terror resulted from the aerial bombardment

---

[5]   *Ibid.*

and the YMCA, a Greek Orthodox Church, and several homes and businesses sustained significant damage and the shelling of these cities continued almost daily for five weeks. Revd Dr Mitri Raheb's Christmas letter for 2000 stated:

> We still remember how, one year ago, the streets of Bethlehem were all lit up with the colourful Christmas lights. Choirs sang the good tidings of the angels and street performers performed their magical shows for children, whose eyes were wide open with wonder. This year these same eyes are filled with anxiety and fear, for the only lights they see this Advent season are the blaze of exploding missiles and beams of helicopters hovering low above their homes. The only sound they hear is that of bullets and shells raining on their schools and playgrounds.[6]

As a result, everyone anticipates that more Palestinian Christians will be forced to emigrate. With another failed peace process and violence all around, most Palestinian Christian families fear that their children will grow up with few job opportunities and face a situation that includes war and military occupation. Whether this present situation will lead to a repeat of the 1948 *Nakba* remains to be seen. These and other questions linger as I conclude the final chapter. With these haunting questions hanging in the balance and the future of a just peace in the Holy Land in doubt, this final chapter will turn with great hesitation to strategies and options available to those Palestinian Christians who choose to remain in Palestine. One is humbled by the task of speculating on a people's future when their very survival is in question. These final pages will seek to articulate certain selected components that Palestinian Christians have shared with me over the past decade that might begin to build an agenda for not only themselves but for concerned Muslims and Jews in the Middle East and their friends around the world. At the same time I must add a note of urgency due to the desperate circumstances in which they find themselves in the year 2001. The scriptures tell us: 'Where there is no vision the people will perish' (Proverbs 29:18). Thus an aggressive but realistic vision is needed for the remnant of Palestinian Christians that will remain to serve their people, their God, their nation, and remind the international community of their responsibilities during the difficult years that lie ahead.

---

[6] Dr Mitri Raheb, 'Christmas Greetings from Bethlehem', The International Centre, Bethlehem, Palestine; 11 December 2000,<annadwa.planet.edu>.

## *The struggle for justice in the Holy Land*

We need to be reminded that the fundamental issues in the one hundred year Israeli/Zionist-Palestinian struggle are essentially political: the struggle for land, sovereignty, international legitimacy, the right of all refugees to return to their homes or be duly compensated for losses, and the right to security and control over ones destiny in an independent state. Political theorists James Bill and Robert Springborg state that there are three principal requirements for successful state formation: a 'state idea' or ideology; vibrant political organizations, and an international community that grants legitimacy to the state project.[7] I would add a fourth component: control over a contiguous portion of the land upon which your people live. Clearly, the Zionist movement achieved statehood by 1948 as it successfully achieved all of these goals between 1897-1948. The Palestinians, on the other hand, have achieved only three of the four, and those in a limited sense. They achieved international legitimacy when the United States and Israel recognized them in 1993, but they have yet to attain statehood (other than in a nominal sense with their Algiers declaration in 1988). Until now, the critical component of controlling their land and resources is in doubt for the Palestinian people. The Israeli-US proposal on land and statehood offered at the Camp David 2000 negotiations offered Palestinians discontinuous islands that were surrounded by areas controlled by Israel that at any time could be the basis for complete closures on the Palestinian population centres. Further, Camp David 2000, provided no end to the persistent expansion and construction of Israeli settlements in the West Bank and Gaza Strip and offered no Palestinian control over East Jerusalem, and no assurances that the Palestinians would be able to access Arab and European countries to develop their sagging economy. The map eventually released after the Camp David II conference divided the Palestinian areas into a series of disconnected cantons and was clearly a step toward implementing an apartheid system in Palestine.

The Palestinian theologian Naim Ateek, founder and Director of the *Sabeel* Centre for Liberation Theology, has reminded us that the fundamental issue in the Israeli-Palestinian conflict is justice, and particularly a theological and political justice based the equality of persons. Whereas much of the prevailing *Realpolitik* orientation of academia and government officials will dismiss the goal of justice as unrealistic and romantic liberalism, it would seem that the religious, peace, and human rights community must embrace

---

[7] James Bill and Robert Springborg, *Politics in the Middle East*, New York: Harper Collins, 1964, page 318.

the concept of justice as their operational mandate if they are to remain true to their respective moral and political heritages. The 'Jerusalem *Sabeel* Document', released in May 2000, concentrates on the justice theme as the basis of a lasting peace in Israel-Palestine:

> 1. God, creator and redeemer, loves all people equally (John 3:16, Acts 17:24-28).
> 2. God demands that justice be done. No enduring peace, security, or reconciliation is possible without the foundation of justice. The demands of justice will not disappear; and the struggle for justice must be pursued diligently and persistently but non-violently (Jeremiah 9:23-24; Isaiah 32:16-17; Romans 12:17-21).
> 3. The Holy Land is God's gift to Palestinians and Israelis. They must live justly and mercifully and be good stewards of it (Micah 6:8).[8]

It is essential that Palestinian Christians remind the international community, especially churches, the peace movement, academia, and the media, to hold fast to such values as universal human rights (as embodied in the Universal Declaration of Human Rights) and the practice of international law as the foundation upon which peace can be established in the Holy Land. In recent years these principles and practices have been abandoned for the sake of pragmatic approaches, most of which have failed to bring a true peace to Israel and Palestine. The religious and legal principles of justice in the Holy Land as articulated in the *Sabeel* document, appeal to the Judeo-Christian-Islamic tradition, in the hope that they will seek a common vision for the three communities to establish a just and durable peace. These principles are embodied in United Nations' resolutions 194 (the refugees' right of return), 242 and 338 (the return of all territories occupied by Israel to their status prior to June 1967). These standards of justice remain the international norm for a just and lasting peace between Israelis and Palestinians. They have been adopted by every nation except Israel and by most Christian organizations throughout the world.

Former President Jimmy Carter recently published an editorial in the *Washington Post* reminding everyone that the official position of the United States has been the full implementation of Resolutions 242 and 338.[9] The Clinton Administration appears to have ignored his position and while

---

[8] The Jerusalem *Sabeel* Document, Jerusalem: The *Sabeel* Ecumenical Center for Liberation Theology, May, 2000, 1

[9] Jimmy Carter, *Washington Post*, 26 November 2000, page B7.

occasionally referring to it in name; the Oslo process became a detour around the resolutions. Despite attempts by the United States and Israel to by-pass or weaken these resolutions during the Madrid and Oslo processes, it would appear that European, Latin American, Asian, African, and Islamic nations could bring pressure upon all member nations of the United Nations as well as other international and transnational agencies to return to these time-tested resolutions. The crisis of October and the *Intifada* of 2000 demonstrate that there are no other workable formulas available at this time.

Thus there is ample evidence that there should be no compromise concerning the international norms for a political settlement in Israel/Palestine, whatever arguments and pressures brought forth by the United States and Israel, the only countries that stand outside the international consensus. If the international community could unite around a significant campaign for a peace process based upon these norms, a new venue for negotiations may be possible. Progressive Israeli and Palestinian human rights and non-governmental organizations, and Palestinian Christian leaders would do well to unite their efforts as quickly as possible and appeal to the international community at multiple levels for new negotiations based on the international consensus. Otherwise, the crisis in the Holy Land could grow into a regional conflict, threatening not only the security of Israel and Palestine, but western nations and their political and economic interests. Since the United Nations resolutions 242 and 338 were issued in 1967 and 1974 respectively, the United States and Israel have steadfastly pursued strategies that by-passed or undermined initiatives that might have convened a peace process based on these formulas. Today over thirty years have been lost with untold suffering for both parties to the conflict with no relief in sight.

Palestinian Christians will have important roles to play as they develop their nation and institutions. On the external level, they can play an important role with western governments and with churches throughout the world n efforts to mobilize support for a new peace process based on the UN resolutions 242 and 338. However, on the internal level, Palestinian Christians must build intimate ties with progressive Israeli organizations as well as with the Palestinian Authority and the important Islamic movements within Palestine and throughout the Islamic world. Additionally, Palestinians inside Israel must continue to struggle for their fundamental civil liberties while becoming engaged at the international level. They must articulate their vision for a future Palestinian state based on the equality of persons and the development of a civil society established on democratic processes and the rule of law.

Returning to their external role, Palestinian Christians will be able to play a pivotal role in building bridges to western Christian churches and organizations as well as governments in Europe, North and South America, Africa and in the Pacific, if they can mobilize the churches, peace organizations, and human rights groups on their behalf. Significant political, moral, and financial support may be available to Palestinians from western governments, religious organizations, and donor agencies. With over half a million Palestinians in South and Central America, many of whom are wealthy and hold high government positions, the Christians of Palestine might concentrate on these 'family members' for significant political, economic and moral support in the future. A high priority should be given to these communities in the next decade.

Palestinian Christians may be able to play an important role in overcoming the Zionist pressures that have traditionally locked them out of the media, Western governments, and funding agencies. Some Palestinian Christians will need to concentrate on opening channels to political leadership and financial institutions as they pursue such controversial issues as remunerations and compensation for property and bank accounts lost since 1948. Just as Herzl and Weizmann found their way to the British media and political elite through such Christian Zionist connections as Lord Arthur Balfour and David Lloyd George, so too will Palestinian Christians be able to make similar informal connections with persons in power today who share moral or religious convictions that match the Palestinian quest for an independent Palestinian state.

More immediate is the need to protect the Palestinians not only in the West Bank and Gaza Strip but also in Jerusalem and Israel. If the present political struggle is to continue in either a high or low-grade form of warfare, or even in a 'cold peace,' all Palestinian civilians will need to be protected not only from the superior Israeli military attacks and from various Jewish militias and vigilante organizations. Such a call for protection was issued in the early days of the *Intifada* of 2000, and found support in human rights organizations such as Amnesty International, Physicians for Human Rights, and the United Nations Human Rights Commission as well as various international church agencies. As the vulnerable community, demonstrated simply by the disproportionate number of Palestinian casualties and the sophisticated weapons available to Israel, there is no question that Israeli military initiatives will lead to an unimaginable number of Palestinian casualties, as most Palestinians remain unprotected. These sobering realities should lead all Palestinian organizations from the political leadership down to the youth in the streets to limit their expressions of violence to forms of non-violent resistance. During the 1987-93 *Intifada,* it was the collective acts of non-violent resistance such as the Beit Sahour tax revolt, boycotts of Israeli products, demonstrations, strikes by merchants, and the stones of children against the tanks of Israel that captured international support. Israel is capable of defeating all Arab armies combined and will simply annihilate Palestinian military strategies. The victory of the Hizbollah in Lebanon cannot be compared to the situation in Palestine, as many Islamic leaders are now suggesting, due to the vulnerability of the Palestinian civilian population and the capacity of Israel to control all resources, the economy, and to market its tactics both at the political level and in the international media. Simply put, Palestinians cannot win a short-term or protracted military struggle. Thus the political, diplomatic, and non-violent vehicles are the only means available to the Palestinians, but these will be successful only if the international community unites with the Palestinian cause, particularly in Europe and the United States. Palestinians cannot achieve this alone. This goal can only be achieved through a collaborative international diplomatic and grassroots campaign, combined with the steadfast efforts of Palestinians on the ground. The South African victory over *apartheid* is the closest parallel and should be studied and replicated by Palestinians and their supporters, both in Palestine/Israel and in the west. As a by-product of this international campaign for a just peace in the Holy Land, the life of the Palestinian Christian community can be extended into the next century.

## *The search for unity*

The search for unity within the Palestinian community and among Palestinian Christians is essential if the Christian community is to survive. Interdenominational division, competition, and inter-communal fighting have often characterized the Christians of the Holy Land. The often petty competition for prominence and space in the Church of the Holy Sepulchre is but one striking example. Palestinian Christians are keenly aware of their diminished numbers and the *Intifada* of the Fall, 2000, points up their utter vulnerability. During the first *Intifada* of 1987-91, the 'Heads of Churches' in the Holy Land united for the first time in history and signed a series of statements that pointed toward their newly emerging unity. Their opposition to Israel's military tactics against the Palestinian community and appeals for assistance were forcefully expressed to the international community. For the most part, their international friends responded in a positive manner with resolutions, volunteers, collections, constructive stories in the press, and soon the Palestinian people were the 'David' going up against the Israeli Goliath. These expressions of unity within the Christian community and simultaneously with international partners is one key to future survival and success.

However, another problem threatens to divide Christians and Muslims. When reports began to reach the international media in late 1997 that the Palestinian Authority was persecuting Christians, it was discovered that the Israeli government had leaked false information to Christian Zionist organizations in Jerusalem. The situation became so serious that a bill was drafted in the United States' House of Representatives that threatened to cut funding for the Palestinian Authority as a consequence of the allegations of persecution, which were not fully substantiated. Most of the leading Palestinian Christian and Muslim organizations or their leadership issued unified statements or reports denouncing the Israeli allegations, and Palestinian Christian and human rights organizations cooperated with western agencies to correct the Israeli accounts.

One of the leading international advocates of religious freedom, Brother Andrew of Open Doors in Holland, joined the North American organization Evangelicals for Middle East Understanding in order to undertake a fact-finding mission in May 1998. Over 150 organizations and leaders on both sides of the conflict from Galilee to the Gaza Strip and throughout the West Bank were interviewed. The fact-finding mission concluded the following in its Jerusalem press statement of 22 May 1998:

> Systematic persecution of Christians by the Palestinian Authority cannot be substantiated, concluded a group of 14 Evangelical scholars, journalists, and charity leaders who just completed a two week fact-finding mission trip to the West Bank, Gaza, and Israel … To the contrary, the group found the earlier reports of abuse to be alarmist, oversimplified, politically motivated, and inaccurate.[10]

The EMEU group learned that close ties between the staunchly pro-Israel International Christian Embassy-Jerusalem (ICEJ) and appointees in the Netanyahu Government had initiated the media campaign. The ICEJ had received information from Prime Minister's Information Office, directed by David Bar-Ilan, that five Muslim converts to Christianity were mistreated by the Palestinian Authority. Research by the Palestinian human rights organization LAW, followed up by EMEU, discovered that indeed the five Muslims had converted to Christianity. However, it was also learned that the converts had previous criminal records and had been engaged in illegal land dealings in the Palestinian territories, facts not reported by the Israelis or the

---

[10] 'Evangelicals Counter Claims of Christian Persecution, Press Release, 22 May 1998', Evangelicals for Middle East Understanding, Chicago, Illinois; see also 'Persecution Propaganda?', *Christianity Today*, 13 July 1998.

ICEJ. The five Palestinians were imprisoned for their criminal activity, not their religious beliefs. An officer in the United States' Consulate also investigated the allegations and learned through an interview with Uri Mor, Director of Religious Affairs for the Israeli Government, that Bar-Ilan was behind the allegations. The EMEU group noted that the strategy was devised by the Israeli officials for purely political reasons, specifically, to undermine the credibility of Arafat's Palestinian Authority and to divide Christians from Muslims.

Christians and Muslims in Palestine and Israel will be forced by events to maintain close cooperation and trust as the political struggle intensifies in the coming years. Clearly, the *Intifada* of 2000 is being led by the Muslim majority in Palestine and the Islamic organizations appear to be the strongest forces in opposition to the Israeli occupation. However, due to the fact that anti-Arab and anti-Islamic stereotypes are still operative in much of Europe and North America, the increased visibility of Hamas and the dominance of Islamic slogans will enable both Israeli public relations experts and American journalists to interpret the conflict in simplistic terms that work to Israel's advantage. Among the themes that have historically worked to Israel's advantage are those that emphasize the 'historic enmity toward the Jews' sentiment or its more sophisticated version seen Harvard University political scientist Samuel Huntington's 'clash of civilizations' (Islamic east vs. 'Christian west'). These interpretative devises are highly marketable in the United States where the majority of the citizenry do not look beyond these 'sound bites.' The danger of these devices lies in the subtle but dangerous shift of the core political questions in the Israeli-Palestinian conflict to a more diversionary religious or pro-Zionist western interpretation. Israel can thus project itself as the west's best defence against the 'Islamic enemies' of western democracy.

Additionally, Israel is keen to take advantage of any occasion in which it can divide Palestinians along religious lines. A recent example occurred in late October 2000 when Israeli military bombardment of the Bethlehem district was interpreted by the *Jerusalem Post* as reflecting Christian-Muslim tension. Soon reports the United States media indicated that Muslim militants were shooting at Israeli settlements from Bethlehem, in order to bring Israeli wrath on the city and force its Christian residents out. Once again, investigations proved the claims to be an Israeli propaganda device and a tool to divide Christians and Muslims. Christian leaders from Jerusalem and Bethlehem responded immediately and issued joint statements that focused their analysis on the core political issues and the disproportionate use of weaponry by Israel and the disproportionate levels of Palestinian civilian population. Christian and Muslim leaders responded with a demonstration of unity and rightly issued statements that focused their statements on the political and military struggle.

In addition to solidarity between Palestinian Christians and Muslims there is also the critical task of unifying Palestinian Christianity from within. Palestinian Christians have been both victim and perpetrator of a series of divisions from the time of Constantine until the present. We have noted throughout this book that Patriarchs and bishops as well as local priests have competed with each other and abused power at the price of fragmenting their community. These practices have destroyed the fragile unity within each church and at times the image projected to the Muslims and Jews, as well as to the tourists and pilgrims, has been overwhelmingly negative. As the Christian community declines to less than 2 percent of the Palestinian population in Jerusalem and the West Bank, unity will be vital to ifs survival. Local Christian leaders and their congregations will find it utterly essential to cooperate in community programs, the sharing of resources, and in a variety of political and economic projects. Western donor agencies will need to bear this in mind as often the most severe forms of competition between Christian leaders and churches will be manifest in the pursuit of financial resources. The task of Palestinian Christians will be to attain what Pope Shenouda, Patriarch of the Coptic Orthodox Church once envisioned: 'Whereas Middle Eastern Christianity brought the curse of division to the Church in the past, let the churches of the Middle East now offer the gift of unity to Christendom.' What better place for the 'gift' to be incarnated than in Jerusalem, Bethlehem, Galilee, and throughout Palestine and Israel. This vision will need to be a guiding principle for all Palestinian Christian communities as well as their friends around the world.

## *A qualitative minority*

As we have observed, the Christian population in Palestine has declined from the time it was the overwhelming majority at the arrival of Islam in the 7th century, maintaining levels around 18-20 percent until the British Mandate phase (1922-1948). Rapid decline began during the 1948 *Nakba*, falling to approximately 13 percent in 1967, and then declining to the shocking level of 1.9 percent today. This is the lowest level that the Christian population in Palestine has been since its founding at the first Pentecost, some 2000 years ago. Nevertheless, throughout this period, Christians have contributed to the Palestinian community in remarkable ways including Palestine's intellectual and cultural life, its political leadership, and in religion. Like the tiny mustard seed in Jesus' parable (Luke 17: 6), or the salt that seasons the food and transforms it (Matthew 5:13), these tiny elements have achieved excellence and brought quality to the larger community in a number of areas. To illustrate this fact I would note that there is no arena in which Christians have excelled more in Palestine than in their commitment to providing quality education for all Palestinians, be they Christian or Muslim.

Palestinians have given a high priority to education for several generations and until the *Intifada* of 1987-92, when schools were closed for extended periods, they had the highest literacy rate in the Arab world. Christian primary and secondary schools have set the pace for quality education in the Palestinian community, but now with diminished resources fewer Christian families to support the schools, there is reason to be concerned about the future of the Christian schools. Perhaps it is time for the Christian educators of Palestine to issue an urgent plea to the international community, including governments, non-governmental agencies, Christian, Muslim and Jewish relief and development agencies, to prioritise the funding and upgrading Christian schools in Israel and Palestine.

Christian primary and secondary schools should be understood not only as vehicles of intellectual development, which in itself is essential, but as laboratories of community-building where Christian, Muslim and in some cases Jewish youth can learn together in a supportive environment that seeks the equality of persons. Most of the schools sponsored by the Greek Orthodox, Latin Patriarchate, Melikite Catholics, Anglicans, Lutherans, Mennonites and Quakers, serve the majority Muslim community with the highest quality education in the region. The schools generally teach respect for democracy, universal human rights, and religious tolerance. As such these schools can be encouraged to pioneer progressive curricula and educational methods that will be used in the United Nations (UNRWA) and government schools. Not only will the Palestinian Christians be strengthened but in the long term Israeli Jews will be more secure and Muslims included as partners in building a new society in the Holy Land.

One of the finest models for this progressive education is the Prophet Elias High School and College in Ibillin, Israel. This vision of Fr Elias Chacour and the staff has achieved excellence in a number of subjects within the secondary and university levels of education while modelling a diverse learning community comprised of Palestinian Christians, Muslims, Druze, and Jews. The high school has been cited by the Education Ministry in the state of Israel for the excellence achieved by students in such fields as Hebrew, where at the third year level, Prophet Elias High School has tested higher than any other high school in all of Israel. This achievement in Hebrew by Palestinian Christian and Muslim youth is somewhat ironic in that the Israeli government had at one time prevented the school from receiving a building permit, and once the school had been constructed, the Government threatened to bulldoze it.

The task of educating the youth of Israel and Palestine within a diverse ethnic and religious community is a spiritual vocation as well as a moral responsibility. In order to implement the task in a consistent and intentional manner it will be necessary to call upon the international community to assist with the financial, curricular, training modules, technological support, and other practical resources in the immediate future as the Palestinian Authority will be limited by its lack of staff and financial resources. One illustration of how the international Christian community and local Palestinians have combined resources in the educational enterprise is in the Latin Patriarch's schools. Patriarch Michel Sabbagh, the first Palestinian to be appointed to the office, has provided leadership and vision with his Director of Education, Fr Emile Salayta (see Chapter 1). With the help of the Vatican and other international partners, the Latin Schools have been implementing significant educational reform for the past decade including the introduction of technology and new teaching methodologies. Fr Emile and the Patriarch have developed several international partnerships between Catholic congregations in Europe and the United States with schools throughout Jordan, the West Bank, Jerusalem, and inside Israel. Not only Catholic but many Protestant churches have twinned with local Palestinian and Jordanian Christians, such as the First Presbyterian Church of Houston, Texas, twinning with Latin churches in Beit Sahour (Palestine) and Smakieh (Jordan). They have also worked with the churches and schools in Madaba, Jordan, a Christian town in southern Jordan and was one of the centres of early Christianity in the 4th-6th century. The Houston church has provided significant funding for specific educational projects but perhaps more important are the relationships between the two communities. During the spring and summer of 2000, Palestinian and Jordanian teachers lived with Houston families as they participated in special training programs offered by Houston universities. In return, volunteers from Houston give a week to ten days of volunteer service with their sister churches and schools before embarking on a Holy Land pilgrimage. It is hoped that this model of sister church or sister school relationships can be expanded rapidly over the next decade to insure the survival and expansion of quality education in Israel and Palestine.

Education is but one illustration of what this small community of Palestinians can offer as important gifts to the larger community by achieving excellence in various endeavours while at the same time becoming a laboratory for the larger community of Jews, Muslims, and Christians to experience true community. During these days of prolonged violence when the gulf between

Palestinians and Jews is widening with each passing week, there must be those who see beyond the present impasse to envision a day when the next generation can experience 'the other' as an equal partner, deserving the same justice, security, and peace. Let the international community take the risks necessary to preserve and indeed strengthen those school in Israel and Palestine who are committed prepare for a day not as yet seen when every citizen in Palestine and Israel will have their dignity guarded by the other.

## Spiritual renewal

Palestinian Christians are facing not only a political and economic crisis, but also a profound spiritual crisis as well. However, they generally interpret their predicament in terms of political and economic realities. Throughout this book I have placed considerable weight on the political aspects of the conflict plus the historical events that have brought these peoples to the present stalemate. Included in this development has been the spiritual realm, which in the Middle East is integral to their worldview and individual identity. In today's Middle East, the Islamic revival is calling Muslims back to a more theocentric view of life, but many Christians and secular Muslims are rejecting the traditional approaches and adopting western or secular models, often without realizing it. There are problems with the secularisation of reality in that it tends to compartmentalize life and give priority to the political, economic, technological, and, in general, the pragmatic dimensions. There are several trends that illustrate this tendency but one need only turn to how the Palestinian Authority is expending its limited resources. With each passing year, more and more of their shrinking budget is expended on internal and external security, albeit under pressure from Israel and the United States. Meanwhile it is education, the development of institutions that enhance democracy, and social services that suffer. Minimal attention has been dedicated to the healing of persons, and in particular, attending to the spiritual and emotional needs of the people.

Until recently Dr Eyad Surraj was the only psychiatrist who served the 1.2 million Palestinians of Gaza, the second most crowded region on the planet. For a population that is poor, the majority of whom are refugees, and are generally confined to their camps inside the small and impoverished Strip, the emotional problems are manifesting themselves in destructive patterns. Dr Sarraj has noted that spousal abuse, child abuse, an increase of heart disease and depression are among the manifestations of unattended spiritual and emotional problems. Dr Surraj is among the growing number of leaders who are calling attention to the emotional and spiritual crisis in Palestinian society. Further, the recent bombardment of the Bethlehem, Ramallah, and Hebron districts has given rise to depression, trauma, and such alarming signs as bedwetting. Who will heal he children? Who will heal their parents? There is great need for an infusion of those skilled in the healing sciences, and to multiply the number of Palestinians who, like Dr Sarraj, can begin the long journey toward wholeness.

Lacking these resources, the *Sabeel* Ecumenical Liberation Theology Centre in Jerusalem has made it a priority do its part in addressing the spiritual needs of the clergy, women, and youth of Palestine. In addition to *Sabeel*, the Latin Catholics, Anglicans, Lutherans, and the small evangelical Palestinian community, led by Bethlehem Bible College, have increasingly focused on the spiritual needs of their people. Palestinian clergy and lay leaders are finding new emotional and spiritual resources from *Sabeel's* retreats. In the peaceful environment of a hotel or retreat centre along the Sea of Galilee, participants find opportunities to share problems and gain support within a trusting small group of colleagues. The retreats begin a healing of people who live each day serving others and carry the stress of military occupation. Participants gain intellectual stimulus from lectures and Bible studies, spiritual renewal through reflection, worship, prayer and meditation. Such experiences have been lacking in Palestine until recently and have been enthusiastically received, but they are minimal and service very limited segment of the Palestinian population due to *Sabeel's* limited resources.

Palestinian communities are developing different strategies to meet these needs and bring healing to their people. Three examples are the Latin Patriarchate, *Sabeel* and the International Centre in Bethlehem. While the Latin Patriarchate is concentrating on education, housing, and congregational renewal, *Sabeel* and the International Centre are working on several projects that strive to recover an authentic Arab Palestinian 'indigenous theology' and spirituality. Raheb has also emphasized renewal through education and the arts, bringing international educators and artists from Europe and the United States together to share their skills and encourage Palestinian youth and artists to develop this other dimension a new Palestinian consciousness within the agony that surrounds them. The emphasis on spirituality, developing an indigenous Palestinian theology, education, and the arts, are all set within the context of building a new Palestinian state that is grounded in democracy and reaching a just and lasting peace with Israel. Palestinian Muslims and Christians come together at every level from children in elementary school to young adults and the elderly at the International Centre. Thanks to significant international partners, the dream is being implemented.

Among the partners are the Government and Lutheran Churches of Germany, Sweden, Norway, and the Evangelical Lutheran Church (USA). All have been partners in building new schools, renovating the Christmas Lutheran Church, and providing training opportunities in Palestine and abroad for the new Palestinian generation that is implementing the program at the International Centre. The Latin Patriarchate, *Sabeel* and the International Centre are but three models of what is occurring in the Anglican, Lutheran, and other churches in an effort to blend the spiritual with the political in renewing Palestinian Christianity and local communities.

Perhaps the time has come for Palestinian Christians with assistance from international partners to consider a revival of a few selected monasteries so as to benefit the whole of Palestinian society. As noted in Chapter 2I, by the 5th or 6th century there were over 400 functioning monasteries throughout Palestine that provided spiritual vitality for the region. Monks were involved in local churches, hospitality was available to international pilgrims, and in cases like St Jerome's academy in Bethlehem, they provided significant biblical and theological instruction for followers from far-away Rome and distant parts of Europe. Building upon the scholarly tradition pioneered by Origen and Jerome, important theological work was generated that provided an important interchange with the new Islamic religion. Today it is worth studying how a number of abandoned or underutilised monasteries might be returned to Palestinian churches or Christian organizations in order to provide a variety of educational and spiritual programs for the community. Several organizations have developed vital programs but they lack the buildings. Considerable funding will be necessary to modernize the monasteries but in many cases the land can and should be returned to the Palestinian Christian community. Grants from UNESCO or European and Asian governments could begin to transform the monasteries into centres of healing, lively theological and inter-religious exchange, and spiritual renewal for Palestinians, Israelis, and international friends.

One could envision the monasteries becoming retreat centres, academies for personal psychological healing, the locus of educational training and workshops, and sites where Christians, Muslims, and Jews could gather in a safe and nurturing environment to seek strategies of peace and reconciliation. These centres could also be an environment for Christian, Muslim, and Jewish theological and political dialogue and debate. Through these and other programs the enormous gap of misunderstand and ignorance between Israelis and Palestinians could be bridged in an effort to build community. The monasteries could be equipped as modern but modest facilities that would provide affordable sites for Palestinians and Israelis to 'retreat' from the intense pressures of everyday life and find rest and renewal.

Leadership could be developed through the churches and universities as well as the highly skilled Israeli and international medical and psychological associations. International pilgrims could be encouraged to utilize the facilities for selected programmes. If the marketing and pricing of the activities is carefully organized there will be no problem with space utilization and financing the programs. The first step would be to assess the methods by which the monasteries and other under-utilised or abandoned Christian buildings could be restored, financed, and transformed into much needed centres of healing and renewal for the whole community.

## The restoration of lost land and financial compensation to Palestinian churches and families

Palestinians live in an environment of increased marginalization where approximately 60 percent of their population exists in some form of refugee status, whether they reside in refugee camps inside historic Palestine or within the growing Israeli *apartheid* system now being established in the Gaza Strip and West Bank. During periods of extreme unrest, such as is occurring in *Intifada* of 2000, unemployment skyrockets to nearly 90 percent and many families are without the bare essentials of existence. Hunger becomes an urgent issue and adequate medical care becomes rare, as the quality of life plummets. Palestinian refugees in Arab countries live under tight restrictions in neighbouring Arab nations. Hundreds of thousands have emigrated to the west and found freedom and new opportunities, but at the price of having to live far from their homeland. In their weakened state the Palestinian diaspora has observed Jews throughout the world granted the right to return to Israel, usually with significant economic and various forms of social services granted to them by the State of Israel. Palestinians have also noted that other Jews are receiving enormous sums of money as reparations for the unspeakable genocidal practices imposed on them by Nazi Germany and other European governments or businesses. To their credit, Zionist organizations have been tireless in researching and tracking down the Nazi criminals, businesses, and governments that collaborated. Remarkable levels of compensation have been turned over to the bereaved families or to the government of Israel and various institutions within the Jewish state. However, Palestinians have not received compensation for the loss of life, homes, land, bank accounts, tax revenue paid to the State of Israel, or compensation for the decades spent in dismal refugee camps. Now it is the Palestinians turn.

The time is long overdue for a sustained, heavily financed,

international campaign directed toward the goal of attaining fair compensation for land, homes and buildings, possessions, and bank accounts taken by Israel and Jewish militias during the hostilities of 1948-9-to the present. It has been over fifty years since the Nazi atrocities devastated the Jews of Europe and the process of remunerations continues. Armenians are beginning to turn a corner that may lead to their just pursuit in receiving compensation for their genocide under the Turks, a tragedy still denied by most Turkish officials. The Palestinian case for reparations for the 1948 atrocities has yet to be officially recognized by the state of Israel but, like the Armenian case, it is only a matter of time before that recognition becomes official. It is abundantly clear that the Government of Israel is anticipating an accelerated campaign by Palestinians and is seeking methods to avoid it, as occurred during the July 2000 negotiations at Camp David. One of the many reasons that the Palestinian Authority balked at the proposals brought by Israeli officials was that the Israelis with US support were forcing the Palestinians to sign an agreement stating the conflict was over and Israel would agree to settle 75,000-100,000 refugees and drop the case of reparations for the remaining 700,000. Such a proposal would never be acceptable to Palestinians.

The first priority concerning 'restoration' is for the Palestinians worldwide and all who support them to unite around their right of return to their homes lost from 1948 to present. This fundamental human right as stipulated in United Nations resolution 194 cannot be revoked by any government, or even by their own Palestinian Authority. This right is at the core of the Zionist-Israeli and Palestinian conflict and as such it must be dealt with in a just and legal manner. Just as Jews continue to be compensated for their losses in Europe during and before World War II, so do Palestinians have a right to return to their homes or receive full compensation for what they lost. Not only Palestinians, but churches, governments, human rights and academic associations, and others, must stand against any political or legal pressures or instruments that would jeopardize this right.

The increased publication of historical records on the atrocities of 1948 and interpretations by highly credible Israeli historians such as Meron Benvenisti's recent volume *Sacred Landscapes*, augur well for an official Israeli apology and eventual remuneration. However, these will be have a long road with repeated delays before they are achieved. Still, Palestinians will need to be remarkably efficient and prepared for extensive legal battles to receive even a portion of what is deserved. Benvenisti's volume is one of the first written by a mainstream Israeli journalist that uses the phrase 'ethnic cleansing' with reference to the forced exodus of Palestinians from their homes in 1948. Israelis inside and outside of political power must be challenged to come to terms with the deeds done in 1948 and redress the aggrieved Palestinians. A small minority of Israeli intellectuals and Israelis in the peace camp appear to be open to accept these claims, among them some of the 'New' Israeli historians, and progressive Israeli organizations such as Rabbis for Human Rights, the New Israel Fund, Peace Now and *B 'tselem*. However, the forces of resistance and maintenance of the status quo govern the political response within the Israeli establishment, but the seeds of healing must be pushed forward now if there is to be peaceful co-existence.

The Palestinian Christian community, through the Palestinian Orthodox Congress, could be one strategic test case among many others for remunerations and achieving the right of return for Palestinian families from the 1948-9 period. The important work already begun by the Palestinian Orthodox Congress is worthy of consideration as a starting point in this process. The Congress has maintained excellent documentation on major land cases and is worthy of international support to implement its goals. Presently the Congress is in a state of severe understaffing and lacks the capacity to mount a serious legal challenge. The Palestinian Christian diaspora could change this situation by creating a trust fund to underwrite a long-term legal challenge to Israel on behalf of the Palestinian victims.

The Congress might consider a two-tiered strategy: first, one that takes selected cases and targets the Greek Orthodox Patriarchate concerning church and family properties sold or leased to the government of Israel and its subsidiary land companies. The second will be to focus on the Jewish National Fund and the government of Israel concerning village, mosque or church, and family properties, including homes and buildings, that were confiscated through various quasi-legal and military means between 1948 and the present. Galilean Palestinian villages such as Bir'am, Ikrit, Fasouta, Beisan, Tiberias, and parts of Haifa are among the 425 cities and villages that are subject to litigation and potential remuneration for Palestinians inside Israel. The villages of Ikrit and Bir'am have already won their case in the Israeli courts but their victory has not been implemented, some 50 years after the court case. The villages of Lifta, Ramle, Lydda, Jaffa, are only some of the many cities and villages that once had massive Palestinian land holdings between West Jerusalem and the Mediterranean and are among the choice land that was lost in 1948. The second strategy is much broader and should include the entire Palestinian community, both Christian and Muslim, while also engaging the international legal and human rights communities through the United Nations and the International Court at The Hague.

The road to compensation and return of refugees will be long, complicated, and expensive. Palestinian Christians will need to be part of the Palestinian organizations that have been working for several decades to bring visibility, financial backing, and political and moral support to the twin issues of reparations and return. Palestinian Christians must be engaged at every level with the rest of the Palestinian community as they have a particular political and moral responsibility in reclaiming what the Christian churches have surrendered to the Zionist movement and later Israel. Western Christians will need to be prepared to assist them at every level for many years to come.

## Redemptive suffering as a vocation of justice and peace

The saga of Israel and the Palestinians in the Holy Land has been filled with tragedy after tragedy during the past one hundred years. The previous nine chapters have attempted to present many but certainly not all of the tragedies experienced by Jews and Palestinians, including the agony they have brought upon themselves. Strategies employing violence and military tactics will continue to be options for large segments of both communities but in the end Israel and the Palestinians will be forced to admit that these have no lasting value. As we have begun another millennium, the two communities have reached a juncture in history when both parties realize that diplomacy is the only viable path to achieve lasting peace, but the old patterns of forging security through military means still linger. The political choices of the past fifty years seem bankrupt and the present *status quo* of persistent insecurity will only accelerate the cycle of terrorism, revenge, and counter-violence. As the Israeli's seek an answer in the imposition of an *Apartheid* arrangement on the Palestinian territories it will evoke unquestionably a pattern of Palestinian resistance, Israeli retaliation, and untold suffering for both communities. It is my conviction that there are clues for a just and peaceful future in the Holy Land that are hidden within the Abrahamic religious traditions. For a variety of reasons these options have been eclipsed by other primary impulses such as the struggle for survival and the understandable pressure to take revenge, annihilate or control the other. Bishop Cragg is helpful at this point when he writes:

> It follows that a capacity to read tragedy is crucial to any religion's claim to interpret society itself. Plainly history is not set to prosper good causes or blandly facilitate good wishes. It is full of what Paul called *athigmata*, 'puzzling reflections in a mirror'...the tragic sense of life understands the legitimacy, already argued, of the rule of law and the 'ought' in the fabric of the world. It also comprehends that suffering belongs inexorably with the human condition. It registers this, of course,

in the hazards of our mortality, 'the ills that flesh is heir to.' The plagues and disasters in nature, the cancers and infections in the body, the atrophy of the brain—all these contribute their grim quota to our tragedy in life. But the more ultimate register is that of inhumanity in the interhuman, the guilt of structures and the wrongs of society, all stemming from the dominion/*khalifah* by which our creaturehood is dignified by the entrusting—and therefore trusting—'Lord of all being'.[11]

This eloquent statement cuts to the core of that which is human in all of us and what our Abrahamic spiritual traditions offer in transforming this 'dominion/*khalifeh*'. Palestinian Christians, Muslims, and the Jews have their respective histories of tragedy that we need not review, except to say that the wounds of the Crusades, western imperialism, the holocaust and Western antisemitism have not been healed, nor has the tragedy of the *Nakba* and its continuing saga of injustice for Palestinians. Some will say these wounds will never heal but the better part of all of us must reach for options that offer healing, hope, security based upon justice, and reconciliation that includes reparations for past suffering. Perhaps there is the seed of healing in the present suffering if members of the two communities can transcend their understandable fear and instinct to protect themselves through revenge strategies and reach a deeper level of their common humanity. If the present climate of abuse and revenge continues another fifty years, it is likely that a significant percentage of one community will be erased or be severely crippled. The victor will celebrate a brief period of domination but simply await a succeeding generation to take revenge. But one point is clear, neither the Israelis nor the Palestinians will disappear as a nation or as a people.

The recent demise of South Africa's *apartheid* regime provides but one illustration of evil forced to collapse under its own weight. South Africa may take two generations to heal but the new leadership has initiated a remarkable process that could heal many of the wounds and move the majority of South Africans to close the chapter n revenge and hatred. The vital role that religious faith has played in the conception and implementation of the 'The Truth and Reconciliation Commission' offers an important and perhaps unique illustration of the wedding of politics and theology in the cause of justice.

Israeli Jews and Palestinians will do well to study the 'Truth and Reconciliation Commission' in order to see if there are aspects that might be

---

[11] Cragg, *Palestine, The Prize and Price of Zion*, 208.

translated into their own context. It would seem that such a prospect is but a distant hope at this time of intense mistrust. Some analysts claim that the South African model is based more on a Christian model and the Muslim and Jewish/Zionist worldviews are incompatible. Clearly, the South African model cannot be imposed on Israel and Palestine. If something similar to the South African model is to emerge in the Israeli-Palestinian situation it will take a different form. There may be different religious and ideological motivations from the three Abrahamic traditions but there is common ground. One of the vital lessons of the South African experience is that the community that was initially judged the victim of *apartheid* became the community that initiated the process of healing and the long path toward reconciliation.

Some Jewish and Christian theologians are finding the 'sacrifice of Isaac' story (Genesis 22:1-19) a paradigm for interpreting the whole of religious reality and possibly finding in it clues for political and interpersonal conflict resolution. This is not a new discovery, of course, as theologians and spiritual leaders through the ages have turned to the story. The great Danish philosopher Soren Kierkegaard used it for what many believe was the finest philosophical and psychological work of the 19th century, *Fear and Trembling*. Kierkegaard would claim at the conclusion of his agonizing work that ultimately, man and woman are essentially spiritual beings when all else is stripped away, and 'faith is the highest passion of the human.'[12] In the midst of their agony, it is faith and an understanding of those life issues that probe the spiritual dimension that provide meaning to those who chose the long and often thankless journey toward peace built upon justice.

The theologians working on this paradigm often find their starting point in the Hebrew term *akedah* or 'the binding', which refers to Isaac's willing sacrifice. Certainly this is a troublesome concept for any era, but particularly for our time that is rightly geared to the empowerment of indigenous minorities, and the rights of women and children to be protected from the violence of the strong over the weak. Religion has too often been used in the past to support such racist institutions and practices as *apartheid*, slavery, masculine domination and abuse in marriage, female genital mutilation, child labour, and even genocide. At first reading it might appear that the sacrifice of Isaac paradigm imposes these unenlightened primitive forms of religious oppression. On closer examination there are deeper meanings that have generally been missed.

Professor Kenneth Vaux of Garrett Evangelical Theological Seminary finds in the Abraham and Isaac story the theme of redemptive suffering that

---

[12] Soren Kierkegaard, *Fear and Trembling* (translation by Walter Lowie), New York, Doubleday-Anchor Books, 1954, 131.

runs through the Hebrew scriptures, the Talmud, as well as the New Testament and subsequent Christian doctrine.[13] *Akedah* is also an important theme in Islam, sustaining Islam's core doctrine of submission (the Arabic word *Islam* means 'one who submits') and even the concept of martyrdom. The martyr is one who in submission to Allah makes the ultimate sacrifice for truth and justice on behalf of the community, which may be different from the military models popularised today by Hizbollah and Hamas suicide missions. Vaux and others note that while the Genesis 22 text may have been used by early Jews to negate Canaanite traditions of child sacrifice, more important is Abraham's struggle against himself, against hopelessness, and his quest for obedience to Yahweh when his beloved son may be lost. This direction of interpretation comes close to the deeper meaning of the Islamic concept of *jihad*, spiritual struggle. Abraham's ultimate 'submission' (*Islam*) becomes his salvation and legacy to succeeding generations. Vaux summarizes *akedah*:

> *Akedah* is the deepest common metaphor joining the Abraham faith of Judaism, Christianity, and Islam. It is the fundamental symbol of atonement and reconciliation, of death and resurrection for those faith communities and cultures who follow that pioneer of 'The Way.' As such its mystery and power can lead the way for Israel, the nascent State of Palestine, and the surrounding world of Islam.[14]

When Abraham binds Isaac to the sacrificial altar (the firewood which Isaac willingly transported up Mt Moriah), he is about to kill his beloved son, his sustaining hope that future generations will fulfil the promises made to him in the Covenant with Yahweh. Here is a foreshadowing of Jesus' death, the suffering of the prophets, and Muhammad's humiliation and suffering at the hands of the Meccan opposition prior to his triumph. At this moment all hope was suspended, all future possibilities placed in question, and Abraham's own sense of meaning and purpose were placed at risk.

Jesus faced a similar test on the eve of his crucifixion when he prayed: 'If it be possible, let this cup pass from me but nevertheless, not my will but thine be done.' Likewise, the Israelites at the Exodus from Egypt had their backs against the wall when the waters opened and Yahweh provided safe passage from the pursuing armies of the pharaoh. As they wandered in the wilderness of Sinai and faced hunger and the harshness of the desert, they quickly lost this trust and submission to Yahweh as many wished to

---

[13] Author's interview with Kenneth Vaux, Evanston, Illinois, 28 August 2000.

[14] Vaux, *op. cit.*

return to slavery in Egypt rather than face the unknown demands of freedom.

Israelis and Palestinians are at a similar juncture of facing an unknown future that may know deeper suffering and yet another war. Perhaps the Palestinian Christians, in their weakened and vulnerable state, can probe the depths of Genesis 22 and the reality to which it points. One of the important components of the *akedeh* tradition is the theme of vicarious suffering for the sake of the other. After a century of suffering from each other and from Western powers, it is difficult to discuss vicarious suffering with the people of the Holy Land. Sheer survival and the need for vengeance often consume Israelis and Palestinians. The *akedeh* emphasis on vicarious suffering claims that those who are truly obedient to God and are secure in themselves will be capable of making truly heroic sacrifices for the society as a whole. Bishop Cragg describes it in this way:

> It suspends the enmity, remits the offence and intends reconciliation, where there is any will to penitence. There comes about then a certain kind of bearing which bears away—not the evil as if it had not been evil, but the evil as now bereaved of the momentum it would have otherwise gathered. This alone is the way in which forgiveness comes—a forgiven–ness turning on a forgiving-ness that has made it possible. Such is the ultimate peacemaking.[15]

There comes a time, as Cragg says, to suspend the enmity and take a courageous step to act with a different spirit toward the enemy. Here I am not suggesting that Palestinians lay down their lives and roll over in submission to the abuses that might annihilate them, nor that Israelis would automatically surrender all their arms and trust that God will protect them from Hamas and Hizbollah. Rather, I am suggesting that in a deteriorating political climate in which armed struggle and military occupation appear to be the primary options, some Palestinians and Jews would do well to consider an alternative approach. Those who choose this path will be among the vilified minority but it seems that there is still wisdom in calling a critical mass of concerned Jews, Muslims, and Christians to seek the path of non-violent resistance and a variety of alternative strategies to armed conflict.

Palestinian Christians, Muslims, and Israeli Jews may have lost the *akedah* dimension of suffering justice due to the historic pain and oppression that has been heaped upon them. Certainly the Jewish victims of Hitler's

---

[15] Cragg, *op. cit.*, 209.

genocide will find it close to impossible to consider redemptive suffering, reconciliation, and even trust in God rather than oneself or the armies of Israel for security and hope. Likewise, Palestinian Christians, who have spent a long history in their *dhimmi* status under Islam and now as a beleaguered minority under Israeli rule, will not be attracted by the concept of *akedah* and suffering justice. The quest for power, vindication, revenge and taking steps to insure security for oneself and ones family will usually be preferred. It is worth considering, however, that Palestinian nationalism and Zionism have both developed strong traditions of secular nationalism that seek liberation and power. The religious nationalisms of Zionism (the Shas Party and others in the Likud coalition) and of Islam (Hamas and Islamic Jihad in Palestine) are opting for a religious nationalism that excludes their opposition and chooses brute power over negotiation and reconciliation. In the present climate of strictly drawn lines of religion, ethnicity, politics, and state power, there is little credence given to the politics of forgiveness.

Could a small community of Palestinian Christians begin to explore the *akedah* and vicarious suffering for justice tradition and call the other faith communities to dialogue and practical action? Could this be one of the prophetic vocations for the Palestinian Christian community within Israel and Palestine, as well as abroad? Are there international partners who will be willing to join the dialogue and action, including those in power, who will come as honest participants rather than as foreign agents with their separate political agendas? Allow me to make a modest proposal that is discussed from time to time in some Palestinian gatherings. Could one Palestinian Christian community that directly experienced the loss of homes, land, and livelihood in the 1948 *Nakba*, take the initiative and forgive Israel for the ethnic cleansing conducted against their village? They need not offer forgiveness on behalf of all Palestinians, only for their village. For the offer to have meaning it must request a simultaneous apology and compensation for their losses from the Government of Israel. However, the forgiveness need not be conditional upon receiving the apology but the forgiving party must be persistent in demanding a clear response from Israel for it to have meaning. Such an initiative is modest and it may lead to silence from the Israelis. But if the apology is sincere, it will send a signal to every Jew as well as to the international community.

The political moment for such a dramatic initiative would need to be carefully studied with full consideration given to the historic memory of both peoples. For example, one would not choose to initiate such an action during Israeli celebrations of national independence nor during one of the major Jewish holy days. On the other hand, Palestinians could select one of their important national holidays, such as 'Land Day' (29-30 March), which recalls Palestinian resistance to Israeli land confiscation). A new force for peace could be unleashed in the Holy Land that may or may not grow in this polarized climate. I am not suggesting this initiative as a mere political manoeuvre nor as an act by religious 'do-gooders' that lacks the teeth of justice, for there is no reconciliation without justice.

The vocation of many Palestinian Christians can best be summed up in the concept of 'suffering love in search of justice'. It is a devotion to God, to one's family, and to the nation. The *akedah* vocation seeks to be faithful to the one who founded Christianity and indeed set the pace by laying down his own life for his followers. The person living into such a vocation must be grounded spiritually and be of exceptional emotional maturity, for the journey will be long and usually thankless. The person must be politically wise as a serpent yet 'harmless as a dove' in the implementation of a just peace. It is also the case that the vocation will call the servant to live in his or her mission knowing that they may see little fruit in their lifetime. After several false starts Abraham developed the maturity and heroism that enabled him to trust the promise that God would honour the Covenant promised him earlier (Genesis 12:1-3) and grant many descendants, a promise that seemed to be at risk as the knife was raised. Palestinian Christians have the same uncertainty today as they may not see a viable Palestinian state or the possibility of a just and free Palestinian society in their lifetime, but they must trust God and hold to that vision of a better society whatever their present conditions, believing that their children or children's children will share in its fruit.

## A prophetic bridge

Palestinian Christians must be willing to address injustices committed by both the Palestinian Authority and various organizations within their community as they have been outspoken against human rights violations by Israel. They will need to find the creative and courageous space that is neither too close to the governments of Israel, Jordan, or the Palestinian Authority, nor can they be beholden to financial sources that could compromise their independence. If the emerging leadership of the Palestinian Christian community can find a moral centre, assemble the financial resources and personnel, and carve out a prophetic role that challenges any government, person, militia, or organization that violates the international norms for justice and international law, they will eventually gain respect and support. However, the first sign of collaboration, receiving financial support from Middle Eastern governmental sources, will undermine their moral ground. The minefields are numerous in the Middle East and the methods of manipulation and discrediting are clever. Jesus' advice to be 'wise as serpents and harmless as doves' will need to be heeded and enforced.

The prophetic task will involve courageous and thoughtful political positions that are theologically sound and politically prudent. One such proposal would be an extensive analysis with an eye toward applying the success of the Truth and Reconciliation Commission in South Africa to the Israeli-Palestinian conflict. The methodology and the theory behind it are both intriguing and applicable. While it looks to the grievances of the past, the task of the commission was (and is) to have an honest airing of the crimes and suffering perpetuated by the *apartheid* regime, but for the ultimate purpose of healing past wounds. The process demands that the past must be faced and the perpetrators of injustice apologize, that both communities begin to move through it to 'reconciliation'. Reconciliation is a profound theological and political concept that necessitates justice and accountability, but it holds out the possibility for healing and forgiveness. The pain of the past may never leave, but life must be lived facing the future. Many of the victims of oppression in South Africa stated that they just wanted the offenders to acknowledge their crimes and apologize. Once this was accomplished they were able to begin the healing process. The Palestinian Christian community can gather progressive Muslim and Israeli Jewish attorneys and academics to initiate research and begin the educational process at both the popular and political levels necessary in order to prepare the way for a Truth and Reconciliation Commission.

A second prophetic task for the community will be a deep, consistent, and open public debate on the advantages and disadvantages of the Oslo Peace Process and appropriate responses to its failure. Is armed resistance an option for Palestinians? Is an Islamic Palestinian state the best remaining model for Palestinians or is there a way to balance the religious and secular models? What will be the shape of democracy and democratic institutions in the future state? How will the Israeli and Palestinian security mechanisms operate and will human rights be protected within the new Palestinian state? Initially, such a debate may be stifled by both the Palestinian Authority and the government of Israel. Avoidance of an open discussion or crushing debate will create a pool of resentment and potential resistance on the Palestinian side, and a deeper division between the two peoples. Israel is assuming that by military might, including nuclear weapons, that Palestinians will be forced to accept the present peace process, whatever the flaws, simply because it is the only option available. The responsibility of the Christian minority, as with the Muslim and Jewish majorities, is to educate the public concerning the flaws and why it will not work. The purpose of the critique is to search for what is just, honourable, and visionary in order to correct the dismal situation of the present. The critique will give perspective and hopefully vision to the process, so people will maintain their bearings and be better able to plan, cope, and discern where hope may lie.

In this regard, it is time for the Christian community to debate, research, and organize for an eventual one state solution in historic Palestine. Most of those reading these words will not be alive when such a state would come into being. However, the foregoing analysis of the political situation makes it clear that the *apartheid*-style 'state' or series of *bantustans* offered to the Palestinians will breed only contempt and hatred of Israel and the United States. The new arrangement will place an unpopular Palestinian regime in power, but everyone knows that the CIA, Mossad (Israeli intelligence), and US funding (via the World Bank) are controlling the situation. In such an impoverished and corrupt system there will be no justice and the quality of life will be dismal. Such a situation will insure the demise of the Christian community in Palestine as a living church rather than a few caretakers of museum pieces that once were vibrant churches.

Thus the type of state offered by the Oslo Process will not be a true state by any method of evaluation, be it political, economic, social, or otherwise. In many ways, the two-state solution (a Jewish and Palestinian state side by side), or the prevailing position of the international community (minus Israel and the United States), is a formula that is no longer viable. It has been replaced by something worse. Thus it is time to develop the ideological political theory and the accompanying theological rationale for a single democratic state in Palestine. Considering the history of partitions or two-state solutions, most do not work. The old dynamics of domination and/ or military build-up and paranoia seem to be the case, particularly when the conflict has been protracted for more than one generation and the seeds of discontent remain. One thinks of the failures in Northern Ireland, Kosovo, Cyprus, India and Pakistan, etc. Palestine is such a case.

The gradual effect of the Israeli peace community on the body politic is slow and often shows few signs of progress, but change is evident. A growing number of Israelis are opposed to their government creating *bantustans* and an *apartheid* system in Palestine. The Oslo Accords are proving to be a vehicle leading to *apartheid*, with Arafat and his regime manipulated into tiny, economically bankrupt and fragmented Bantustans in the West Bank and Gaza. The ethical dimensions of Judaism must be appealed to concerning the 'neighbour', justice, and keeping Torah equally in the treatment of Palestinians as in treatment of Jews. Zionists and the State of Israel must be held accountable for its violence and abuses inflicted on Palestinians and the long, arduous campaign must not end. Bishop Cragg puts it this way:

> The radical depth of the issue lies simply in the fact that another people have been tragically invaded and distressed. It has often been observed that how people relate to Jews is a test-case of what humanity they are. The dictum might be reversed, so that the Jewishness of Jewry is tested by their relation to humanity.[17]

Thus Palestinians are the test case for Jews to see if they are truly keeping Torah, loving justice, and walking humbly with their God.

## A parable

I recently heard an old Arabic parable that seems relevant in the charged politics of Israel and Palestine. An old Jerusalem family had three sons.

One son left home to study abroad and converted to Judaism, becoming in time an Orthodox rabbi. Eventually he returned to Jerusalem and gained great respect as the leader of a prominent synagogue. He was know internationally for his mystical devotion to the land of Israel, his deep commitment to the Zionist cause, and especially for his passion about Jerusalem. The second son left home and studied in Greece, where he became an important Greek Orthodox priest and theologian. Eventually he was sent to Jerusalem where he was assigned to be the leading Palestinian archbishop assigned to the patriarch. He became an expert on the Orthodox land holdings and he too became passionate about the land still held by the Orthodox Church. The third son converted to Islam and set off for Cairo where he studied for several years at Al-Azhar, the great Islamic university. He became an expert on Umayyad Jerusalem and was a specialist on the Islamic properties that were established during this period. In time he became the grand mufti of Jerusalem and openly preached at Al-Aqsa Mosque about his vision that Palestine must move toward becoming an Islamic state with Shari'a law as its foundation.

One day the three religious leaders received word that their father was dying. The father still lived in the family home in the Old City of Jerusalem. Naturally, each of the three brothers coveted that land and had been

---

[17] Cragg, *Palestine: The Prize and Price of Zion*, 197.

formulating legal arguments from their religious perspective to gain control of the land. Each of the religious leaders arrived at the house in their respective religious attire and was told the father was prepared to make a decision about the land.

They entered the father's room and he greeted each one with a warm hug from his bed but was too weak to utter more than their name. After greeting the last son he somehow mustered up enough energy to say: 'I am unable to make a decision for each of you has brought dignity to our family. My parting wish is that I would have you here with me during my final hours. Please, carry me to basement where there still remains a dirt floor of ancient Jerusalem's soil. Perhaps I can make a final decision about the house down there.' Tenderly and carefully they carried descended down three stories into the bowels of the old home and reached the dirt floor. The father then said: 'Place me down to the ground that my ear will touch the ground. I cannot decide who will receive this land unless I touch the earth and seek its guidance.'

The three sons lowered the father until his ear touched the earth. There was absolute silence in this sacred moment in the candlelight as the father touched the earth. An intense but peaceful spirit came over the father's face. He seemed to be praying. He closed his eyes and five minutes went by, then ten, perhaps 30 minutes passed. Each brother grew impatient as his dream of possessing the priceless land was in question.

Then the father opened his eyes and began to speak: 'The land has spoken to me and she has said: I do not belong to you because you belong to me, and I belong to God.'

Then he closed his eyes and died, leaving the three brothers to learn to share the land and learn before God the lessons of faith.

## Conclusion: a vulnerable witness for justice and peace

During his visit to the Holy Land in April, 2000, Pope John Paul II was more a symbol of the Christian faith than the international religious celebrity that the media coverage implied. His carefully organized itinerary seemed to have touched on the critical aspects of the crisis including the places and people of Palestine and Israel: a visit to Deheishe refugee camp outside Bethlehem as a first order of business; a stop at Yad Vashem (Holocaust museum); meetings with Israeli Prime Minister Ehud Barak and Palestinian President Yasser Arafat; meetings with the Muslim Grand Mufti of Jerusalem and the Chief Rabbi of Israel with both religious leaders criticizing the Church for its past indiscretions; and several opportunities for worship and prayer with the faithful. The pope was careful neither to overstate his position nor to appear arrogant, but he came in humility as a frail, shuffling figure, to be in solidarity with Muslims and Jews, victims of the Holocaust and victims of the *Nakba*. On his last day the pope asked to change his itinerary and despite an exhausting week, the aged leader requested that he return to pray at the Church of the Holy Sepulchre. We are told that the pope personally called the Franciscan responsible to grant permission for a private visit to the great church. The telephone rang and the friar, thinking it was a prank call, laughed and nearly hung up the telephone. The pope identified himself again and the friar was convinced. Special arrangements quickly went into effect, the church was cleared by Israeli security, and Pope John Paul II made his way alone, climbing the steep staircase to the site of Jesus' sacrificial death and resurrection.

Tom Getman, Director of the World Vision Office in Jerusalem, followed the Pope's visit closely and participated in several of the major events. He wrote this commentary on Palm Sunday, 2000:

> In a region where there is a serious shortage of hope after years without peace, the Pope exclaimed it with his very body on the site which symbolizes like no other the realm of the cosmic battleground for the human soul. The place which Greeks call the 'Center' of the world near the site the Muslims call the 'navel of the universe,' half way between heaven and earth, he boldly proclaimed non-verbally that the cross should no longer be seen as an 'offence to the Jews' or an instrument of imposed guilt by Christians. Rather he lifted up the possibility, by this one final act of his pilgrimage, that the ultimate sacrificial table could be a gathering point of merciful understanding. His exclamatory and painful ascent was the embracing of other peoples' suffering, Jewish and Arab Israeli and Palestinian alike. Indeed his word of 'fear not' proclaimed in this deed was the embracing of all our suffering and fear.[18]

Tom Getman expressed well the call to Palestinian Christians and perhaps all people who care about Israelis and Palestinians, Christians, Muslims, and Jews. All have been consumed by their fears and their desire to dominate or eliminate the other. All are victims. In a deteriorating climate of suffering and talk of a future war within the Holy Land, the time is long overdue to not only feel the very real wounds and pain of the other, but to

---

[18] Tom Getman, *Reflection #35*, Jerusalem: World Vision, 21 April 2000.

move with open hearts toward healing. Perhaps the frail and weakened pope was a sign of the future role of not only Palestinian Christians, but all who wish to transcend the violent and hateful *status quo*. The way forward may be hidden in what a courageous minority of Palestinian Christians, Muslims, and Israeli Jews manifest in the coming years in their quest for a just and durable peace in the Holy Land.

# Epilogue
# A PROPOSAL FOR THE TRANSFORMATION OF PALESTINIAN CHRISTIANITY

## Summary

The historical, theological, and political assumptions that have informed this volume and the following proposal should be read as preliminary suggestions designed to stimulate dialogue, reflection, and strategic planning among Palestinian Christians and concerned international organizations and friends. As a result of the preceding analysis, I propose the immediate formation of a Selection Committee who after careful deliberation will appoint a Committee of Experts who will guide a year long preparation period, leading to the convening of an 'International Congress on the Transformation of Palestinian Christianity'. Prior to convening the Congress, a Palestinian Christian Guidance Committee will be formed to be comprised of Palestinian Christians living inside historic Palestine and the Diaspora as well as experts they select for particular tasks (research, governmental relations, fundraising, legal counsel, etc.). The primary goal of the Guidance Committee will be to provide oversight and resources for a multi-dimensional international movement for the renewal of Palestinian Christianity and its churches through legal, educational, economic, theological, spiritual, political, and archaeological initiatives. The Guidance Committee and its programmes will need to chart an independent theological, ecclesiastical, and political course in terms of its relations with the churches worldwide, with the Muslim and Jewish communities in the Middle East, and with various political parties in Israel and the Palestinian Authority and the future state of Palestine.

## Stage One: a feasibility study on the present crisis and future prospects of Palestinian Christianity in the Holy Land

*Formation and immediate objectives*
The Committee of Experts (COE) will be the primary body to oversee a year-long period of preparation and research. The COE will be chosen by a Selection Committee consisting of the Heads of four international organizations and the Patriarch of one major church, all of whom have maintained a record of

absolute integrity and independence. I would propose the following members of the Selection Committee: Nora Kort, Director of Orthodox Relief Services; the Revd Dr Mitri Raheb, Pastor of the Christmas Lutheran Church in Bethlehem and Director of the International Centre; the Latin Patriarch, His Grace Patriarch Michel Sabbah; Fr Elias Chacour, President of Prophet Elias College and Educational Institutions in Ibillin, Galilee-Israel; and the Revd Dr Naim Ateek, Director of the Sabeel Ecumenical Liberation Theology Centre. At this initial stage it may be important to involve leaders who are tied to the grass roots of Palestinian Christianity rather than those in the church hierarchy, with the exception of Patriarch Sabagh. The five leaders mentioned above have significant international and local support networks as well as distinctive careers and reputations for independence from political and ecclesiastical conflict. It will be absolutely mandatory that the Committee gain support from the Heads of Churches, clergy, the Palestinian National Authority, and the majority of the NGOs in Jerusalem, the West Bank and Gaza Strip. Their work will lead to the formation of the Palestinian Christian Guidance Committee and convening the 'International Congress on the Transformation of Palestinian Christianity'. Given the political, economic, and demographic crises facing Palestinian Christians in the Holy Land. The sole purpose of the COE will be to select leadership who will develop a detailed feasibility study on various aspects of the present status and future prospects of the Palestinian Christian community. Most of this information already exists and needs to be updated and compiled into a manageable form with the addition of strategies for the transformation of Palestinian Christianity. The COE will be comprised of a select group of Christian clergy, academics, business, and laypersons from the local churches plus a limited number of international experts. The feasibility study will consist a series of documents that analyse the present political, economic, demographic, and spiritual needs of the Palestinian Christian community. Each document will conclude with a series of strategies and practical steps that can be undertaken over the next 10-25 years in order to transform the Palestinian Christianity into a revitalized community. The documents will propose theological, archaeological, developmental, legal, economic, spiritual, and other practical principles that will form the basis for an international movement whose central goal will be nothing less than the transformation of Palestinian Christianity into a growing and living reality. An important component of the feasibility study will be the development of the legal infrastructure, various organizational mechanisms, personnel, and funding necessary to convene an international Palestinian Christian Congress that would receive the feasibility study and begin to implement it.

## Stage Two: interim responsibilities of the Committee of Experts and select committees and working groups

At its initial meeting, the COE will begin the selection of highly skilled researchers and experts who will be divided into committees or task forces. They will be given clear job descriptions, financial resources, and a timeline within which they will need to complete their documents. Among the committees of experts that should be considered are the following: (partial list): Finance and Fundraising; Economic Development; Right of Return and Reparations; Palestinian Archaeology; Local Arrangements for the International Palestinian Congress; Legal Advisory; Inter-religious; Spiritual Renewal; the Return and Restoration of Monasteries and Church Property; Interdenominational and Ecumenical Affairs; and Political Advisory. The Committee of Experts shall be convened and begin their work no later than Pentecost 2001. The COE as well as all subcommittees and working groups shall be charged to conclude their work by mid-January 2002. Their preliminary findings, including interim documents, will be presented to the Selection Committee by 15 January 2002 in a private 'Hearing'. At the conclusion of the initial hearing, the Selection Committee and COE will jointly agree upon a date for an open public hearing that will be convened within three months. Following the second and larger hearing, a date will be announced for the convening of the first International Congress on the Transformation of Palestinian Christianity, with a target date for the meeting to be no later than the end of January 2003. At that point selected portions of the 'transformation' documents shall be distributed to the delegates, the international support agencies, and governments plus selected portions that will be distributed to the media. The Selection Committee in cooperation with the COE will nominate a slate of leaders for the International Guidance Committee. The names will be presented at the open public hearing on the COE's interim report. The COE will receive feedback from the persons attending the hearing, refine their slate of leaders, and make final decisions within one week of the conclusion of the hearing. At this point the International Guidance Committee will be convened and assume primary responsibility for the preparations for and convening of the International Congress. The COE and Selection Committee members may or may not be part of the Guidance Committee, but they will all be involved in the selection of delegates to the Congress.

# Stage Three: preparation for and convening of the international Congress on the transformation of Palestinian Christianity

*A. The selection of delegates and the invitation process*
Representatives from the Palestinian churches and the international and ecumenical church community plus partner organizations will be invited to select delegates to the Congress. The Committee of Experts in cooperation with the newly selected Guidance Committee will oversee the invitation process, select the location for the Congress, and conduct local arrangements. They may appoint separate subcommittees or task forces for such important tasks as oversight of local arrangements, fundraising for the Congress, publicity, and church relations at the local and international levels. They will also need to establish a preliminary budget at the initial meeting.

*B. Prominent persons in solidarity with Palestinian Christians*
An important function of the COE's invitation process will be to draw up a list of 25-30 prominent persons who will simply serve as 'International Sponsors' of the Congress. Among the names that will give credibility to the Congress will be Billy Graham, Jimmy Carter, Edward Said, Archbishop Desmond Tutu, Nelson Mandela, Daniel Barenboim, Kofi Anan, the Archbishop of Canterbury, Coptic Orthodox Patriarch Pope Sheneuda, Pope John Paul II, and other recognizable personalities. The list should be international, inter-religious, and enlist prominent personalities who have proven and principled positions on human rights and the implementation of international law.

*C. Factors in the selection of delegates and oversight of the Congress*
The Congress will invite delegates from all Palestinian Christian churches within historic Palestine and in the Diaspora plus Non-Governmental Organizations, international donor agencies, governments, Christian and non-Christian partner organizations around the world. Each agency and the local organizations will be asked to send 2-3 delegates to the Congress and be responsible for their travel, accommodations, and meals. Such an investment will hopefully facilitate the commitment of the sponsoring churches and agencies to the overall project. Additional invitations can be extended to leading clergy, intellectuals, religious, women, humanitarian, women, youth organizations, United Nations agencies, and laity including the business, legal, media, and technology sectors.

*D. Considerations for the First International Congress on the transformation of Palestinian Christianity*

It is suggested that the Congress be convened prior to the end of January 2003 and earlier if possible. The meeting should take place in historic Palestine at a location where the largest number of Palestinian Christians from inside historic Palestine and the Diaspora will be able to attend. The Congress should be approximately four days in duration. During the morning and afternoon periods, the final documents of the Committee of Experts and Working Groups will be presented on the critical issues facing Palestinian Christians. Time should be allowed for questions and responses from the delegates. A Resolution Committee will be responsible to listen to each session and meet throughout the Congress to draft the final document. The evenings of the Congress will be dedicated to cultural events, worship, and presentations by international personalities. One afternoon will be spent visiting sites of suffering and transformation, so as to give delegates contact with people at the grass roots level and to see projects that are beginning to transform the local community. The final day will be dedicated to receiving the report of the Resolution Committee and to take additional proposals from the floor. The entire Congress will be televised throughout Israel, Palestine and the Middle East with satellite television broadcasts made available to an international audience.

It is important to reiterate that most of the preparatory research and an embryonic form of ecumenical cooperation already exists within the Palestinian Christianity community and the expatriate Non-Governmental and religious organizations that are their partners. However, until now there has not been international support, a marked degree of urgency, and a commitment to such practical components as a strategy for remuneration, reclaiming and renovating lost property from 1948 present, the reconstruction and designating new contemporary spiritual and practical programs in the monasteries, an investment in research on Palestinian Christianity from the first Christian Pentecost until today, and a commitment to the spiritual components of renewal.

Several local churches and organizations such as Sabeel, the Middle East Council of Churches, and the Washington DC-based Holy Land Christian Ecumenical Foundation have distinguished themselves in recent years for their spirit of ecumenicity, indigenous nature, degree of political and ecclesiastical independence, and the spiritual and political issues they have chosen to address. The time has come a local and international ecumenical and independent Palestinian Christian movement focused for theological, spiritual, and political transformation of Palestinian Christianity.

The scriptures remind us that 'Where there is no vision the people will perish' (Proverbs 29:19). May the world respond with their prayers, time, energy, financial and technological resources, and may the Holy Spirit bless this effort in transformation while time still allows for it.

# Appendix
# THE JERUSALEM *SABEEL* DOCUMENT
# PRINCIPLES FOR A JUST PEACE IN
# PALESTINE-ISRAEL
## 'Seek peace and pursue it.' (1 Peter 3:11)

In pursuit of peace and out of our faith commitment, *Sabeel* Ecumenical Liberation Theology Center, Jerusalem has formulated a set of principles by which we, as Palestinian Christians, feel a just, secure, and lasting peace can be achieved.

## THEOLOGICAL BASIS
### Our faith teaches us that,

1.  God, creator and redeemer, loves all people equally (John 3:16, Acts 17:24-28).

2.  God demands that justice be done. No enduring peace, security, or reconciliation is possible without the foundation of justice. The demands of justice will not disappear; and the struggle for justice must be pursued diligently and persistently but non-violently (Jeremiah 9:23-24, Isaiah 32:16-17, Romans 12:17-21).

3.  The Holy Land is God's gift to Palestinians and Israelis. They must live justly and mercifully and be good stewards of it (Micah 6:8).

4.  'Love your neighbour as yourself' is an inclusive principle that must be honoured and sought after (Mark 12:31). The Golden Rule continues to apply, 'Do to others what you want them to do to you' (Matthew 7:12).

5.  Faithfulness to God obliges us to work for justice, peace, forgiveness, reconciliation, and healing (Matthew 5:9, 43-45).

## MORAL BASIS

1.  We acknowledge the sufferings and injustices committed against Jews by the West, especially those inflicted in the holocaust. Nevertheless, they do not justify the injustices committed against Palestinians. Justice claimed by one people at the expense of another is not justice.

2.  Since Israel has, by force, displaced the Palestinians, destroyed their villages and towns, denied them their basic human rights, and illegally dominated and oppressed them, it is morally bound to admit its injustice against the Palestinians and assume responsibility for it.

3.  Since Israel acquired by force 77 percent of the land of Palestine in 1948,

approximately 20 percent more than the United Nations had allotted, and established its state there, it is moral and right for Israel to return the whole of the areas captured in 1967, i.e. the Gaza Strip and West Bank, including East Jerusalem, to the millions of Palestinians who need their own small sovereign state.

4.  Israel's 'Law of Return' which allows any Jewish person to immigrate to Israel while denying Palestinians the right of return to their homeland is immoral and discriminatory.

5.  Sharing the sovereignty of Jerusalem is imperative to a moral and just peace.

6.  The ideology of militarism as well as the stockpiling of weapons of mass destruction are morally wrong. They sabotage the spirit and viability of peace and will not provide security either.

## LEGAL BASIS: international legitimacy

The following principles have been affirmed and repeatedly reaffirmed by the international community:

1.  Palestinian refugees have the right of return—*UN General Assembly Resolution 194*.

2.  The Gaza Strip and the West Bank, including East Jerusalem, are occupied territories and the Israeli forces must withdraw from them—*UN Security Council Resolution 242 and 338* based on the international principle of the inadmissibility of the acquisition of territory by force.

3.  The Israeli settlements in the Gaza Strip and West Bank, including East Jerusalem, are illegal. Moreover, it is illegal for the occupying power to transfer its population to, or to change the status of, the occupied territories—*Fourth Geneva Convention*.

4.  East Jerusalem is occupied territory. Israel's unilateral actions to alter the status of Jerusalem are illegal and invalid—*UN Security Council Resolutions 252 and 478*.

5.  Violations of human rights such as home demolitions, land confiscation, torture, revocation of residency rights, restriction of movement, closures, and the monopolization of resources are an insult to the dignity of human beings and contravene international law—*United Nations Universal Declaration of Human Rights*.

## THE PRINCIPLES FOR WHICH *SABEEL* STANDS

The people of the region—Palestinians and Israelis—both need and deserve a lasting peace, and security. With peace and security in place, bonds of acceptance and friendship can grow. It is no service to either community to promote a peace which flouts international law, ignores justice, and ultimately cannot endure since this will lead to continued bitterness and violence.

The following principles are therefore, based on international legitimacy. The international community has a responsibility to see that they are fulfilled. Once achieved, the strongest international guarantees must be given to ensure that the people of Palestine and Israel will live in peace and security.

1.  Israel must admit that it has committed an injustice against the Palestinian people and must accept responsibility for that. This means that reparation must be paid to all Palestinians who have suffered as a result of the conflict since 1948 whether they are Palestinian citizens of Israel, Palestinians living on the West Bank and the Gaza Strip, or Palestinians living in the Diaspora. The road to healing and reconciliation passes through repentance, forgiveness and redress.

2.  The Palestinians must have their own sovereign, independent, and democratic state established on the whole of the Gaza Strip and West Bank, including East Jerusalem. Israel must withdraw to the June 4, 1967 borders. No solution is acceptable if it does not guarantee the Palestinians' and Israelis' right to self-determination, independence, and sovereignty.

3.  Jerusalem's sovereignty must be shared by the two states of Palestine and Israel. The city must remain open for Palestinians, Israelis, and all. East Jerusalem can be the capital of Palestine while West Jerusalem can be the capital of Israel. Any agreement must protect the sanctity of the holy places and guarantee the rights of the three religions, Christianity, Islam, and Judaism on an equal basis. All illegal confiscation of land or expansion of areas by Israel within the walled city of Jerusalem since 1967 must be reversed.

4.  The right of return to Palestinian refugees must be guaranteed according to international law. All refugees must be fully compensated.

5.  All Israeli Jewish settlements on the Gaza Strip and West Bank, including East Jerusalem, are illegal under international law. All the settlements built on Palestinian soil since 1967 must be part of Palestine.

6.  Once the principles of an acceptable justice are applied, a peace treaty must be drawn up between the two states of Palestine and Israel guaranteeing the full sovereignty and territorial integrity of each including recognized borders, water rights, and other resources.

7.  Furthermore, both states must fully guarantee the respect and protection of the human rights of all their citizens, including freedom of religion, in accordance with all international conventions.

## POLITICAL BACKGROUND

In 1948 a grievous injustice was committed by the Zionists (forerunners of the state of Israel) against the Palestinian people. The Zionists acquired by force 77 percent of the land of Palestine and displaced three quarters of a million Palestinians. Consequently, the state of Israel was declared as a Jewish state. Since then, most of the displaced Palestinians have lived in refugee camps and their national rights have been denied. Despite UN Resolution 194, passed in December 1949 and reaffirmed annually by the UN, Israel has adamantly refused the right of return of Palestinian refugees to their homes. The 150,000 Palestinians who remained within that part of Palestine which became the state of Israel were given Israeli citizenship. However, they have been discriminated against and have been treated as second class citizens. In 1967, the state of Israel acquired by force the rest of the country of Palestine (the 23 percent) further displacing approximately 325,000 Palestinians. The Palestinians living in the Gaza Strip and the West Bank came under Israeli military rule. The occupation has been oppressive, brutal, and dehumanising. Palestinian land has been systematically confiscated, human rights violated, and people systemically humiliated, as documented by a number of international, Israeli, and Palestinian human rights organizations, such as Amnesty International, B'Tselem, LAW and Al-Haq. Furthermore, Israel assumed control of Palestine's water supply (unfairly restricting water to Palestinians and charging them exorbitant prices), began building exclusively Jewish settlements on Palestinian land and, through hundreds of military laws, persisted in its oppression of the Palestinians. As to East Jerusalem, Israel annexed it and, in 1993, closed it and cut it off from the rest of the West Bank and Gaza Strip, thus denying Palestinians the right of access to it. Consequently, even the right to worship in its churches and mosques is obstructed. Moreover, Israel enacted a policy to limit the Palestinian presence in Jerusalem to 27 percent of the city's population, through demolition of homes, confiscation of land, revocation of Palestinian residency rights as well as other means.

In 1991 at the end of the Gulf War, the peace process was initiated by the United States and Russia. In spite of its initial promise in the Madrid Conference to achieve a just peace, it became, in its Oslo form, an instrument for furthering the injustice. As it evolved, certain portions of the occupied territories were returned by Israel to the Palestinian Authority. By the end of March 2000, only 18.2 percent of the area of the West Bank has been returned to full Palestinian Authority; 24.7 percent is under Israeli security and Palestinian civil control. The remaining 57.1 percent of the West Bank is still under full Israeli control. The areas that have been returned to the Palestinians are not geographically linked together. The Israeli Army controls the highways and major roads throughout the occupied territories, as well as everything below the ground and sky above. It is important to note that in the Gaza Strip, only 60 percent of the land is under Palestinian control where over a million Palestinians live; while Israel controls the 40 percent of the Strip for the benefit of 6100 Jewish settlers. Furthermore, some of the 194 Israeli settlements (166 in the West Bank and Gaza Strip and 28 in East Jerusalem— all illegal under international law) have expanded to sizable towns. It is estimated that the number of settlers, including those who live in the settlement ring in and around Jerusalem, is approximately 400,000.

The two sides, Israelis and Palestinians, have more recently been engaged in the final status negotiations which include the thorniest issues, namely, Jerusalem, borders, refugees, water, and settlements.

We feel we are standing at a most important juncture in our history. The United States Government has been working to broker a peace agreement between Israel and Syria as well as to keep alive the negotiations between the Palestinians and the Israelis. Many of us are afraid that what might ensue in Palestine is an unjust peace. We at Sabeel feel we have a Christian responsibility to speak our mind for the sake of a lasting peace that will bring an acceptable justice to the Palestinians and security for all the peoples of our region. We fear that the Palestinian Authority might be forced to accept an unjust peace which will be attractively packaged by the state of Israel and the United States Government. We are, however, sure that an unjust peace will only be temporary and will inevitably plunge our region into greater violence and bloodshed. We will not be silent. We lift our voice prophetically in pointing to the pitfalls of injustice. The following points comprise the different scenarios. We would like to present them clearly with their probable consequences.

### THE GREATEST CONCERN: a *bantustan* state

Taking a good look at the Gaza Strip and the West Bank, it is clear that Israel's eye is focused on the West Bank which includes East Jerusalem. The confiscation of Palestinian land, the building and expansion of the settlements have never stopped. Israel continues to insist that the settlements will remain under Israeli rule. If this is done, Israel will maintain its military presence on the West Bank while allowing the Palestinian Authority to have autonomous rule over its own people. The areas under Palestinian rule will be called Palestine. They will have the semblance of a state but will exist under the suzerainty of Israel and will not enjoy genuine sovereignty. What we are witnessing, therefore, is a *bantustan*-type state, home rule, just like what was proposed by the former apartheid government of South Africa to its black citizens. From all indications, this is the picture which is emerging on the ground.

If pressured, Israel may even concede the Gaza Strip, where it currently has only 6100 settlers and controls approximately 40 percent of the land and one third of the water. It might withdraw totally from the Gaza Strip, which now has a damaged aquifer and a serious lack of usable water, and allow the Palestinians to have their sovereign state there. That area will be small and contained in one corner of Palestine and, from Israel's perspective, will, presumably, not pose any serious threat to Israel. On the West Bank, however, the Palestinians will only be given autonomous rule, a homeland, in the guise of a state yet void of actual sovereignty.

This we believe is an unnatural, unhealthy, and unjust scenario and will only lead to a bloodier conflict. History teaches us that oppressed nations will not give up their struggle for freedom and independence. Under this scenario, Israel will not achieve the security it seeks because the forced and unjust peace settlement cannot be permanent.

**Sabeel rejects outright this peace formula or any variation of it and warns that its imposition will be ultimately catastrophic for both peoples.**

## THE GENUINE HOPE: two sovereign and fully democratic states

This scenario envisages the total withdrawal of Israel from all the occupied territories including East Jerusalem according to United Nations resolutions 242 and 338. The Palestinians will establish their sovereign state on the whole of the 23 percent of the land of Palestine. One way to redeem the settlements is to make them the new towns for the returning Palestinian refugees. This can constitute a part of Israel's reparations to the Palestinians. Israel must compensate the owners from whom the land was confiscated. The Jewish settlers who choose to remain in Palestine can become Palestinian citizens and live under Palestinian sovereignty.

As to Jerusalem, it will have to be shared. The city must remain open to all. A peace treaty will be drawn up and the two countries will become inter-dependent economically and will help each other develop their resources for the well being of both their peoples.

This is the formula which the Palestinians have been hoping and working for. Indeed, it is not the ideal solution, but it carries within it an acceptable justice which most Palestinians are willing to live with for the sake of peace and prosperity. Furthermore, as this scenario agrees with United Nations resolutions since 1967, it will ensure the support of the international community of nations. This formula gives the Palestinians a state as sovereign as Israel, rids them of the Israeli occupation, and restores to them the whole of the occupied territories of 1967. Indeed, a state within the West Bank and Gaza, composed of only 23 percent of Palestine instead of the 43 percent allotted by the UN in 1947, is already a very signficant compromise by the Palestinians. The Palestinians would have to give up their right to most of historic Palestine. Obviously, Israel, with the help of the United States and the international community, will have to compensate the Palestinian people.

## THE VISION FOR THE FUTURE

Our vision involves two sovereign states, Palestine and Israel, who will enter into a confederation or even a federation, possibly with other neighboring countries and where Jerusalem becomes the federal capital. Indeed, the ideal and best solution has always been to envisage ultimately a bi-national state in Palestine-Israel where people are free and equal, living under a constitutional democracy that protects and guarantees all their rights, responsibilities, and duties without racism or discrimination. One state for two nations and three religions.

## STANDING FOR JUSTICE

At every turn, the principle of justice must be upheld. Unless justice is rendered and security is achieved, the solution must be rejected because it will not endure. A just solution must include an equal measure of justice and security for both sides to make it viable. Otherwise it will not lead to a permanent peace. This is the basic principle that must be upheld and used as the measure for every one of the above points.

This is where Sabeel takes its stand. We will stand for justice. We can do no other. Justice alone guarantees a peace that will lead to reconciliation and a life of security and prosperity to all the peoples of our land. By standing on the side of justice, we open ourselves to the work of peace; and working for peace makes us children of God.

**'Blessed are the peacemakers for they shall be called children of God'**
**(Matthew 5:9)**

*Sabeel* Ecumenical Liberation Theology Center
PO Box 49084, Jerusalem 91491
telephone 972 2 532 7136; fax 972 2 532 7137
website: www.sabeel.org; email: sabeel@sabeel.org

Friends of *Sabeel* UK: Mrs Janet Davies, 46 Timms Lane, Formby, Merseyside, L37 7ND UK, tel. +44 (0) 1704 872788; fax: +44 (0) 1704-878843; email: fos@globalnet.co.uk

Friends of *Sabeel* North America: Mrs Elizabeth Barlow; PO Box 4214; Ann Arbor, MI. 48106 USA; tel. +1 734-665-5773; email: fos-na-admin@umich.edu.

# SELECTED BIBLIOGRAPHY

*Abstracts of the Census of 1922*, Jerusalem: Government of Palestine, 1923.

Abu ESl-Assal, Riah, *Caught in Between*, London: SPCK, 1999.

Abu-Lughod, Ibrahim (Editor), *The Transformation of Palestine*, Evanston: Northwestern University Press, 1971.

Armstrong, Karen, *Jerusalem: One City, Three Faiths*, New York: Alfred A Knopf, 1996.

Ateek, Naim. S, *Justice and Only Justice*, Maryknoll, New York: Orbis Books, 1989.

*B'Tselem*, 'Disputed Waters: Israel's Responsibility for the Water Shortage in the Occupied Territories', Jerusalem: B'Tselem, 1998.

Bender, D L and R Bruno Leone, *Israel: Opposing Viewpoints*, San Diego: Greenhaven Press, 1989.

Brayer, Lynda, 'Decimation of Palestinians in the Occupied Territories of Palestine', Jerusalem: Catholic Information Network, 1997.

Brown, Peter, *The Making of Late Antiquity*, Cambridge, Massachusetts: Harvard University Press, 1979.

Chacour,Elias, *Blood Brothers*, Grand Rapids, Michigan: Chosen Books, 1984.

Chapman, Colin, *Whose Promised Land?* Batavia, Illinois: Lion Publishing Company, 1992.

Childers, Erskine, 'The Other Exodus', *The Spectator*, 12 May 1961.

Colbi, Saul S., *Christianity in the Holy Land, Past and* Present: Tel Aviv, 1968.

Cragg, Kenneth, *Palestine: The Prize and Price of Zion,* London: Cassell Publications, 1997.

Cragg, Kenneth, *The Arab Christian*, Louisville: Westminster/John Knox Press, 1991.

Dalrymple, William, *From the Holy Mountain: A Journey Among the Christians of the Middle East,* New York: Henry Holt and Company, 1998.

Daniszewski, John, 'Christians Feel Under Siege in the Mideast', *Los Angeles Times*, 14 August 1997.

Diamond, John, 'Clinton Reports Some Progress in Negotiations', *Chicago Tribune*, 17 July 2000.

Eusebius of Caesarea, Ecclesiastical History (trans. by J E L Oulton, Cambridge, Massachusetts: Harvard University Press, 1932.

Farsoun, Samih with Christina Zacharia, *Palestine and the Palestinians*, Boulder, Colorado, Westview Press, 1997.

Finkelstein, Norman, *Image and Reality in the Israeli-Palestine Conflict*, New York: Verso Press, 1995.

Freund, W H C, *The Rise of Christianity*, Philadelphia: Fortress Press, 1984

Getman, Tom, Reflection #35, Jerusalem: World Vision Jerusalem, 2000.

Gilmour, Ian and David, 'Pseudo-Travellers', *London Review of Books*, 7 February 1985

Government of Israel, *Refugees in the Middle East*, Tel Aviv: Israel Information Service, 1967.

Gresh, Alain, *The PLO: The Struggle Within,* London: Zed Books Ltd., 1985.

Griffith, Sidney, *Arabic Christianity in the Monasteries of the Ninth Century*, London: Variorum Press, 1992.

Grossman, Ron, 'Remembering One of Israel's Founding Fathers: A Protestant Scotsman', *Chicago Tribune*, 29 April 1998.

Hadawi, Sami, Palestinian Rights and Losses in 1948, Amman, Jordan: Saqi Books, 1988.

Hertzberg, Arthur, *The Zionist Idea*, New York: Athenium Press, 1959.

Herzl, Theodor, *The Complete Diaries*, New York: Herzl Press and Thomas Yoseloff, 1960.

Herzog, Ze'ev. 'Deconstructing the Walls of Jericho', *Ha'aretz*, 29 October 1999.

Hummel, Thomas, Kevork Hintlian, and Ulf Carmesund, *Patterns of the Past, Prospects for the Future*, London: Melisende, 1999.

Igrams, Doreen, *Palestine Papers: 1917-22*, London: John Murray, 1972.

Jeremias, Joachim, *Jerusalem in the Time of Jesus*, Philadelphia, Fortress Press, 1969

Kamin, Leon, *The Science and Politics of IQ*, New York: John Wiley and Sons, 1974.

Khalidi, Rashid, *Palestinian Identity: The Construction of a Modern National Consciousness*, New York: Columbia University Press, 1997.

Litani, Yehuda, 'The Harsh Summer of the Patriarch', *Ha'aretz*, 25 September 1992.

Malik, Habib Charles, 'Christians in the Land Called Holy', *First Things*, (January 1999).

Mallison, Thomas and Sally, *The Palestine Problem in International Law*, Harlow, England: Longman Ltd., 1986.

Masalha, Nur, *A Land Without a People*, London: Faber and Faber, 1997.

McDowell, David, *Palestine and Israel: The Uprising and Beyond*, Berkeley: University of California Press, 1989.

Morris, Benny, *Righteous Victims*, New York: Alfred A Knopf, 1999.

Morris, Benny, *The Birth of the Palestinian Refugee Problem,* New York: Oxford University Press, 1987.

O'Mahony, Anthony (ed.), *Palestinian Christians: Religion, Politics, and Society in the Holy Land,* London: Melisende, 1999

O'Mahony, Anthony with Göran Gunner and Kevork Hintlian, *The Christian Heritage in the Holy Land*, London: Scorpion-Cavendish, 1995.

Orme, William, 'Ulster and Israel Look in a Mirror at Each Other', *New York Times*, 16 July 2000.

Pacini, Andrea, *Christian Communities in the Middle East, The Challenge of the Future,* Oxford: Clarendon Press, 1998.

Palumbo, Michael, *The Palestinian Catastrophe,* London: Faber and Faber, 1987.

Pappe, Ilan, *The Making of the Arab-Israeli Conflict: 1947-51*, New York: St Martins Press, 1994.

Peretz, Don, *The Middle East Today*, Westport, Connecticut: Praeger Publishers, 1994.

Peters, Joan, *From Time Immemorial*, New York: Harper and Row, 1984.

Porath, Yehoshua, 'Mrs. Peter's Palestine', *New York Review of Books*, 16 January 1985.

Prior, Michael, *The Bible and Colonialism*, Sheffield, Sheffield Academic Press, 1997.

Prior, Michael and William Taylor, *Christians in the Holy Land*, London: World of Islam Festival Trust, 1994

*Promises, Promises, The Realities of Oslo*, London: World Vision UK, 1999.

Raheb, Mitri, *I Am A Palestinian Christian*, Minneapolis: Fortress Press, 1995.

Rantisi, Audeh, *Blessed Are the Peacemakers*, Grand Rapids: Zondervan Publishing House, 1990.

Roy, Sara, 'De-development Revisited: Palestinian Economy and Society Since

Oslo', *Journal of Palestine Studies,* Volume XXVIII, No. 3, Spring 1999.

Ruether, Herman and Rosemary, *The Wrath of Jonah*, San Francisco: Harper and Row, 1989.

Ryan, Joseph L, 'Refugees Within Israel', *Journal of Palestine Studies*, Vol, II, no. 4, 1973.

Sabeel, *The Jerusalem Sabeel Document,* Jerusalem: The Sabeel Ecumenical Centre for Liberation Theology, May 2000.

Sabella, Bernard, 'A Century Apart', *Christian Voices from the Holy Land,* London: The Palestinian Delegation in the United Kingdom, 1998.

Said, Edward W, *Out of Place*, New York: Alfred A Knopf, 1999.

Segev, Tom, *1949: The First Israelis*, New York: The Free Press, 1986.

Shick, Robert, *The Christian Communities of Palestine From Byzantium to Islamic Rule*, Princeton, New Jersey: Darwin Press, 1995.

Shriver, Donald W, *An Ethic for Enemies*, New York: Oxford University Press, 1994.

Sinclair, Andrew, *Jerusalem: The Endless Crusade*, New York: Crown Publishers, 1995.

Stauffer, Thomas R, 'Water and War in the Middle East', Washington, DC: Center for Policy Analysis on Palestine, 1996.

Sternhell, Zeev, *The Founding Myths of Israel*, Princeton: Princeton University Press, 1998.

Sykes, Christopher, *Crossroads to Israel,* Cleveland: World Publishing, 1965.

Thomas, Bayliss, *How Israel Was Won*, Boston: Lexington Books, 2000.

Trimingham, J S, *Christianity Among the Arabs in Pre-Islamic Times,* London: Longman, and Librairie du Liban, 1979.

Tsimhoni, Daphne, *Christian Communities in Jerusalem and the West Bank Since 1948*, Westport, Connecticut: Praeger Press, 1991.

Tuchman, Barbara, *Bible and Sword*, New York: Ballentine Books, 1984.

Uris, Leon, *Exodus*, New York: Simon and Schuster, 1963.

Vester, Bertha Spafford, *Our Jerusalem*, Beirut: Middle East Export Press, 1950.

Wagner, Donald, *Anxious for Armageddon*, Scottsdale, Pennsylvania: Herald Press, 1995.

Wenger, Martha, 'Jerusalem', *Middle East Report*, May-June 1993.

Whitelam, Keith, *The Invention of Ancient Israel*, New York: Routledge, 1996.

Wilson, Harold, *The Chariot of Israel*, London: W W Norton, 1981.

Young, Kenneth, *Arthur James Balfour*, London: J Bell and Sons, 1963.

# INDEX

Ayyubids  69
Azouri, Najib  168

**B**

Ba'ath  198
Baghdad  65,  198
Baha al-Din  68
Baker, James  216
Baldwin  67
Balfour, Arthur  95,  98,  99,  101,
        105,  124,  127,  192,  246
Balfour Declaration  102,  103,  104,
        108,  109,  111,  112,  115,
        122,  126,  127,  158,  162
*bantustans*  223,  224,  227,  236,  267
Bar Kochba revolt  45
Bar-Ilan, David  248
Bara'am  164
Barak, Ehud  199,  220,  239,  269
Barenboim, Daniel  156
Begin, Menachem  107,  121,  122,
        136,  139,  175,  180,  202
Beilin, Yossi  218
Beirut  84,  198,  199,  212,  241
Beisan  63,  141,  143,  160,  258
Beit Jala  82,  170, 210,  239,  241
Beit Safafa  151
Beit Sahour  82,  210,  241,  246,  252
Bellow, Saul  146
Ben-Gurion, David  121,  129,  130,
        134,  136,  138,  141,  148,
        166,  190,  204,  205,  211,  225
Benvenisti, Meron  196,  212,  257
Bernadotte, Folke  149, 153,  154
Bethlehem  21,  23,  27,  28,  32,  36,
        44,  52,  53,  57,  68,  69,  75,
        84,  113,  136,  173,  177,  208,
        210,  228,  239,  241,  250,
        254,  269
Bethlehem Bible College  254
Bethlehem University  20,  87, 228
Bevin, Ernest  122,  125
Biltmore Hotel  120,  144,  163
Biltmore Program  120, 128
Bir Zeit  37,  82, 228,  229

Bir Zeit University  217
Bir'am  164,  165,  184,  258
Blackstone, William E  93
British Foreign Office  124
British Mandate  19,  112,  113,  132,
140,  151,  159,  171,  250
British Mandatory Government  133
Brother Andrew, Open Doors  248
*B'tselem*  228, 257
Buber, Martin  90,  195
Bush, George  216,  217
Butros al-Bustani  86
Byzantine Christianity  51
Byzantine empire  24,  36
Byzantine Orthodoxy  56
Byzantine theology  48
Byzantines  33,  58,  61,  67
Byzantium  55,  59,  65,  69

**C**

Caesarea  44,  47,  50,  51,  52,  56,  59
Cairo  198,  212,  241,  268
Cairo Agreement  221,  235
Camp David  240,  257
Camp David 2000  243
Camp David Accords  162,  180
Canaan  161,  191,  193,  194,  195
'Canaanite Waters'  176
Canaanites  11, 32,  33,  190
Canada Park  165
Capitulations  71
Cappadocia  56
Cappucci, Hilarian  161
Carter, Elliot  156
Carter, Jimmy  175,  180,  244
Chacour, Elias  23,  164,  165,  251
Chalcedonian Christianity  36
Chalcedonian creed  56
Charlemagne  66
Charter of the State of Israel  165
Childers, Erskine  148
Christ  11,  15,  40,  51, see also Jesus
Christian Zionism  17,  40,  100,  102,
105
Christian Zionists  19,  23,  31,  72,

## Other related titles from Melisende

THEY CAME AND THEY SAW, WESTERN CHRISTIAN EXPERIENCES OF THE HOLY LAND
*ed. Michael Prior* £12.50 ppr, 272 pages, 2000

PATTERNS OF THE PAST, PROSPECTS FOR THE FUTURE: THE CHRISTIAN HERITAGE IN THE HOLY LAND
*eds.Thomas Hummel, Kevork Hintlian and Ulf Carmesund* £15.00 ppr, 330 pages, 1999

THE CHRISTIAN HERITAGE IN THE HOLY LAND
*eds. A O'Mahony with G Gunner and K Hintlian* £15.95 ppr, 320 pages, 1995

THE NOBLE HERITAGE, A PORTRAIT OF THE CHURCH OF THE RESURRECTION
*Alistair Duncan* £15.00 hbk, 80 pages, 1986

MAMLUK JERUSALEM: AN ARCHITECTURAL STUDY
*Michael Burgoyne* £125.00 hbk, 622 pages, 1987 (World of Islam Festival Trust)

LIFE AT THE CROSSROADS. A HISTORY OF GAZA
*Gerald Butt* £16.95 hbk, 208 pages, 1995 (Rimal)

JERUSALEM: WHAT MAKES FOR PEACE! A PALESTINIAN CHRISTIAN CONTRIBUTION TO PEACEMAKING
*eds. Naim Ateek, Cedar Duaybis and Marla Schrader* £12.50 ppr, 372 pages, 1997

WESTERN SCHOLARSHIP AND THE HISTORY OF PALESTINE
*ed. Michael Prior* £8.50 ppr, 128 pages, 1998

CHRISTIANS IN THE HOLY LAND
*eds. Michael Prior and William Taylor* £12.50 ppr, 254 pages, 1995 (World of Islam Festival Trust)

HOLY LAND–HOLLOW JUBILEE: GOD, JUSTICE AND THE PALESTINIANS
*eds. Naim Ateek and Michael Prior* £12.50 ppr, 334 pages, 1999

PALESTINIAN CHRISTIANS: RELIGION, POLITICS AND SOCIETY IN THE HOLY LAND
*A. O'Mahony* £12.50 ppr, 224 pages, 1999

A THIRD MILLENNIUM GUIDE TO PILGRIMAGE TO THE HOLY LAND
*ed. Duncan Macpherson* £7.95 ppr, 2000

OTTOMAN JERUSALEM: THE LIVING CITY 1517-1917
*eds. Sylvia Auld and Robert Hillenbrand architectural survey by Yusuf Natsheh* £145.00 hbk, 1168 pages, 2 parts, 2000 (Altajir World of Islam Trust)

ISLAM AMONG THE SPIRES
*Kenneth Cragg* £12.50 ppr, 232 pages, 2000

FUSTAT GLASS OF THE EARLY ISLAMIC PERIOD
*George T Scanlon and Ralph Pinder-Wilson* £18.00, ppr 2001 (Altajir World of Islam Trust)

**MELISENDE**
39 Chelmsford Road, London E18 2PW England
tel. +44 (0)20 8498 9768; fax +44 (0)20 8504 2558
e-mail: melisende@cwcom.net; www.melisende.cwc.net